Volume 4

by
Koge-Donbo

LOS ANGELES • TOKYO • LONDON • HAMBURG

Translator - Nan Rymer
English Adaptation - Adam Arnold
Copy Editors - Troy Lewter and Carol Fox
Retouch and Lettering - Abelardo Bigting
Cover Layout - Raymond Makowski
Graphic Designer - James Lee

Editor - Paul Morrissey
Digital Imaging Manager - Chris Buford
Pre-Press Manager - Antonio DePietro
Production Managers - Jennifer Miller and Mutsumi Miyazaki
Art Director - Matt Alford
Managing Editor - Jill Freshney
VP of Production - Ron Klamert
President & C.O.O. - John Parker
Publisher & C.E.O. - Stuart Levy

E-mail: info@TOKYOPOP.com
Come visit us online at www.TOKYOPOP.com

A  Manga

TOKYOPOP Inc.
5900 Wilshire Blvd. Suite 2000
Los Angeles, CA 90036

Pita-Ten Volume 4
© 2001 Koge-Donbo.
First published in Japan in 2001 by Media Works Inc., Tokyo, Japan.
English publication rights arranged through Media Works Inc.

English text copyright ©2004 TOKYOPOP Inc.

ISBN: 1-59182-630-6

First TOKYOPOP printing: July 2004

10 9 8 7 6 5 4 3 2

Printed in the USA

contents

Characters

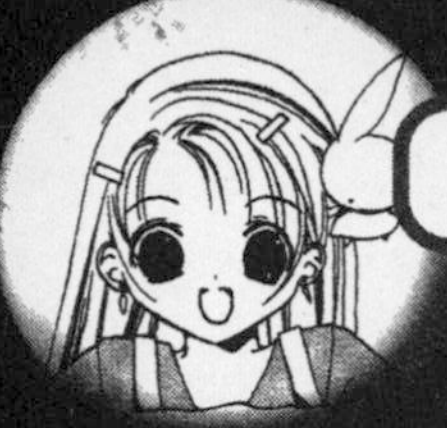

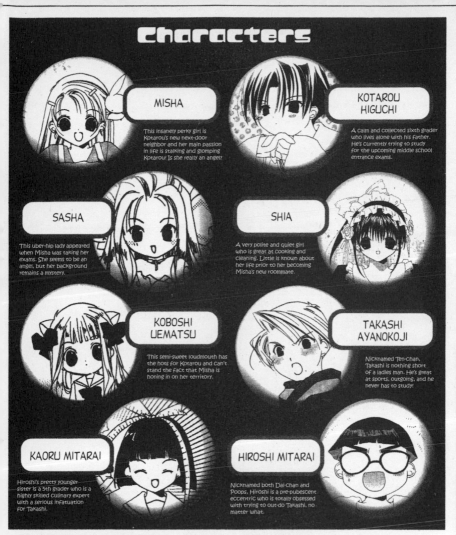

MISHA

This insanely perky girl is Kotarou's new next-door neighbor and her main passion in life is stalking and glomping Kotarou! Is she really an angel?

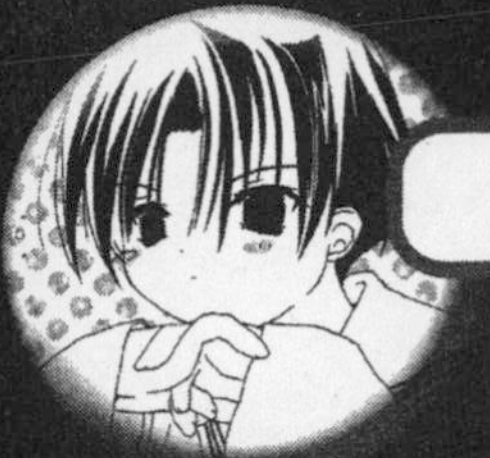

KOTAROU HIGUCHI

A calm and collected sixth grader who lives alone with his father. He's currently trying to study for the upcoming middle school entrance exams.

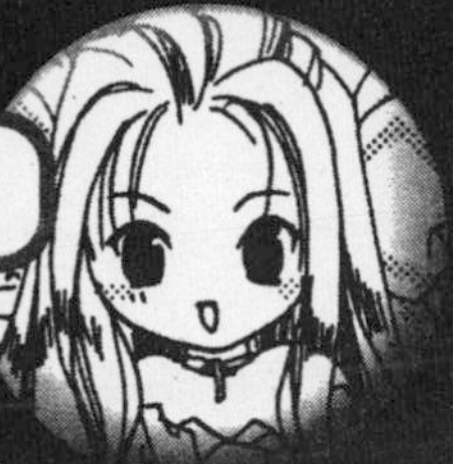

SASHA

This uber-hip lady appeared when Misha was taking her exams. She seems to be an angel, but her background remains a mystery.

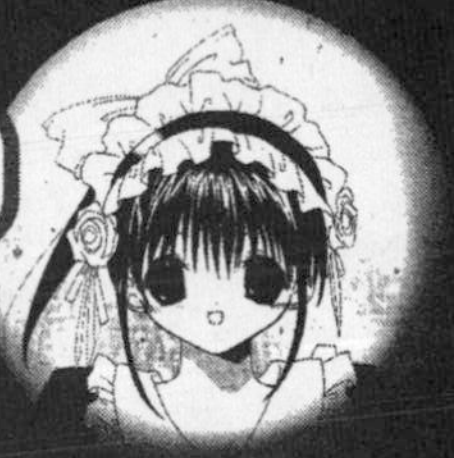

SHIA

A very polite and quiet girl who is great at cooking and cleaning. Little is known about her life prior to her becoming Misha's new roommate.

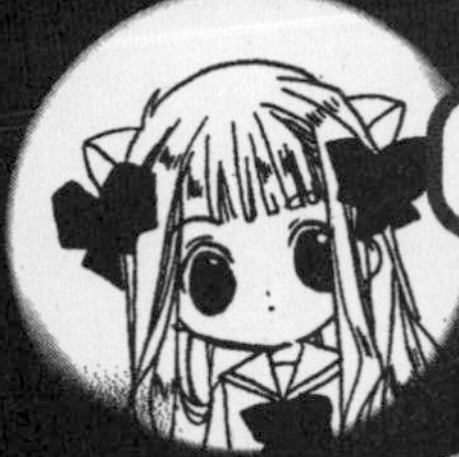

KOBOSHI UEMATSU

This semi-sweet loudmouth has the hots for Kotarou and can't stand the fact that Misha is honing in on her territory.

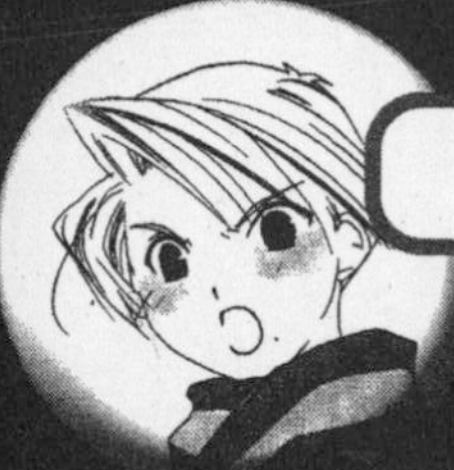

TAKASHI AYANOKOJI

Nicknamed Ten-chan, Takashi is nothing short of a ladies man. He's great at sports, outgoing, and he never has to study!

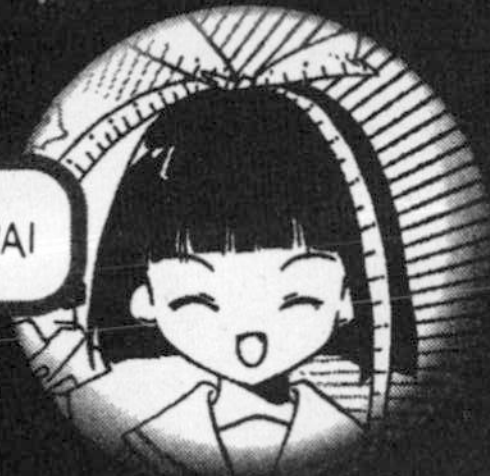

KAORU MITARAI

Hiroshi's pretty younger sister is a 5th grader who is a highly skilled culinary expert with a serious infatuation for Takashi.

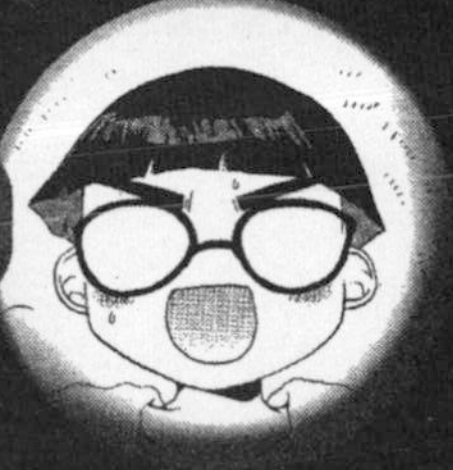

HIROSHI MITARAI

Nicknamed both Dai-chan and Poops, Hiroshi is a pre-pubescent eccentric who is totally obsessed with trying to out-do Takashi, no matter what.

The Story Until Now:

Quiet elementary school student Kotarou Higuchi is worse off than most kids. His mother died in a traffic accident and his workaholic father is never at home. This leaves Kotarou struggling to make it to school on time, cook his own meals, go shopping and keep up with his studies.

His so-called normal life throws him a curve ball in the form of a mysterious girl named Misha who has not only moved in next door, but has also started to attend the very same middle school! Sensing his loneliness and sorrow, Misha decides to make it her life's work to chase after, "abuse" and latch onto Kotarou. Not long after her appearance, another strange girl by the name of Shia appears and ends up as Misha's new roommate!

Just as Kotarou begins to get accustomed to his topsy-turvy new life, Misha announces that in order for her to take her exams, she must take a brief leave of absence. While she is gone, yet another strange girl—Sasha—appears, brimming with an arsenal of magical powers. Sasha's powers are so strong that even the tight-lipped Ten-chan is coaxed into confessing his love for Shia. Unknown to Ten-chan, Kotarou has witnessed the confession and cannot help but feel a variety of new emotions surge through him. It seems that Kotarou has begun to have feelings for Shia as well. Not long after, however, Misha returns...

Lesson 20

How to Make Yummy Curry

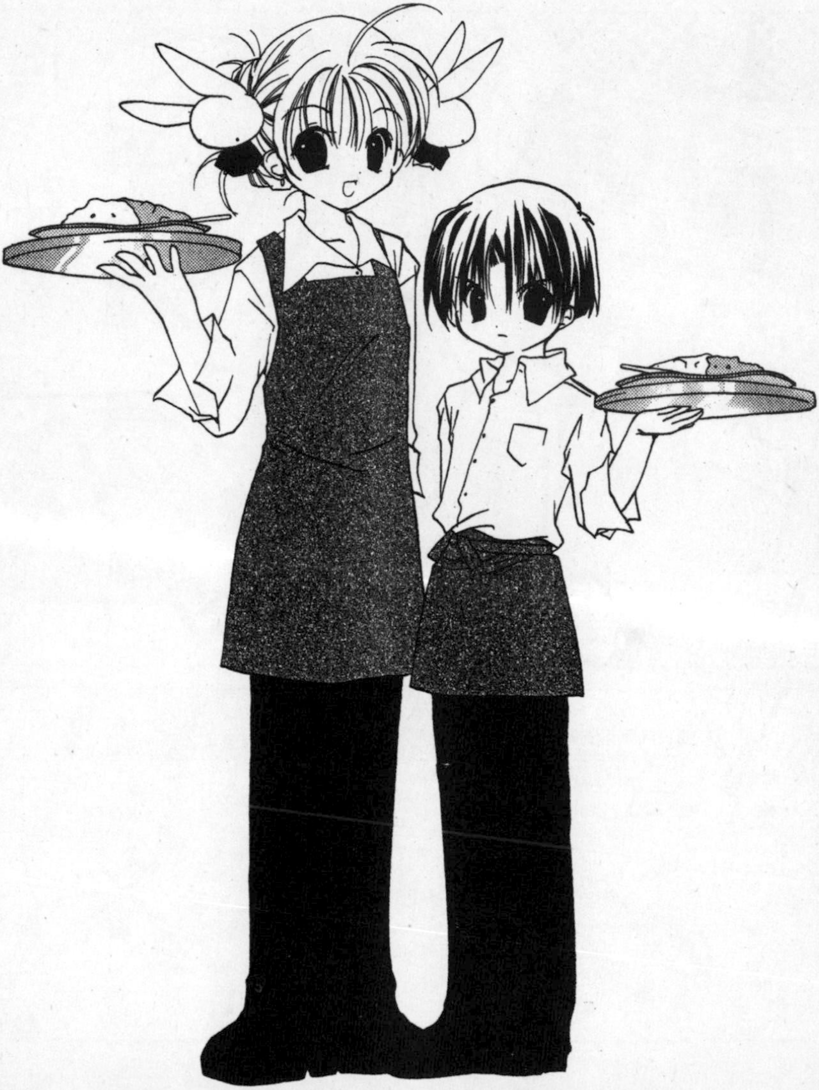

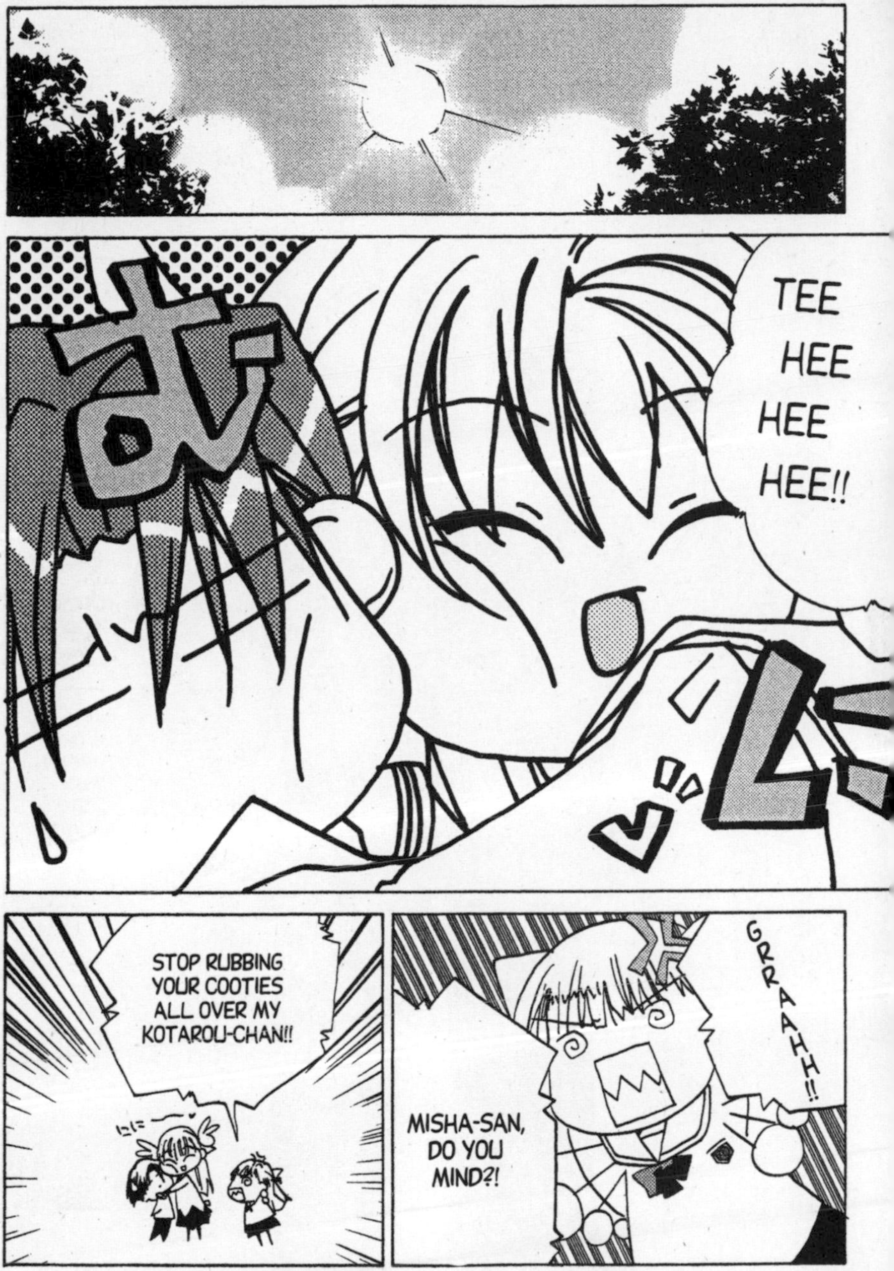
TEE HEE HEE HEE!!
GRRAAHH!!
MISHA-SAN, DO YOU MIND?!
STOP RUBBING YOUR COOTIES ALL OVER MY KOTAROU-CHAN!!

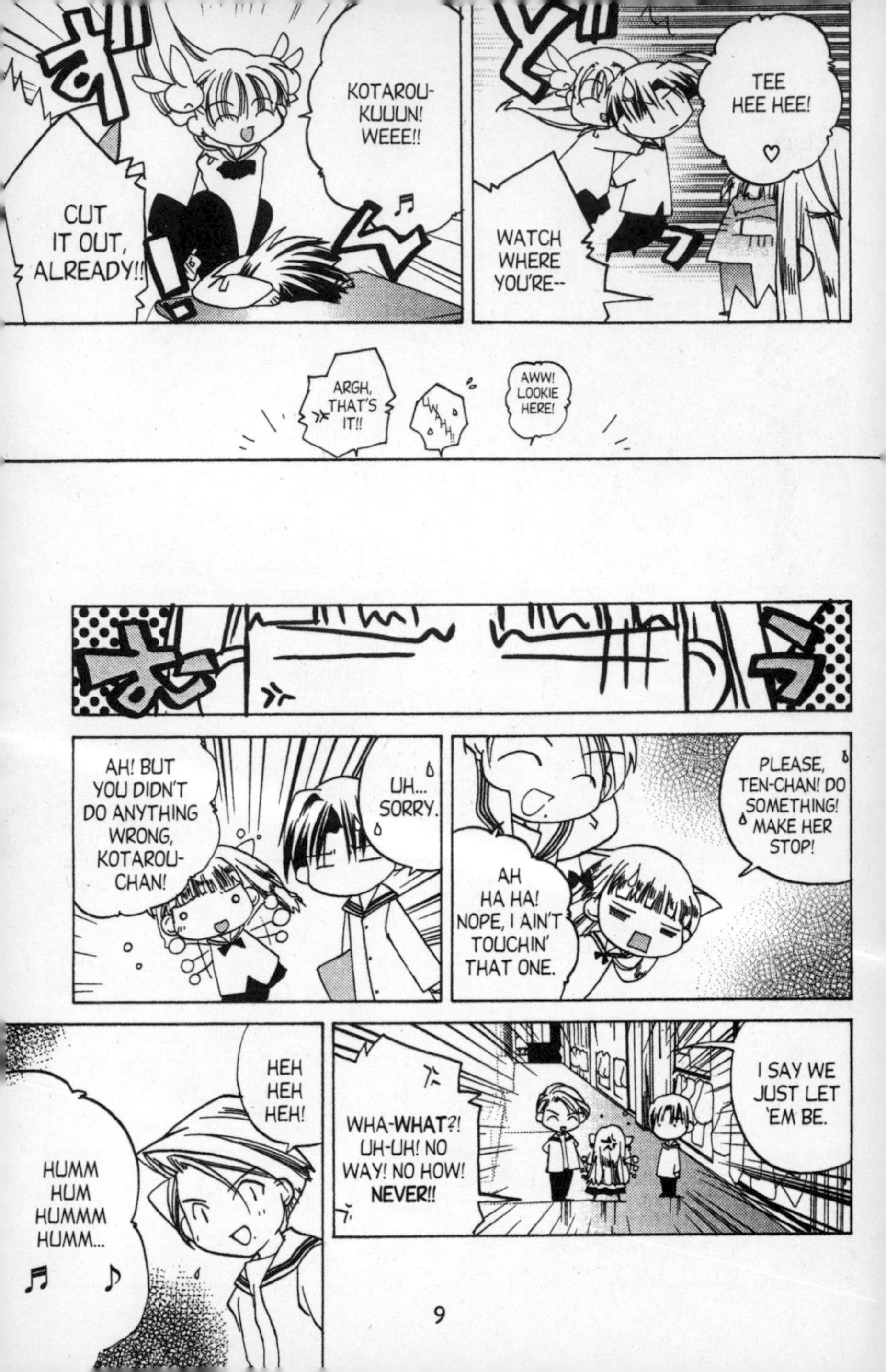
TEE HEE HEE! ♡
WATCH WHERE YOU'RE--
KOTAROU-KUUUN! WEEE!!
CUT IT OUT, ALREADY!!
AWW! LOOKIE HERE!
UWAHH!!
ARGH, THAT'S IT!!
PLEASE, TEN-CHAN! DO SOMETHING! MAKE HER STOP!
AH HA HA! NOPE, I AIN'T TOUCHIN' THAT ONE.
UH... SORRY.
AH! BUT YOU DIDN'T DO ANYTHING WRONG, KOTAROU-CHAN!
I SAY WE JUST LET 'EM BE.
WHA-**WHAT**?! UH-UH! NO WAY! NO HOW! **NEVER**!!
HEH HEH HEH!
HUMM HUM HUMMM HUMM...

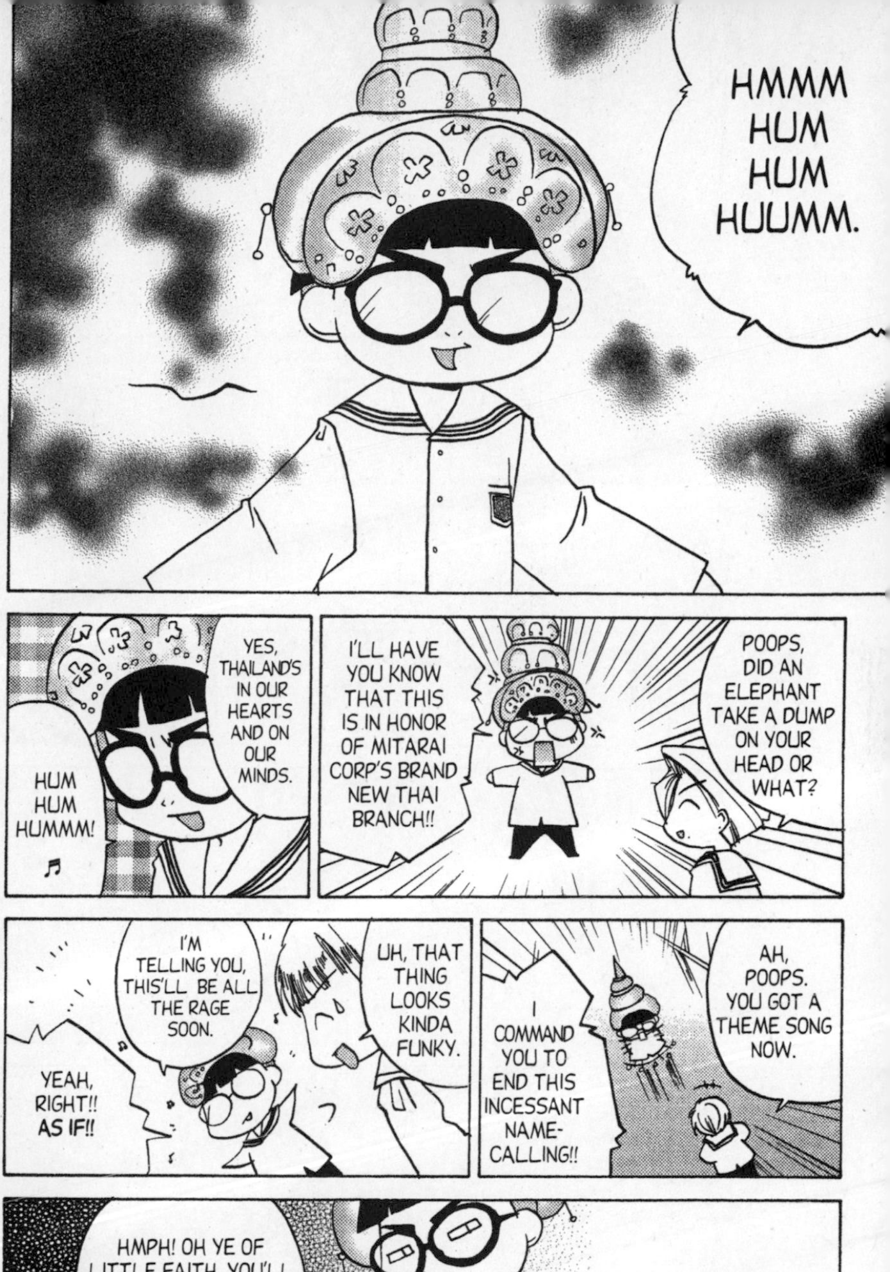
HMMM HUM HUM HUUMM.
POOPS, DID AN ELEPHANT TAKE A DUMP ON YOUR HEAD OR WHAT?
I'LL HAVE YOU KNOW THAT THIS IS IN HONOR OF MITARAI CORP'S BRAND NEW THAI BRANCH!!
YES, THAILAND'S IN OUR HEARTS AND ON OUR MINDS.
HUM HUM HUMMM!
AH, POOPS. YOU GOT A THEME SONG NOW.
I COMMAND YOU TO END THIS INCESSANT NAME-CALLING!!
UH, THAT THING LOOKS KINDA FUNKY.
I'M TELLING YOU, THIS'LL BE ALL THE RAGE SOON.
YEAH, RIGHT!! AS IF!!
HMPH! OH YE OF LITTLE FAITH. YOU'LL SEE SOON ENOUGH.

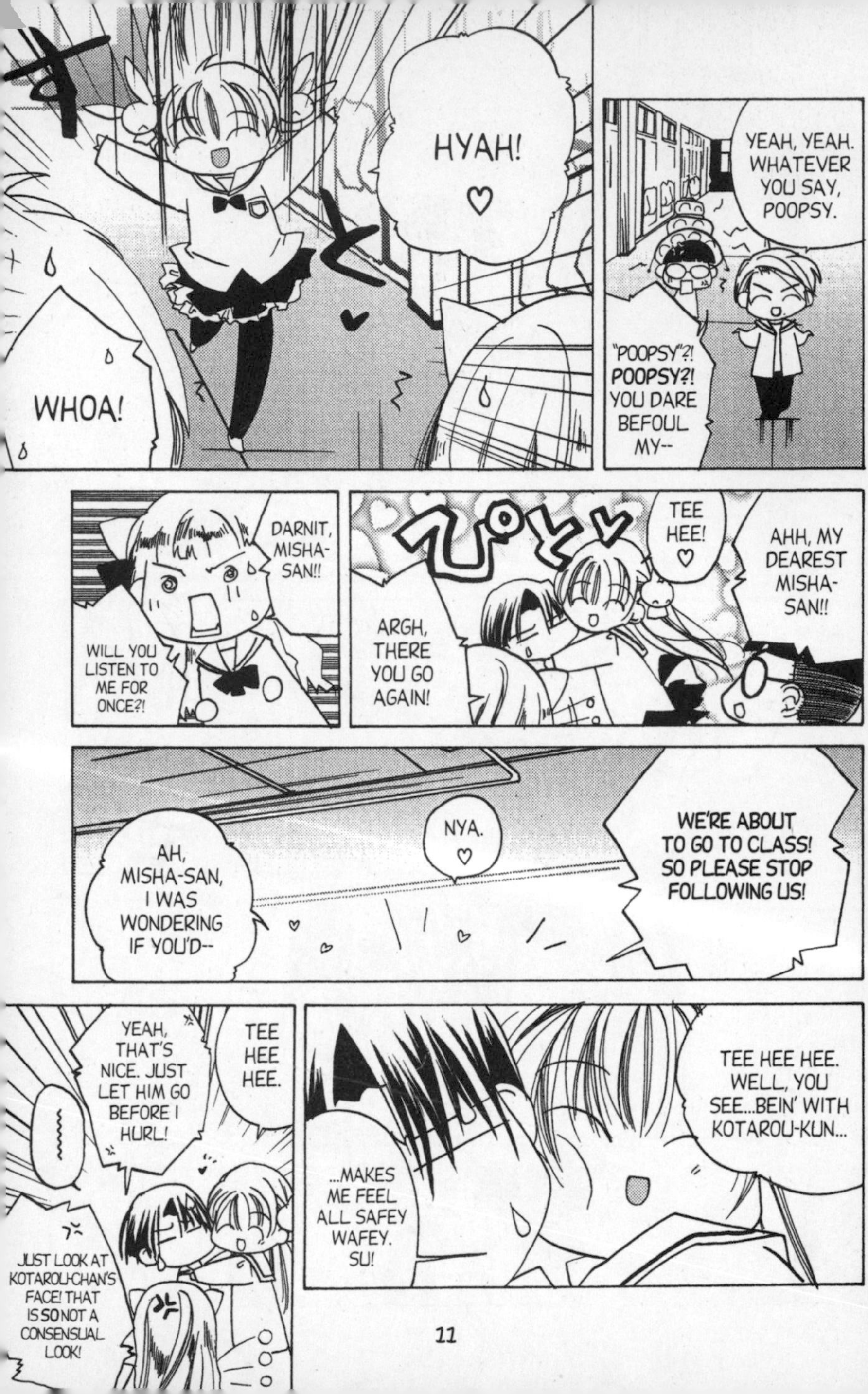
YEAH, YEAH. WHATEVER YOU SAY, POOPSY.
"POOPSY"?! POOPSY?! YOU DARE BEFOUL MY--
HYAH! ♡
WHOA!
TEE HEE! ♡
AHH, MY DEAREST MISHA-SAN!!
ARGH, THERE YOU GO AGAIN!
DARNIT, MISHA-SAN!!
WILL YOU LISTEN TO ME FOR ONCE?!
WE'RE ABOUT TO GO TO CLASS! SO PLEASE STOP FOLLOWING US!
NYA. ♡
AH, MISHA-SAN, I WAS WONDERING IF YOU'D--
TEE HEE HEE. WELL, YOU SEE...BEIN' WITH KOTAROU-KUN...
...MAKES ME FEEL ALL SAFEY WAFEY. SU!
TEE HEE HEE.
YEAH, THAT'S NICE. JUST LET HIM GO BEFORE I HURL!
JUST LOOK AT KOTAROU-CHAN'S FACE! THAT IS SO NOT A CONSENSUAL LOOK!

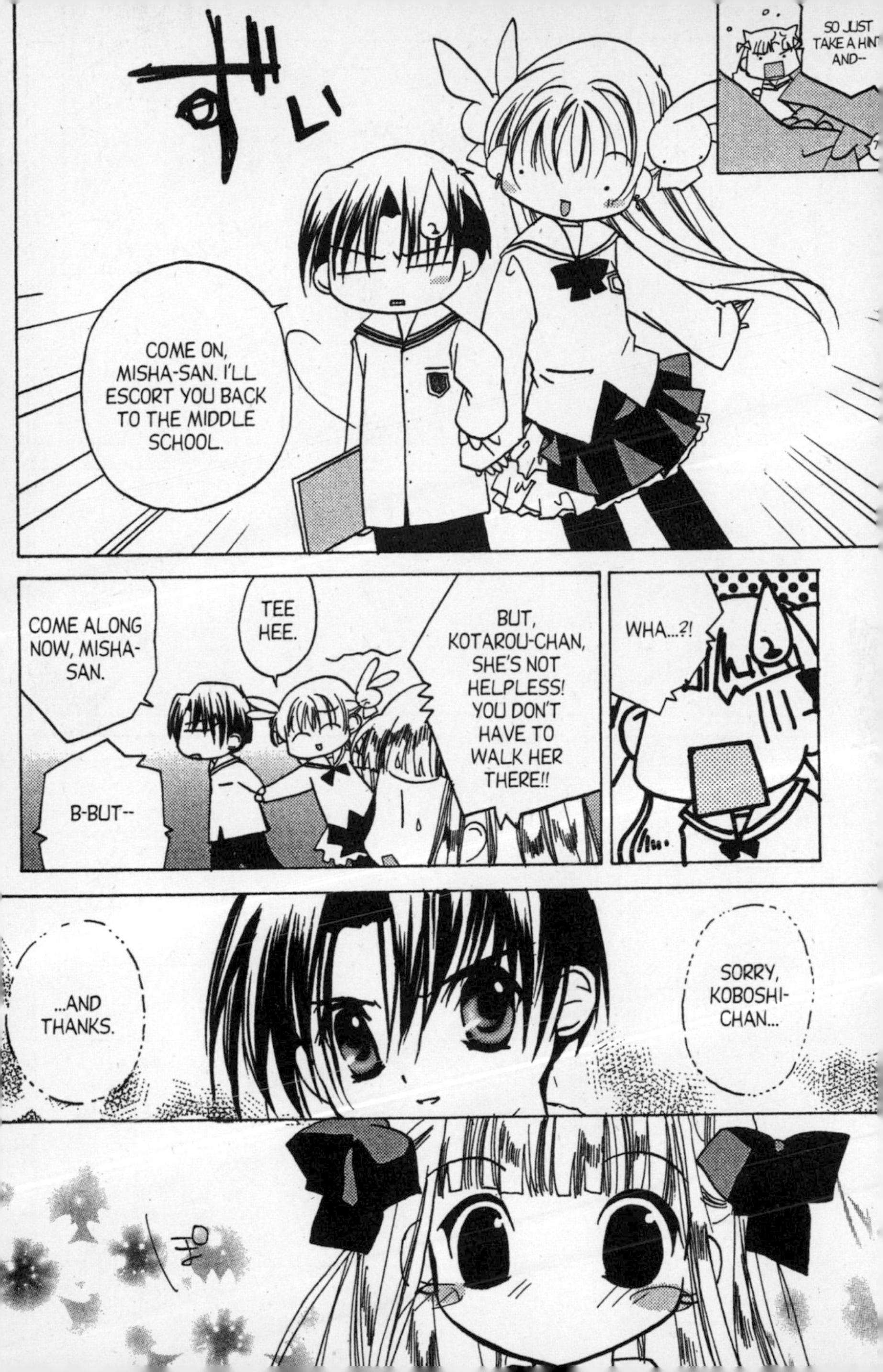
SO JUST TAKE A HINT AND--
ずい
COME ON, MISHA-SAN. I'LL ESCORT YOU BACK TO THE MIDDLE SCHOOL.
WHA...?!
BUT, KOTAROU-CHAN, SHE'S NOT HELPLESS! YOU DON'T HAVE TO WALK HER THERE!!
TEE HEE.
COME ALONG NOW, MISHA-SAN.
B-BUT--
SORRY, KOBOSHI-CHAN...
...AND THANKS.
ぽ

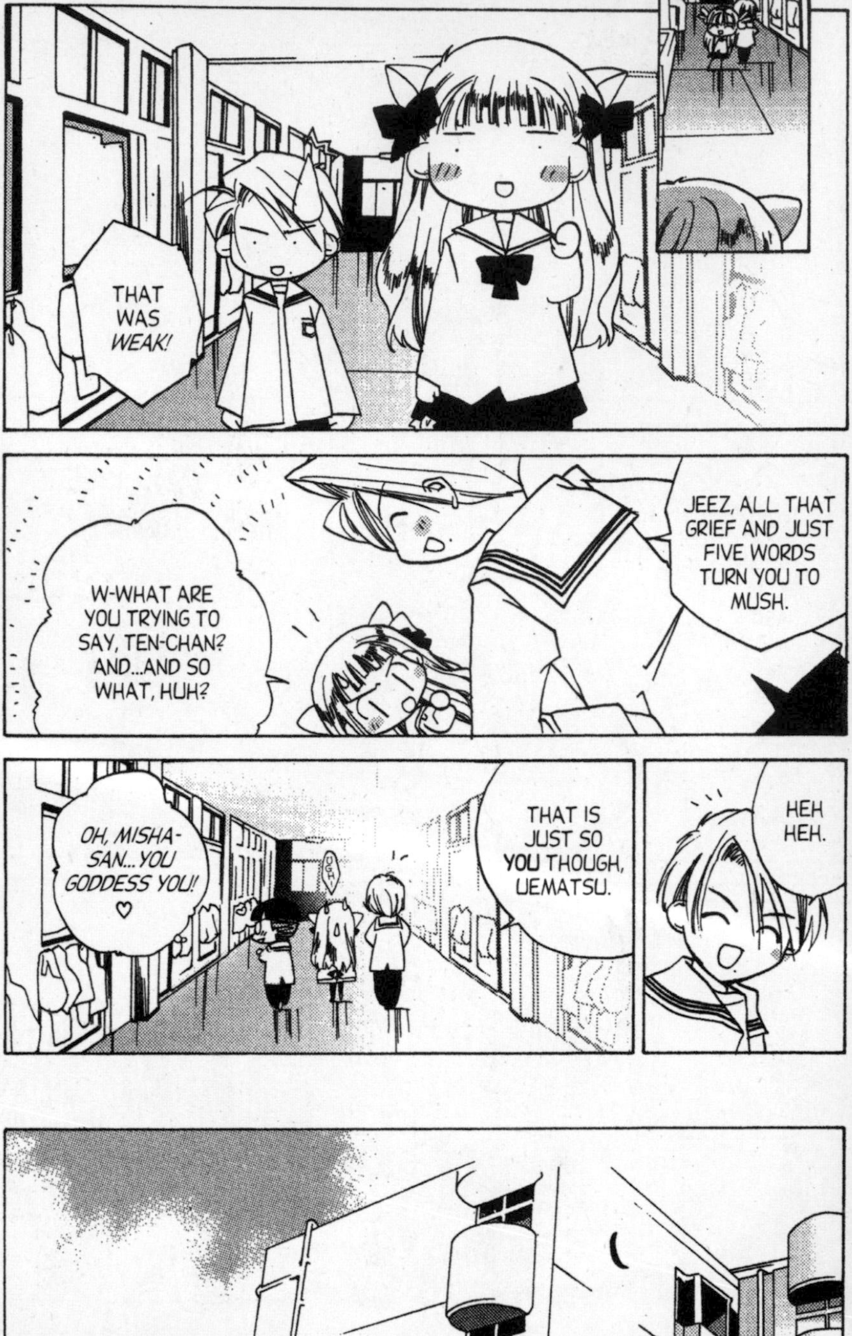
THAT WAS WEAK!
JEEZ, ALL THAT GRIEF AND JUST FIVE WORDS TURN YOU TO MUSH.
W-WHAT ARE YOU TRYING TO SAY, TEN-CHAN? AND...AND SO WHAT, HUH?
HEH HEH.
THAT IS JUST SO YOU THOUGH, UEMATSU.
OH, MISHA-SAN...YOU GODDESS YOU! ♡

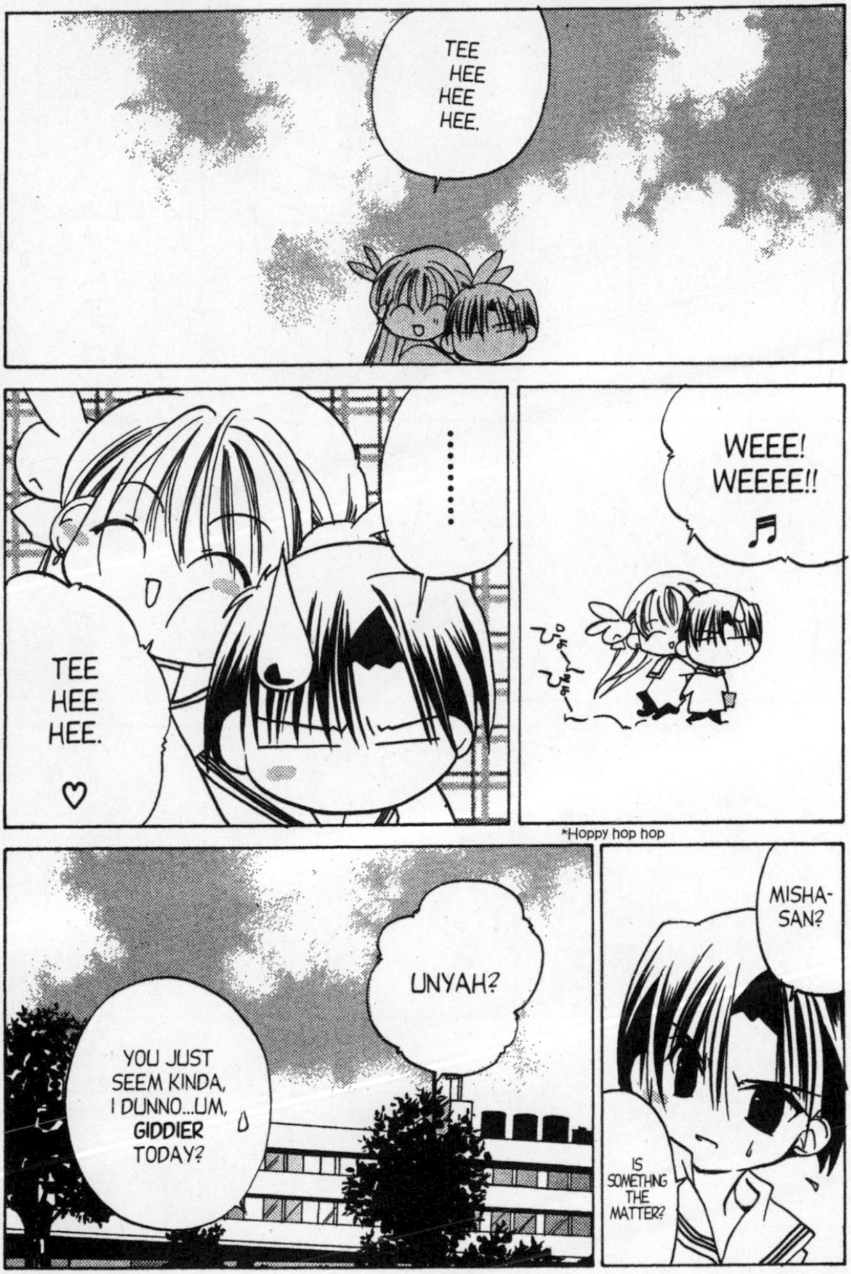
TEE HEE HEE HEE.
WEEE! WEEEE!! ♫
*Hoppy hop hop
....
TEE HEE HEE. ♡
MISHA-SAN?
IS SOMETHING THE MATTER?
UNYAH?
YOU JUST SEEM KINDA, I DUNNO...UM, **GIDDIER** TODAY?

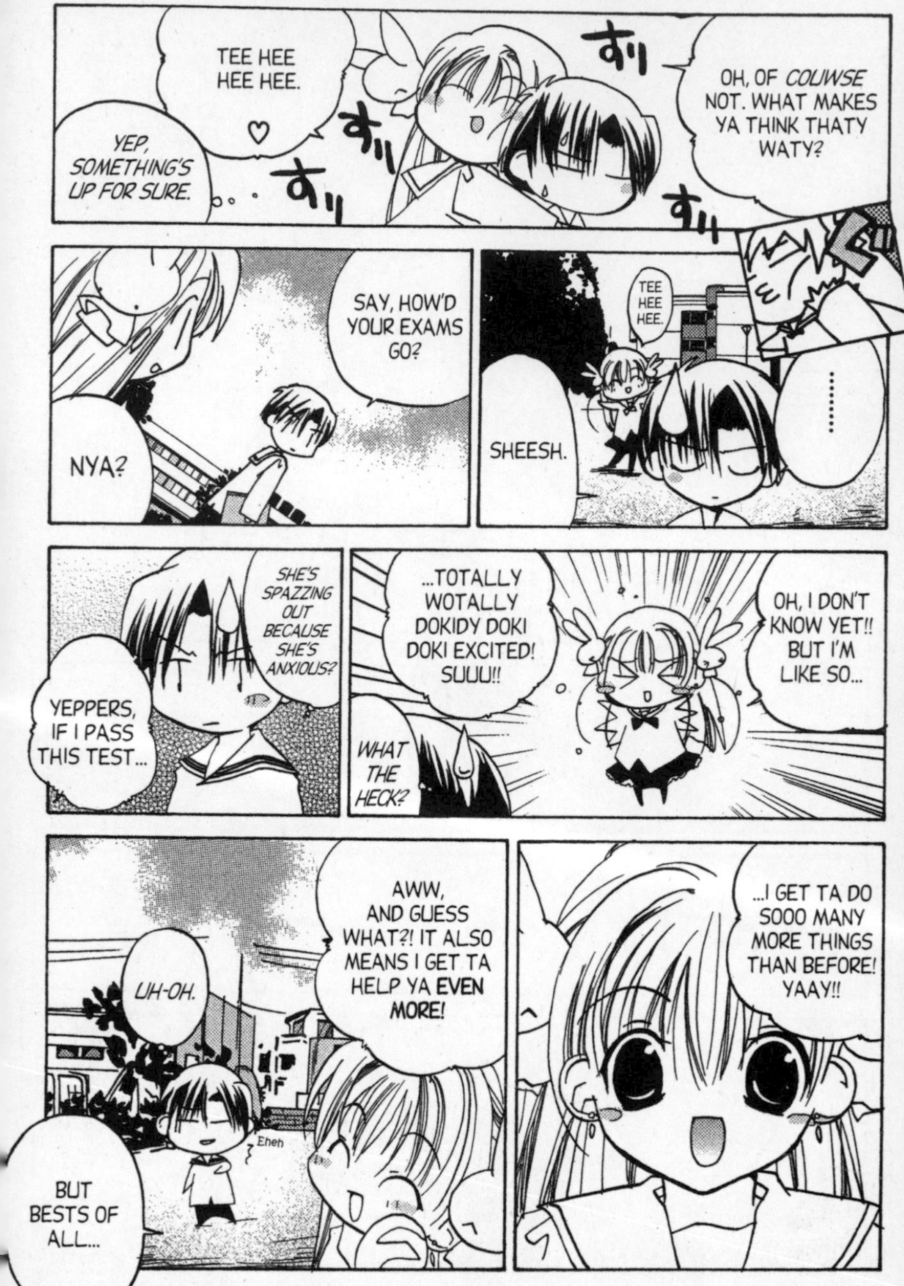
OH, OF COUWSE NOT. WHAT MAKES YA THINK THATY WATY?
すり
すり
すり
すり
TEE HEE HEE HEE. ♥
YEP, SOMETHING'S UP FOR SURE.
......
TEE HEE HEE.
SHEESH.
SAY, HOW'D YOUR EXAMS GO?
NYA?
OH, I DON'T KNOW YET!! BUT I'M LIKE SO...
...TOTALLY WOTALLY DOKIDY DOKI DOKI EXCITED! SUUU!!
WHAT THE HECK?
SHE'S SPAZZING OUT BECAUSE SHE'S ANXIOUS?
YEPPERS, IF I PASS THIS TEST...
...I GET TA DO SOOO MANY MORE THINGS THAN BEFORE! YAAY!!
AWW, AND GUESS WHAT?! IT ALSO MEANS I GET TA HELP YA EVEN MORE!
UH-OH.
Eheh
BUT BESTS OF ALL...

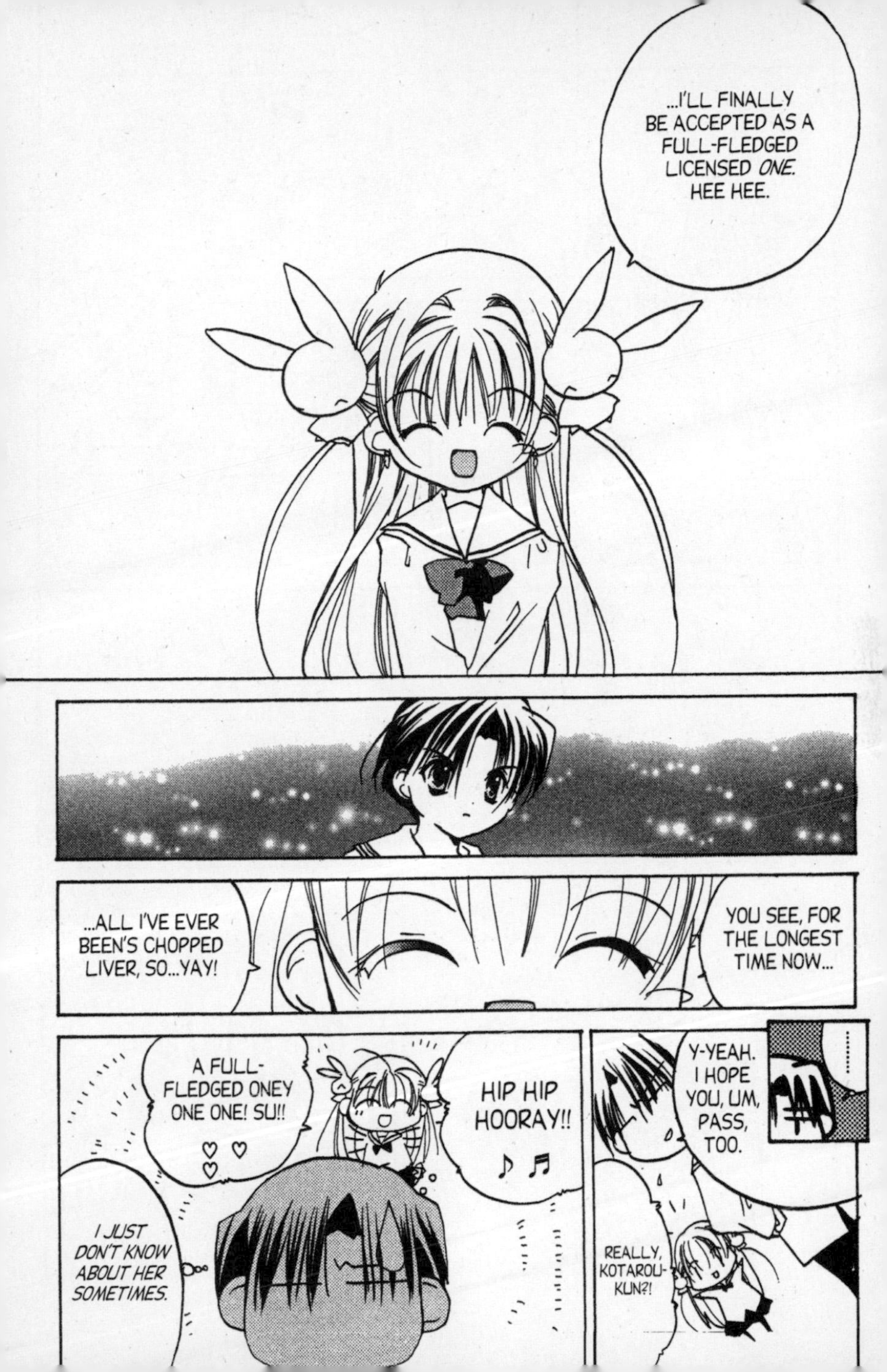
...I'LL FINALLY BE ACCEPTED AS A FULL-FLEDGED LICENSED *ONE.* HEE HEE.
YOU SEE, FOR THE LONGEST TIME NOW...
...ALL I'VE EVER BEEN'S CHOPPED LIVER, SO...YAY!
......
Y-YEAH. I HOPE YOU, UM, PASS, TOO.
REALLY, KOTAROU-KUN?!
HIP HIP HOORAY!!
A FULL-FLEDGED ONEY ONE ONE! SU!!
I JUST DON'T KNOW ABOUT HER SOMETIMES.

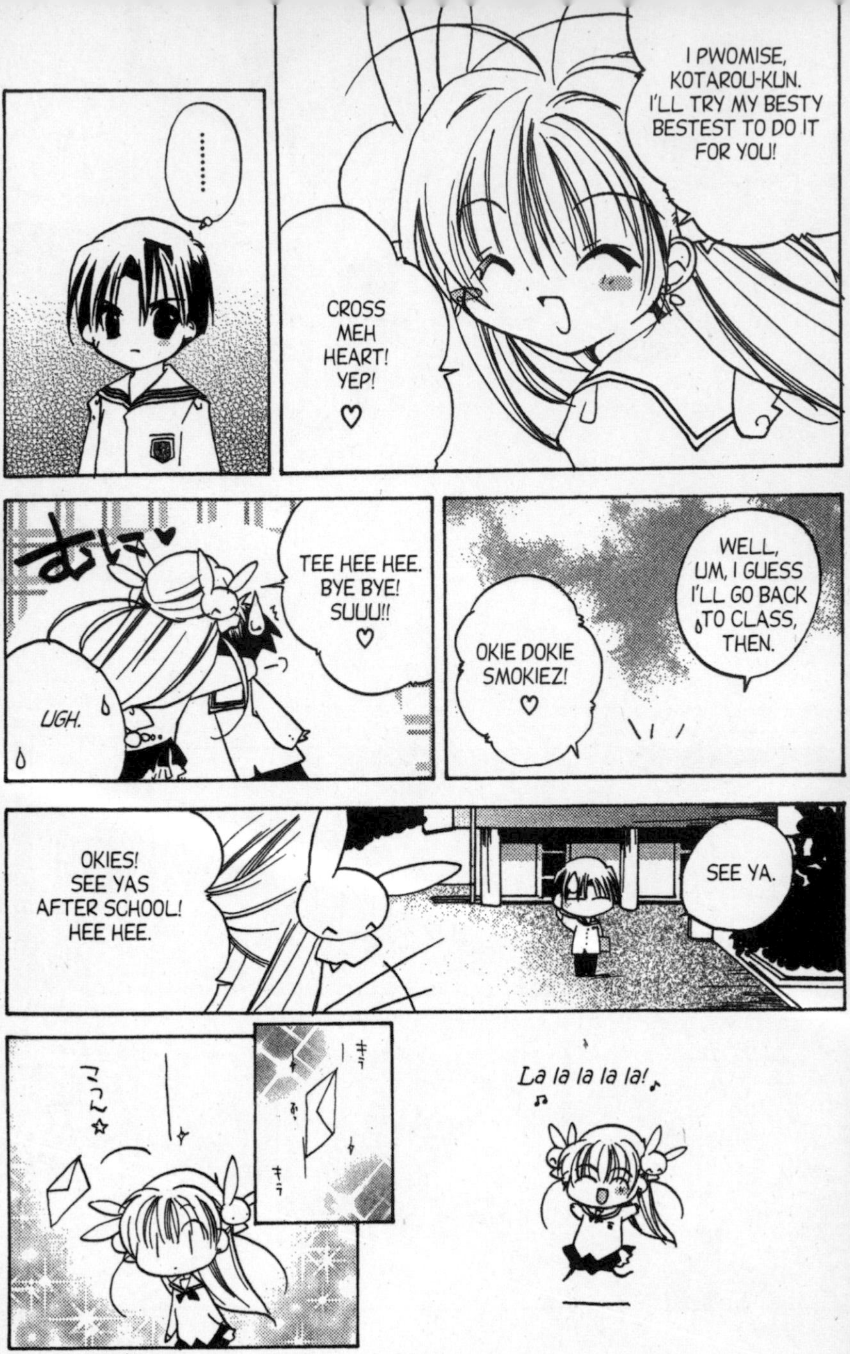
I PWOMISE, KOTAROU-KUN. I'LL TRY MY BESTY BESTEST TO DO IT FOR YOU!
CROSS MEH HEART! YEP! ♡
......
WELL, UM, I GUESS I'LL GO BACK TO CLASS, THEN.
OKIE DOKIE SMOKIEZ! ♡
TEE HEE HEE. BYE BYE! SUUU!! ♡
むに
UGH.
SEE YA.
OKIES! SEE YAS AFTER SCHOOL! HEE HEE.
La la la la la!
キラ
キラ
こつん☆
*poink

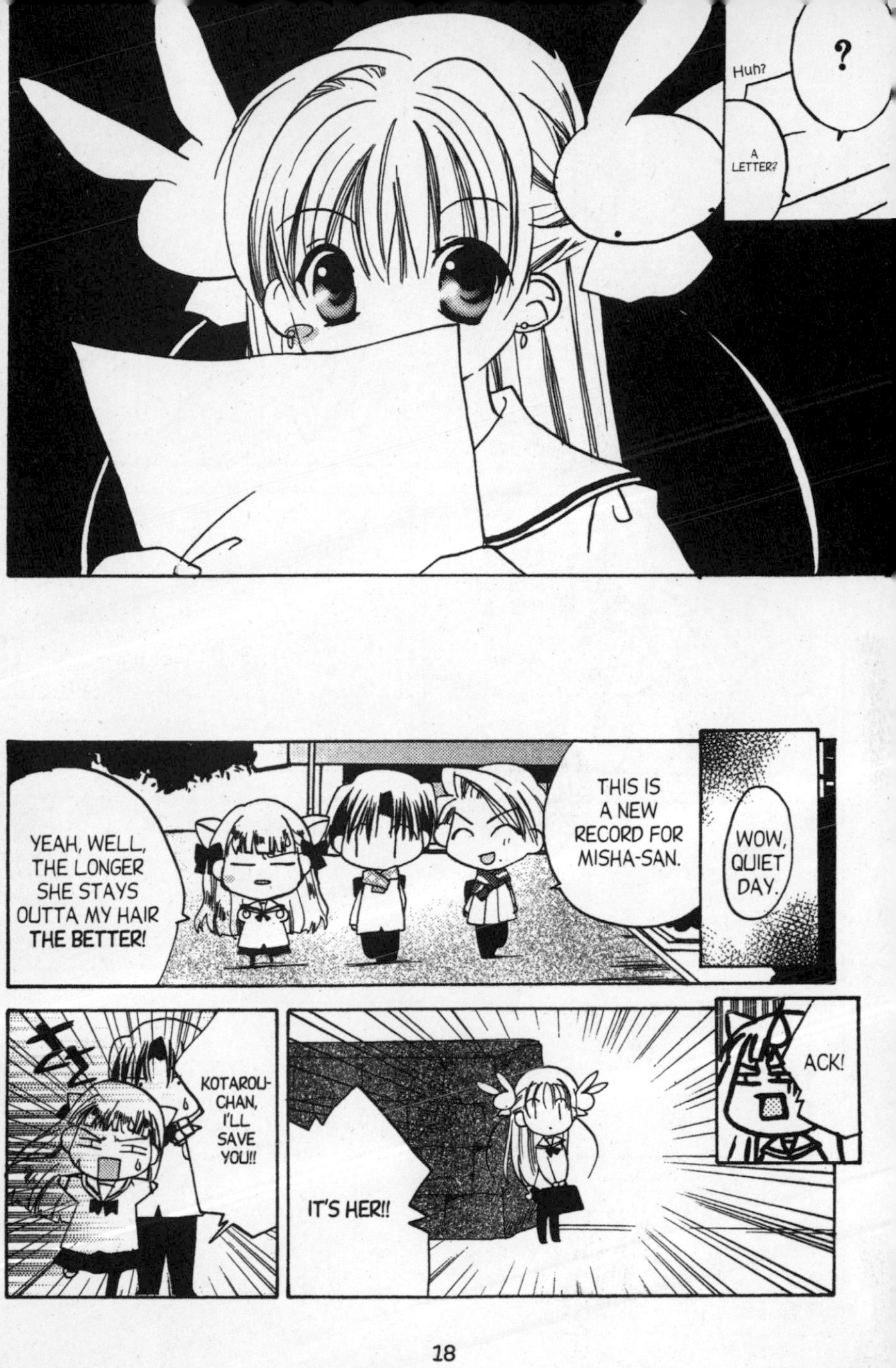
?
Huh?
A LETTER?
WOW, QUIET DAY.
THIS IS A NEW RECORD FOR MISHA-SAN.
YEAH, WELL, THE LONGER SHE STAYS OUTTA MY HAIR THE BETTER!
ACK!
IT'S HER!!
KOTAROU-CHAN, I'LL SAVE YOU!!

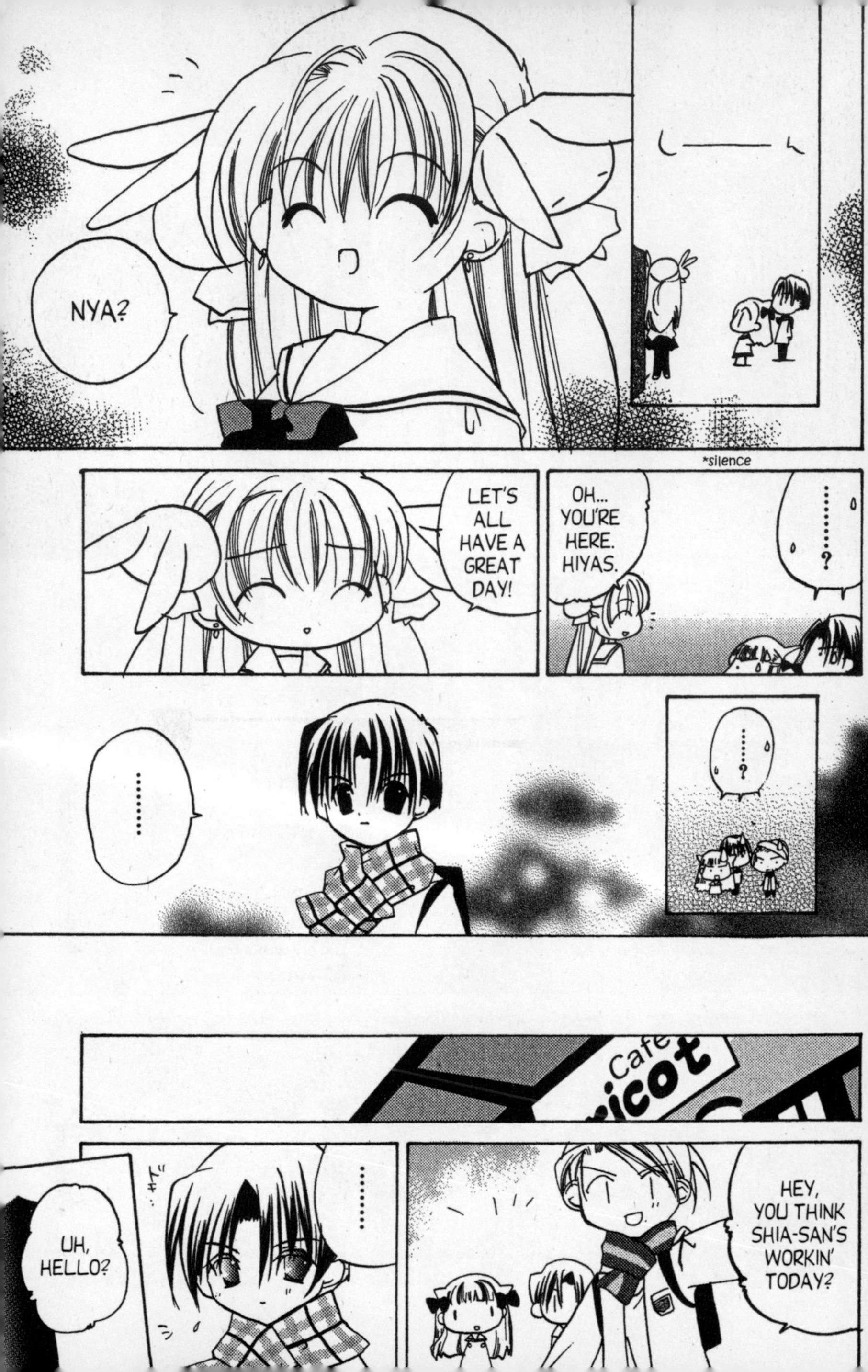
*silence
NYA?
......?
OH... YOU'RE HERE. HIYAS.
LET'S ALL HAVE A GREAT DAY!
......?
......
Cafe
HEY, YOU THINK SHIA-SAN'S WORKIN' TODAY?
......
UH, HELLO?

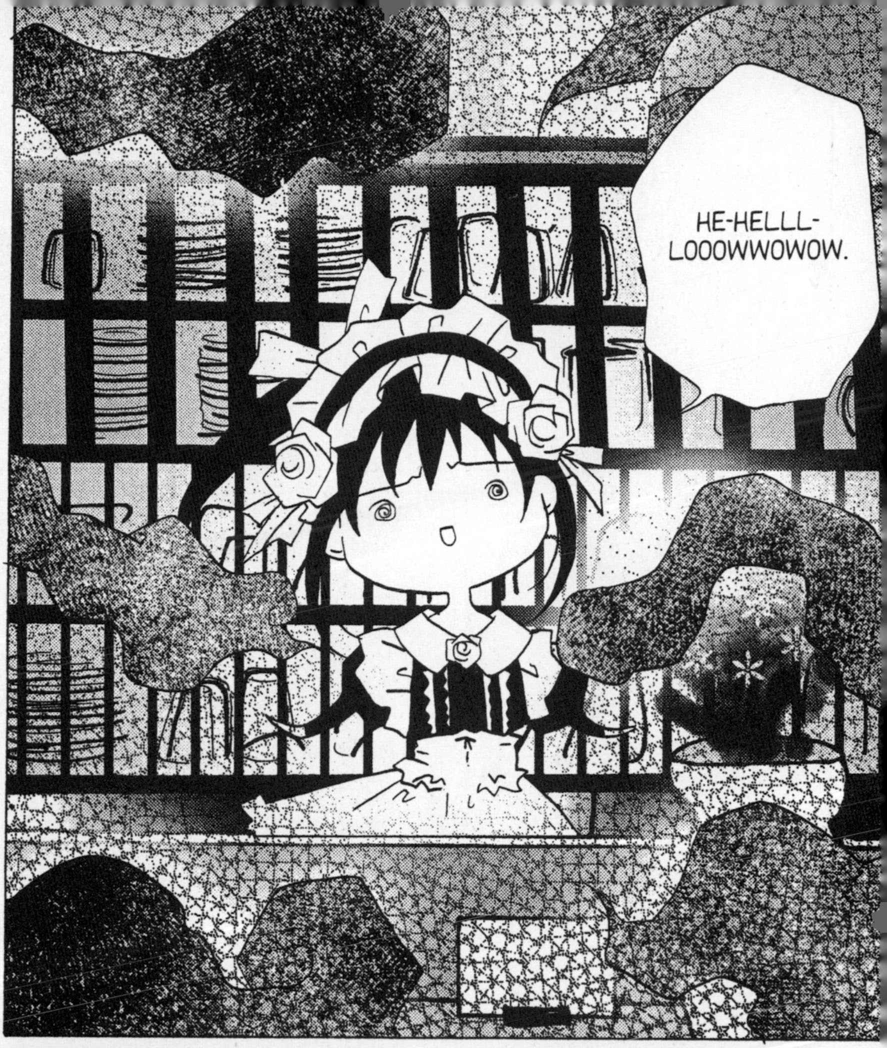
HE-HELLLL-
LOOOWWOWOW.
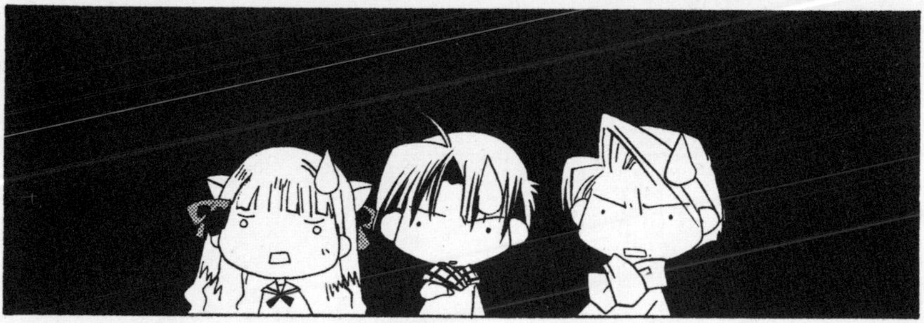

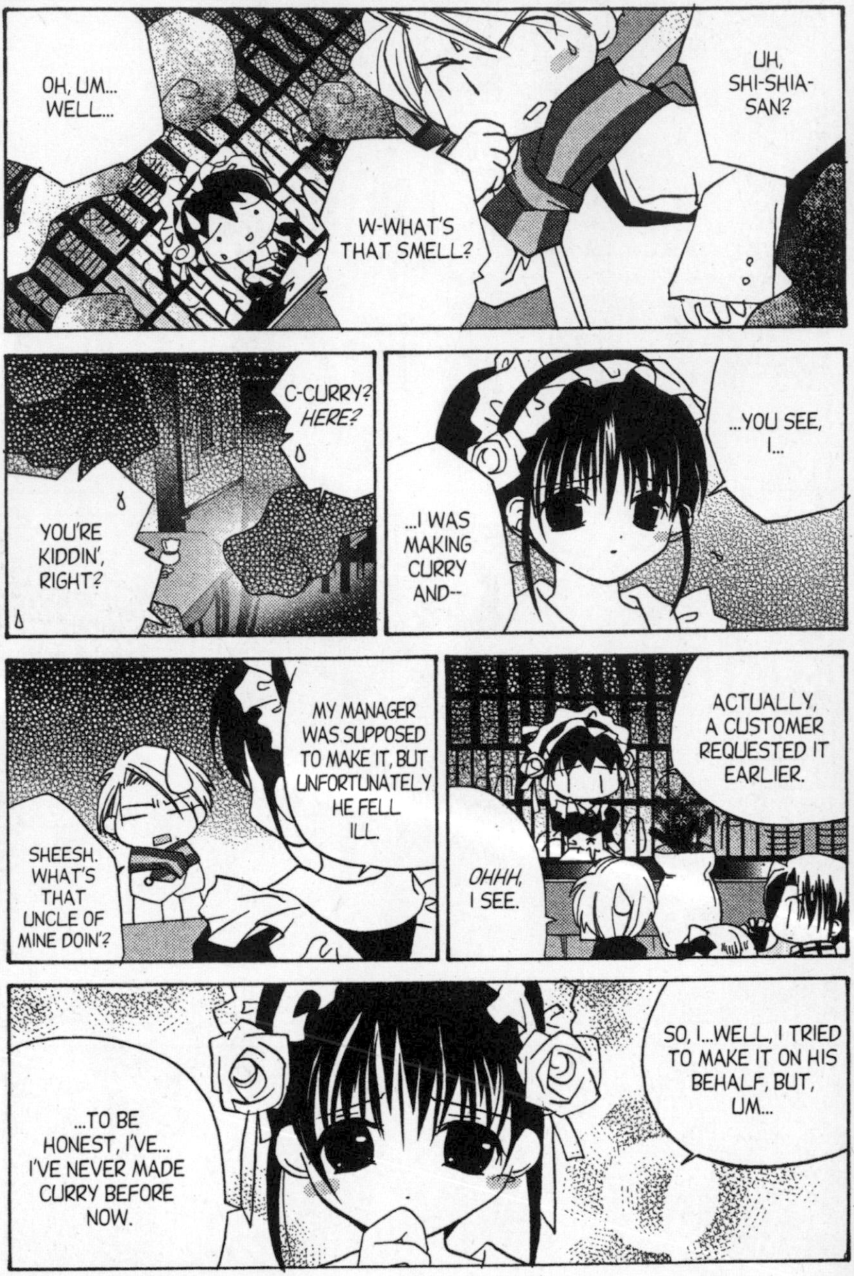
UH, SHI-SHIA-SAN?
W-WHAT'S THAT SMELL?
OH, UM... WELL...
...YOU SEE, I...
...I WAS MAKING CURRY AND--
C-CURRY? *HERE?*
YOU'RE KIDDIN', RIGHT?
ACTUALLY, A CUSTOMER REQUESTED IT EARLIER.
OHHH, I SEE.
MY MANAGER WAS SUPPOSED TO MAKE IT, BUT UNFORTUNATELY HE FELL ILL.
SHEESH. WHAT'S THAT UNCLE OF MINE DOIN'?
SO, I...WELL, I TRIED TO MAKE IT ON HIS BEHALF, BUT, UM...
...TO BE HONEST, I'VE... I'VE NEVER MADE CURRY BEFORE NOW.

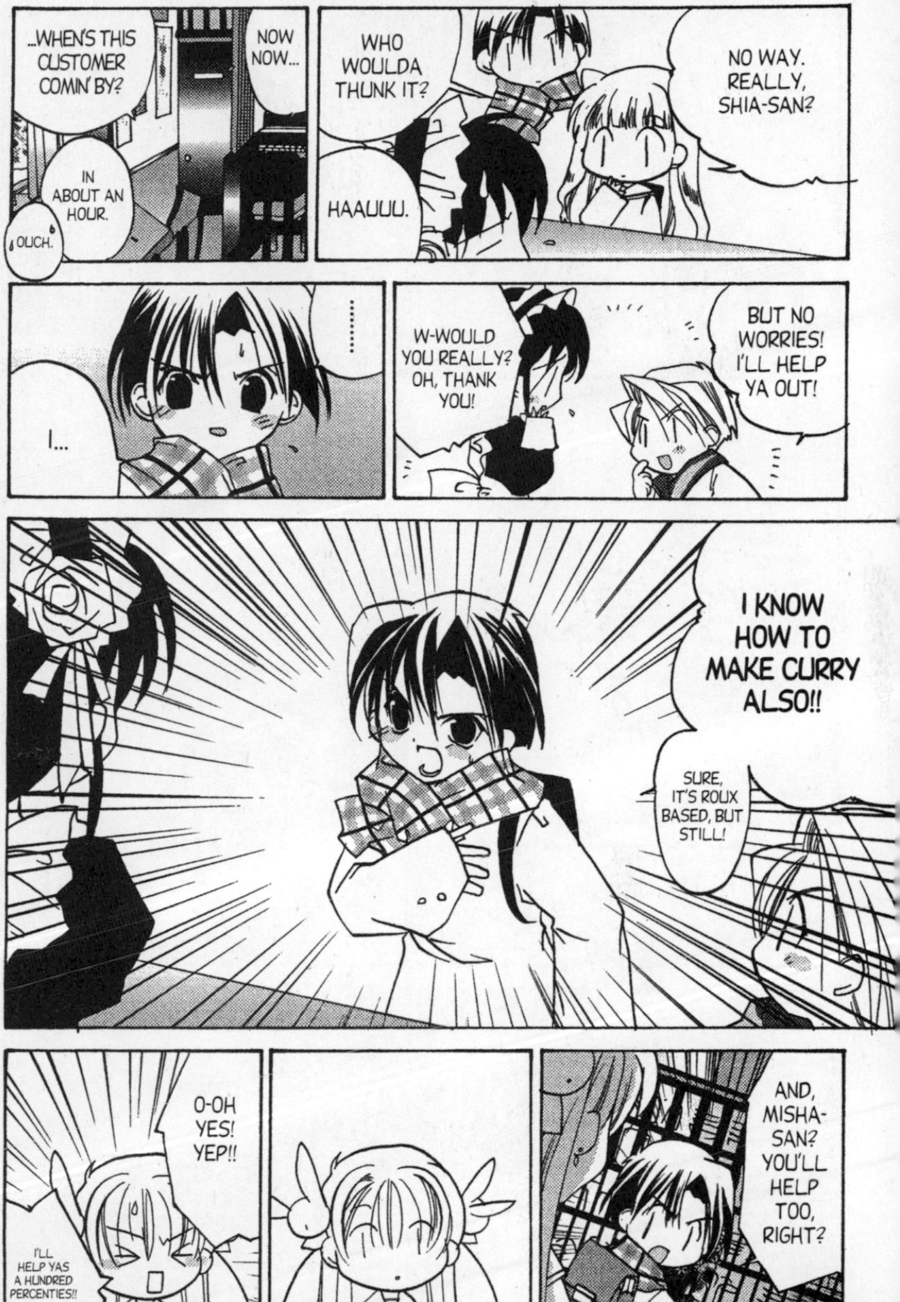
NO WAY. REALLY, SHIA-SAN?
WHO WOULDA THUNK IT?
HAAUUU.
NOW NOW...
...WHEN'S THIS CUSTOMER COMIN' BY?
IN ABOUT AN HOUR.
OUCH.
BUT NO WORRIES! I'LL HELP YA OUT!
W-WOULD YOU REALLY? OH, THANK YOU!
......
I...
I KNOW HOW TO MAKE CURRY ALSO!!
SURE, IT'S ROUX BASED, BUT STILL!
AND, MISHA-SAN? YOU'LL HELP TOO, RIGHT?
O-OH YES! YEP!!
I'LL HELP YAS A HUNDRED PERCENTIES!!

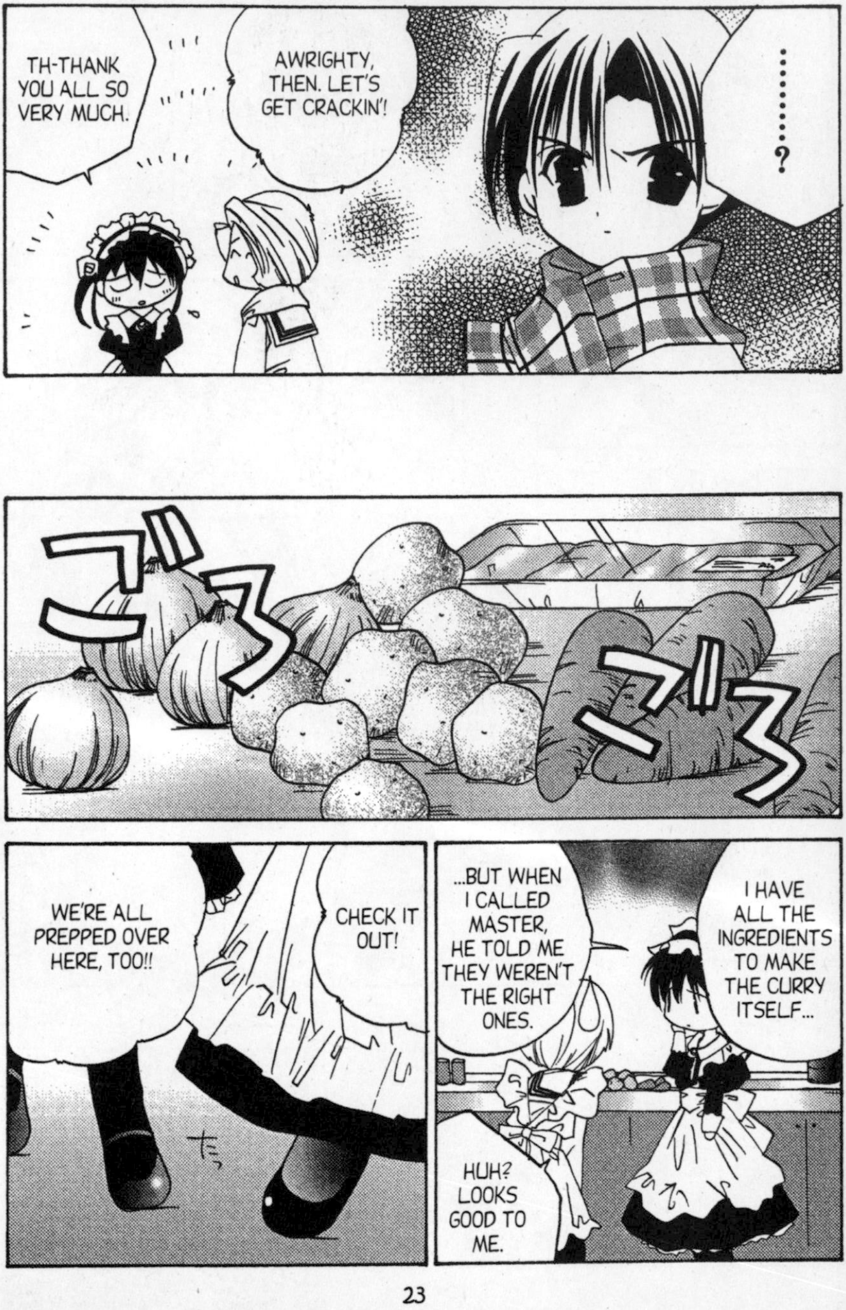
......?
AWRIGHTY, THEN. LET'S GET CRACKIN'!
TH-THANK YOU ALL SO VERY MUCH.
ごろ
ごろ
I HAVE ALL THE INGREDIENTS TO MAKE THE CURRY ITSELF...
...BUT WHEN I CALLED MASTER, HE TOLD ME THEY WEREN'T THE RIGHT ONES.
HUH? LOOKS GOOD TO ME.
CHECK IT OUT!
WE'RE ALL PREPPED OVER HERE, TOO!!

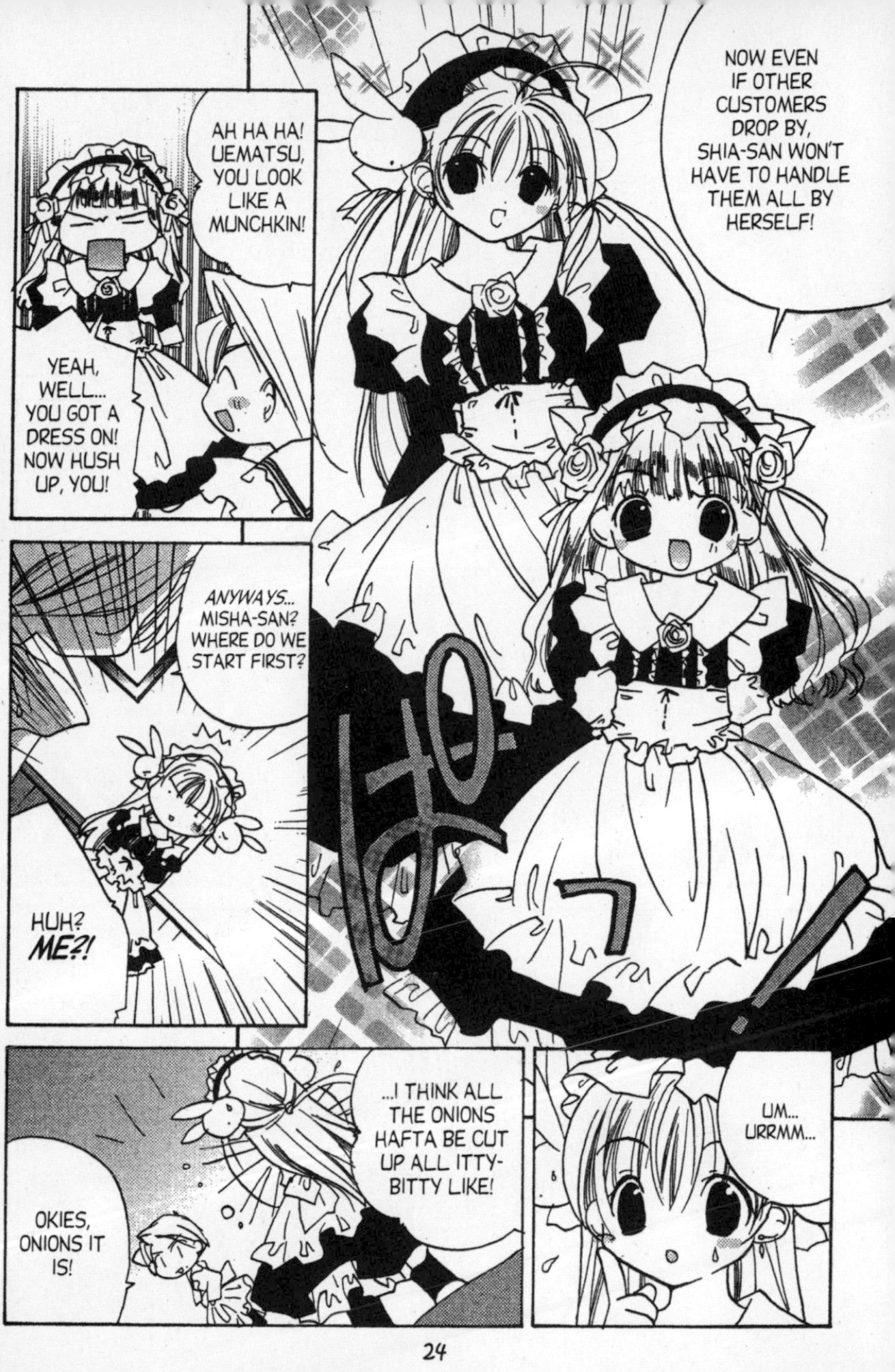
NOW EVEN IF OTHER CUSTOMERS DROP BY, SHIA-SAN WON'T HAVE TO HANDLE THEM ALL BY HERSELF!
AH HA HA! UEMATSU, YOU LOOK LIKE A MUNCHKIN!
YEAH, WELL... YOU GOT A DRESS ON! NOW HUSH UP, YOU!
ANYWAYS... MISHA-SAN? WHERE DO WE START FIRST?
HUH? ***ME?!***
UM... URRMM...
...I THINK ALL THE ONIONS HAFTA BE CUT UP ALL ITTY-BITTY LIKE!
OKIES, ONIONS IT IS!

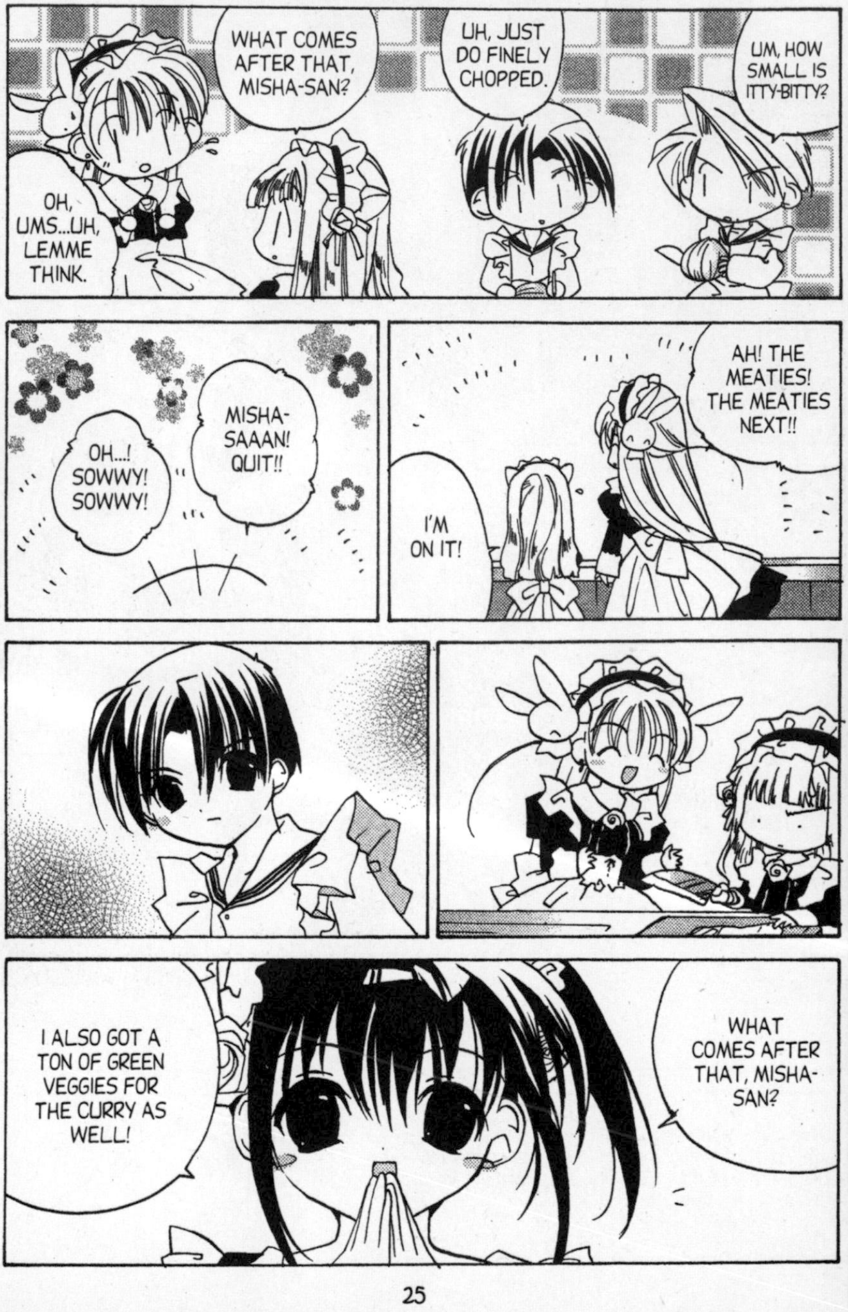
UM, HOW SMALL IS ITTY-BITTY?
UH, JUST DO FINELY CHOPPED.
WHAT COMES AFTER THAT, MISHA-SAN?
OH, UMS...UH, LEMME THINK.
AH! THE MEATIES! THE MEATIES NEXT!!
I'M ON IT!
MISHA-SAAAN! QUIT!!
OH...! SOWWY! SOWWY!
WHAT COMES AFTER THAT, MISHA-SAN?
I ALSO GOT A TON OF GREEN VEGGIES FOR THE CURRY AS WELL!

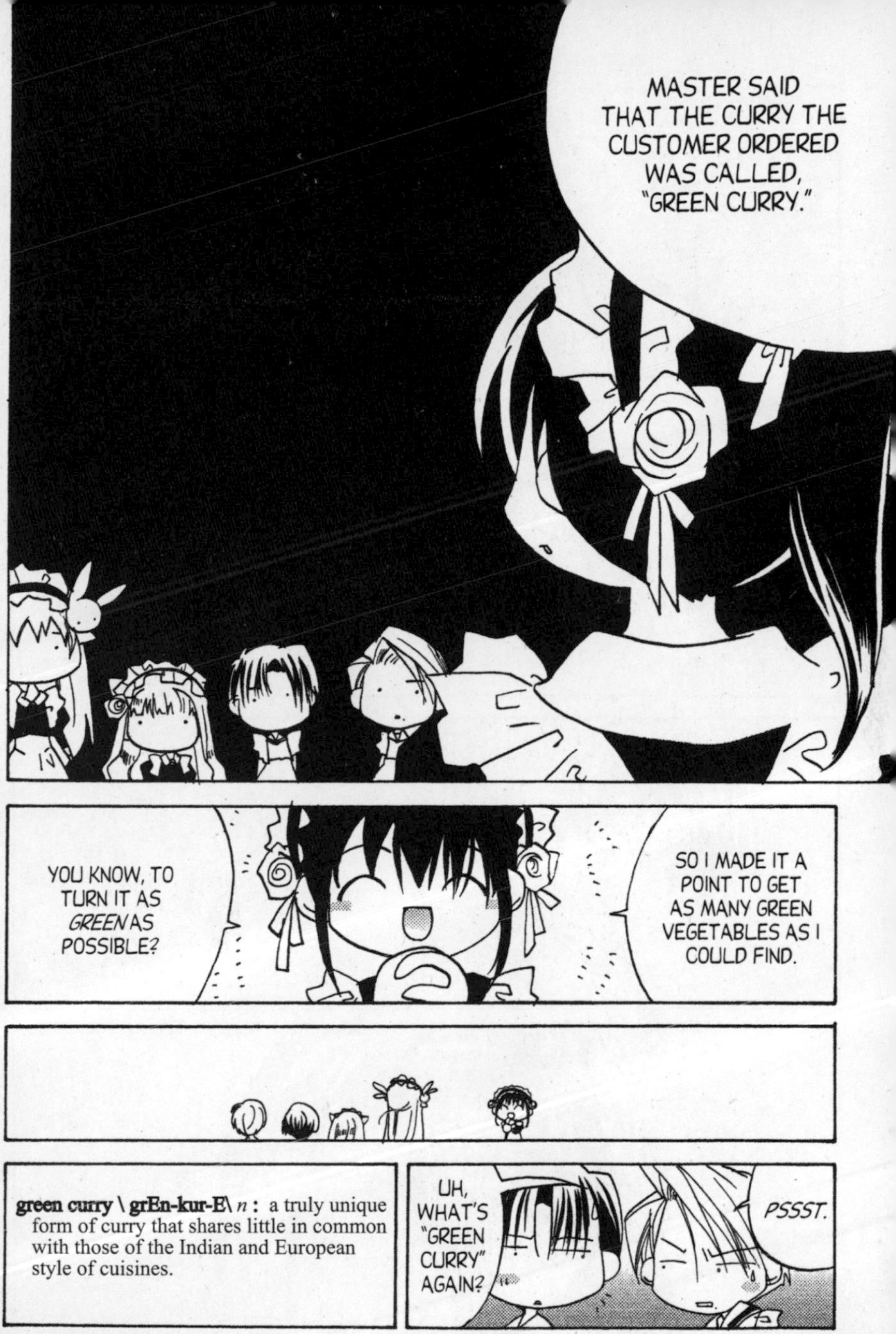
MASTER SAID THAT THE CURRY THE CUSTOMER ORDERED WAS CALLED, "GREEN CURRY."
SO I MADE IT A POINT TO GET AS MANY GREEN VEGETABLES AS I COULD FIND.
YOU KNOW, TO TURN IT AS *GREEN* AS POSSIBLE?
PSSST.
UH, WHAT'S "GREEN CURRY" AGAIN?
green curry \ grEn-kur-E *n* **:** a truly unique form of curry that shares little in common with those of the Indian and European style of cuisines.

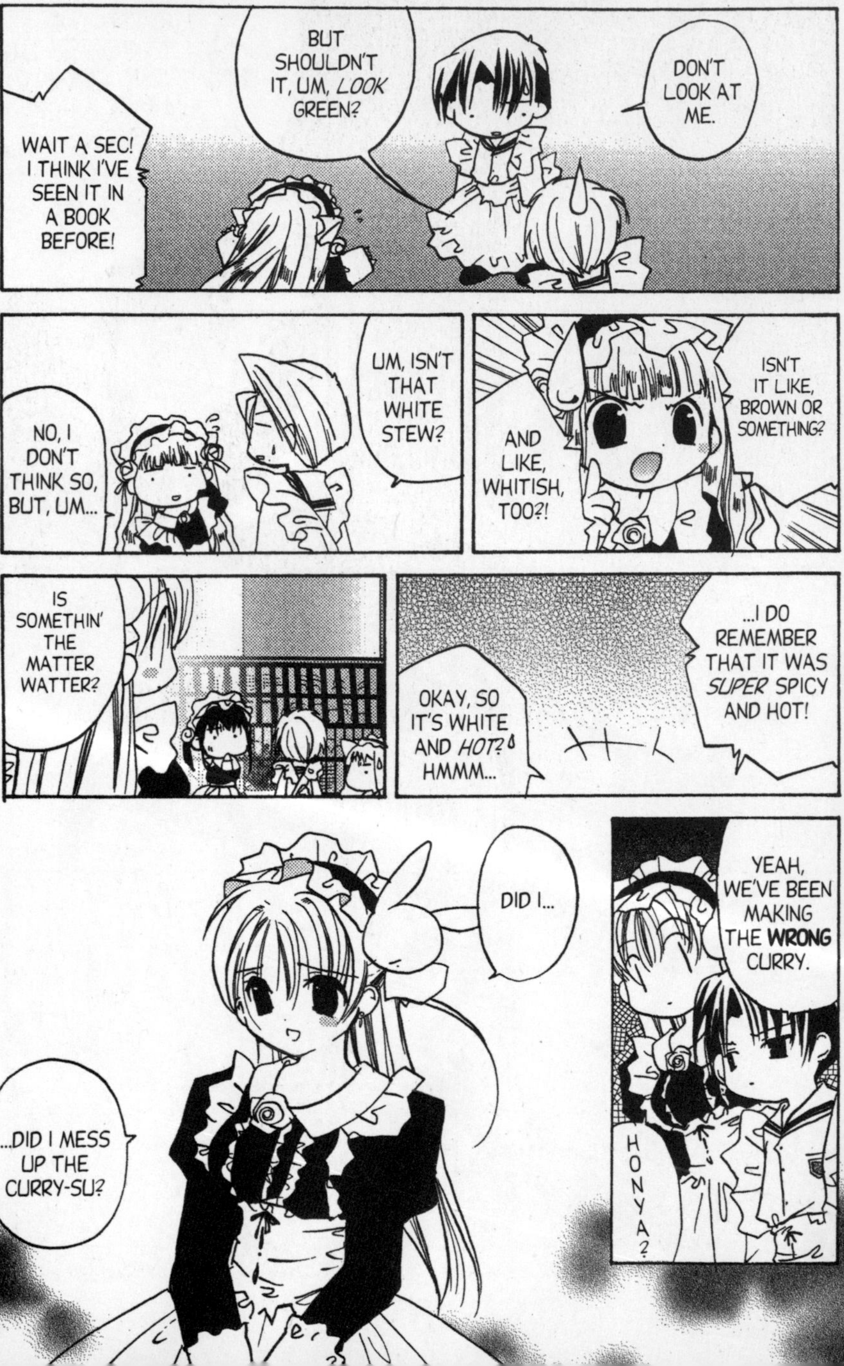
DON'T LOOK AT ME.
BUT SHOULDN'T IT, UM, *LOOK* GREEN?
WAIT A SEC! I THINK I'VE SEEN IT IN A BOOK BEFORE!
ISN'T IT LIKE, BROWN OR SOMETHING?
AND LIKE, WHITISH, TOO?!
UM, ISN'T THAT WHITE STEW?
NO, I DON'T THINK SO, BUT, UM...
...I DO REMEMBER THAT IT WAS *SUPER* SPICY AND HOT!
OKAY, SO IT'S WHITE AND *HOT*? HMMM...
IS SOMETHIN' THE MATTER WATTER?
YEAH, WE'VE BEEN MAKING THE **WRONG** CURRY.
HONYA?
DID I...
...DID I MESS UP THE CURRY-SU?

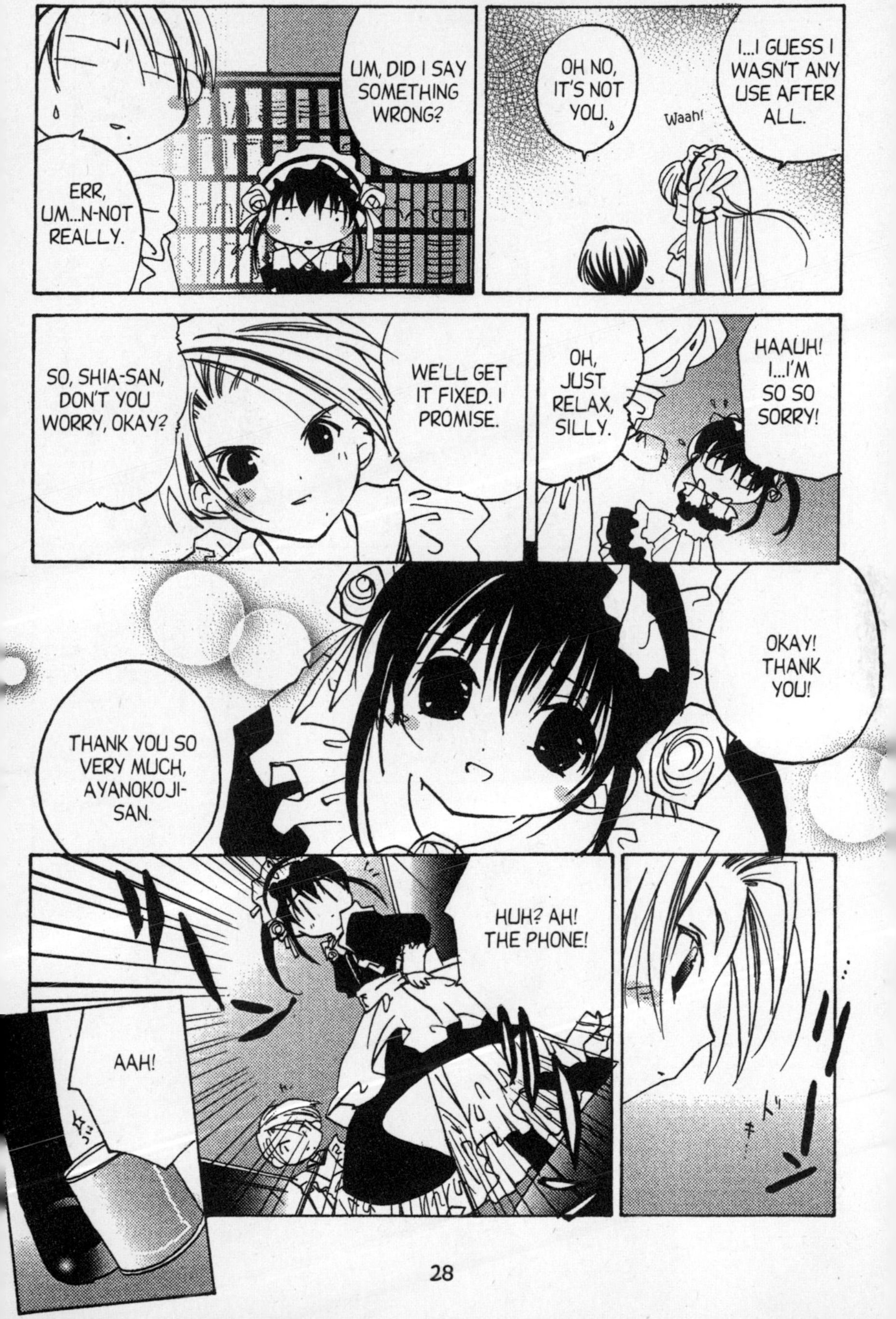
I...I GUESS I WASN'T ANY USE AFTER ALL.
Waah!
OH NO, IT'S NOT YOU.
UM, DID I SAY SOMETHING WRONG?
ERR, UM...N-NOT REALLY.
HAAUH! I...I'M SO SO SORRY!
OH, JUST RELAX, SILLY.
WE'LL GET IT FIXED. I PROMISE.
SO, SHIA-SAN, DON'T YOU WORRY, OKAY?
OKAY! THANK YOU!
THANK YOU SO VERY MUCH, AYANOKOJI-SAN.
HUH? AH! THE PHONE!
AAH!

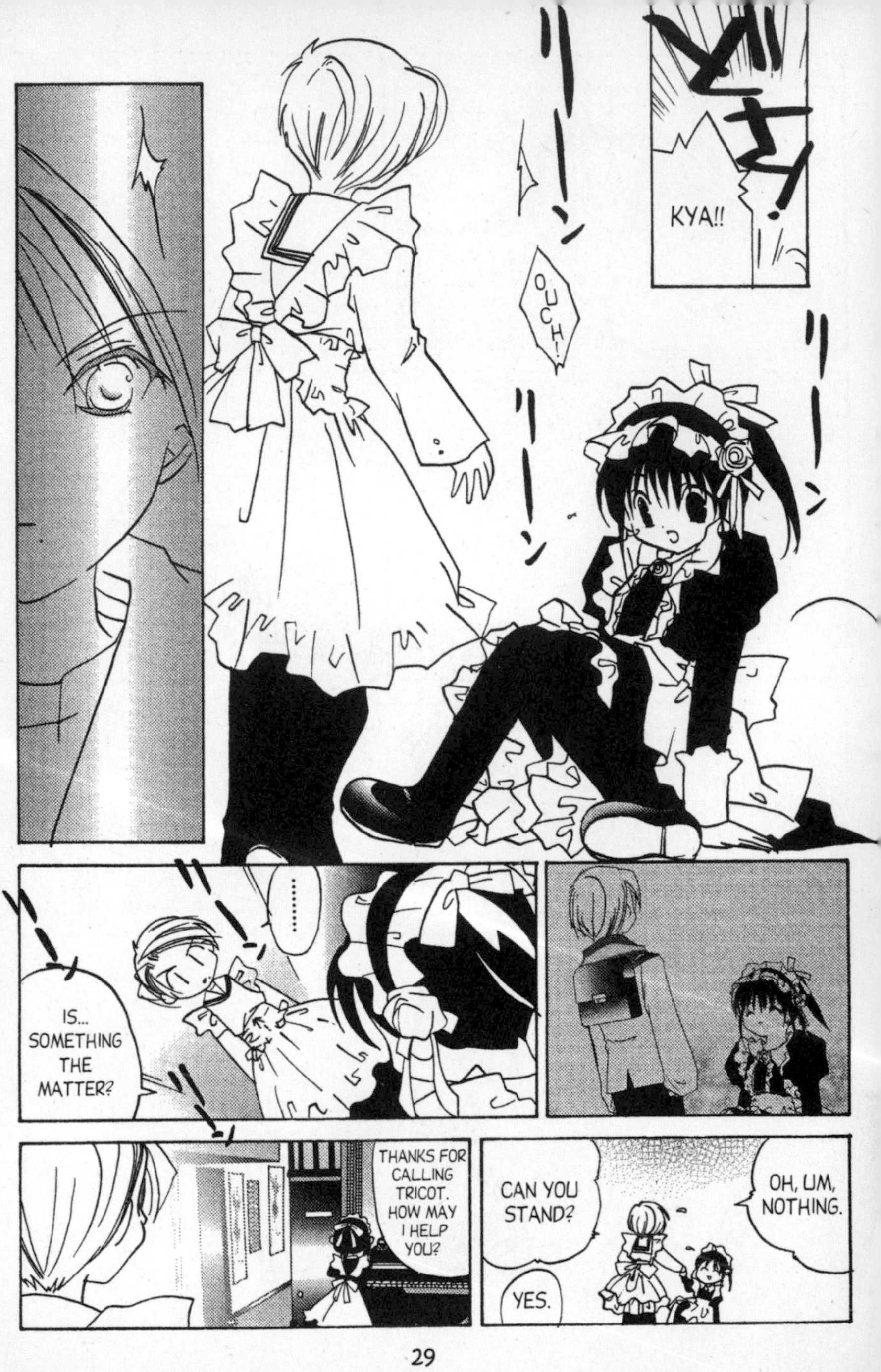
どさっ!
KYA!!
リーーン
OUCH!
リーーン
リーーン
......
IS... SOMETHING THE MATTER?
OH, UM, NOTHING.
CAN YOU STAND?
YES.
THANKS FOR CALLING TRICOT. HOW MAY I HELP YOU?

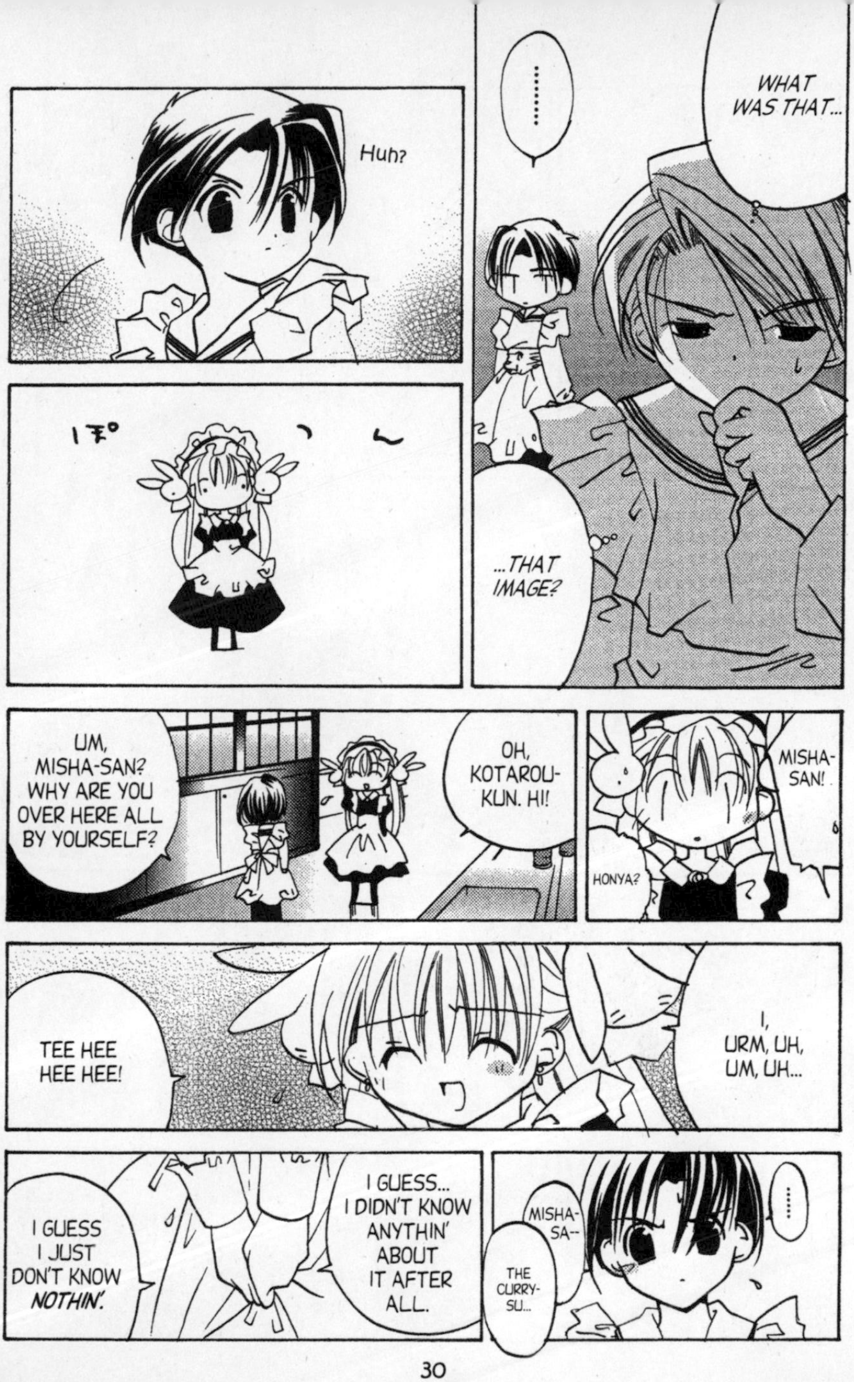
WHAT WAS THAT...
......
...THAT IMAGE?
Huh?
ぽ〜ん
MISHA-SAN!
HONYA?
OH, KOTAROU-KUN. HI!
UM, MISHA-SAN? WHY ARE YOU OVER HERE ALL BY YOURSELF?
I, URM, UH, UM, UH...
TEE HEE HEE HEE!
......
MISHA-SA--
THE CURRY-SU...
I GUESS... I DIDN'T KNOW ANYTHIN' ABOUT IT AFTER ALL.
I GUESS I JUST DON'T KNOW *NOTHIN'*.

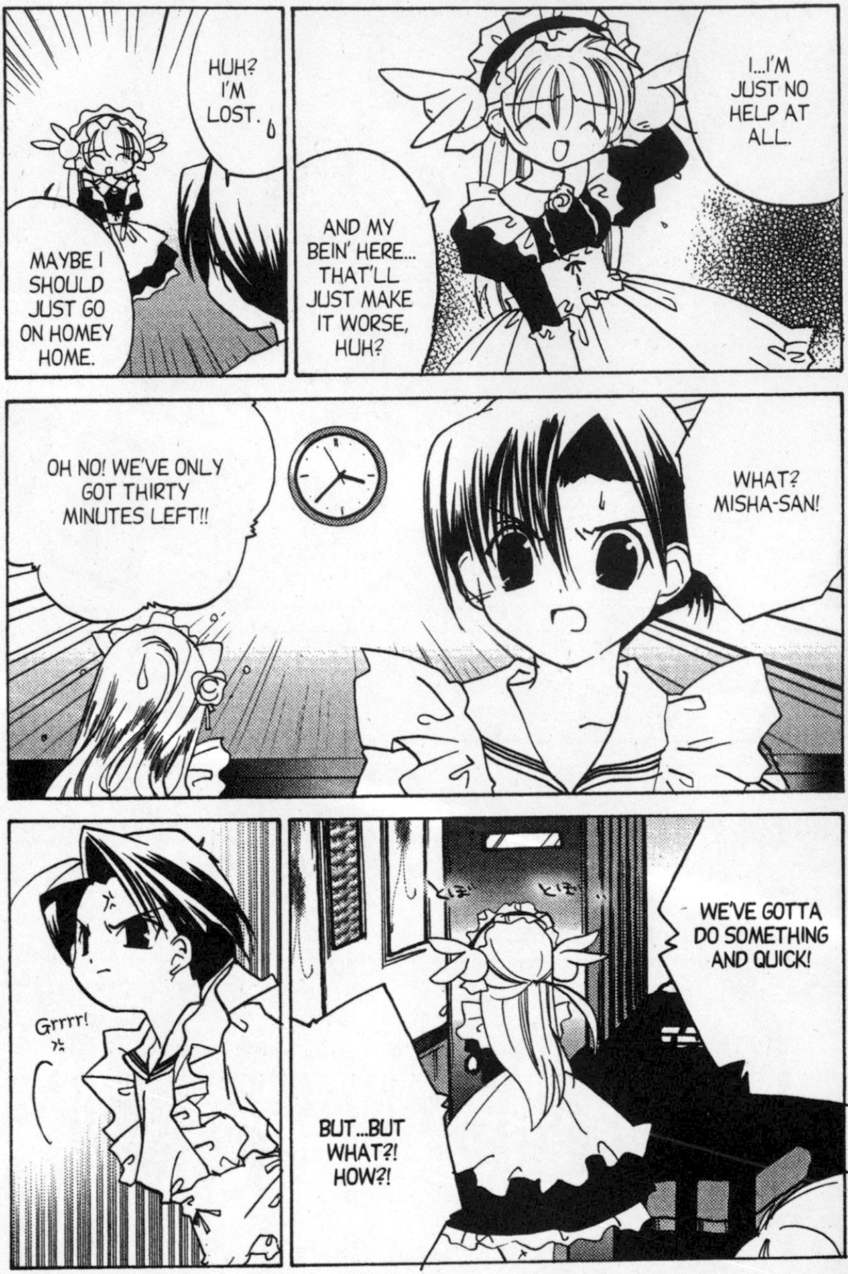
I...I'M JUST NO HELP AT ALL.
AND MY BEIN' HERE... THAT'LL JUST MAKE IT WORSE, HUH?
HUH? I'M LOST.
MAYBE I SHOULD JUST GO ON HOMEY HOME.
WHAT? MISHA-SAN!
OH NO! WE'VE ONLY GOT THIRTY MINUTES LEFT!!
WE'VE GOTTA DO SOMETHING AND QUICK!
BUT...BUT WHAT?! HOW?!
Grrrr!

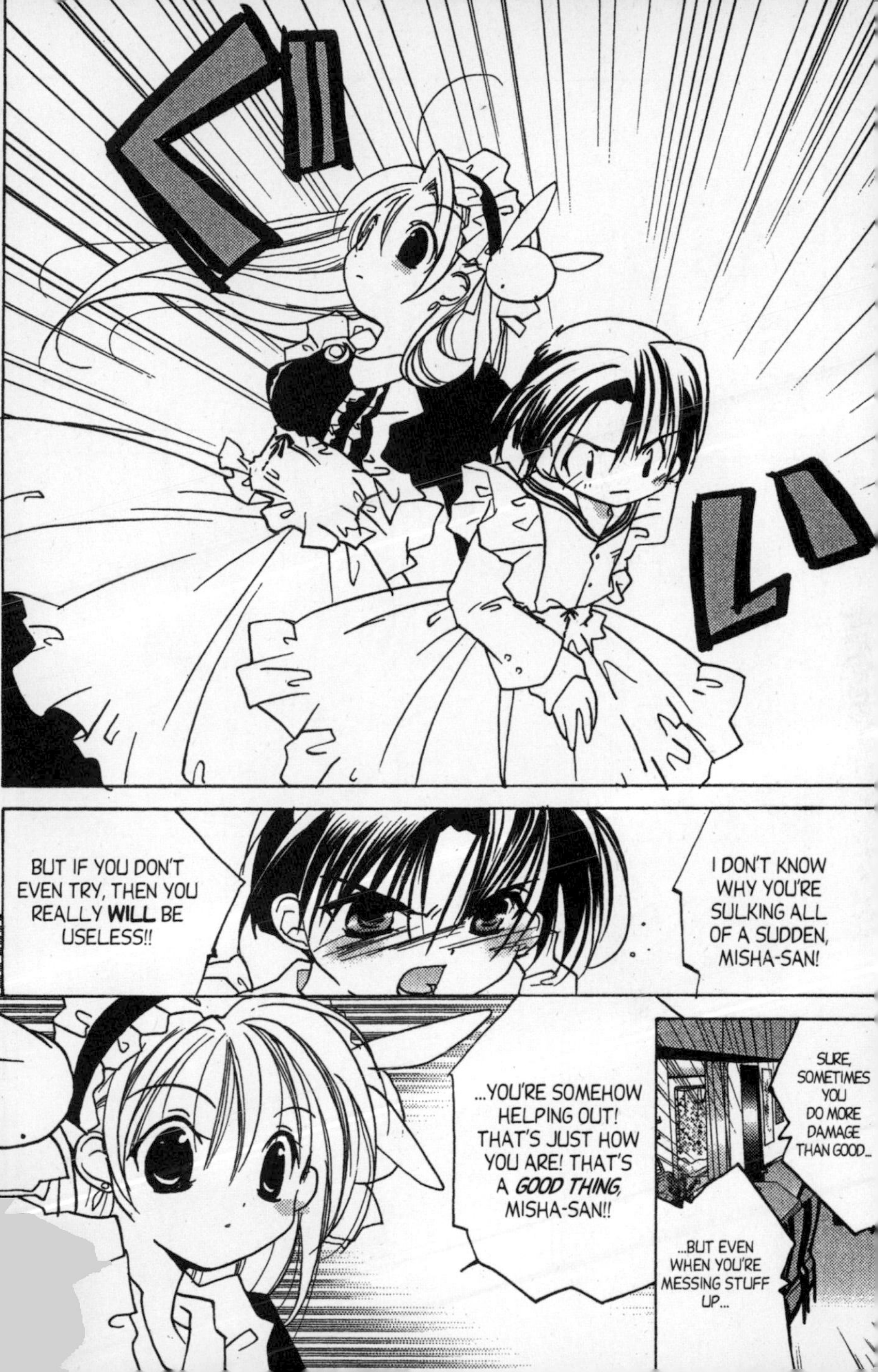
I DON'T KNOW WHY YOU'RE SULKING ALL OF A SUDDEN, MISHA-SAN!
BUT IF YOU DON'T EVEN TRY, THEN YOU REALLY **WILL** BE USELESS!!
SURE, SOMETIMES YOU DO MORE DAMAGE THAN GOOD...
...BUT EVEN WHEN YOU'RE MESSING STUFF UP...
...YOU'RE SOMEHOW HELPING OUT! THAT'S JUST HOW YOU ARE! THAT'S A ***GOOD THING,*** MISHA-SAN!!

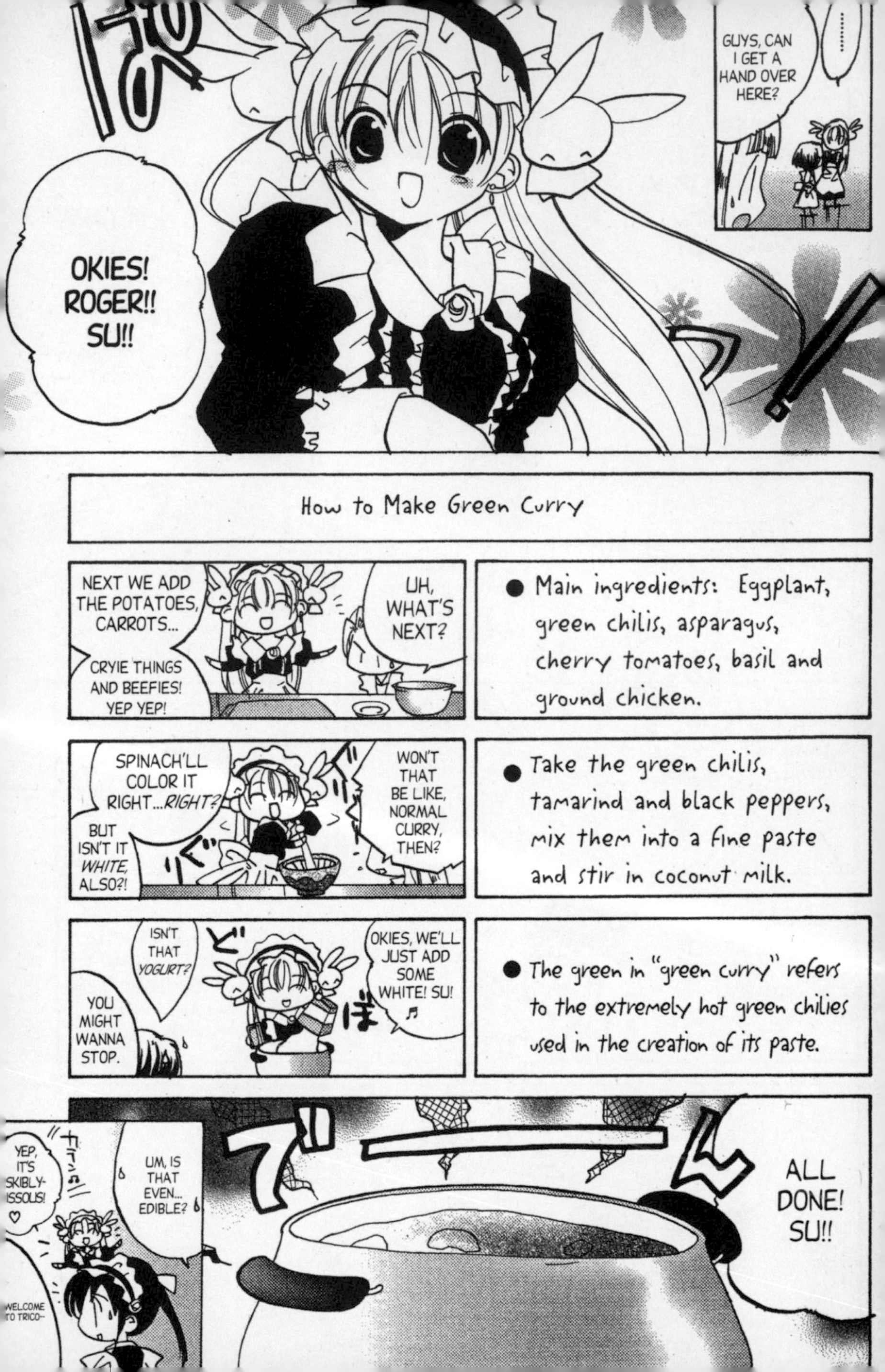
GUYS, CAN I GET A HAND OVER HERE?
......
OKIES! ROGER!! SU!!
How to Make Green Curry
● Main ingredients: Eggplant, green chilis, asparagus, cherry tomatoes, basil and ground chicken.
UH, WHAT'S NEXT?
NEXT WE ADD THE POTATOES, CARROTS...
CRYIE THINGS AND BEEFIES! YEP YEP!
● Take the green chilis, tamarind and black peppers, mix them into a fine paste and stir in coconut milk.
WON'T THAT BE LIKE, NORMAL CURRY, THEN?
SPINACH'LL COLOR IT RIGHT...*RIGHT?*
BUT ISN'T IT *WHITE*, ALSO?!
● The green in "green curry" refers to the extremely hot green chilies used in the creation of its paste.
OKIES, WE'LL JUST ADD SOME WHITE! SU! ♪
ISN'T THAT *YOGURT?*
YOU MIGHT WANNA STOP.
ALL DONE! SU!!
UM, IS THAT EVEN... EDIBLE?
YEP, IT'S SKIBLY-ISSOUS! ♡
WELCOME TO TRICO--

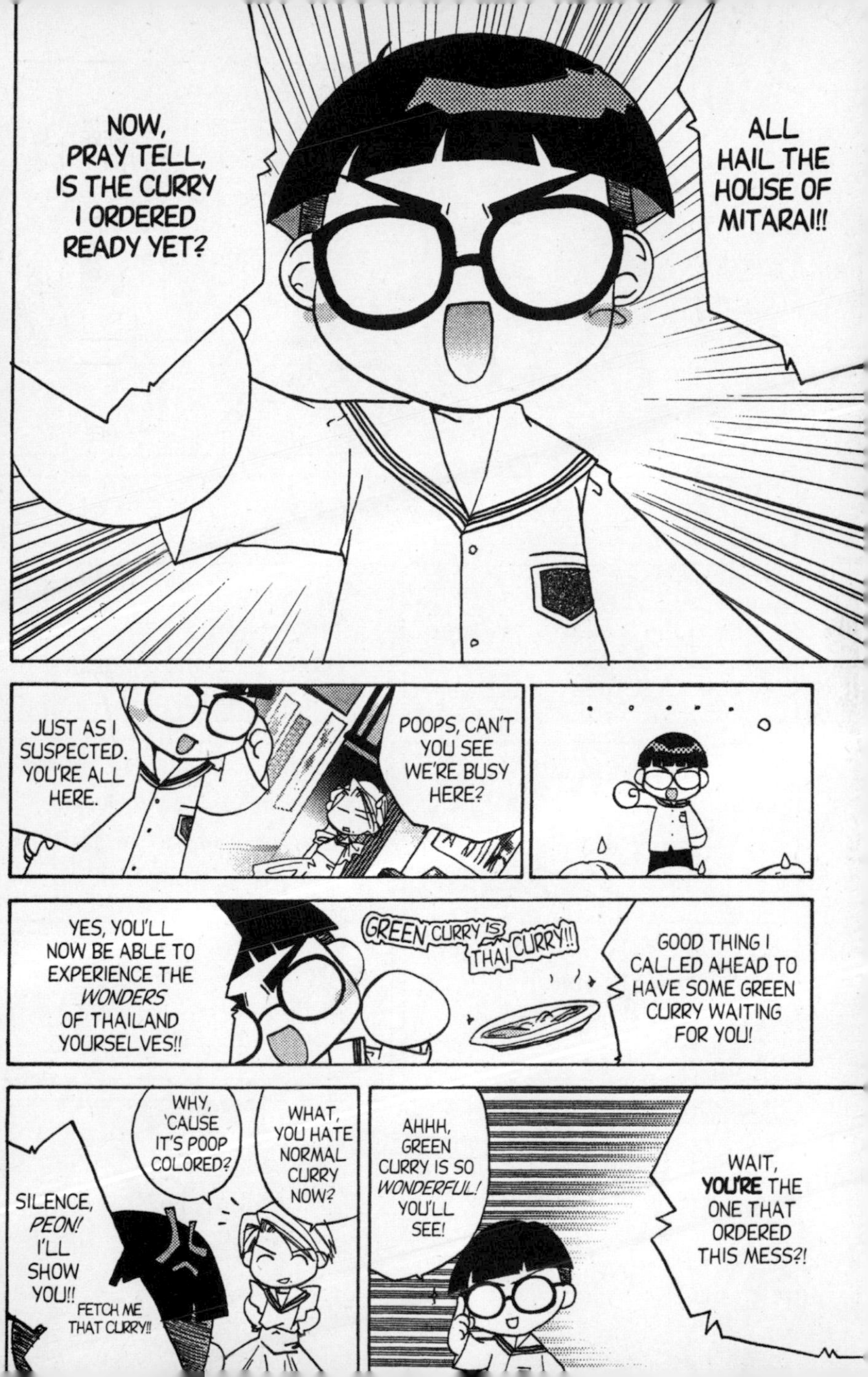
ALL HAIL THE HOUSE OF MITARAI!!
NOW, PRAY TELL, IS THE CURRY I ORDERED READY YET?
POOPS, CAN'T YOU SEE WE'RE BUSY HERE?
JUST AS I SUSPECTED. YOU'RE ALL HERE.
GOOD THING I CALLED AHEAD TO HAVE SOME GREEN CURRY WAITING FOR YOU!
GREEN CURRY IS THAI CURRY!!
YES, YOU'LL NOW BE ABLE TO EXPERIENCE THE *WONDERS* OF THAILAND YOURSELVES!!
WAIT, **YOU'RE** THE ONE THAT ORDERED THIS MESS?!
AHHH, GREEN CURRY IS SO *WONDERFUL!* YOU'LL SEE!
WHAT, YOU HATE NORMAL CURRY NOW?
WHY, 'CAUSE IT'S POOP COLORED?
SILENCE, *PEON!* I'LL SHOW YOU!!
FETCH ME THAT CURRY!!

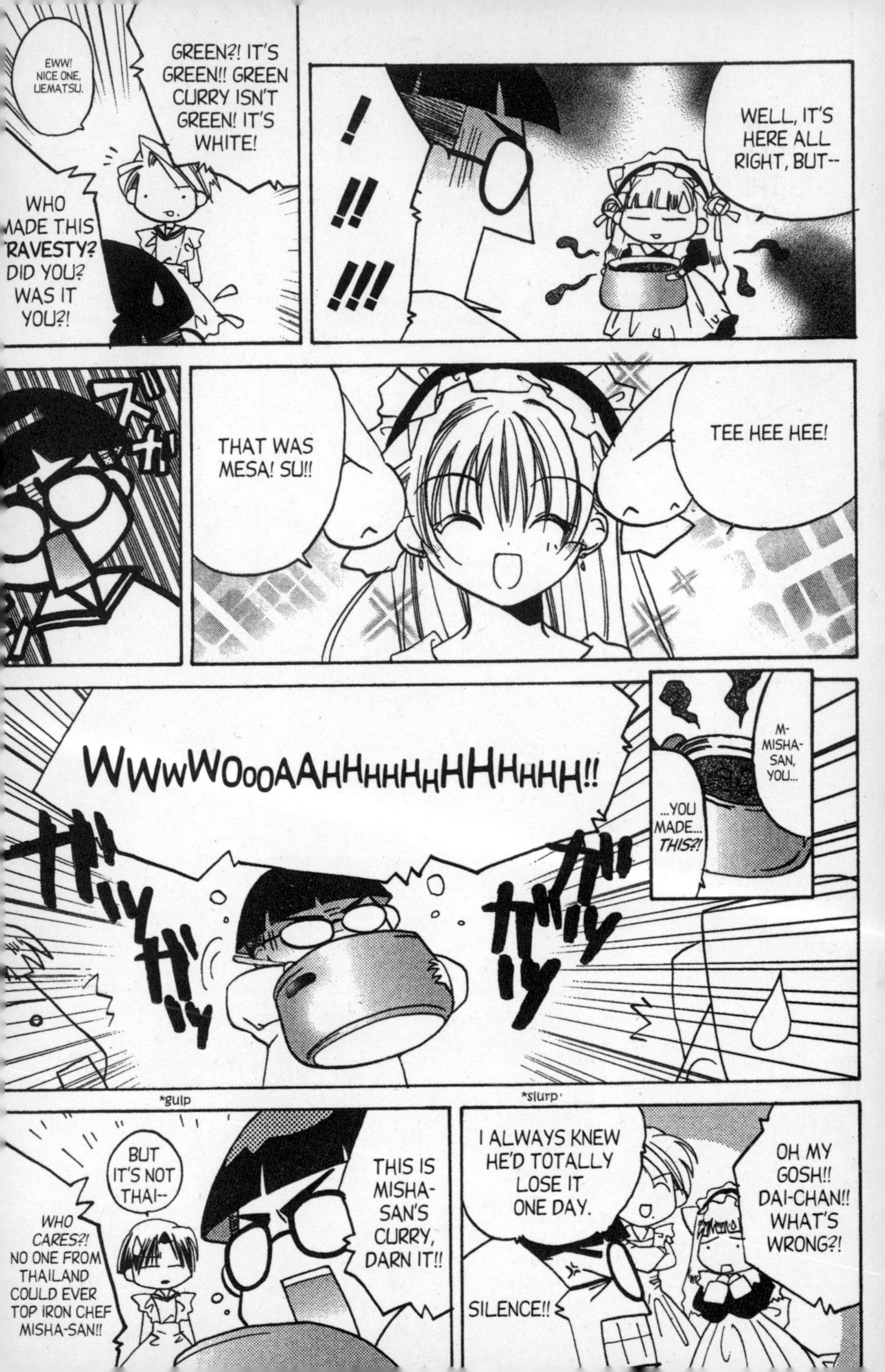
WELL, IT'S HERE ALL RIGHT, BUT--
!
!!
!!!
GREEN?! IT'S GREEN!! GREEN CURRY ISN'T GREEN! IT'S WHITE!
EWW! NICE ONE, UEMATSU.
WHO MADE THIS TRAVESTY? DID YOU? WAS IT YOU?!
TEE HEE HEE!
THAT WAS MESA! SU!!
M-MISHA-SAN, YOU...
...YOU MADE... *THIS?!*
WWWWOOOAAHHHHHHHHHHHH!!
*slurp
*gulp
OH MY GOSH!! DAI-CHAN!! WHAT'S WRONG?!
I ALWAYS KNEW HE'D TOTALLY LOSE IT ONE DAY.
SILENCE!!
THIS IS MISHA-SAN'S CURRY, DARN IT!!
BUT IT'S NOT THAI--
WHO CARES?! NO ONE FROM THAILAND COULD EVER TOP IRON CHEF MISHA-SAN!!

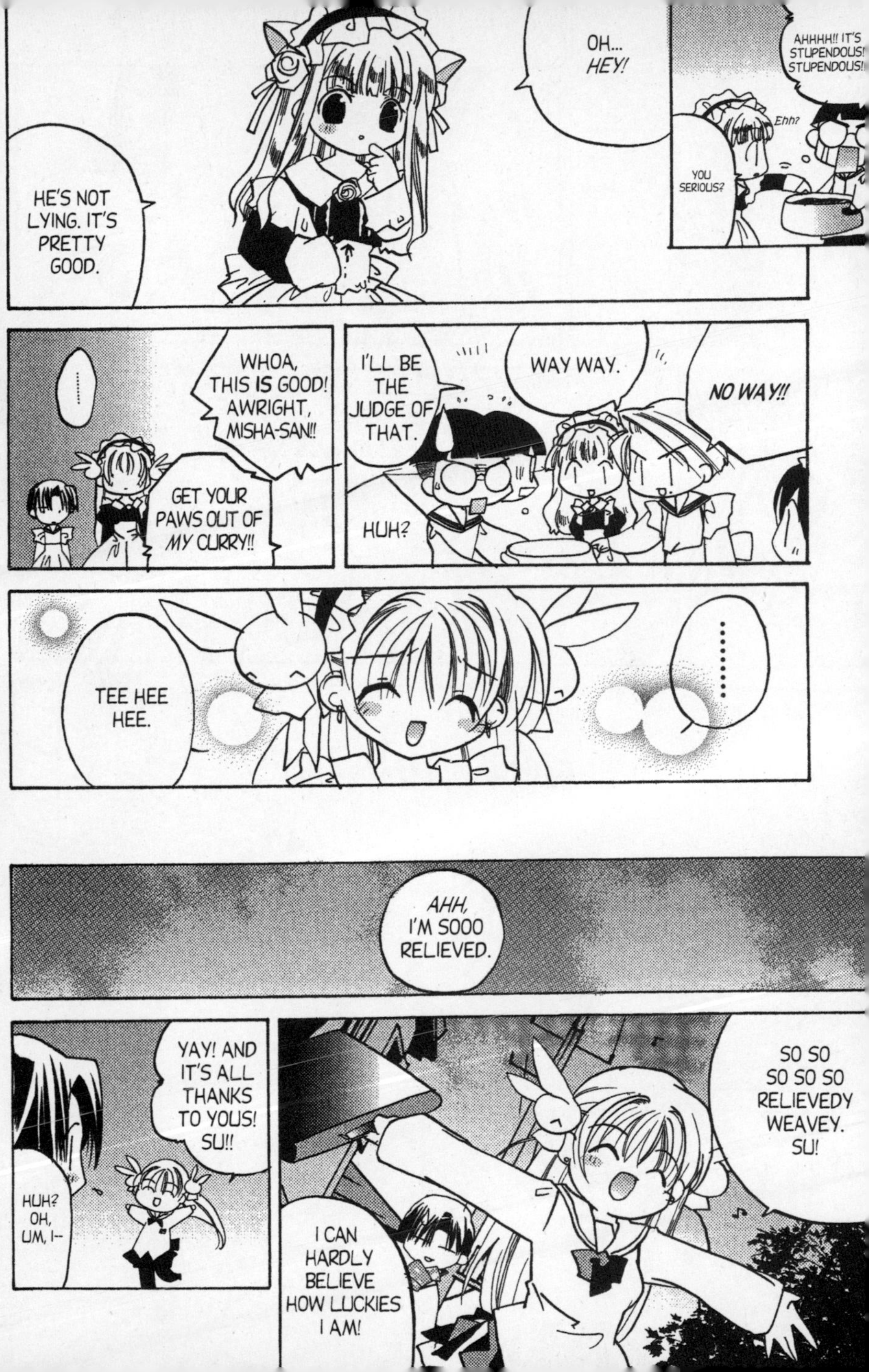
AHHHH!! IT'S STUPENDOUS! STUPENDOUS!
Ehh?
YOU SERIOUS?
OH... HEY!
HE'S NOT LYING. IT'S PRETTY GOOD.
NO WAY!!
WAY WAY.
I'LL BE THE JUDGE OF THAT.
HUH?
WHOA, THIS IS GOOD! AWRIGHT, MISHA-SAN!!
......
GET YOUR PAWS OUT OF MY CURRY!!
......
TEE HEE HEE.
AHH, I'M SOOO RELIEVED.
SO SO SO SO SO RELIEVEDY WEAVEY. SU!
I CAN HARDLY BELIEVE HOW LUCKIES I AM!
YAY! AND IT'S ALL THANKS TO YOUS! SU!!
HUH? OH, UM, I--

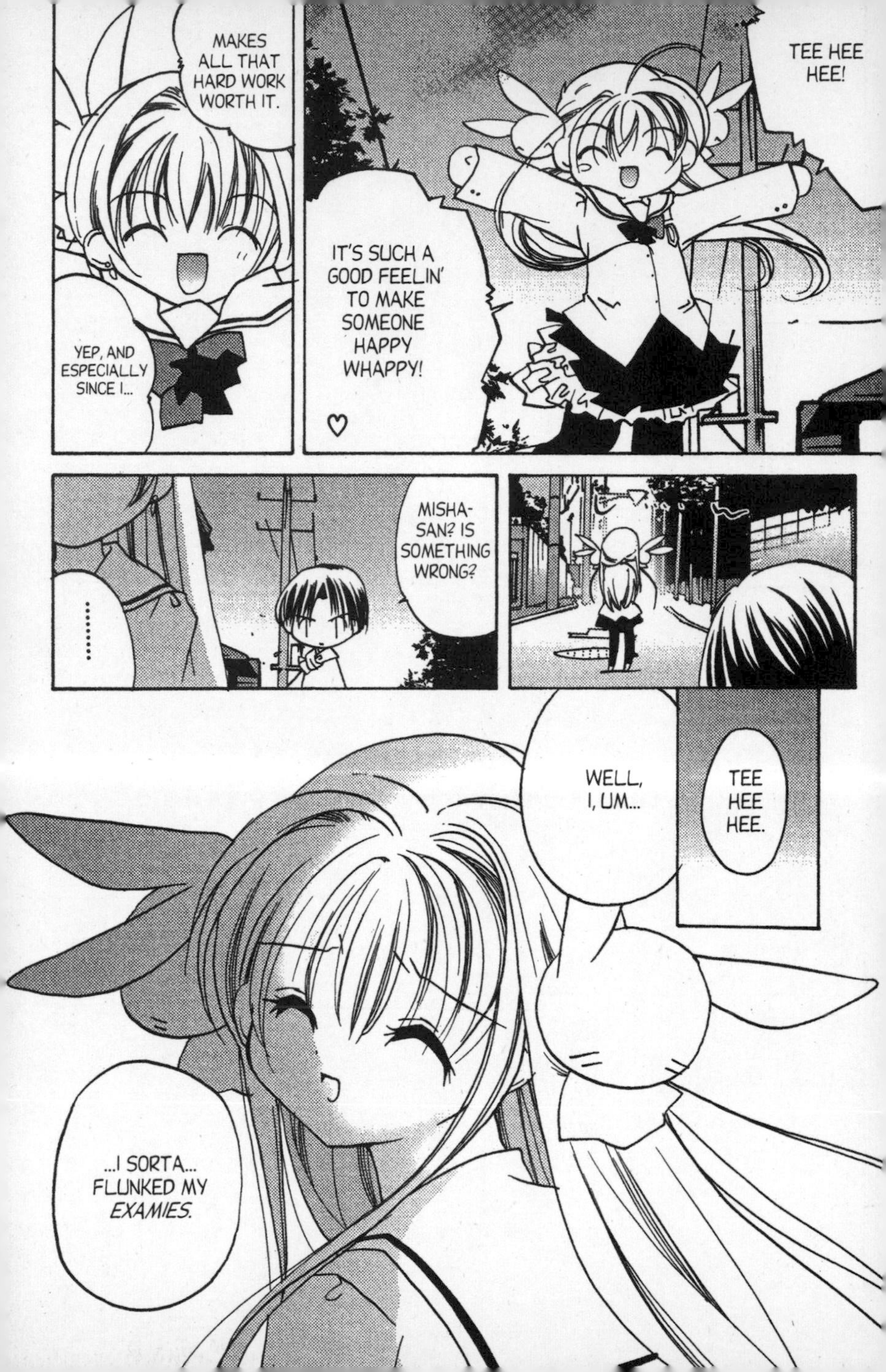
TEE HEE HEE!
IT'S SUCH A GOOD FEELIN' TO MAKE SOMEONE HAPPY WHAPPY! ♡
MAKES ALL THAT HARD WORK WORTH IT.
YEP, AND ESPECIALLY SINCE I...
MISHA-SAN? IS SOMETHING WRONG?
....
TEE HEE HEE.
WELL, I, UM...
...I SORTA... FLUNKED MY *EXAMIES.*

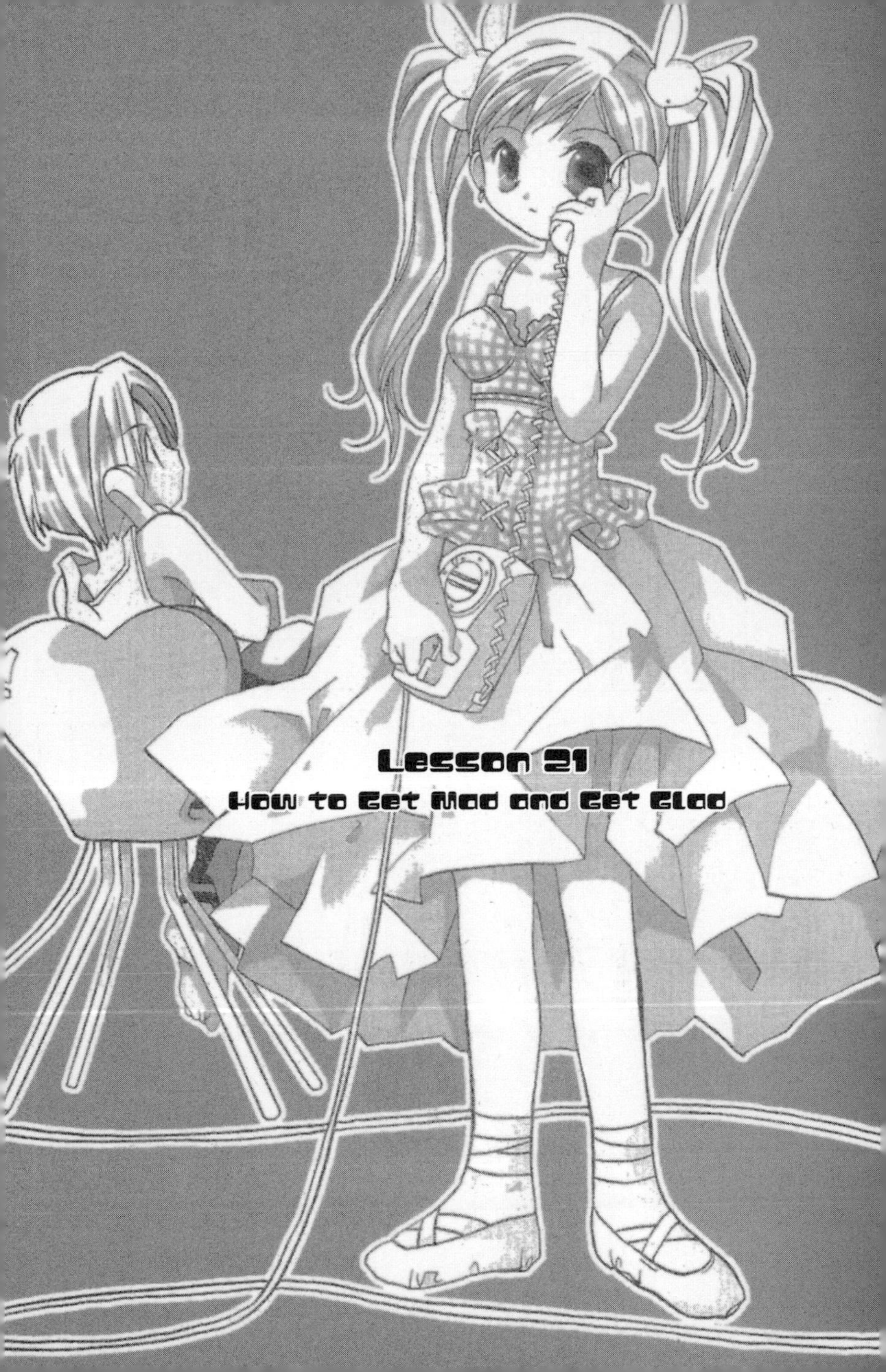
Lesson 21
How to Get Mad and Get Glad

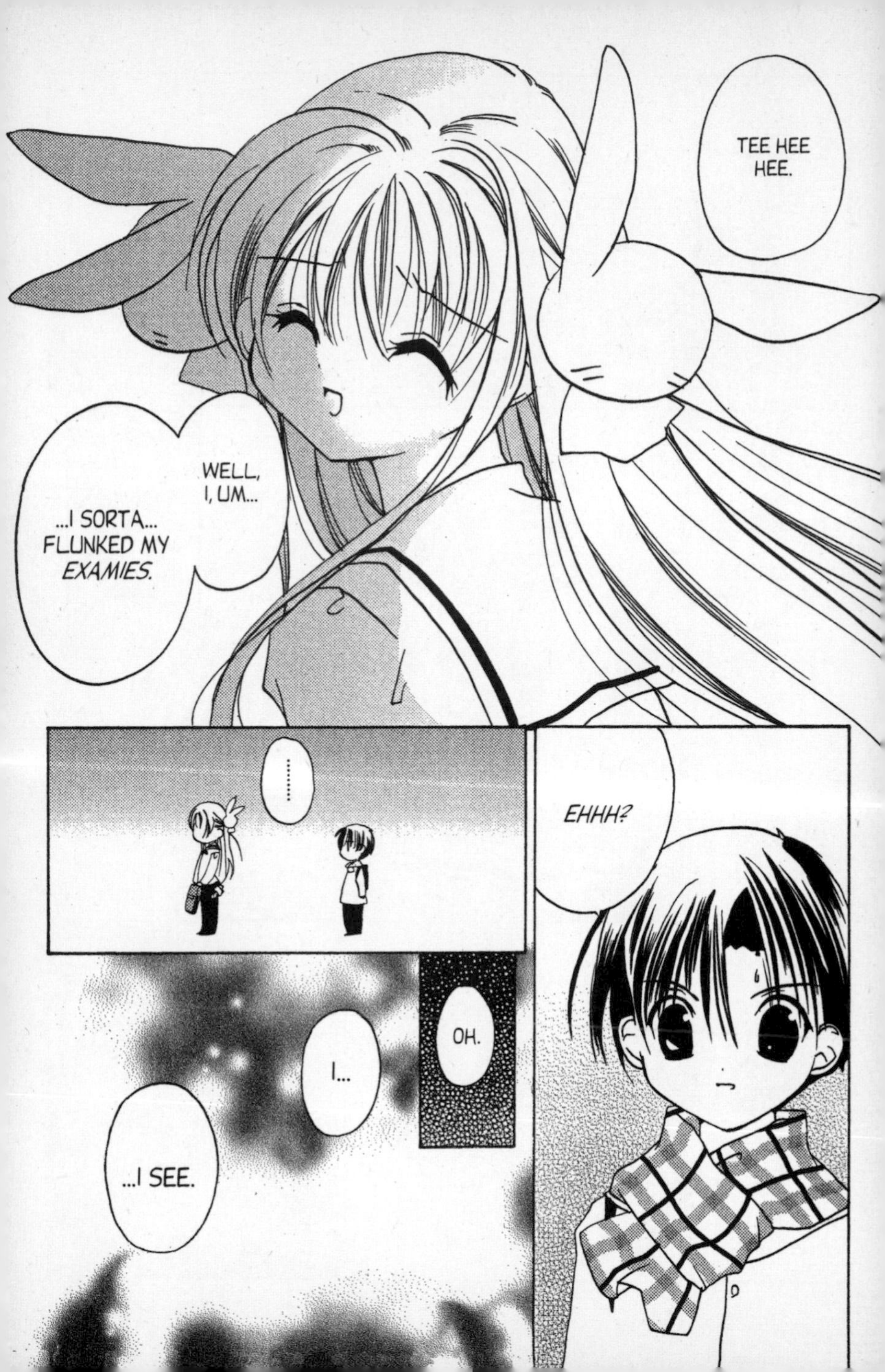
TEE HEE HEE.
WELL, I, UM...
...I SORTA... FLUNKED MY *EXAMIES.*
EHHH?
......
OH.
I...
...I SEE.

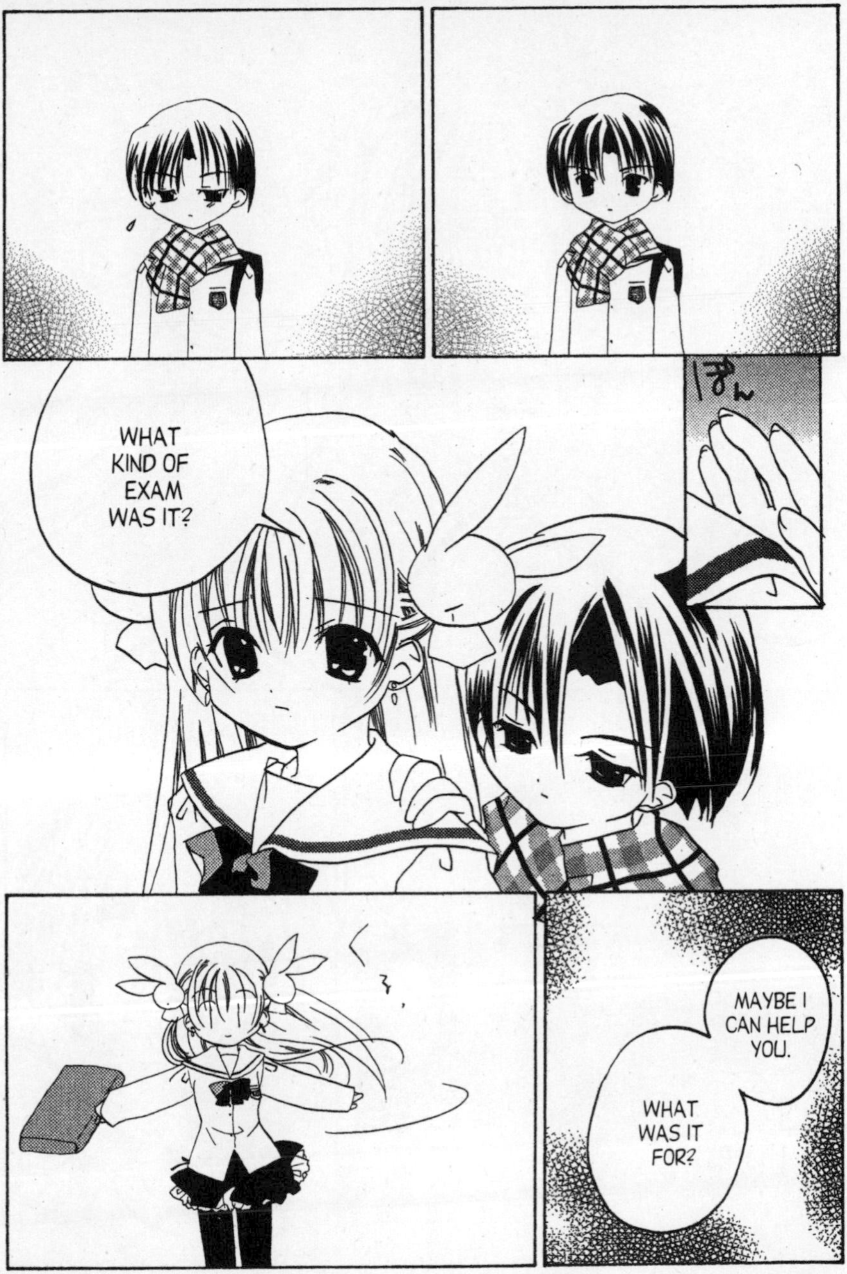
ぽん
WHAT KIND OF EXAM WAS IT?
MAYBE I CAN HELP YOU.
WHAT WAS IT FOR?

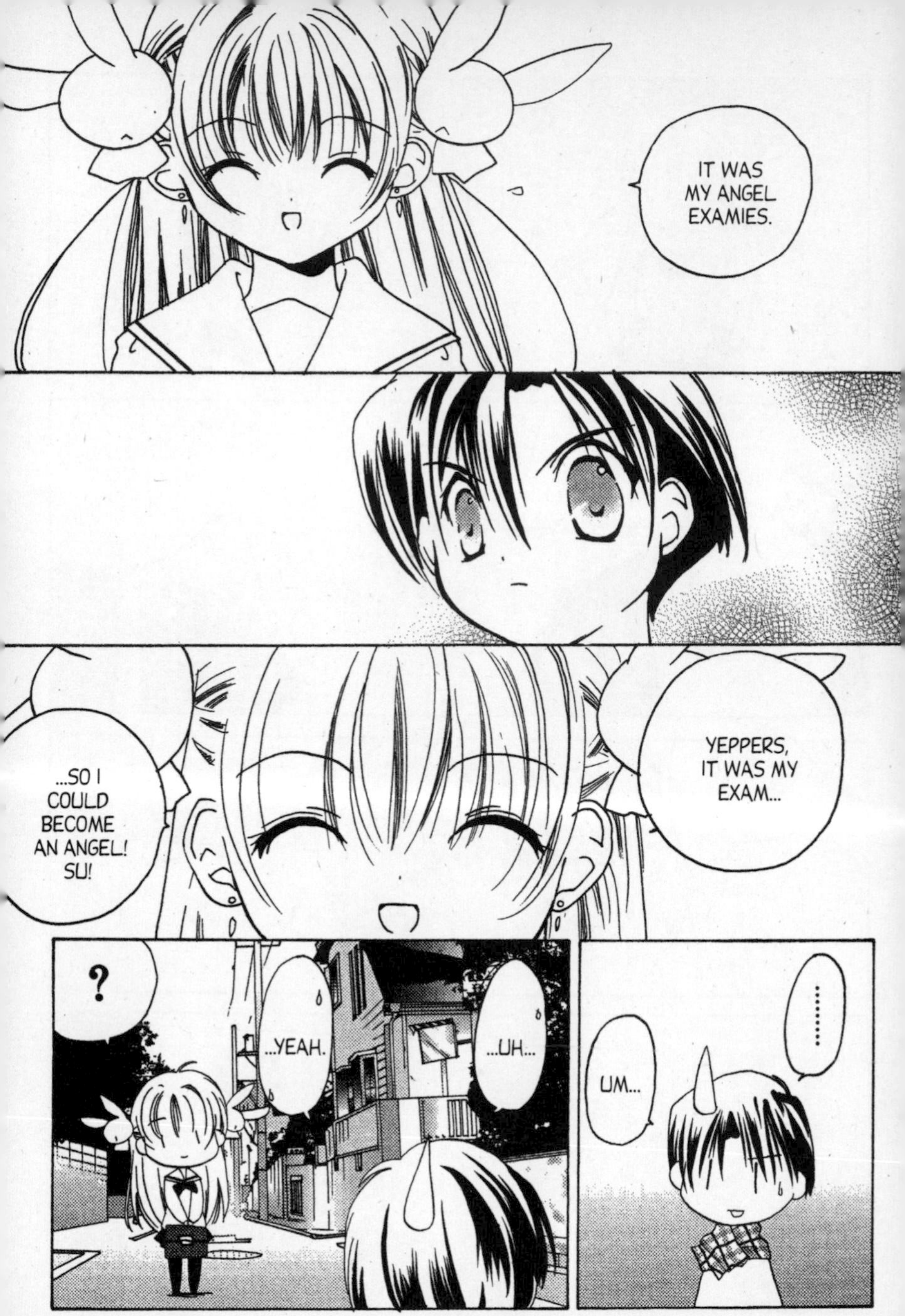
IT WAS MY ANGEL EXAMIES.
YEPPERS, IT WAS MY EXAM...
...SO I COULD BECOME AN ANGEL! SU!
....
UM...
...UH...
...YEAH.
?

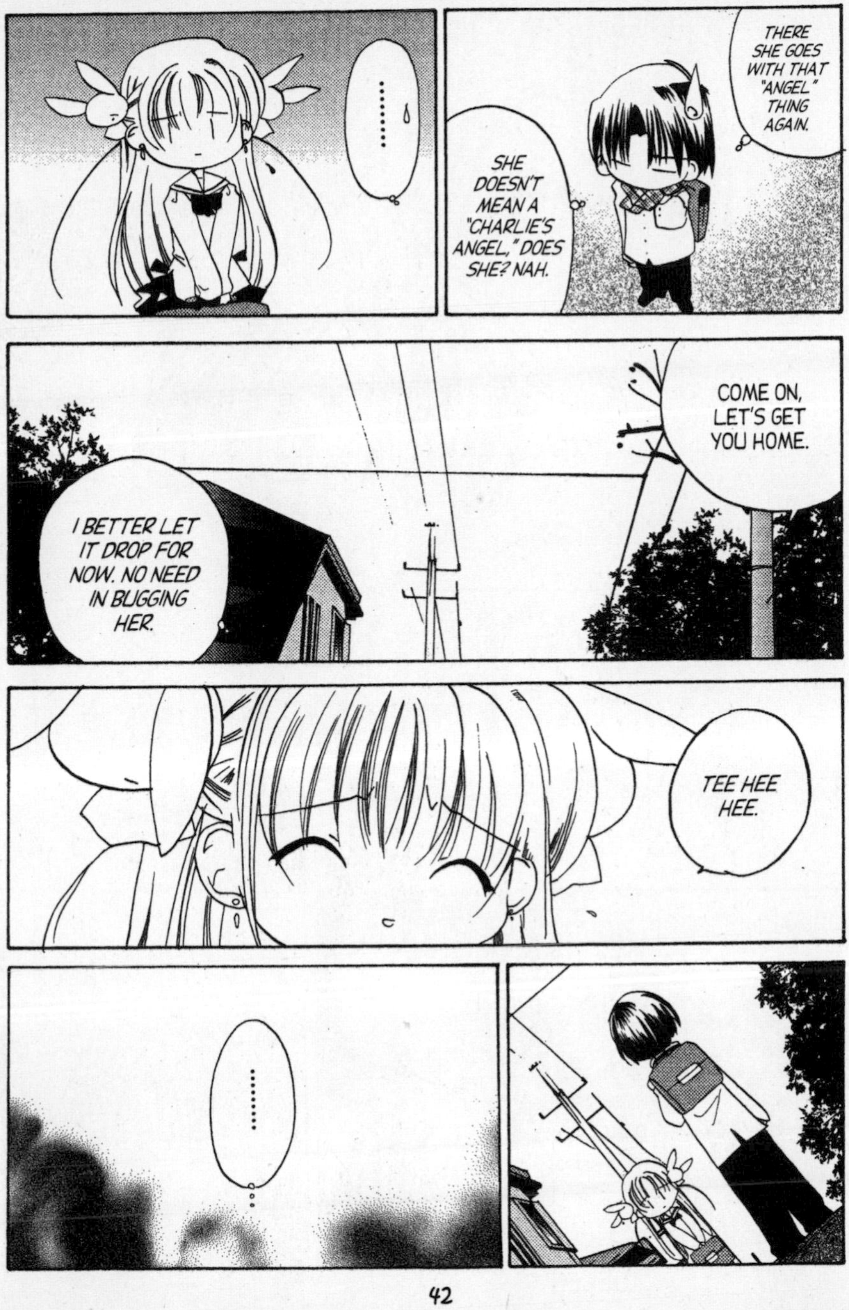
THERE SHE GOES WITH THAT "ANGEL" THING AGAIN.
SHE DOESN'T MEAN A "CHARLIE'S ANGEL," DOES SHE? NAH.
....
COME ON, LET'S GET YOU HOME.
I BETTER LET IT DROP FOR NOW. NO NEED IN BUGGING HER.
TEE HEE HEE.
....

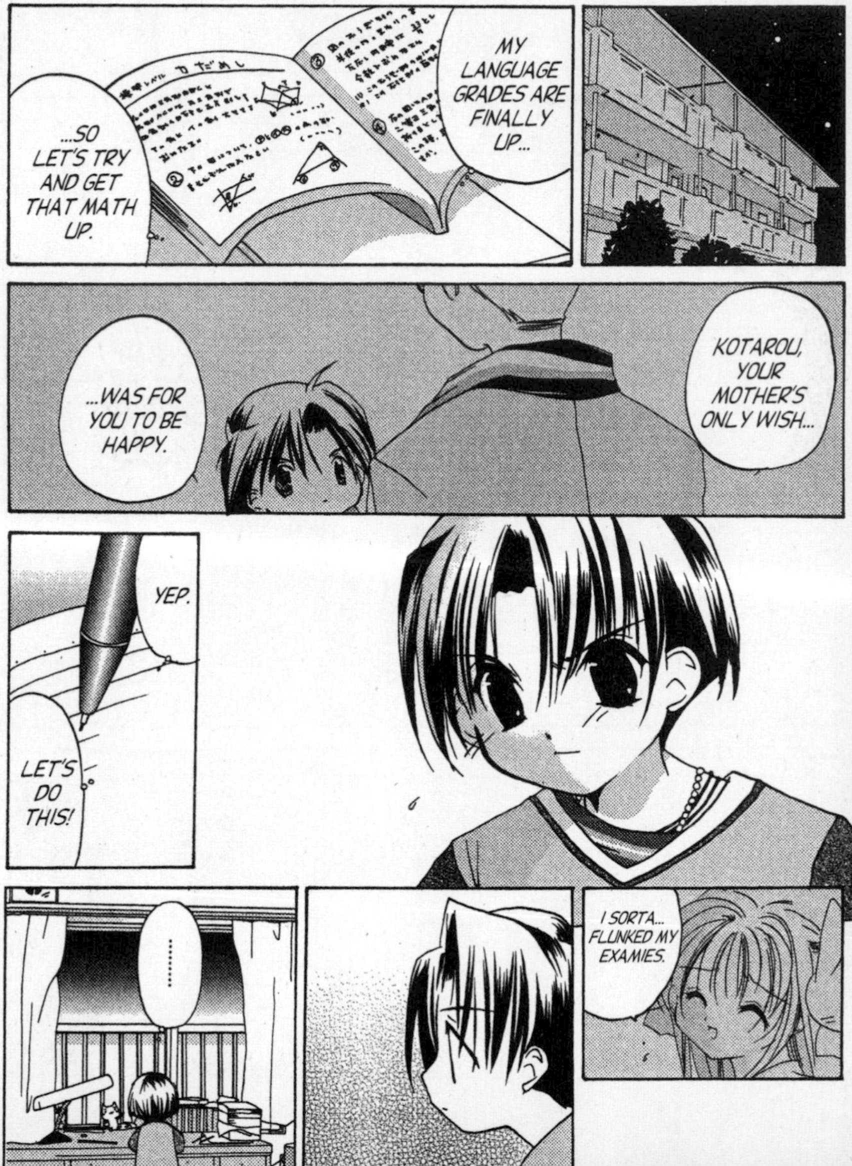
MY LANGUAGE GRADES ARE FINALLY UP...
...SO LET'S TRY AND GET THAT MATH UP.
KOTAROU, YOUR MOTHER'S ONLY WISH...
...WAS FOR YOU TO BE HAPPY.
YEP.
LET'S DO THIS!
I SORTA... FLUNKED MY EXAMIES.
....

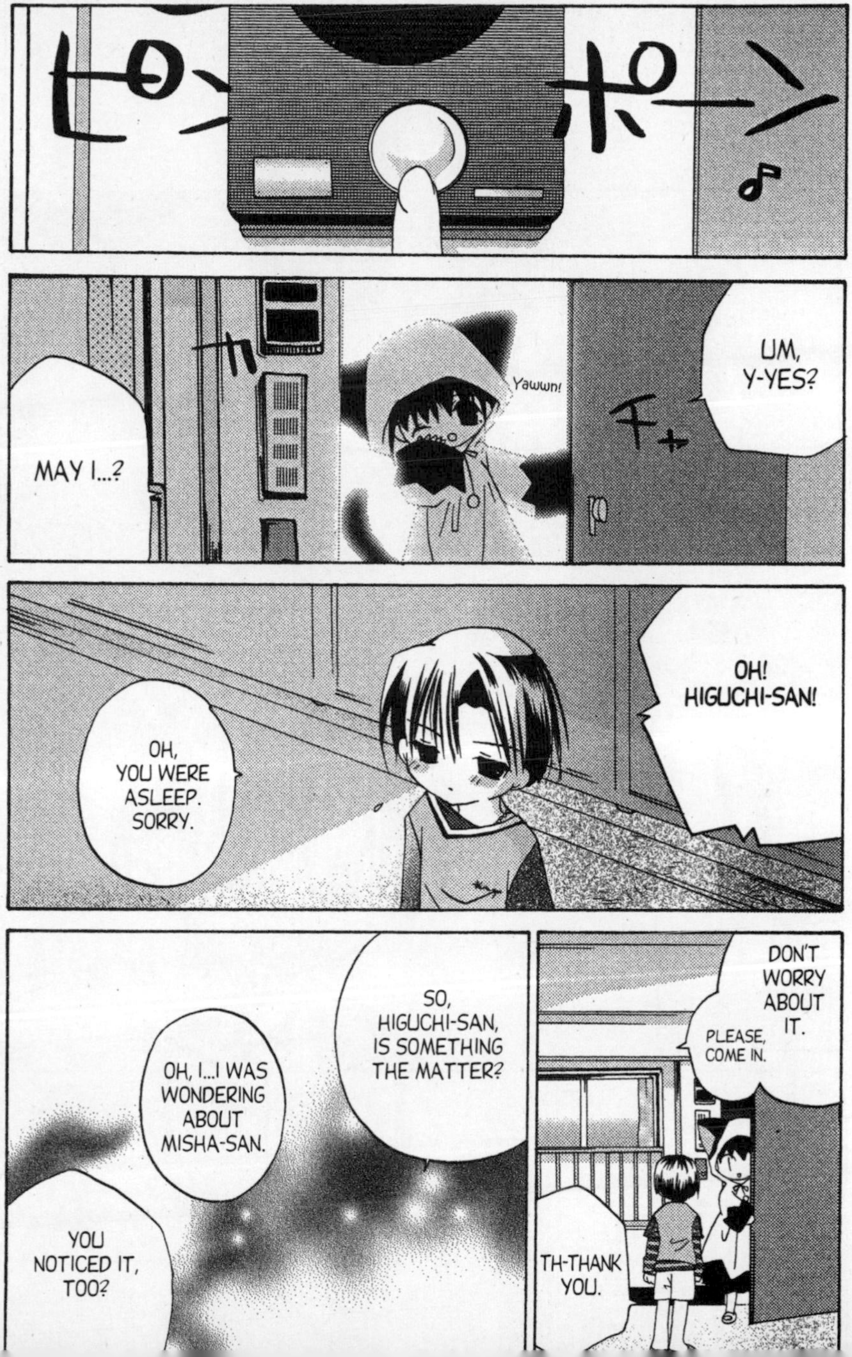
ピン
ポーン
UM, Y-YES?
Yawwn!
MAY I...?
OH! HIGUCHI-SAN!
OH, YOU WERE ASLEEP. SORRY.
DON'T WORRY ABOUT IT.
PLEASE, COME IN.
TH-THANK YOU.
SO, HIGUCHI-SAN, IS SOMETHING THE MATTER?
OH, I...I WAS WONDERING ABOUT MISHA-SAN.
YOU NOTICED IT, TOO?

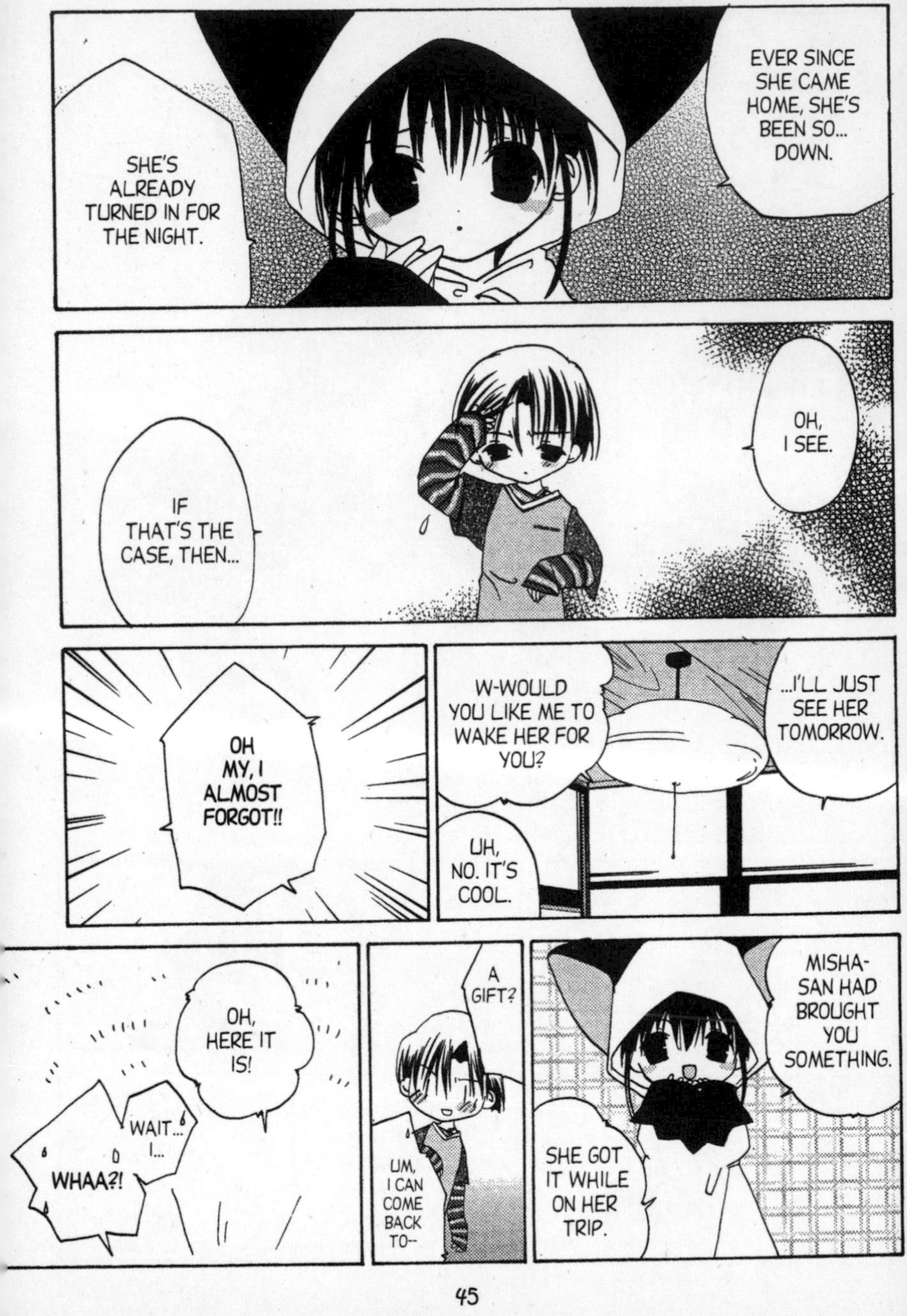
EVER SINCE SHE CAME HOME, SHE'S BEEN SO... DOWN.
SHE'S ALREADY TURNED IN FOR THE NIGHT.
OH, I SEE.
IF THAT'S THE CASE, THEN...
...I'LL JUST SEE HER TOMORROW.
W-WOULD YOU LIKE ME TO WAKE HER FOR YOU?
UH, NO. IT'S COOL.
OH MY, I ALMOST FORGOT!!
MISHA-SAN HAD BROUGHT YOU SOMETHING.
SHE GOT IT WHILE ON HER TRIP.
A GIFT?
UM, I CAN COME BACK TO--
OH, HERE IT IS!
WAIT... I...
WHAA?!

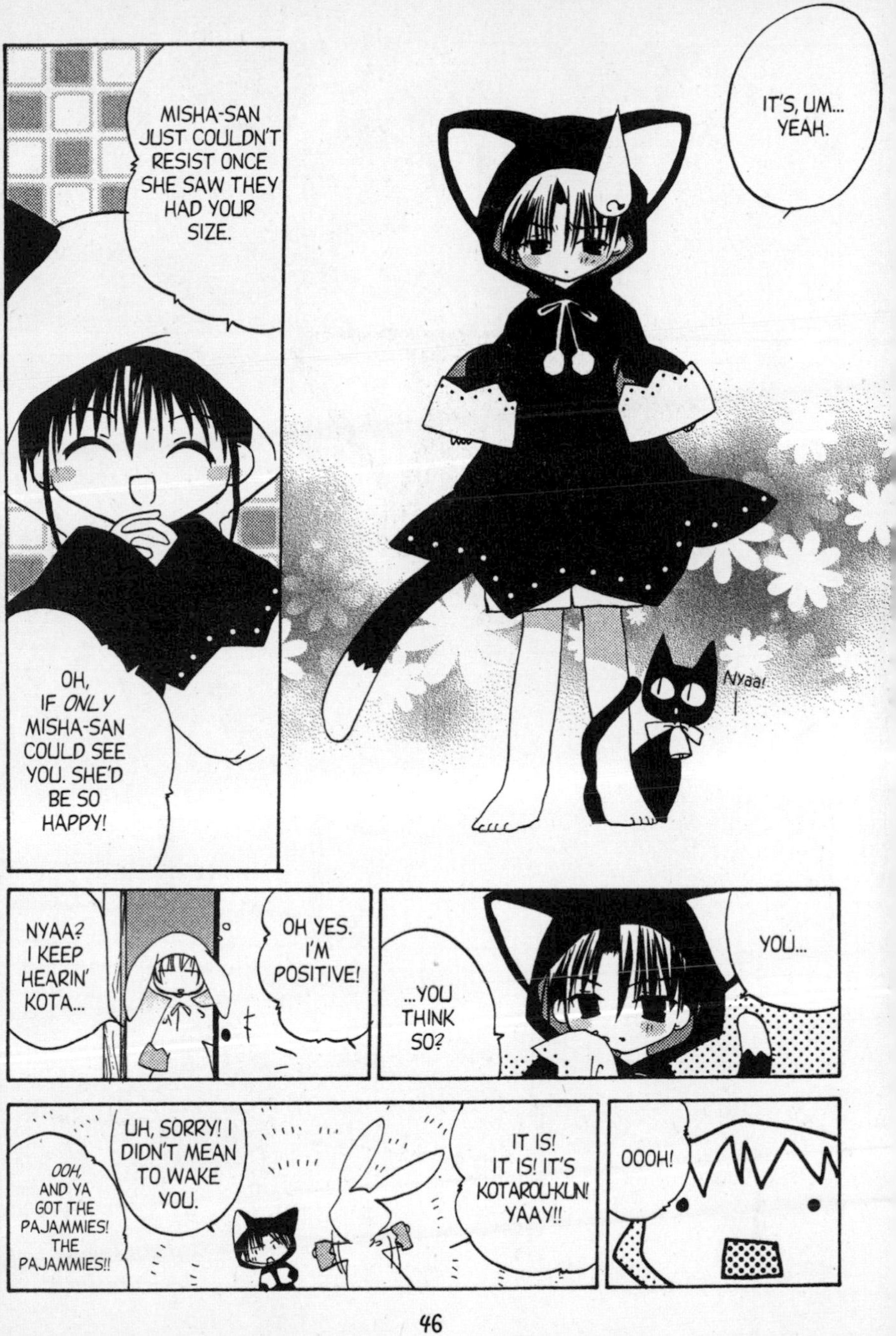
IT'S, UM... YEAH.
Nyaa!
MISHA-SAN JUST COULDN'T RESIST ONCE SHE SAW THEY HAD YOUR SIZE.
OH, IF *ONLY* MISHA-SAN COULD SEE YOU. SHE'D BE SO HAPPY!
YOU...
...YOU THINK SO?
OH YES. I'M POSITIVE!
NYAA? I KEEP HEARIN' KOTA...
OOOH!
IT IS! IT IS! IT'S KOTAROU-KUN! YAAY!!
UH, SORRY! I DIDN'T MEAN TO WAKE YOU.
OOH, AND YA GOT THE PAJAMMIES! THE PAJAMMIES!!

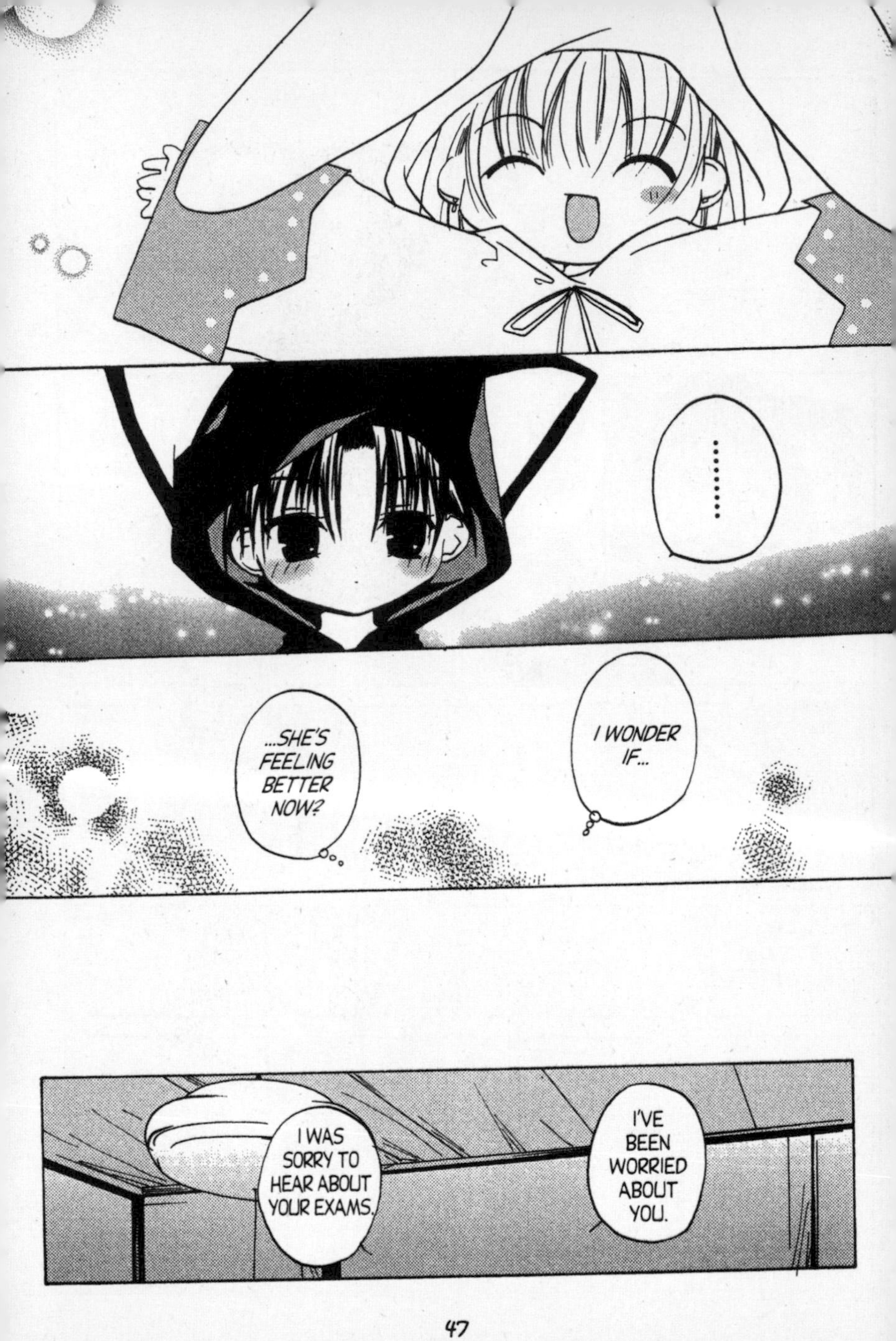
......
I WONDER IF...
...SHE'S FEELING BETTER NOW?
I'VE BEEN WORRIED ABOUT YOU.
I WAS SORRY TO HEAR ABOUT YOUR EXAMS.

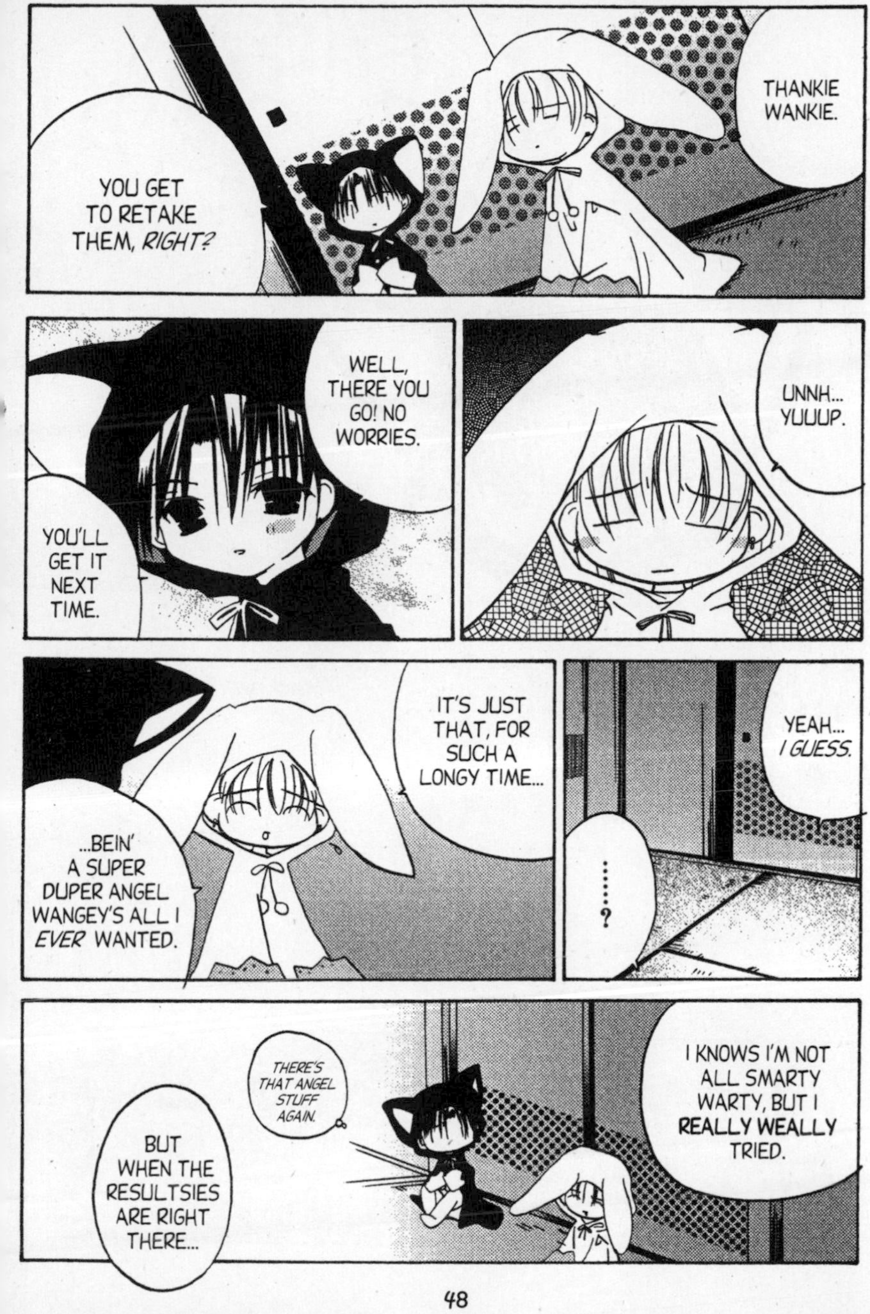
THANKIE WANKIE.
YOU GET TO RETAKE THEM, *RIGHT?*
UNNH... YUUUP.
WELL, THERE YOU GO! NO WORRIES.
YOU'LL GET IT NEXT TIME.
YEAH... *I GUESS.*
......?
IT'S JUST THAT, FOR SUCH A LONGY TIME...
...BEIN' A SUPER DUPER ANGEL WANGEY'S ALL I *EVER* WANTED.
I KNOWS I'M NOT ALL SMARTY WARTY, BUT I **REALLY WEALLY** TRIED.
THERE'S THAT ANGEL STUFF AGAIN.
BUT WHEN THE RESULTSIES ARE RIGHT THERE...

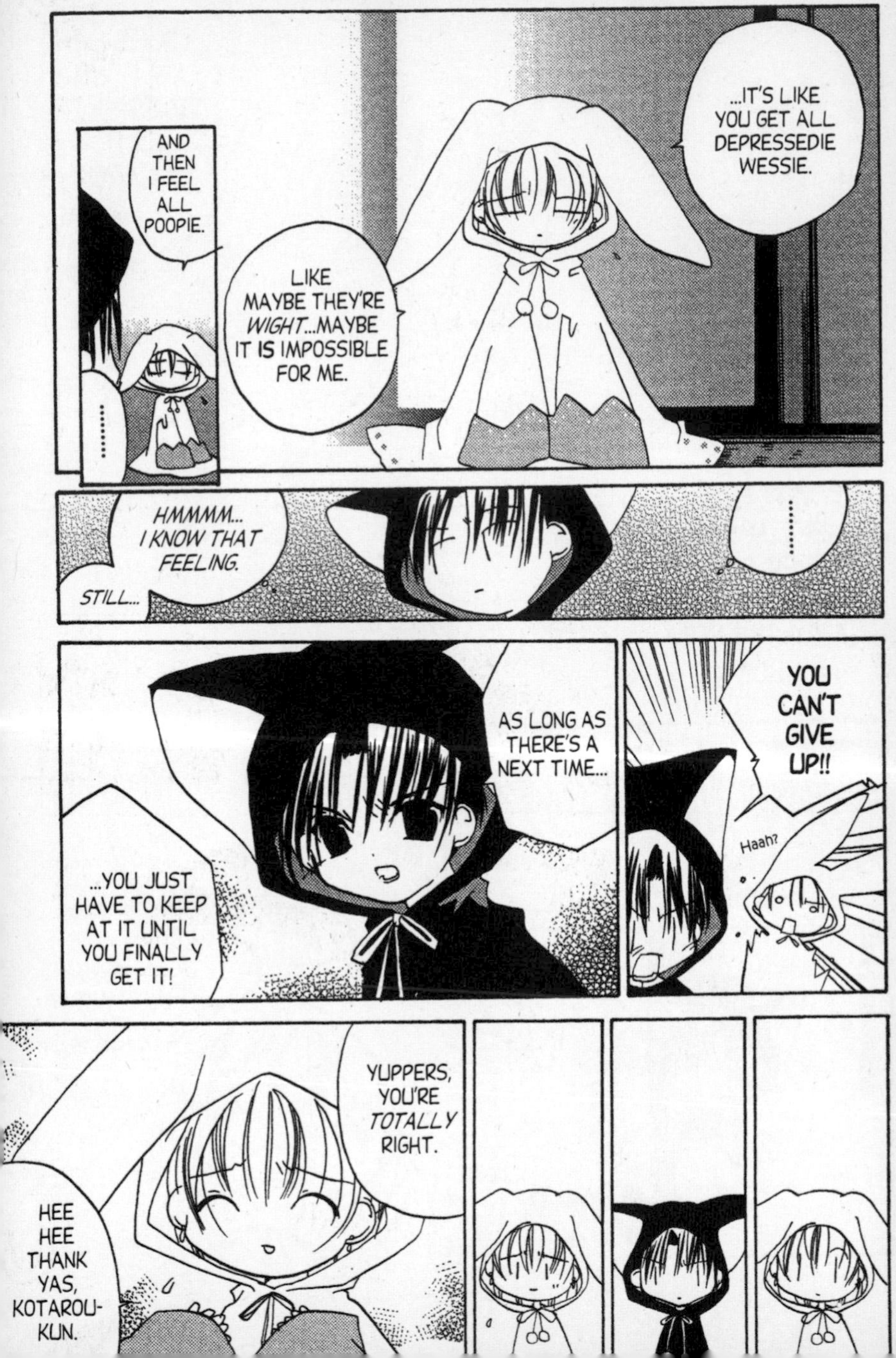
...IT'S LIKE YOU GET ALL DEPRESSEDIE WESSIE.
LIKE MAYBE THEY'RE *WIGHT*...MAYBE IT IS IMPOSSIBLE FOR ME.
AND THEN I FEEL ALL POOPIE.
......
......
HMMMM... I KNOW THAT FEELING.
STILL...
YOU CAN'T GIVE UP!!
Haah?
AS LONG AS THERE'S A NEXT TIME...
...YOU JUST HAVE TO KEEP AT IT UNTIL YOU FINALLY GET IT!
YUPPERS, YOU'RE *TOTALLY* RIGHT.
HEE HEE THANK YAS, KOTAROU-KUN.

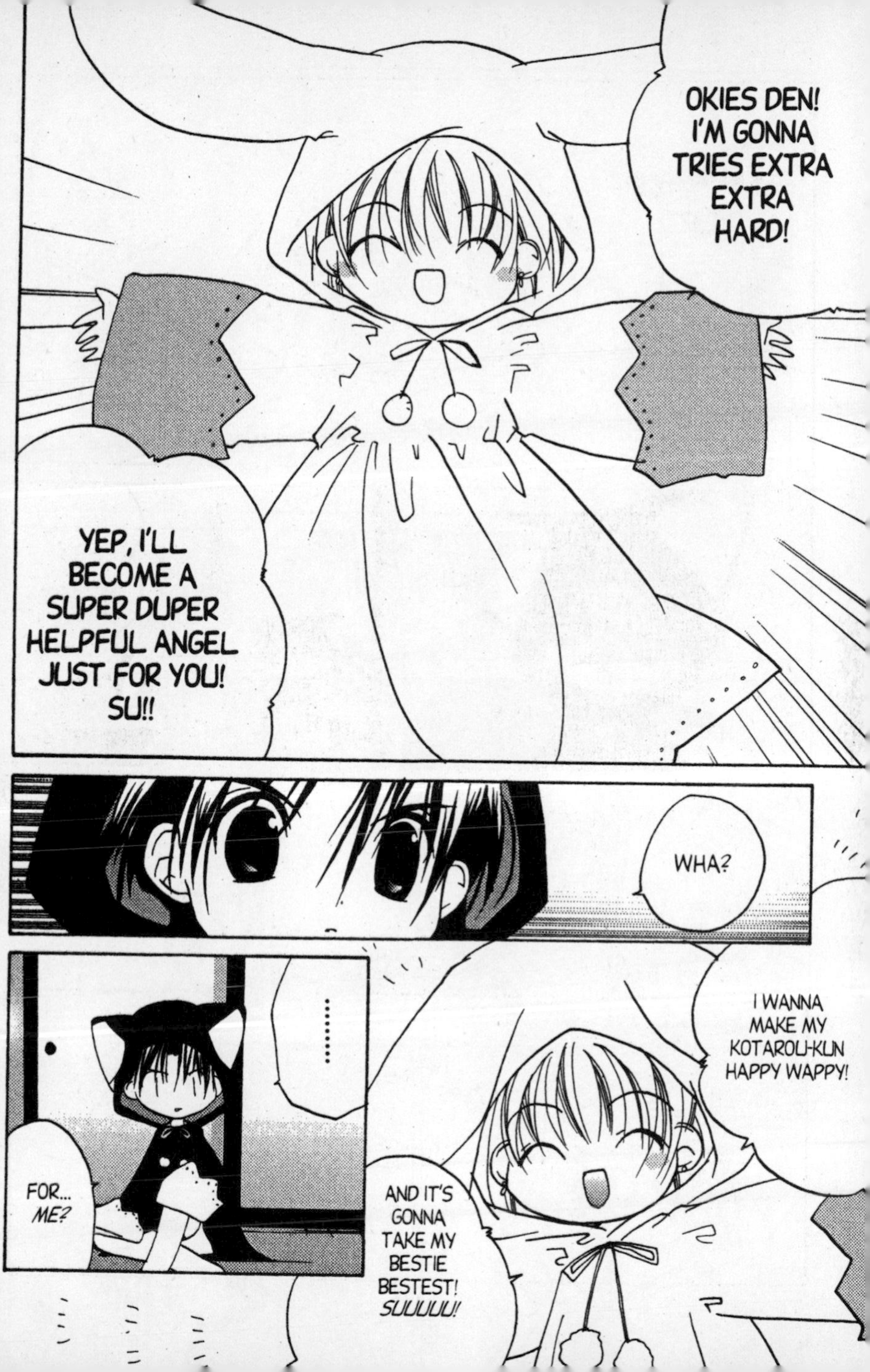
OKIES DEN! I'M GONNA TRIES EXTRA EXTRA HARD!
YEP, I'LL BECOME A SUPER DUPER HELPFUL ANGEL JUST FOR YOU! SU!!
WHA?
I WANNA MAKE MY KOTAROU-KUN HAPPY WAPPY!
AND IT'S GONNA TAKE MY BESTIE BESTEST! *SUUUUU!*
……
FOR... *ME?*

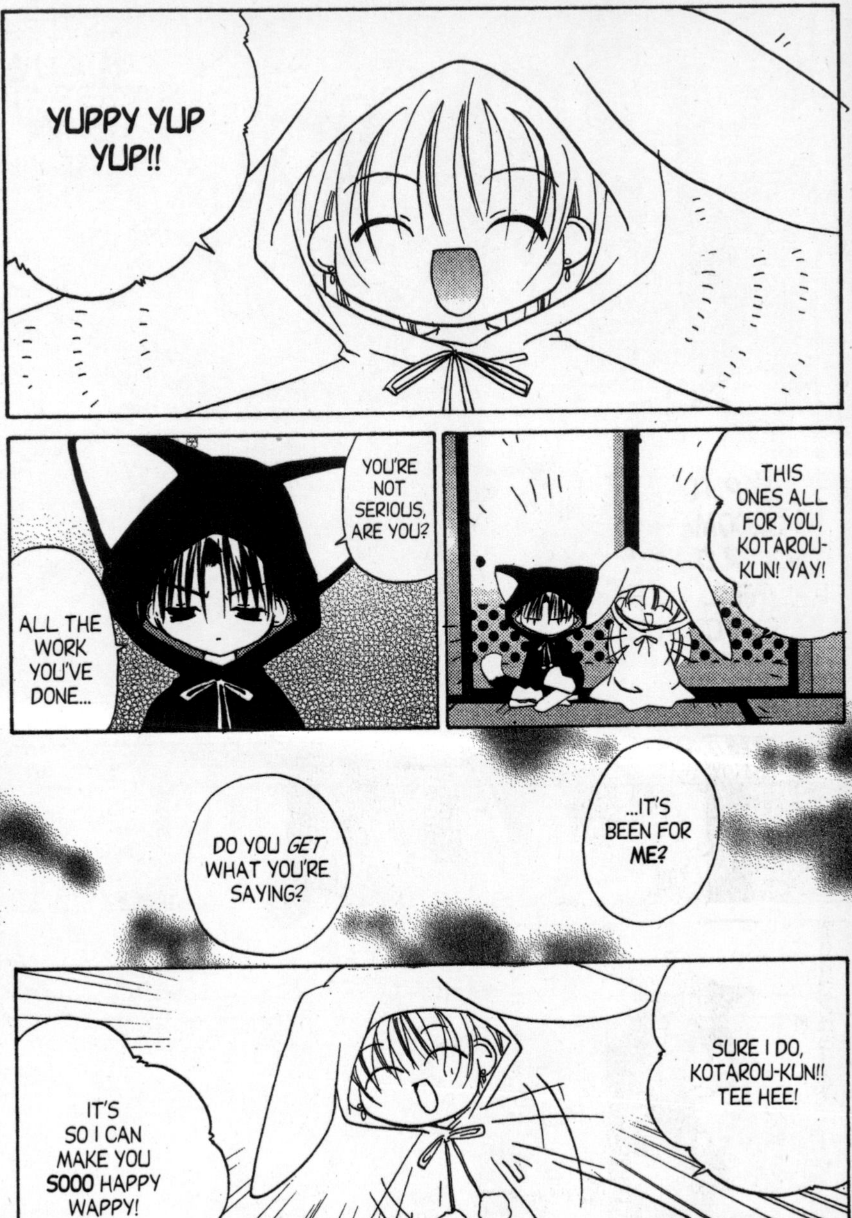
YUPPY YUP YUP!!
THIS ONES ALL FOR YOU, KOTAROU-KUN! YAY!
YOU'RE NOT SERIOUS, ARE YOU?
ALL THE WORK YOU'VE DONE...
...IT'S BEEN FOR ME?
DO YOU GET WHAT YOU'RE SAYING?
SURE I DO, KOTAROU-KUN!! TEE HEE!
IT'S SO I CAN MAKE YOU SOOO HAPPY WAPPY!

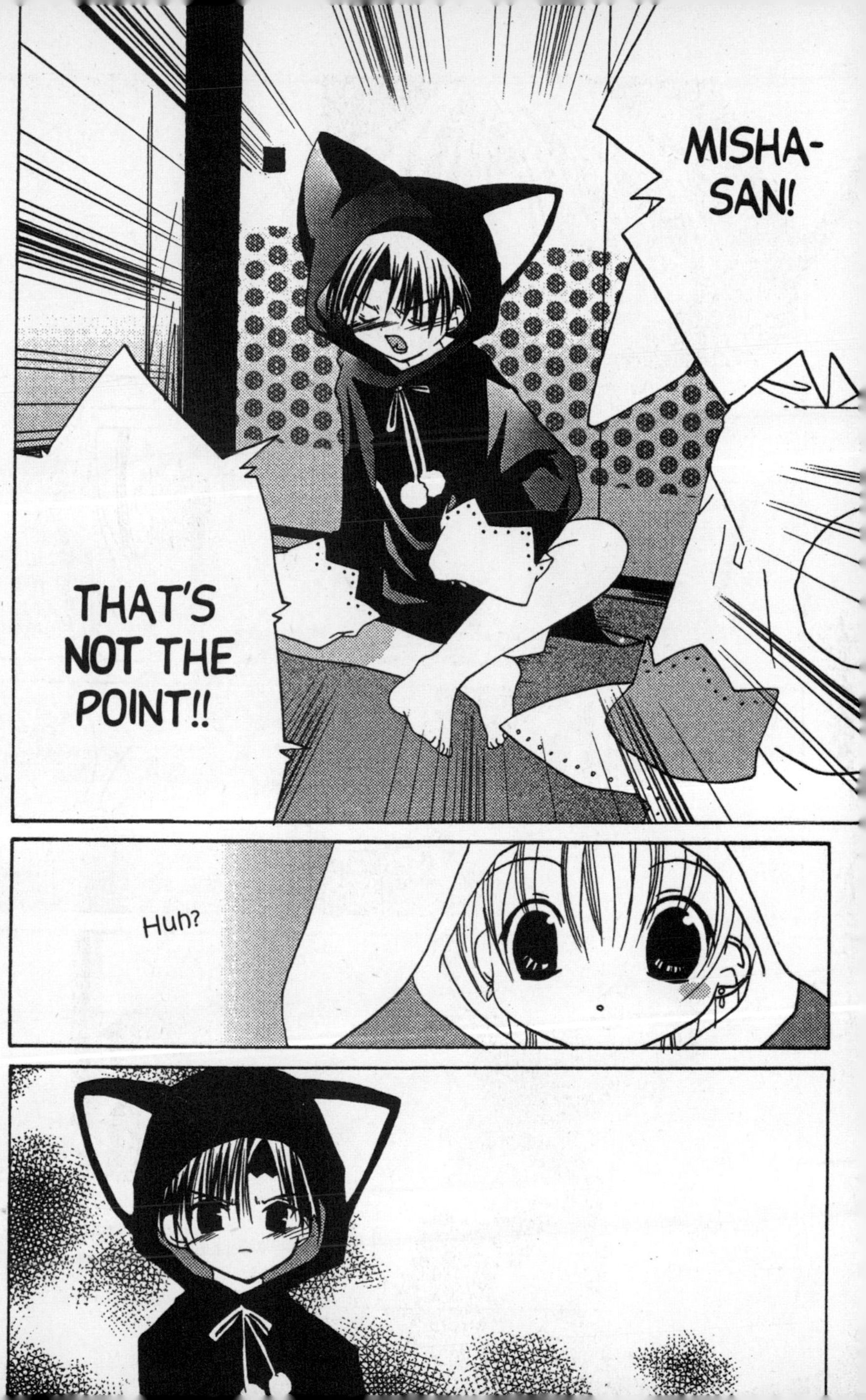
MISHA-SAN!
THAT'S NOT THE POINT!!
Huh?

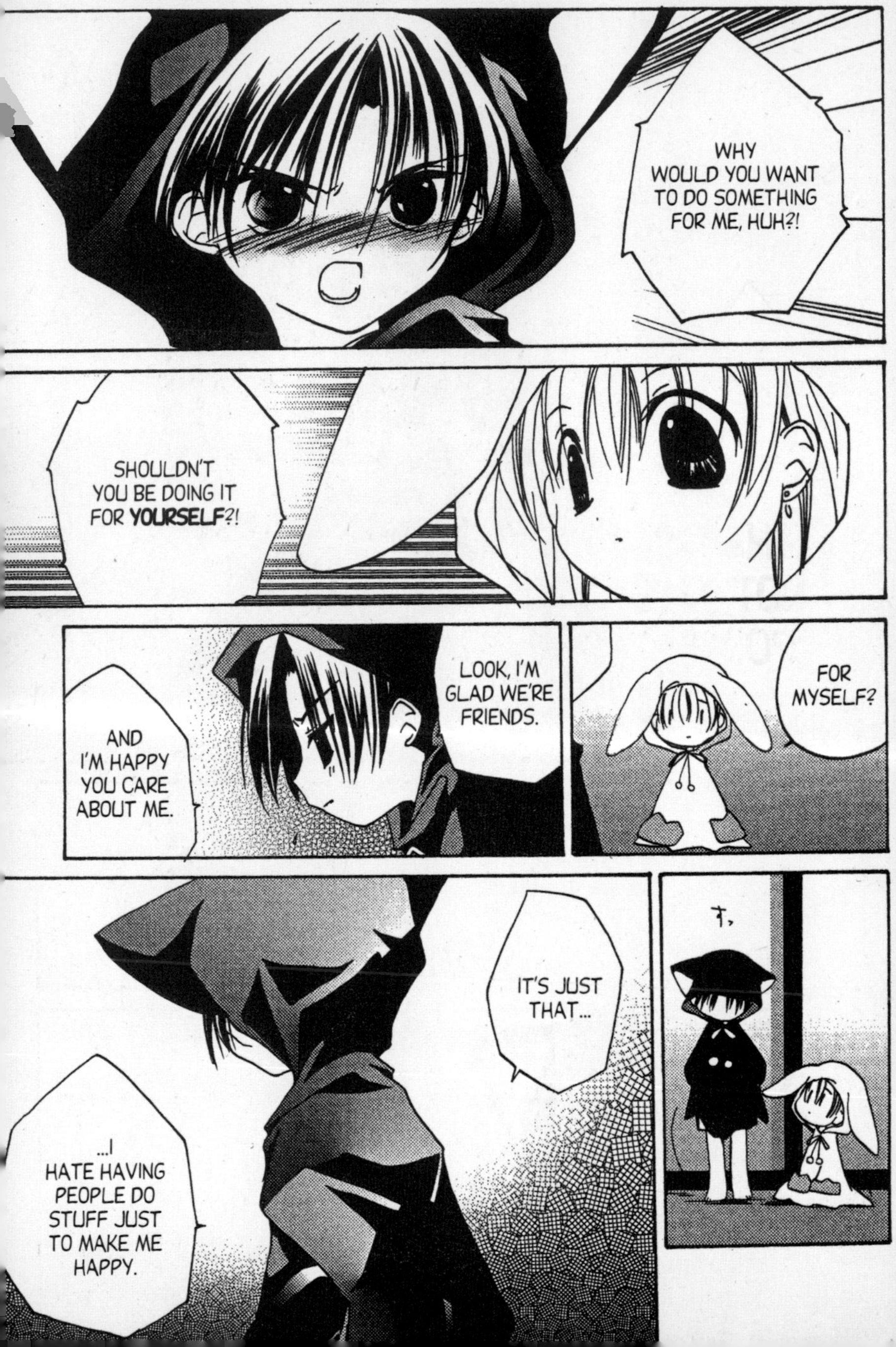
WHY WOULD YOU WANT TO DO SOMETHING FOR ME, HUH?!
SHOULDN'T YOU BE DOING IT FOR **YOURSELF**?!
FOR MYSELF?
LOOK, I'M GLAD WE'RE FRIENDS.
AND I'M HAPPY YOU CARE ABOUT ME.
すっ
IT'S JUST THAT...
...I HATE HAVING PEOPLE DO STUFF JUST TO MAKE ME HAPPY.

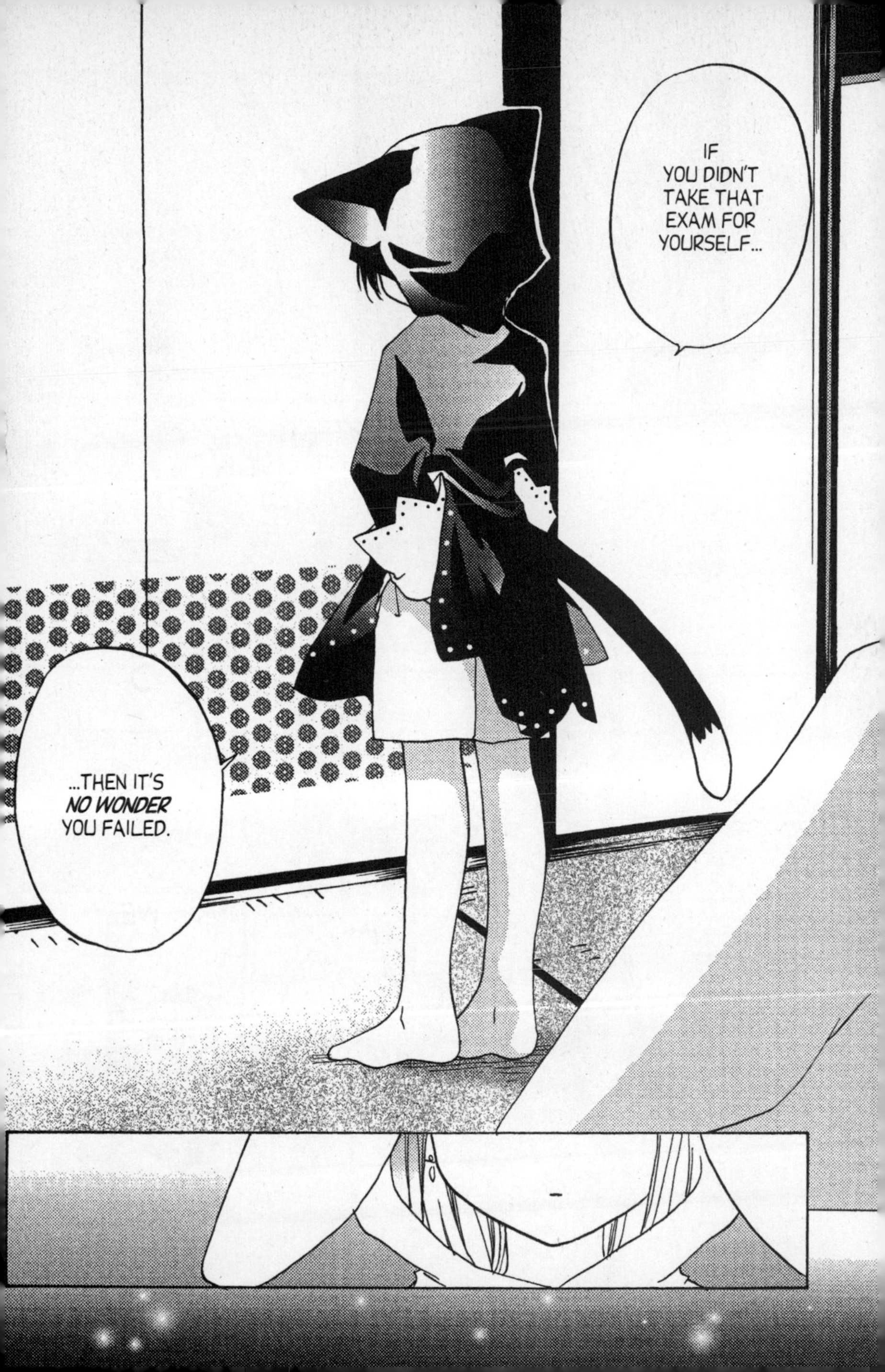
IF YOU DIDN'T TAKE THAT EXAM FOR YOURSELF...
...THEN IT'S NO WONDER YOU FAILED.

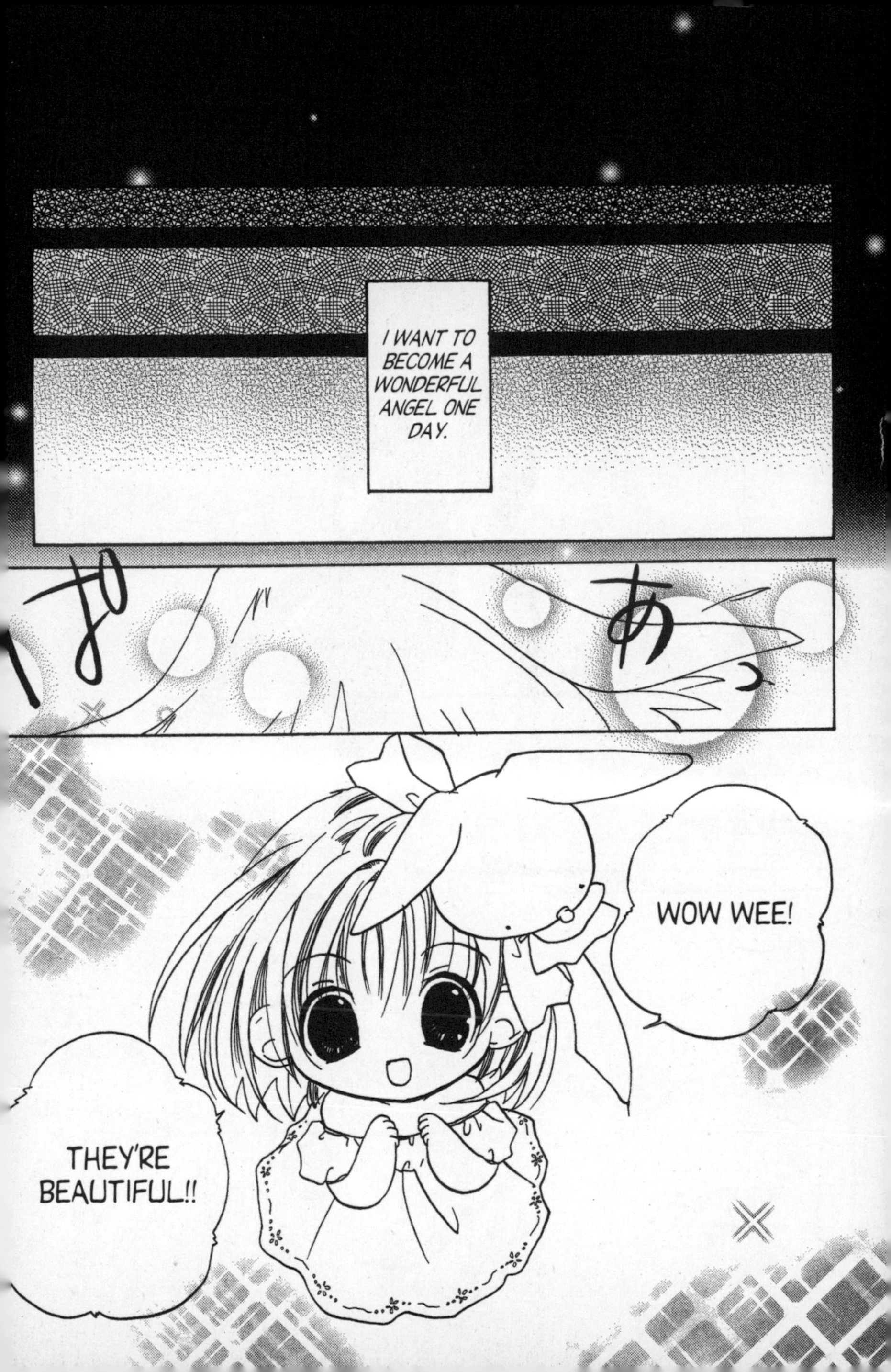
I WANT TO BECOME A WONDERFUL ANGEL ONE DAY.
あっ
ぱ
WOW WEE!
THEY'RE BEAUTIFUL!!

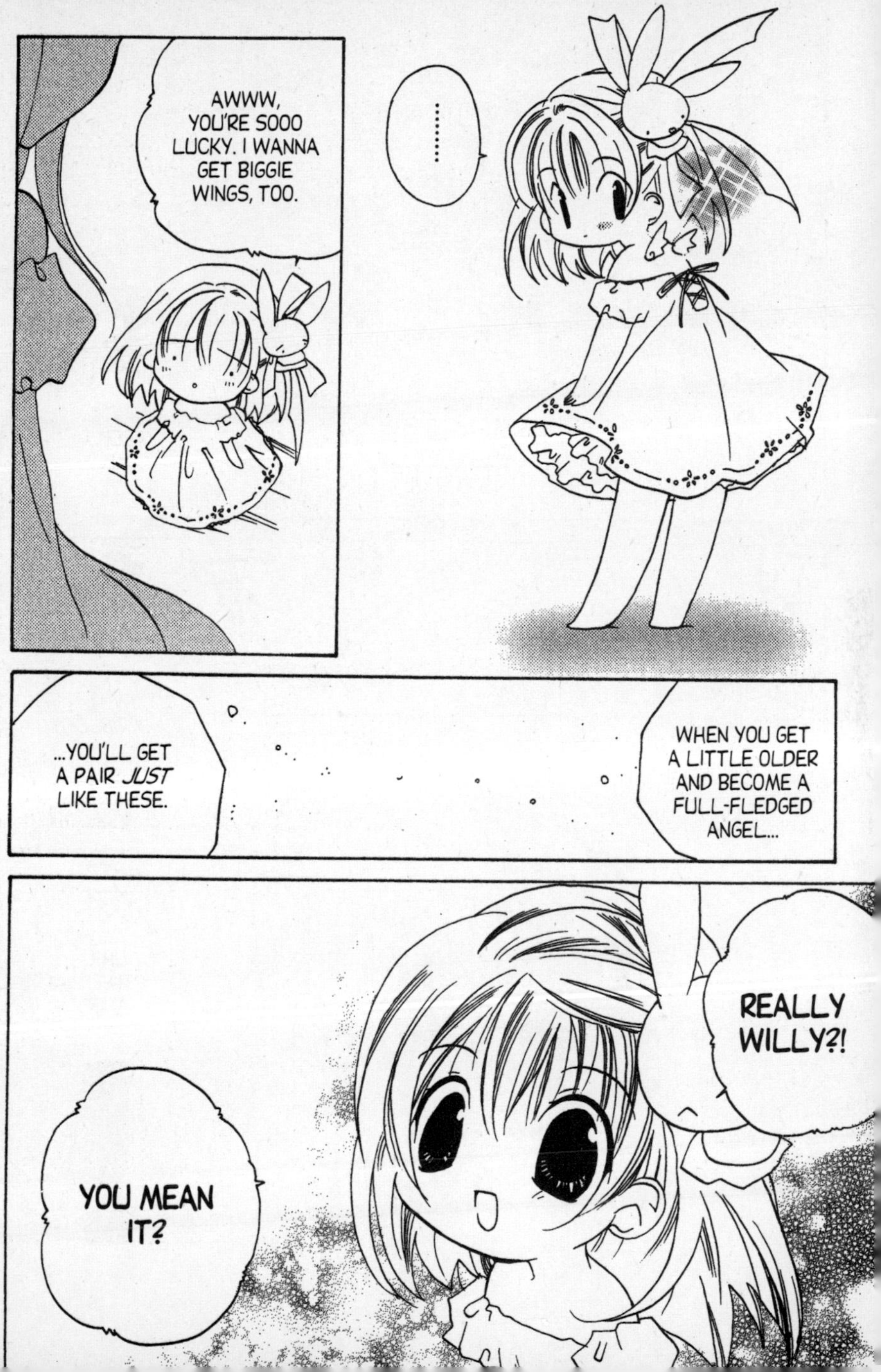
......
AWWW, YOU'RE SOOO LUCKY. I WANNA GET BIGGIE WINGS, TOO.
WHEN YOU GET A LITTLE OLDER AND BECOME A FULL-FLEDGED ANGEL...
...YOU'LL GET A PAIR *JUST* LIKE THESE.
REALLY WILLY?!
YOU MEAN IT?

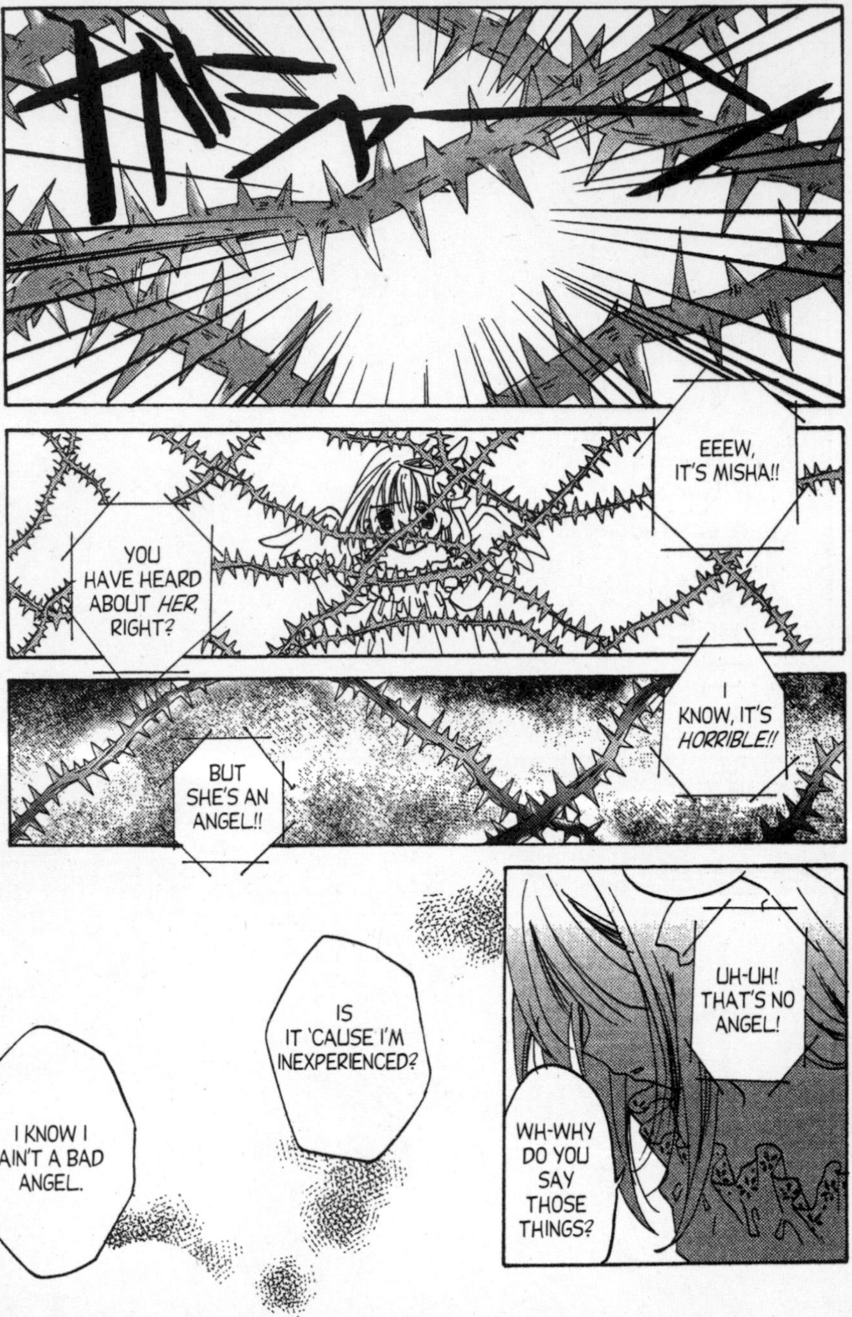
EEEW, IT'S MISHA!!
YOU HAVE HEARD ABOUT *HER*, RIGHT?
I KNOW, IT'S *HORRIBLE!!*
BUT SHE'S AN ANGEL!!
UH-UH! THAT'S NO ANGEL!
WH-WHY DO YOU SAY THOSE THINGS?
IS IT 'CAUSE I'M INEXPERIENCED?
I KNOW I AIN'T A BAD ANGEL.

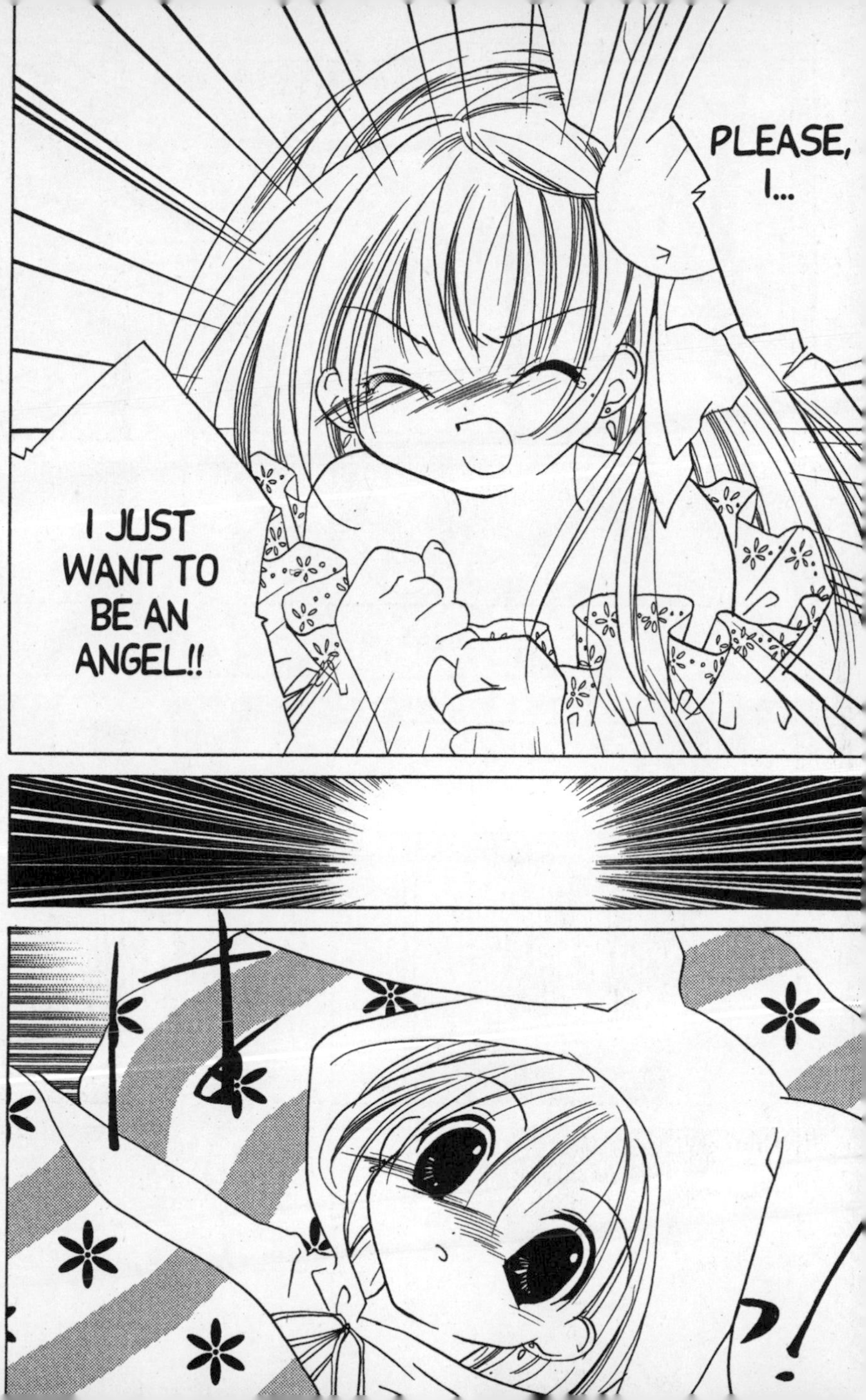
PLEASE, I...
I JUST WANT TO BE AN ANGEL!!
?!

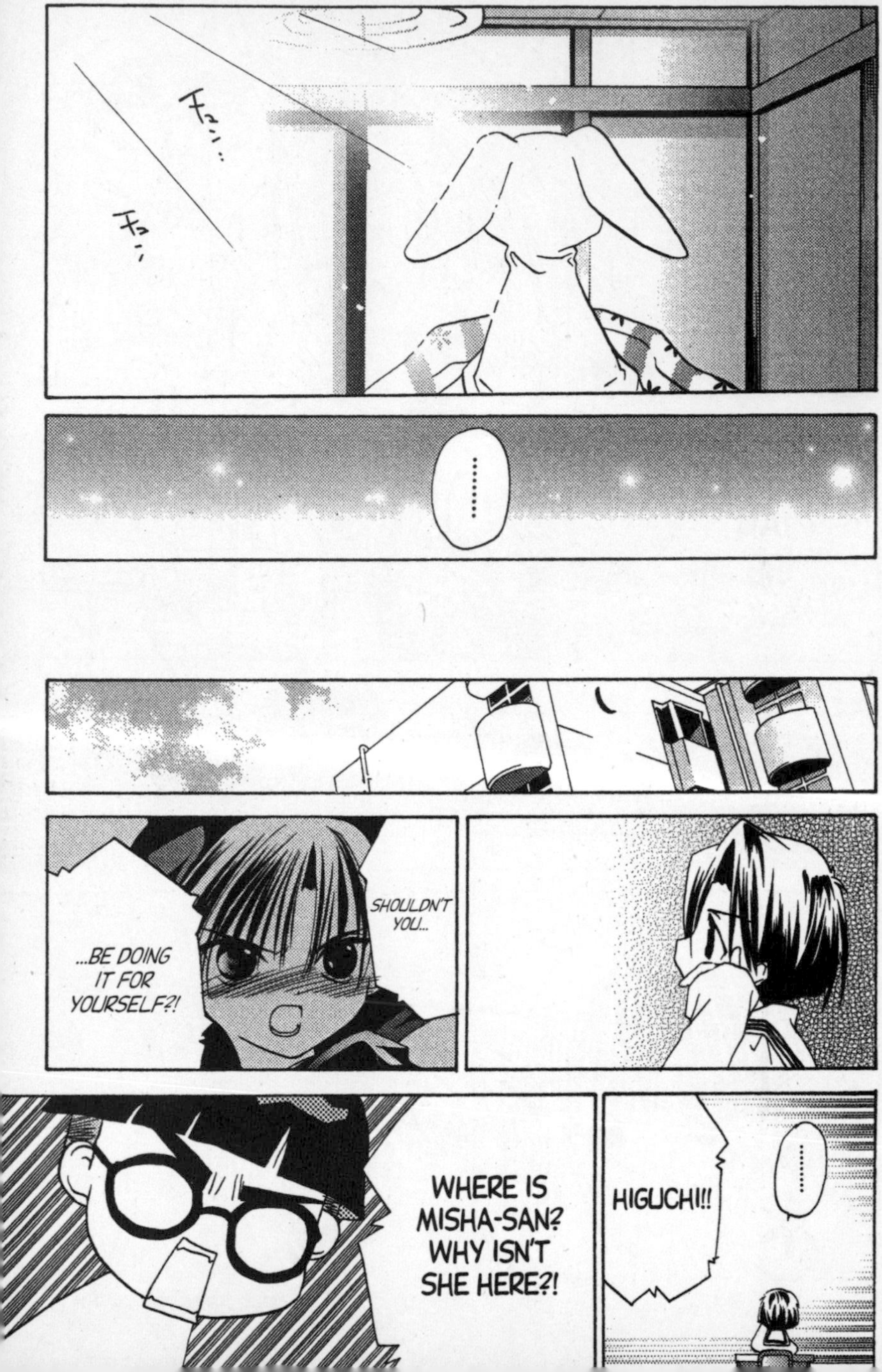
....
SHOULDN'T YOU...
...BE DOING IT FOR YOURSELF?!
....
HIGUCHI!!!
WHERE IS MISHA-SAN? WHY ISN'T SHE HERE?!

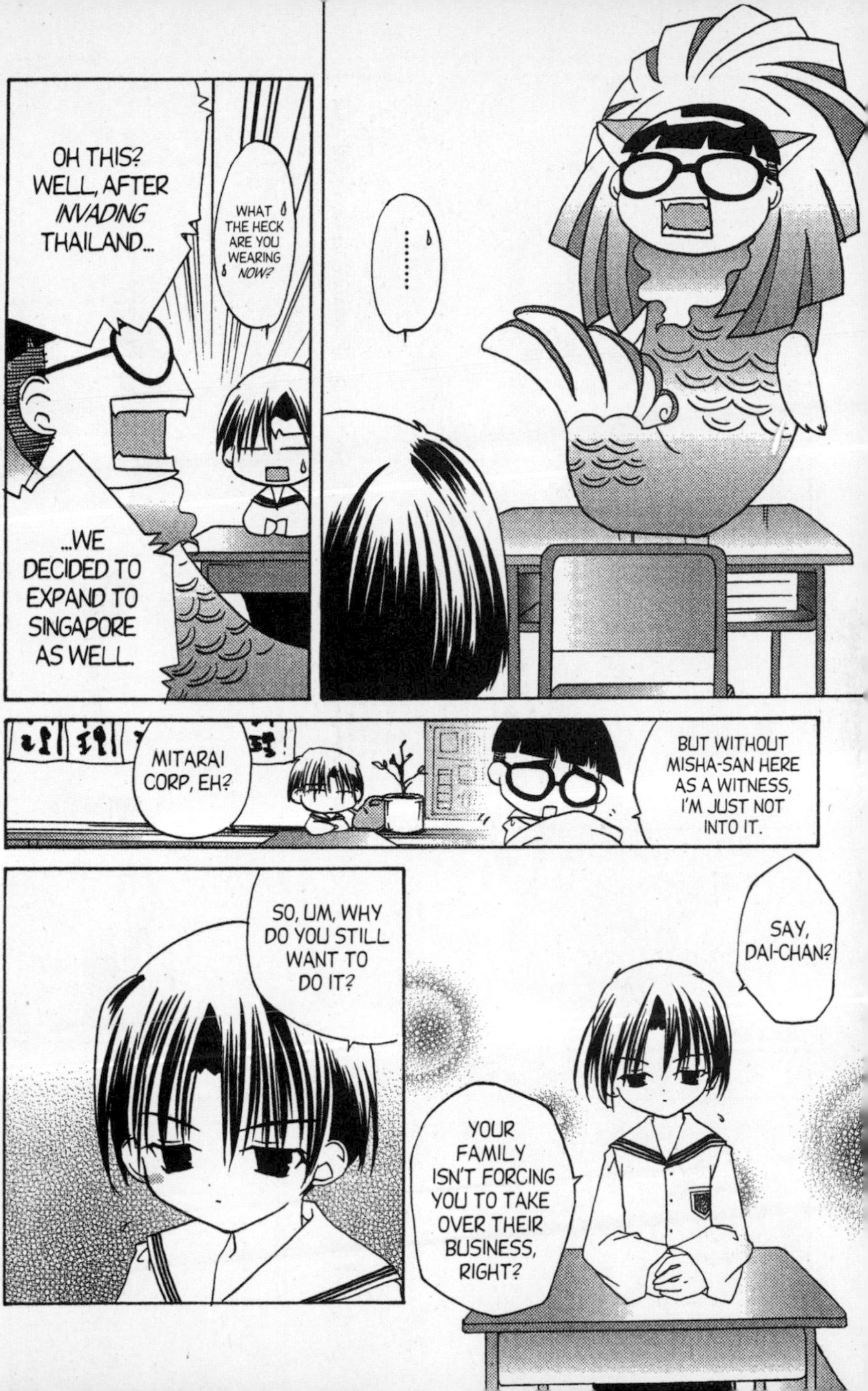
......
WHAT THE HECK ARE YOU WEARING NOW?
OH THIS? WELL, AFTER INVADING THAILAND...
...WE DECIDED TO EXPAND TO SINGAPORE AS WELL.
BUT WITHOUT MISHA-SAN HERE AS A WITNESS, I'M JUST NOT INTO IT.
MITARAI CORP, EH?
SAY, DAI-CHAN?
YOUR FAMILY ISN'T FORCING YOU TO TAKE OVER THEIR BUSINESS, RIGHT?
SO, UM, WHY DO YOU STILL WANT TO DO IT?

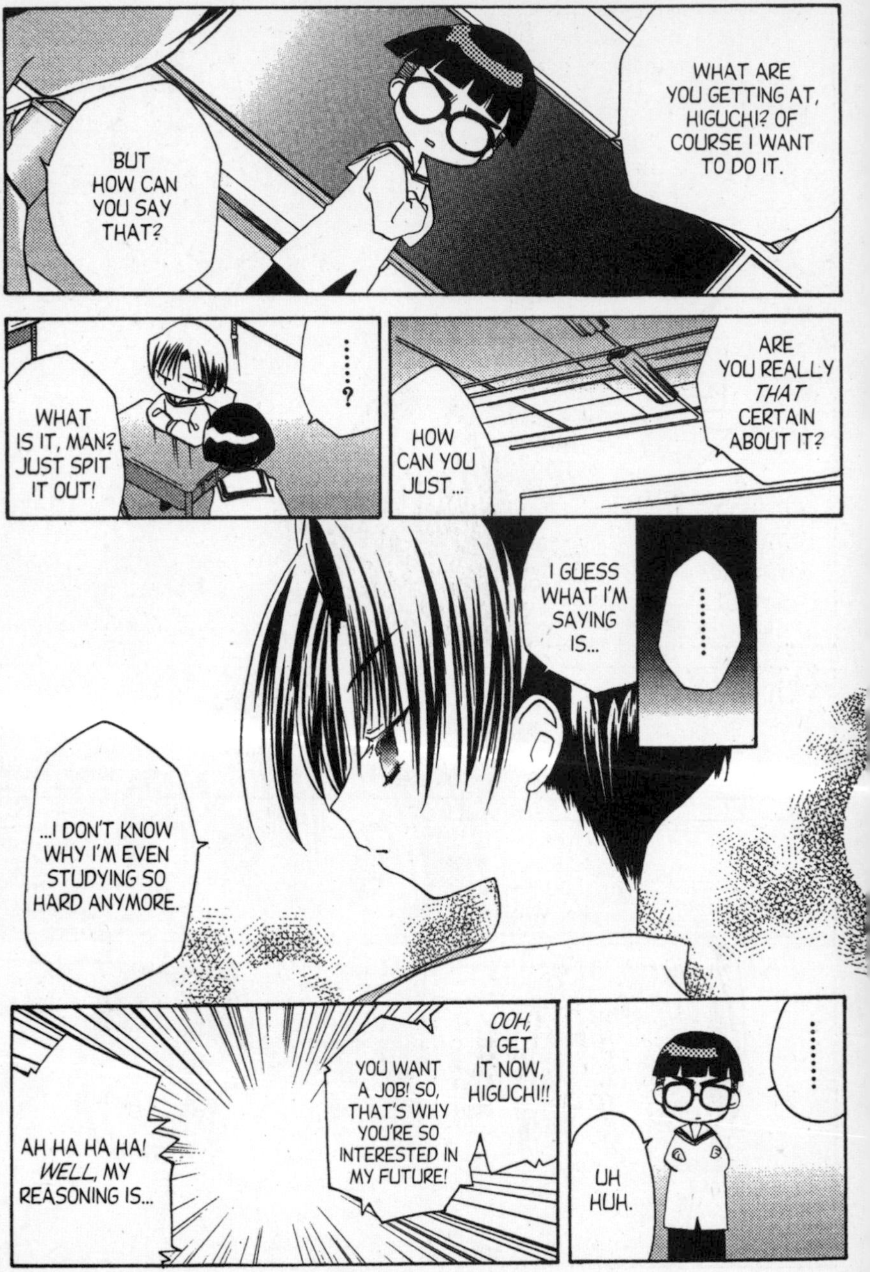
WHAT ARE YOU GETTING AT, HIGUCHI? OF COURSE I WANT TO DO IT.
BUT HOW CAN YOU SAY THAT?
ARE YOU REALLY *THAT* CERTAIN ABOUT IT?
HOW CAN YOU JUST...
......?
WHAT IS IT, MAN? JUST SPIT IT OUT!
....
I GUESS WHAT I'M SAYING IS...
...I DON'T KNOW WHY I'M EVEN STUDYING SO HARD ANYMORE.
....
UH HUH.
OOH, I GET IT NOW, HIGUCHI!!
YOU WANT A JOB! SO, THAT'S WHY YOU'RE SO INTERESTED IN MY FUTURE!
AH HA HA HA! *WELL,* MY REASONING IS...

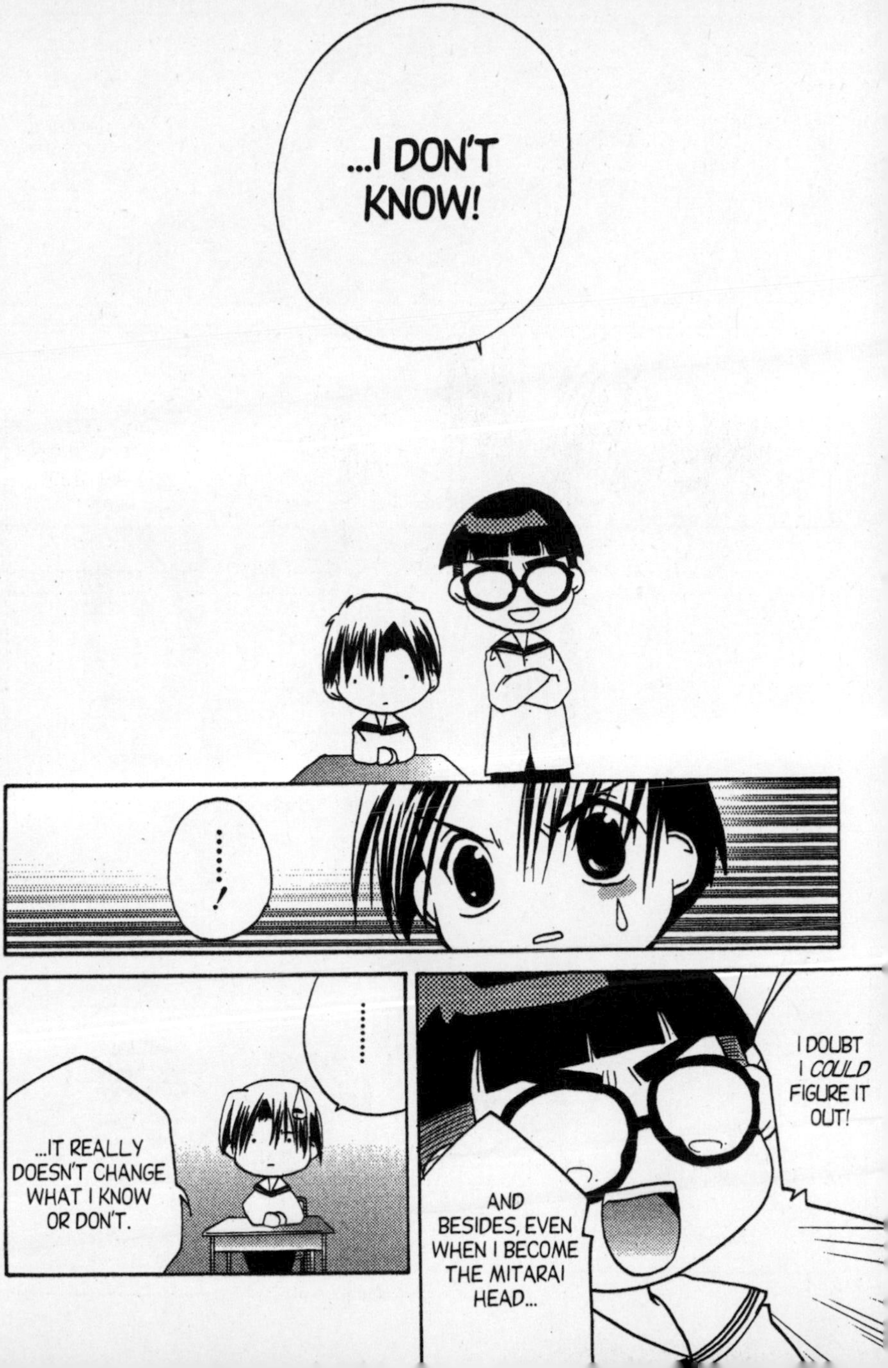
...I DON'T KNOW!
......!
I DOUBT I *COULD* FIGURE IT OUT!
AND BESIDES, EVEN WHEN I BECOME THE MITARAI HEAD...
......
...IT REALLY DOESN'T CHANGE WHAT I KNOW OR DON'T.

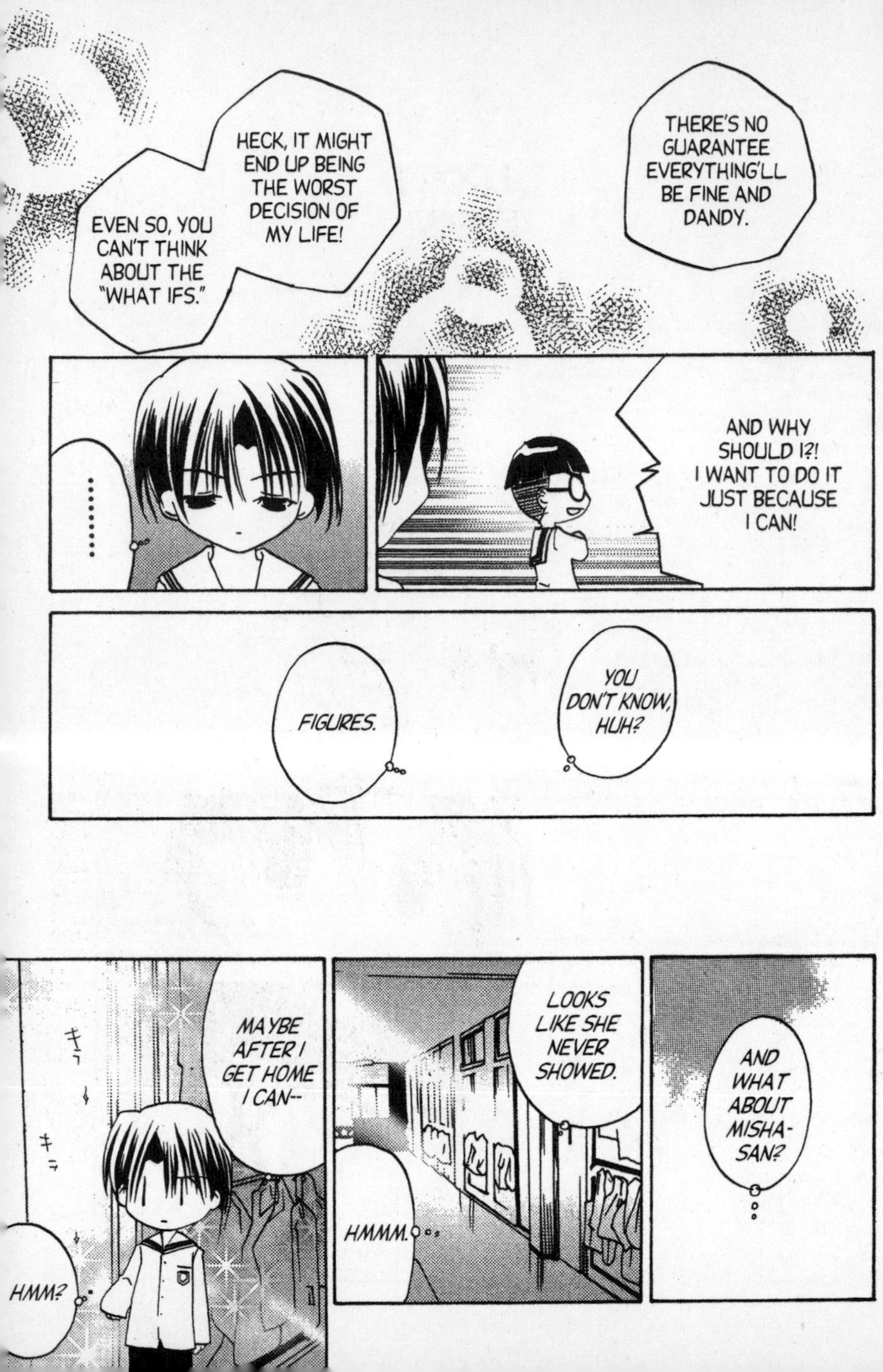
THERE'S NO GUARANTEE EVERYTHING'LL BE FINE AND DANDY.
HECK, IT MIGHT END UP BEING THE WORST DECISION OF MY LIFE!
EVEN SO, YOU CAN'T THINK ABOUT THE "WHAT IFS."
AND WHY SHOULD I?! I WANT TO DO IT JUST BECAUSE I CAN!
......
YOU DON'T KNOW, HUH?
FIGURES.
AND WHAT ABOUT MISHA-SAN?
LOOKS LIKE SHE NEVER SHOWED.
HMMM.
MAYBE AFTER I GET HOME I CAN--
キラ
キラ
HMM?

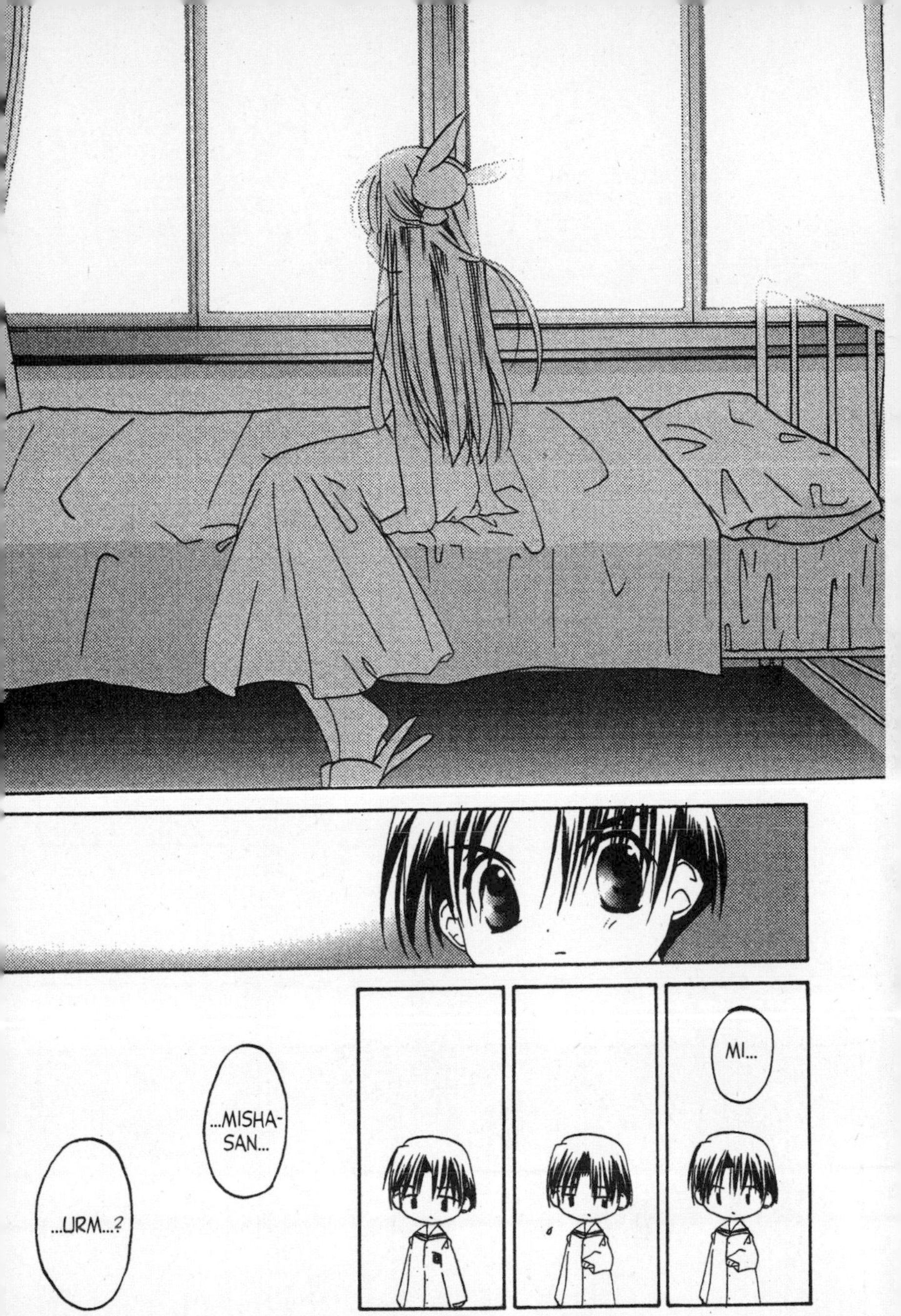
MI...
...MISHA-SAN...
...URM...?

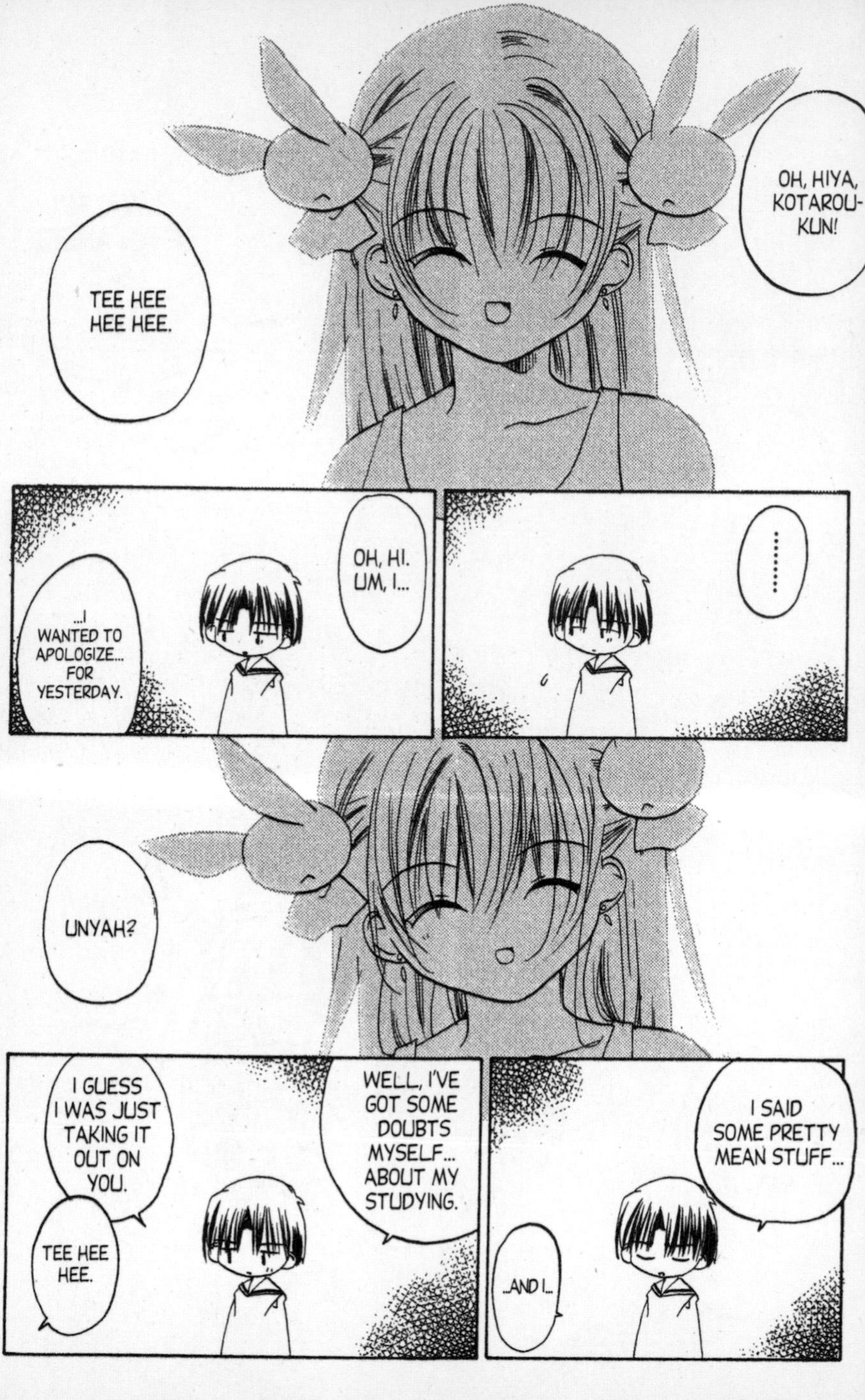
OH, HIYA, KOTAROU-KUN!
TEE HEE HEE HEE.
......
OH, HI. UM, I...
...I WANTED TO APOLOGIZE... FOR YESTERDAY.
UNYAH?
I SAID SOME PRETTY MEAN STUFF...
...AND I...
WELL, I'VE GOT SOME DOUBTS MYSELF... ABOUT MY STUDYING.
I GUESS I WAS JUST TAKING IT OUT ON YOU.
TEE HEE HEE.

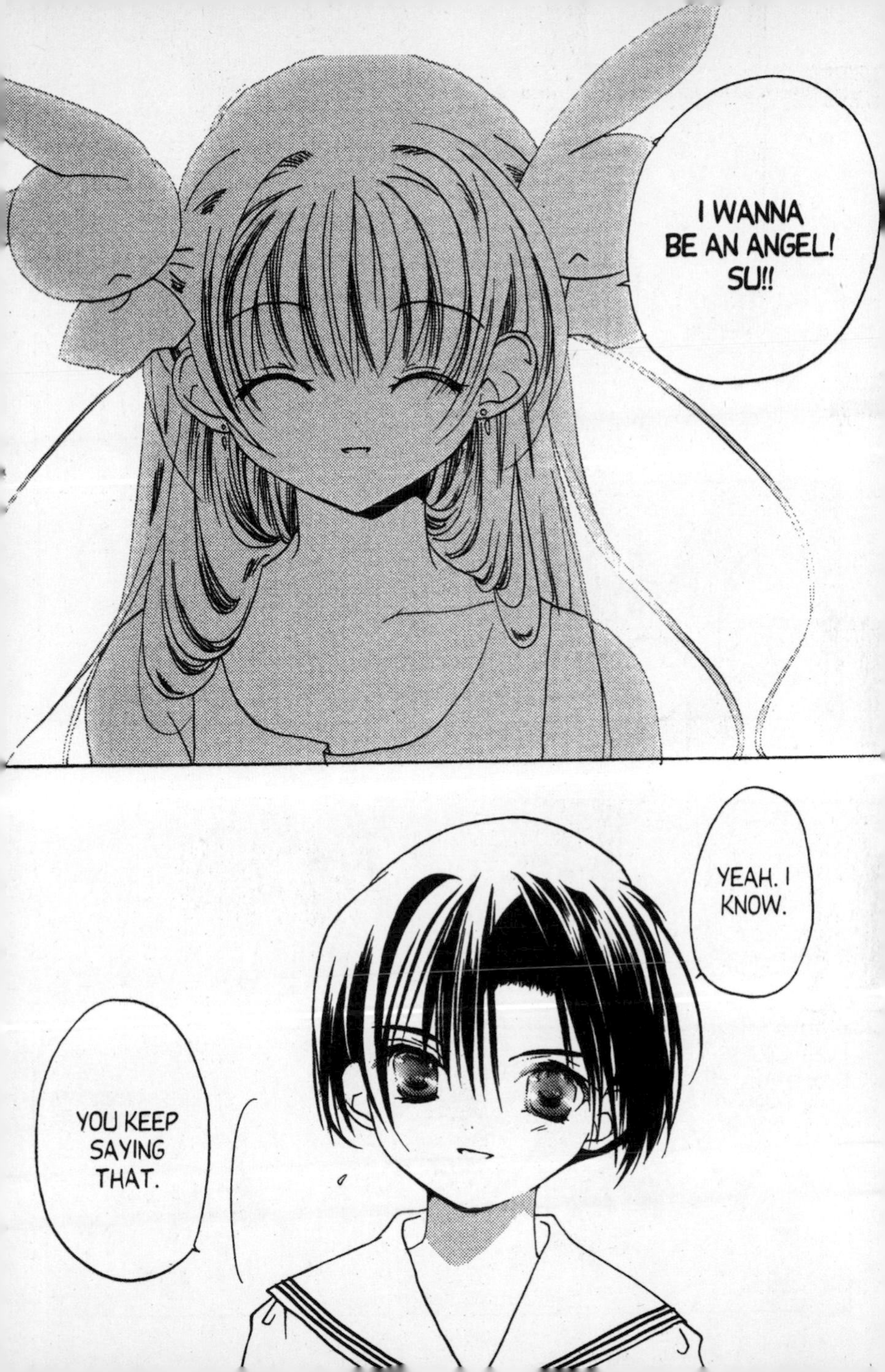
I WANNA BE AN ANGEL! SU!!
YEAH. I KNOW.
YOU KEEP SAYING THAT.

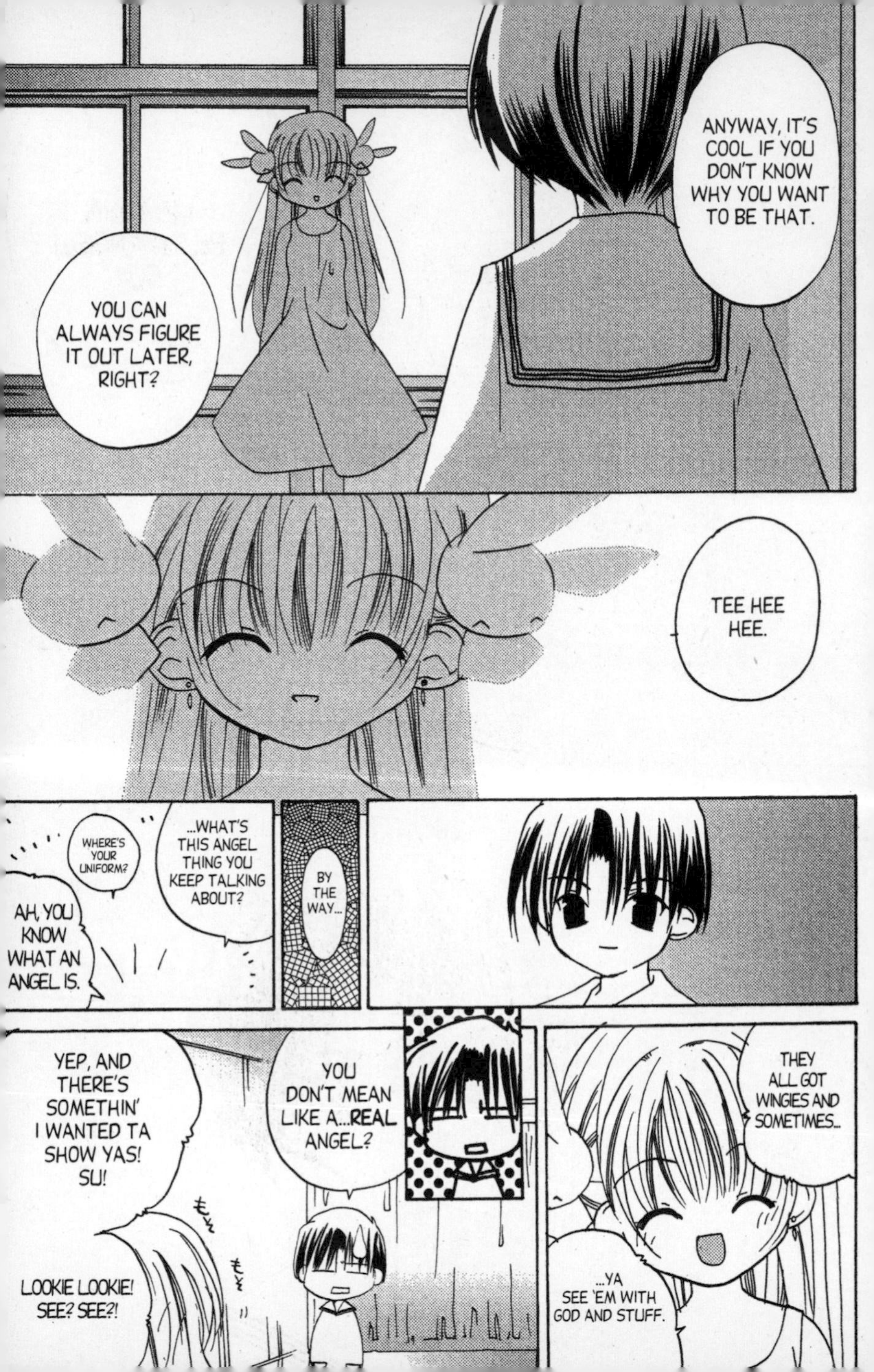
ANYWAY, IT'S COOL IF YOU DON'T KNOW WHY YOU WANT TO BE THAT.
YOU CAN ALWAYS FIGURE IT OUT LATER, RIGHT?
TEE HEE HEE.
BY THE WAY...
...WHAT'S THIS ANGEL THING YOU KEEP TALKING ABOUT?
WHERE'S YOUR UNIFORM?
AH, YOU KNOW WHAT AN ANGEL IS.
THEY ALL GOT WINGIES AND SOMETIMES...
...YA SEE 'EM WITH GOD AND STUFF.
YOU DON'T MEAN LIKE A...REAL ANGEL?
YEP, AND THERE'S SOMETHIN' I WANTED TA SHOW YAS! SU!
LOOKIE LOOKIE! SEE? SEE?!

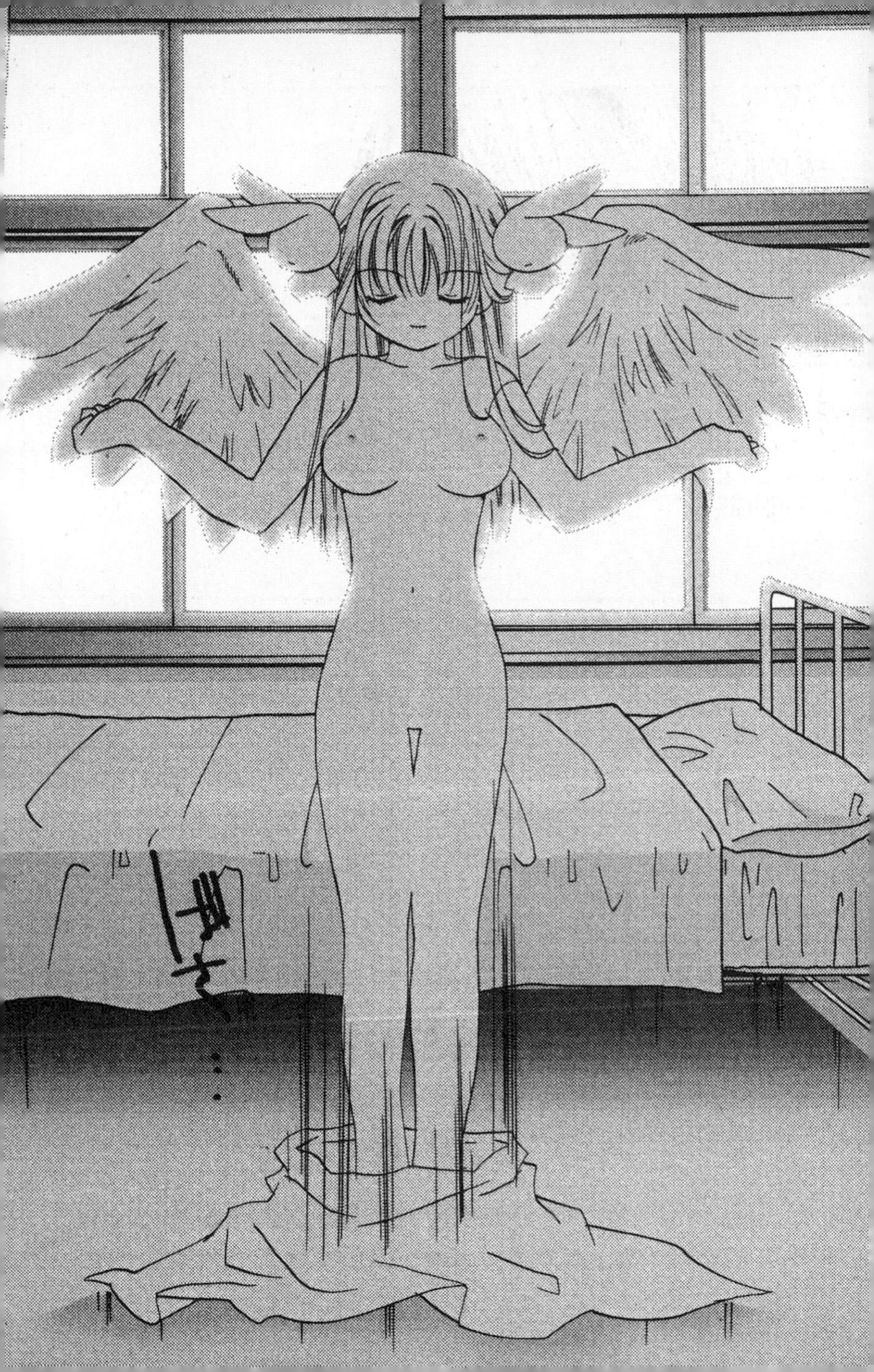
ばさ…

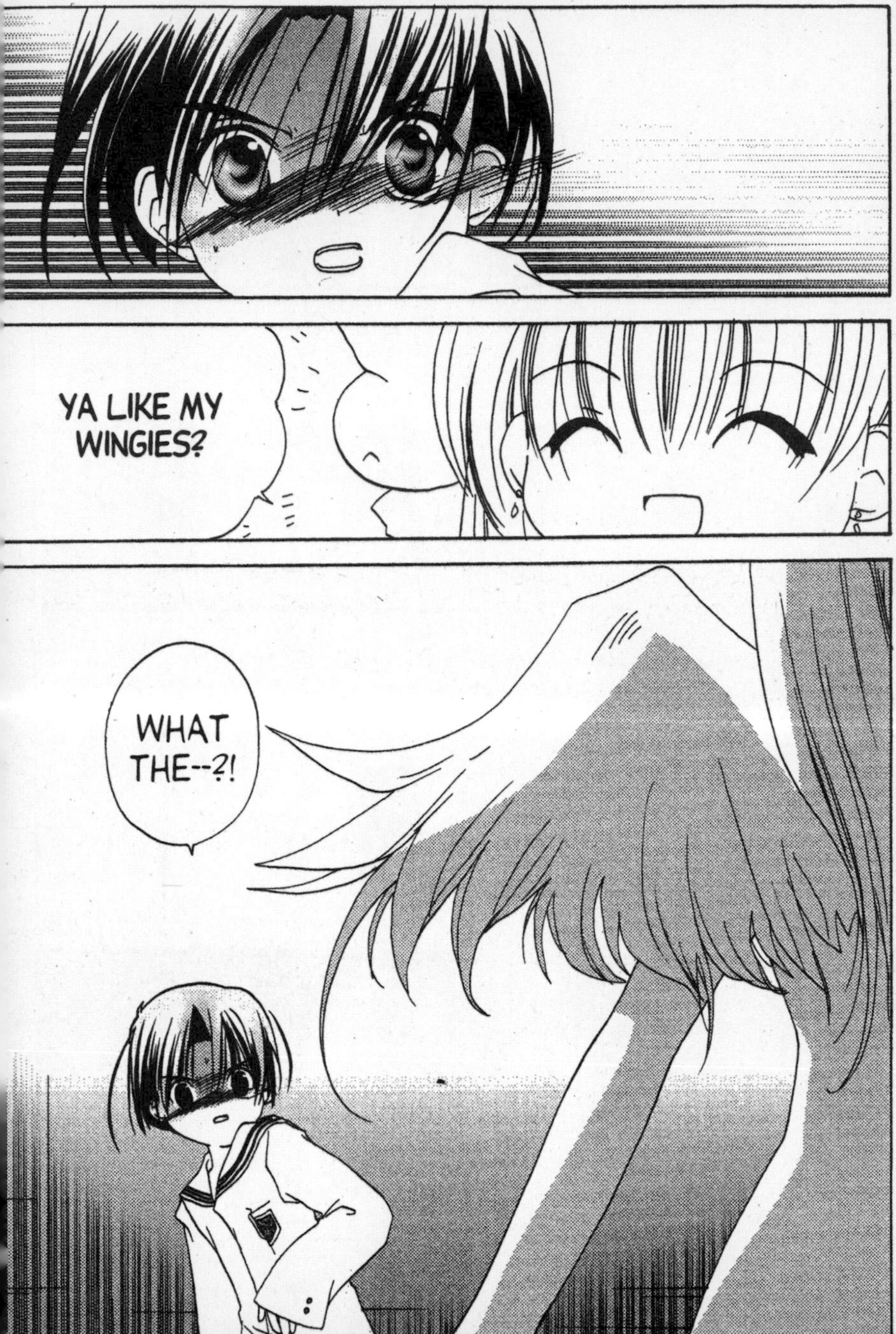
YA LIKE MY WINGIES?
WHAT THE--?!

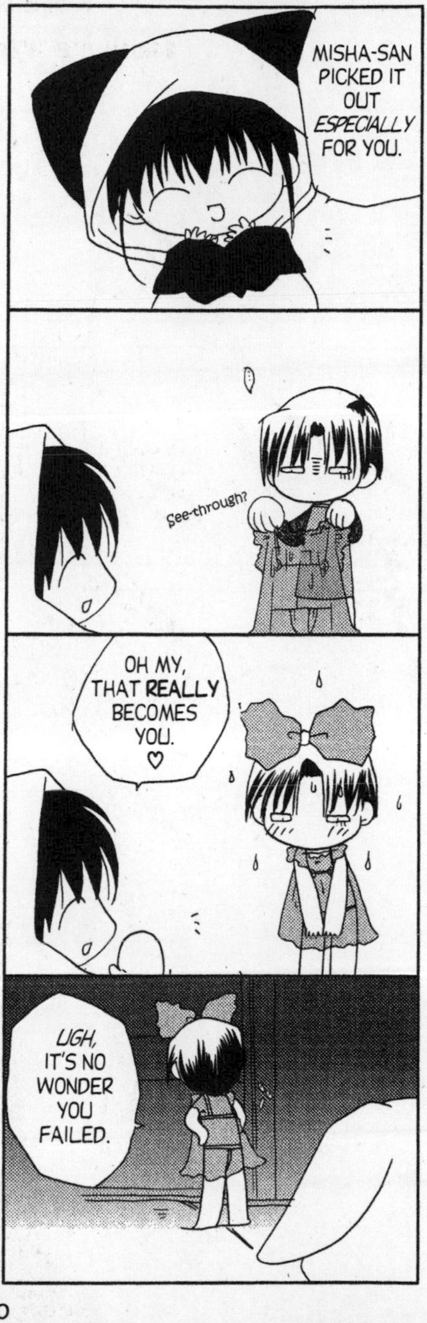
MISHA-SAN PICKED IT OUT *ESPECIALLY* FOR YOU.
See-through?
OH MY, THAT **REALLY** BECOMES YOU. ♡
UGH, IT'S NO WONDER YOU FAILED.

Lesson 22

How to Find an Angel

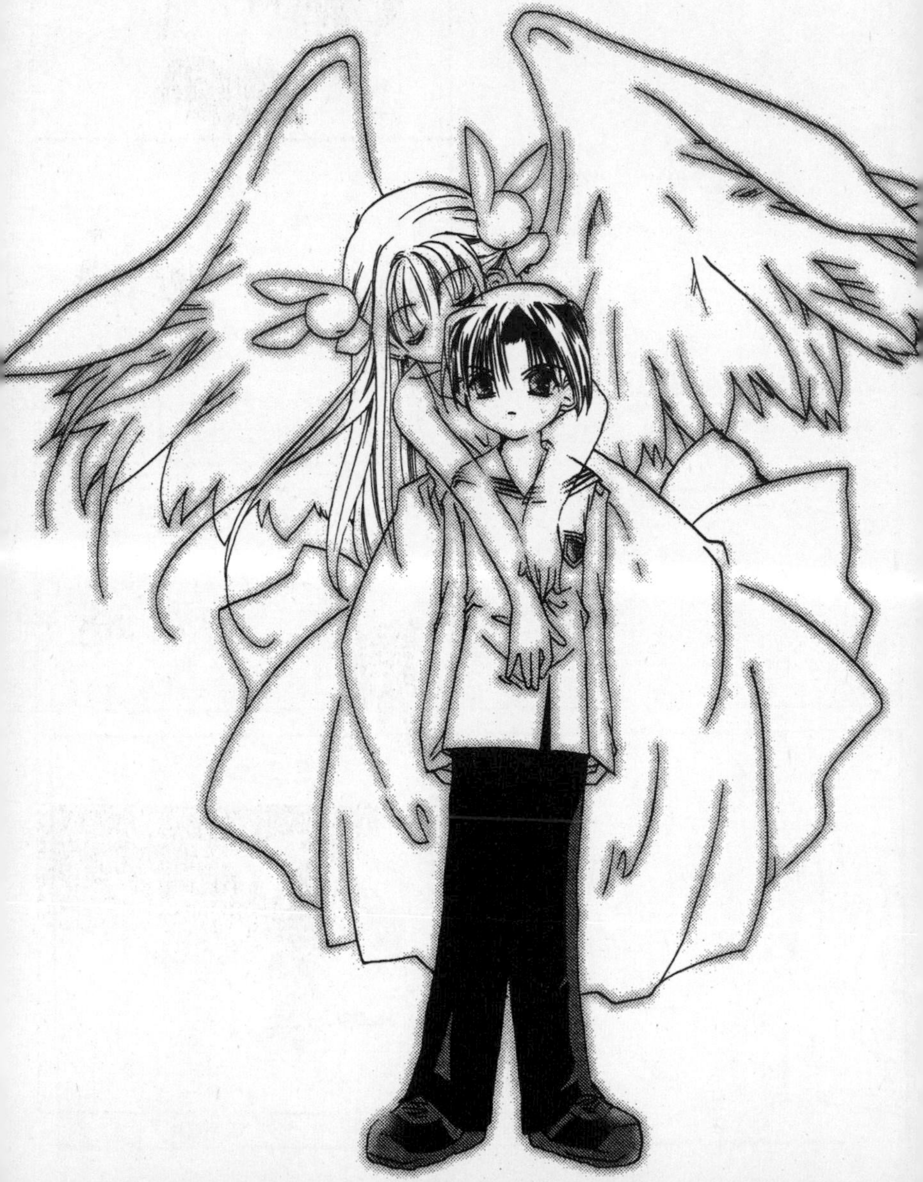

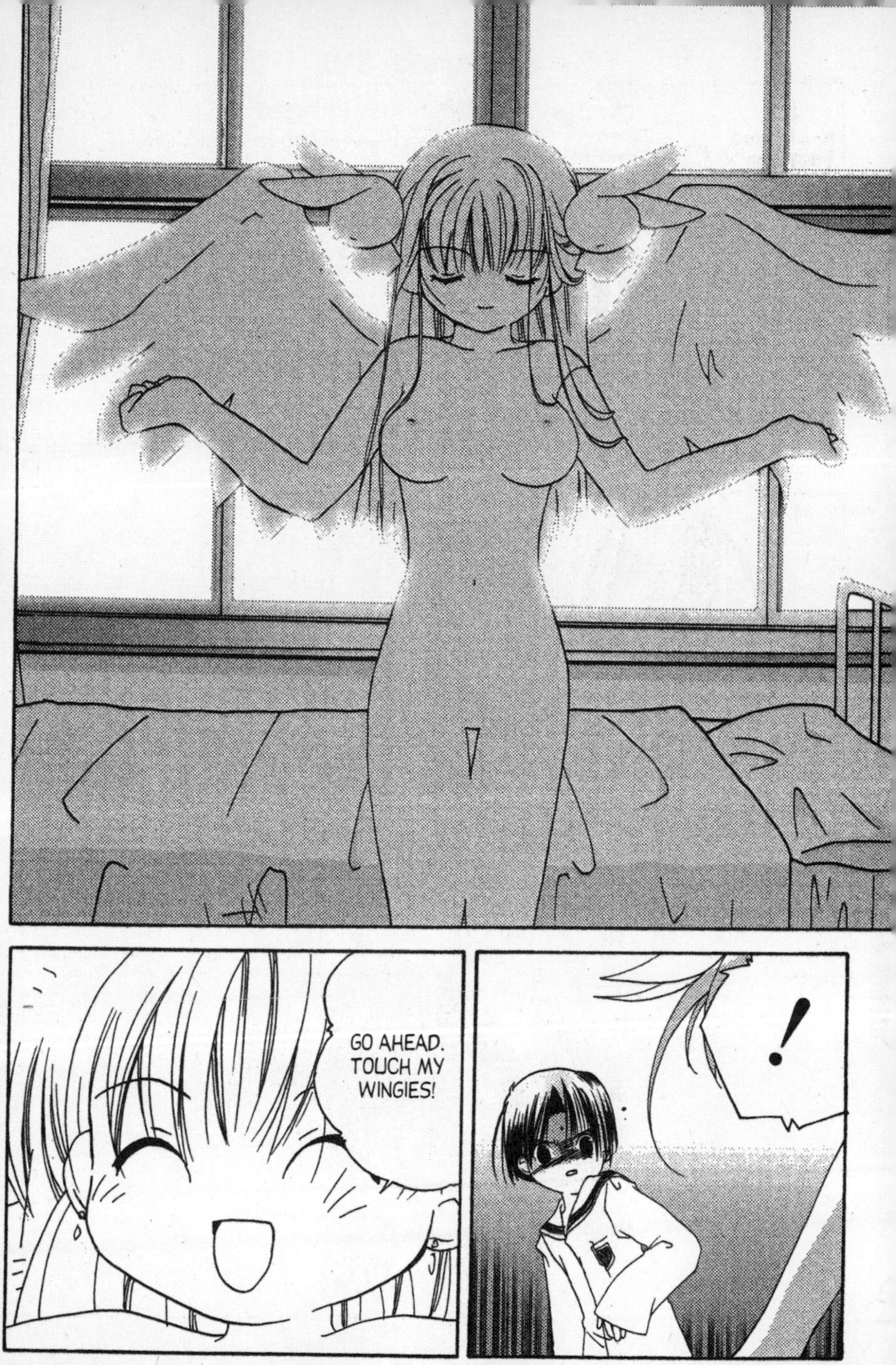
!
GO AHEAD. TOUCH MY WINGIES!

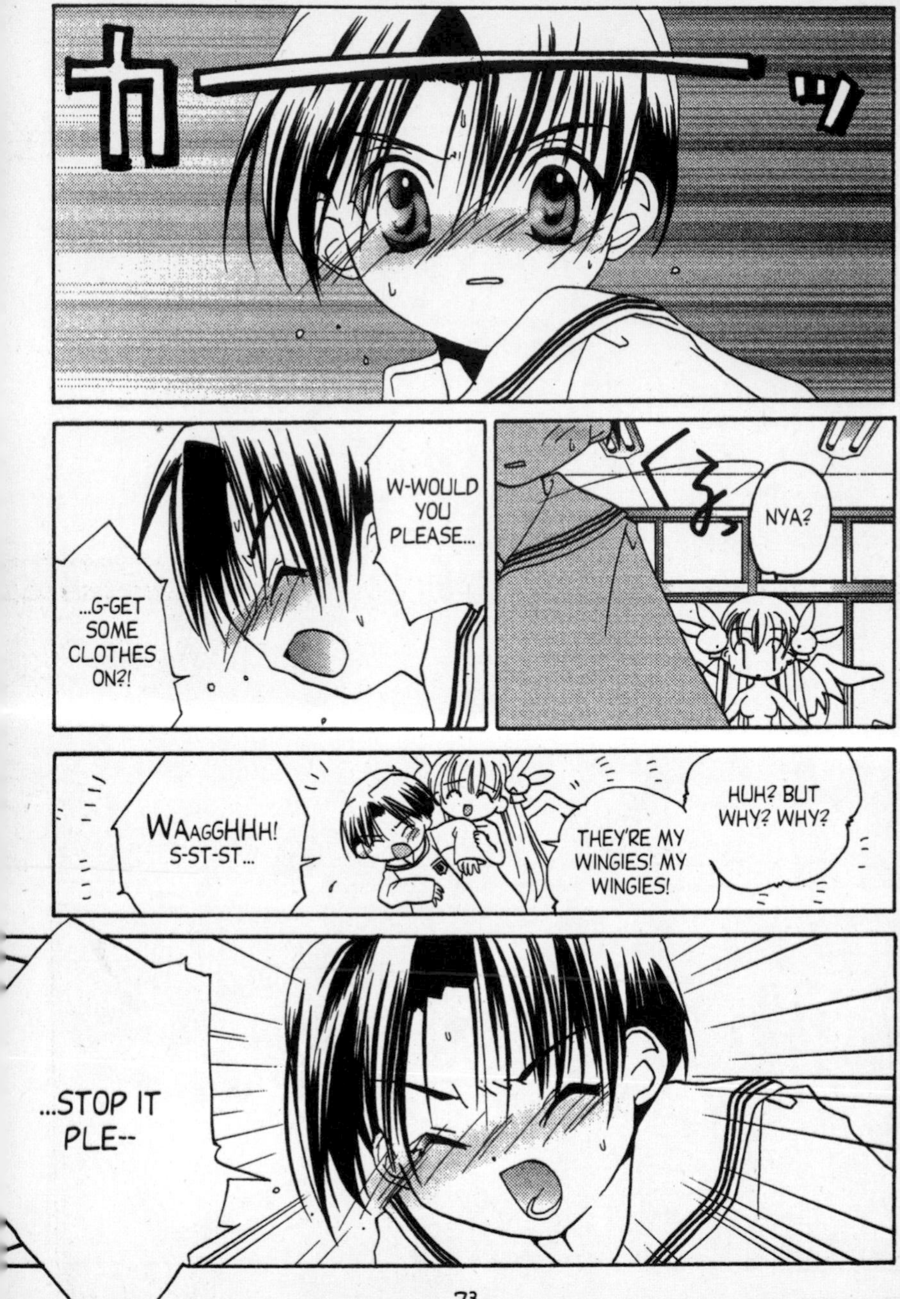
カーッ
NYA?
W-WOULD YOU PLEASE...
...G-GET SOME CLOTHES ON?!
HUH? BUT WHY? WHY?
THEY'RE MY WINGIES! MY WINGIES!
WAaGHHH! S-ST-ST...
...STOP IT PLE--

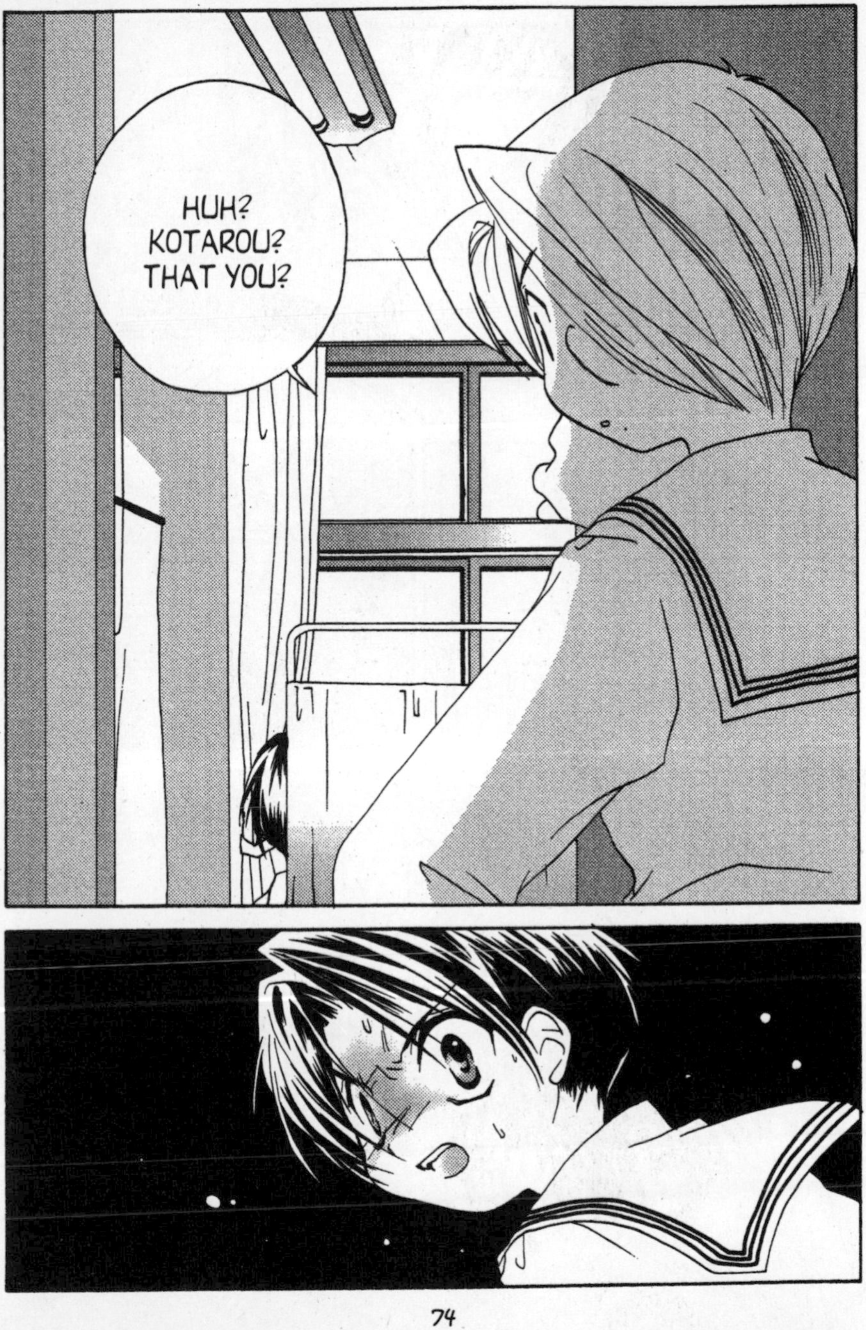
HUH? KOTAROU? THAT YOU?

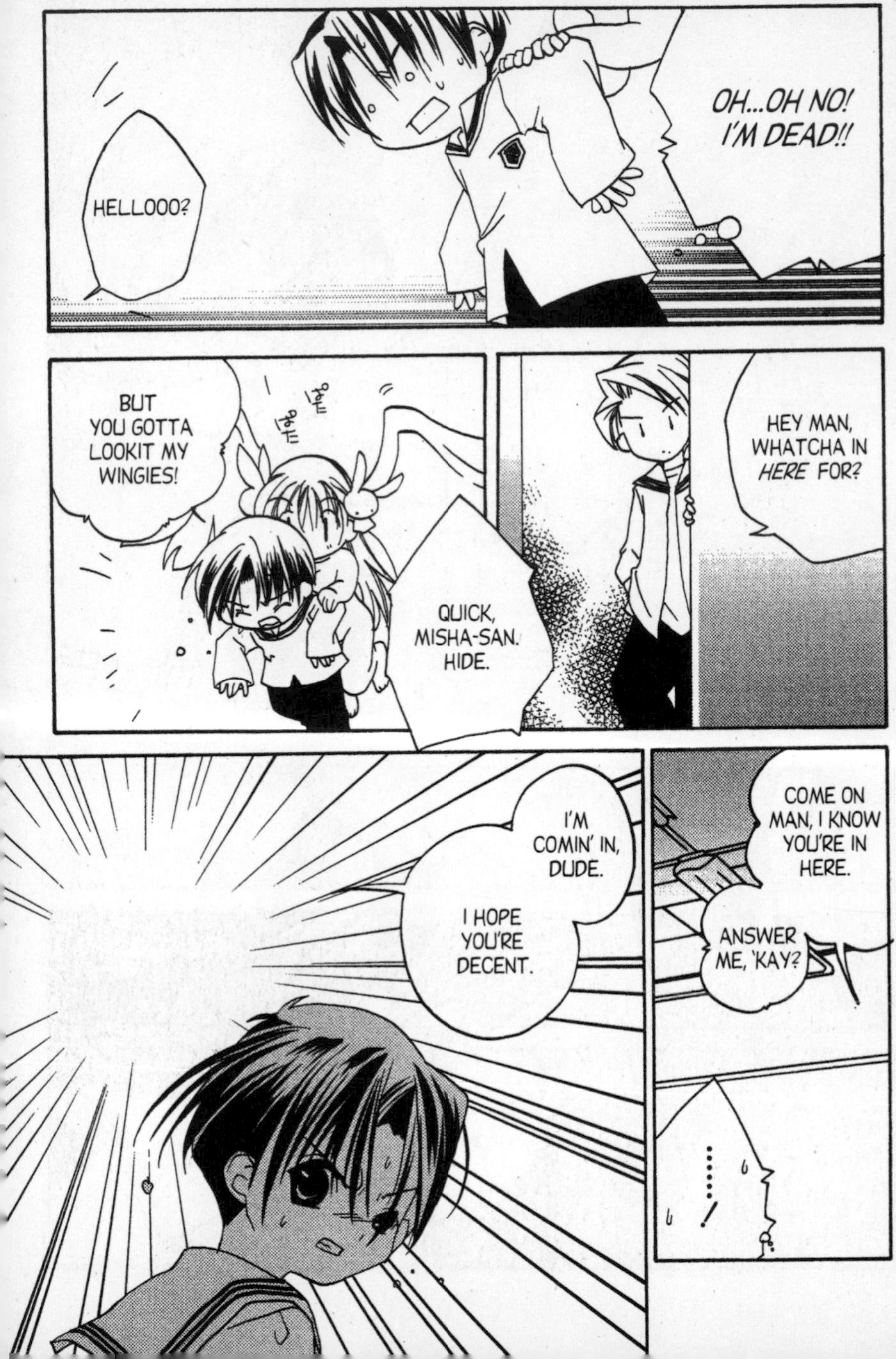
OH...OH NO! I'M DEAD!!
HELLOOO?
HEY MAN, WHATCHA IN *HERE* FOR?
QUICK, MISHA-SAN. HIDE.
BUT YOU GOTTA LOOKIT MY WINGIES!
COME ON MAN, I KNOW YOU'RE IN HERE.
ANSWER ME, 'KAY?
......!
I'M COMIN' IN, DUDE.
I HOPE YOU'RE DECENT.

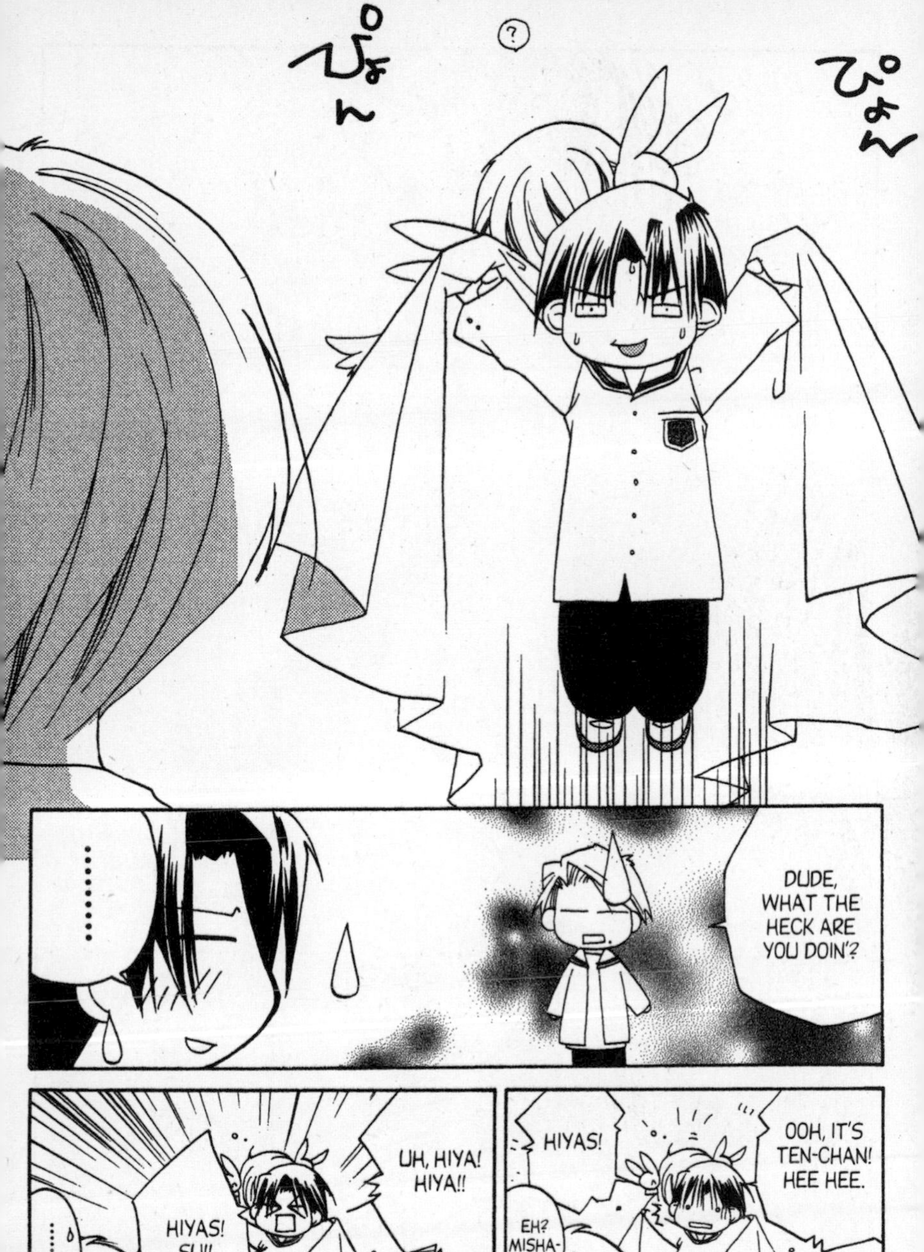
ぴょん
?
ぴょん
DUDE, WHAT THE HECK ARE YOU DOIN'?
....
OOH, IT'S TEN-CHAN! HEE HEE.
HIYAS!
EH? MISHA-SAN?
UH, HIYA! HIYA!!
HIYAS! SU!!
....

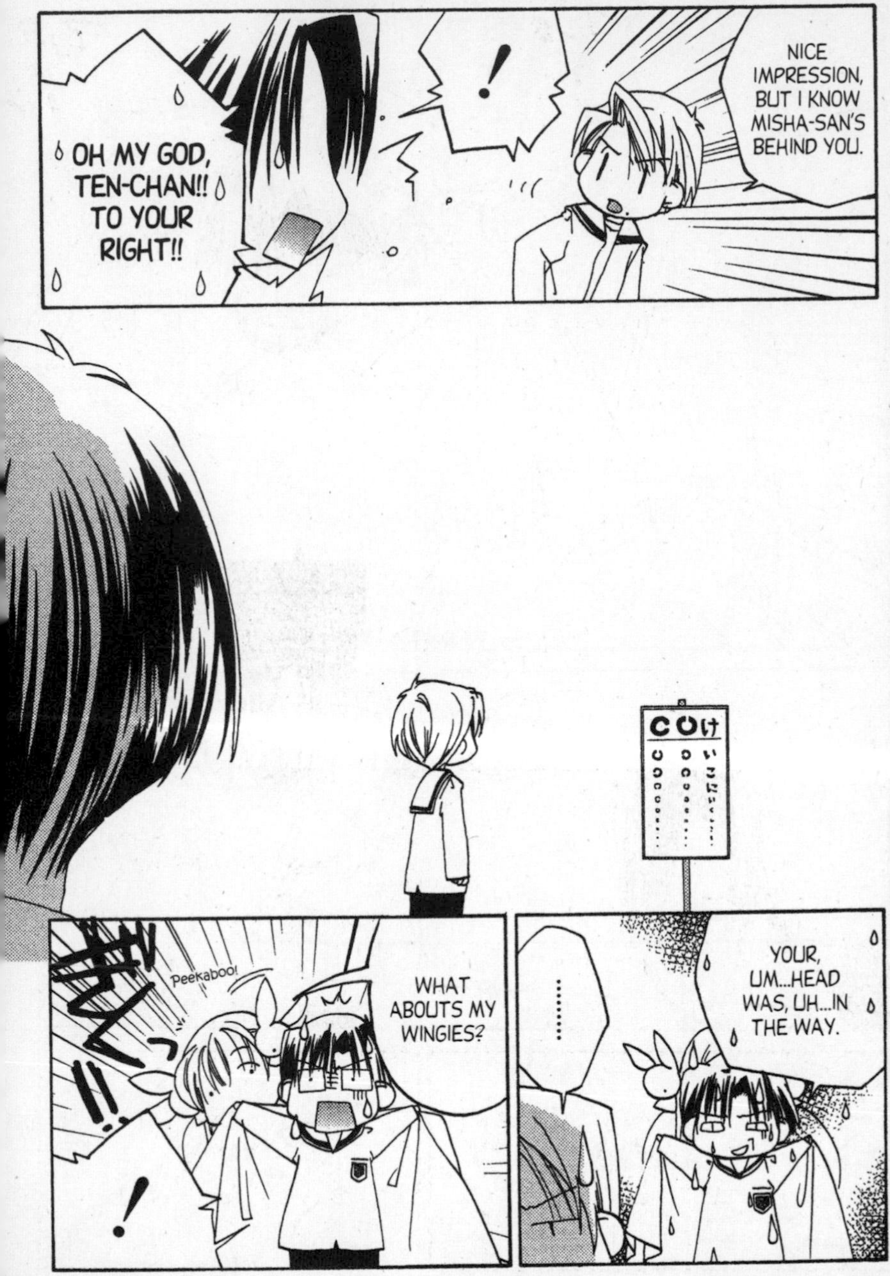
NICE IMPRESSION, BUT I KNOW MISHA-SAN'S BEHIND YOU.
!
OH MY GOD, TEN-CHAN!! TO YOUR RIGHT!!
YOUR, UM...HEAD WAS, UH...IN THE WAY.
......
WHAT ABOUTS MY WINGIES?
Peekaboo!
!

*GYAH!

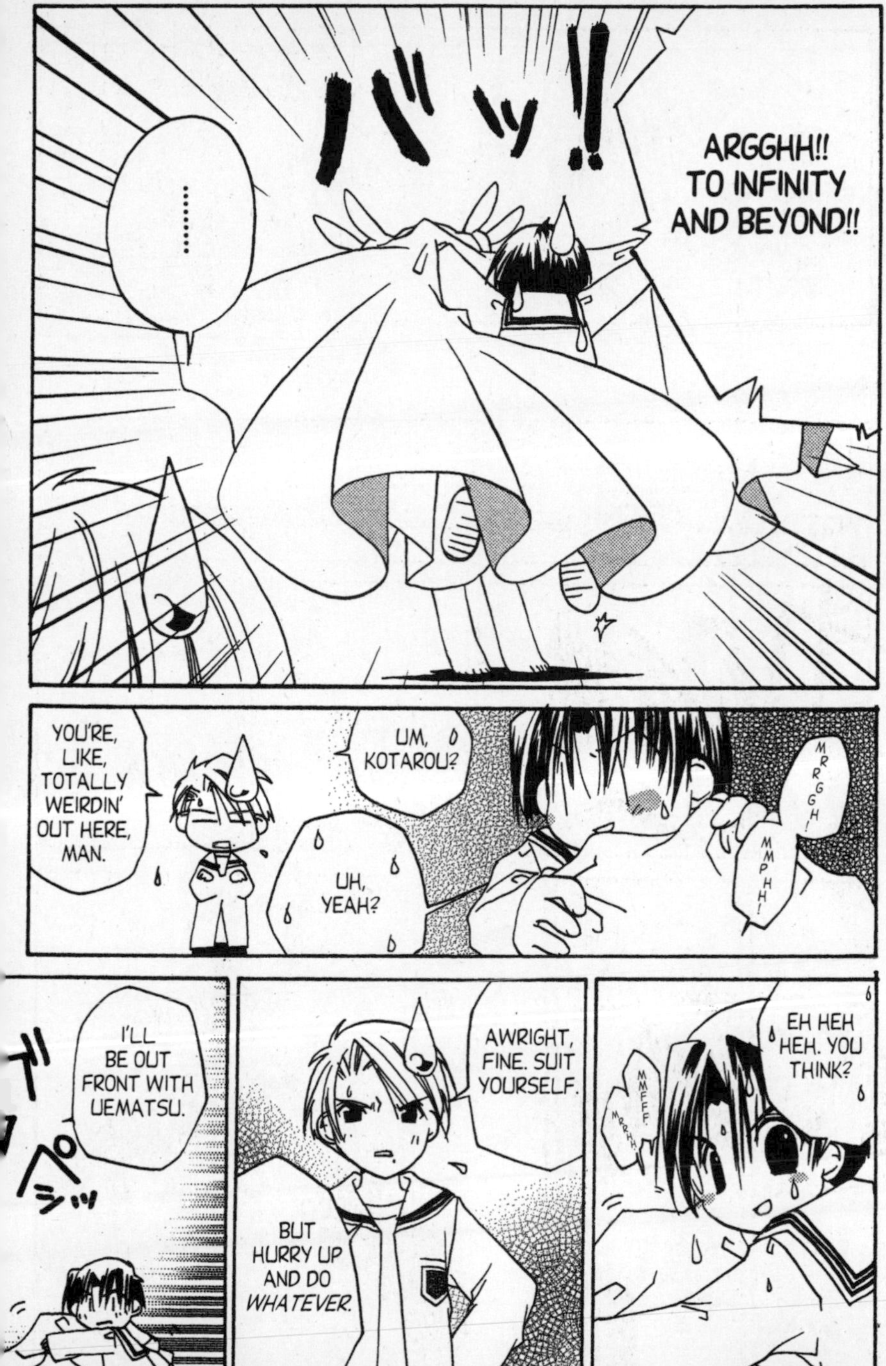
ARGGHH!! TO INFINITY AND BEYOND!!
バッ!!
....
MRRGH!
MMPHH!
UM, KOTAROU?
UH, YEAH?
YOU'RE, LIKE, TOTALLY WEIRDIN' OUT HERE, MAN.
EH HEH HEH. YOU THINK?
MMFFF.
MRRHH!
AWRIGHT, FINE. SUIT YOURSELF.
BUT HURRY UP AND DO *WHATEVER*.
I'LL BE OUT FRONT WITH UEMATSU.

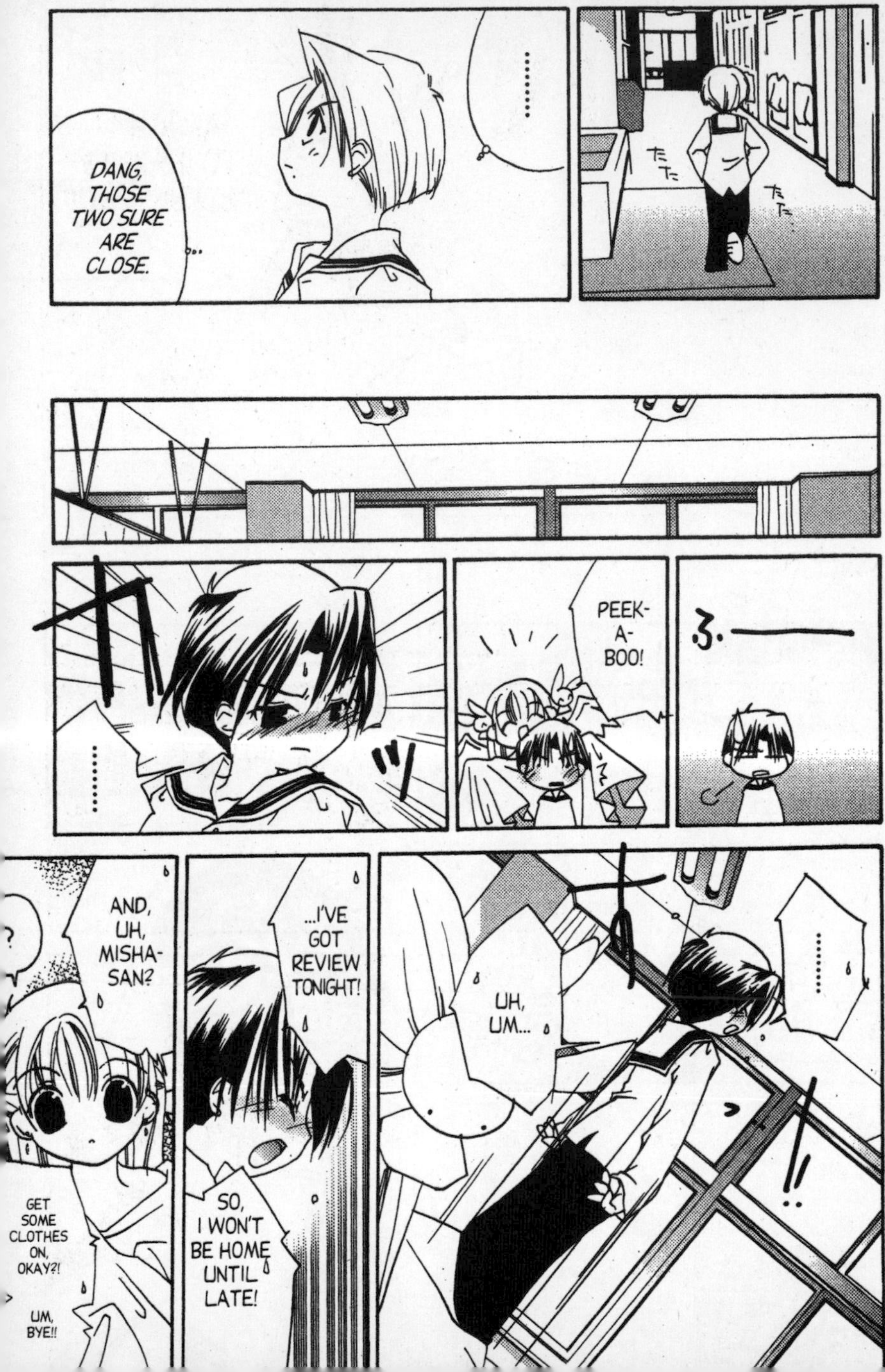
......
DANG, THOSE TWO SURE ARE CLOSE...
PEEK-A-BOO!
......
......
!!
UH, UM...
...I'VE GOT REVIEW TONIGHT!
SO, I WON'T BE HOME UNTIL LATE!
?
AND, UH, MISHA-SAN?
GET SOME CLOTHES ON, OKAY?!
UM, BYE!!

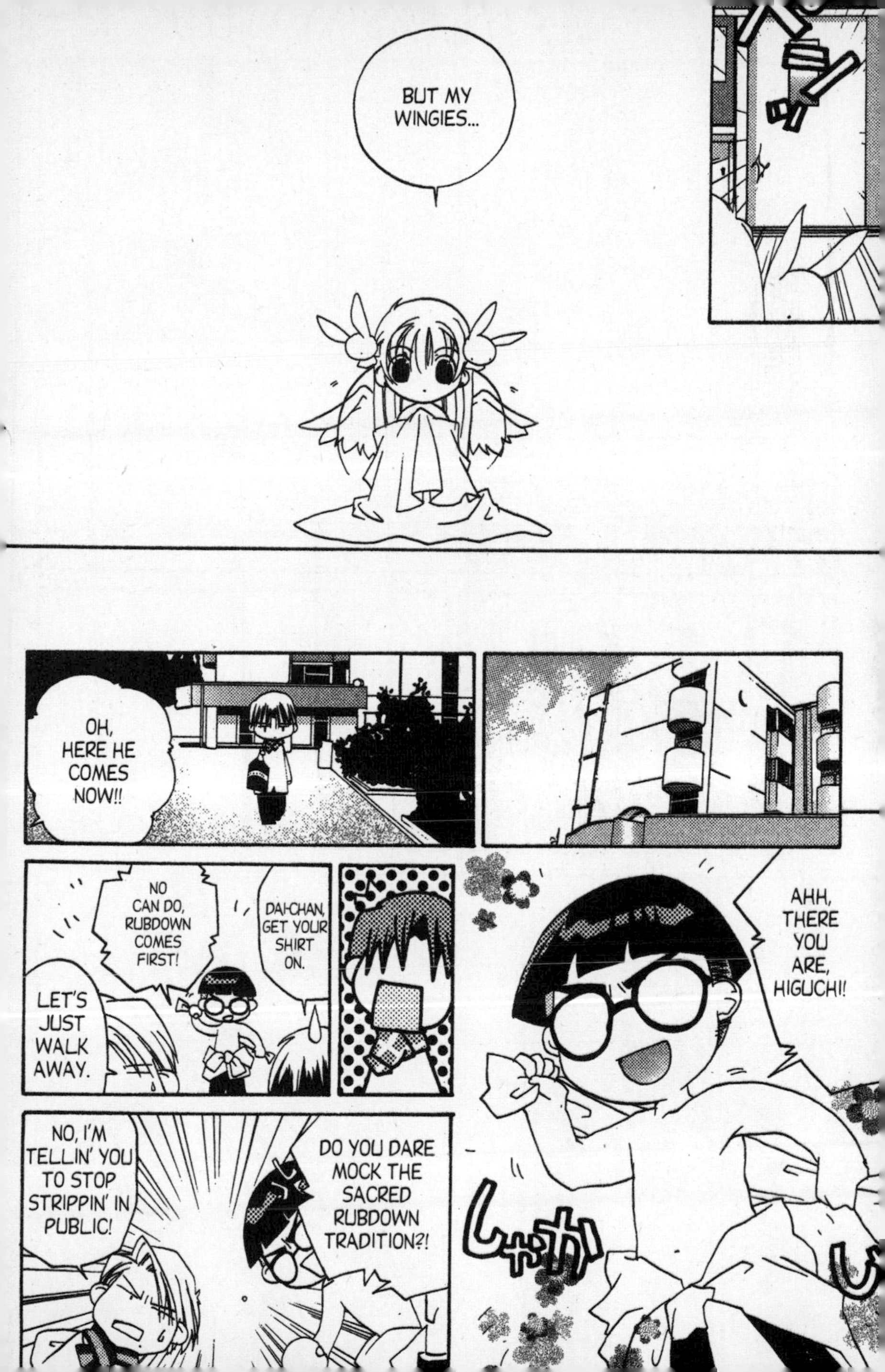

BUT MY WINGIES...
OH, HERE HE COMES NOW!!
AHH, THERE YOU ARE, HIGUCHI!!
DAI-CHAN, GET YOUR SHIRT ON.
NO CAN DO, RUBDOWN COMES FIRST!
LET'S JUST WALK AWAY.
DO YOU DARE MOCK THE SACRED RUBDOWN TRADITION?!
NO, I'M TELLIN' YOU TO STOP STRIPPIN' IN PUBLIC!

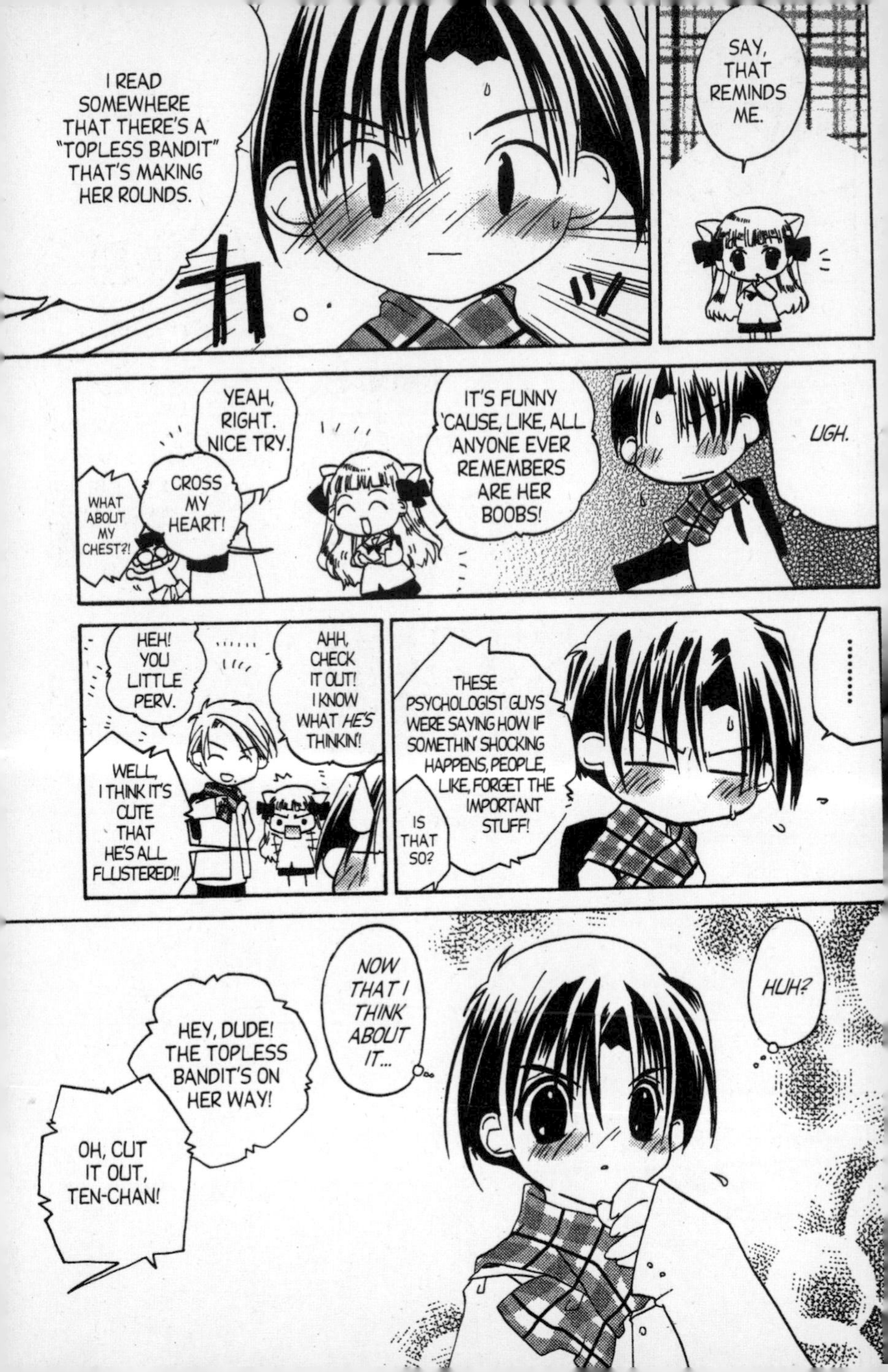
SAY, THAT REMINDS ME.
I READ SOMEWHERE THAT THERE'S A "TOPLESS BANDIT" THAT'S MAKING HER ROUNDS.
UGH.
IT'S FUNNY 'CAUSE, LIKE, ALL ANYONE EVER REMEMBERS ARE HER BOOBS!
YEAH, RIGHT. NICE TRY.
CROSS MY HEART!
WHAT ABOUT MY CHEST?!
......
THESE PSYCHOLOGIST GUYS WERE SAYING HOW IF SOMETHIN' SHOCKING HAPPENS, PEOPLE, LIKE, FORGET THE IMPORTANT STUFF!
IS THAT SO?
AHH, CHECK IT OUT! I KNOW WHAT *HE'S* THINKIN'!
HEH! YOU LITTLE PERV.
WELL, I THINK IT'S CUTE THAT HE'S ALL FLUSTERED!!
HUH?
NOW THAT I THINK ABOUT IT...
HEY, DUDE! THE TOPLESS BANDIT'S ON HER WAY!
OH, CUT IT OUT, TEN-CHAN!

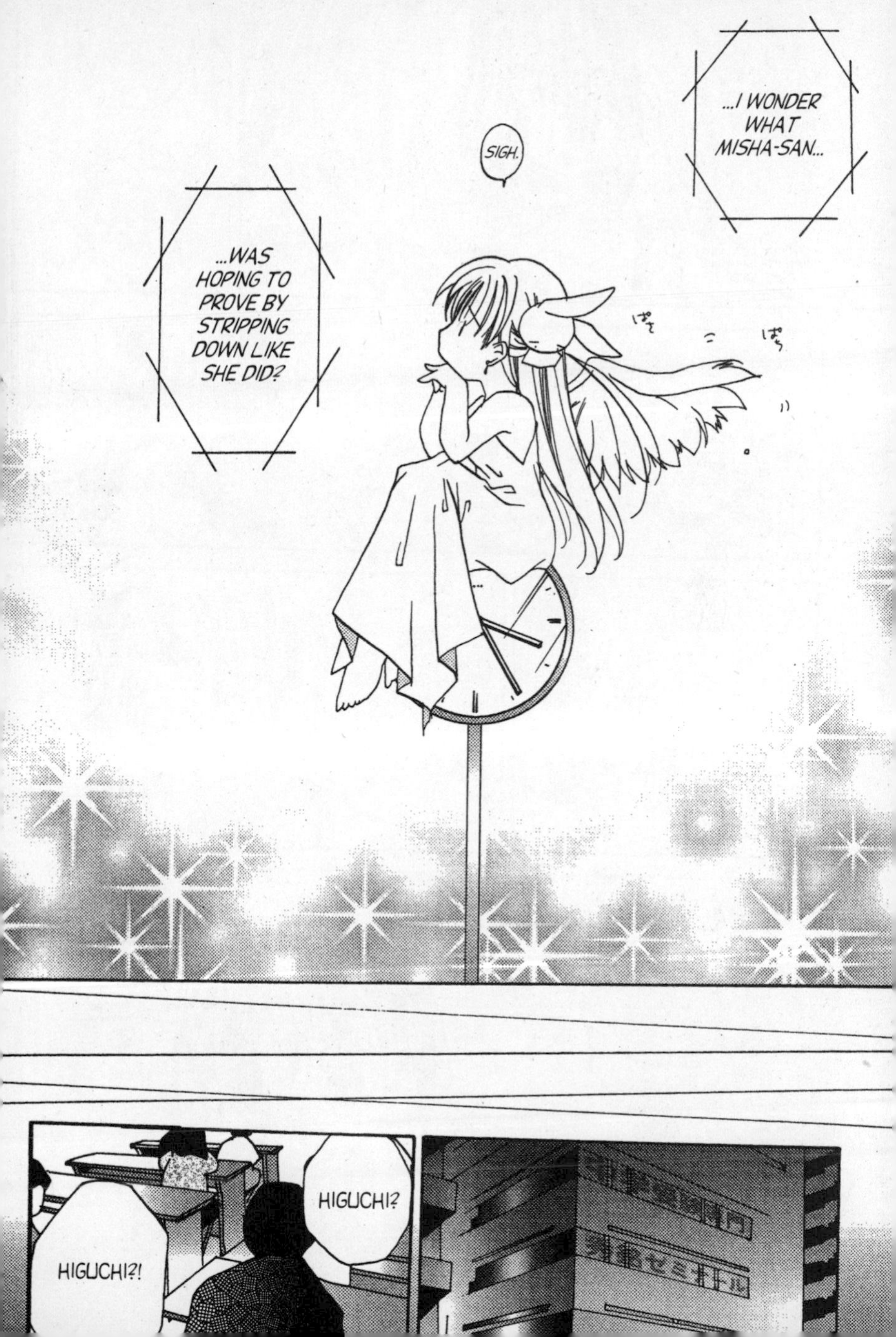
...I WONDER WHAT MISHA-SAN...
SIGH.
...WAS HOPING TO PROVE BY STRIPPING DOWN LIKE SHE DID?
HIGUCHI?
HIGUCHI?!

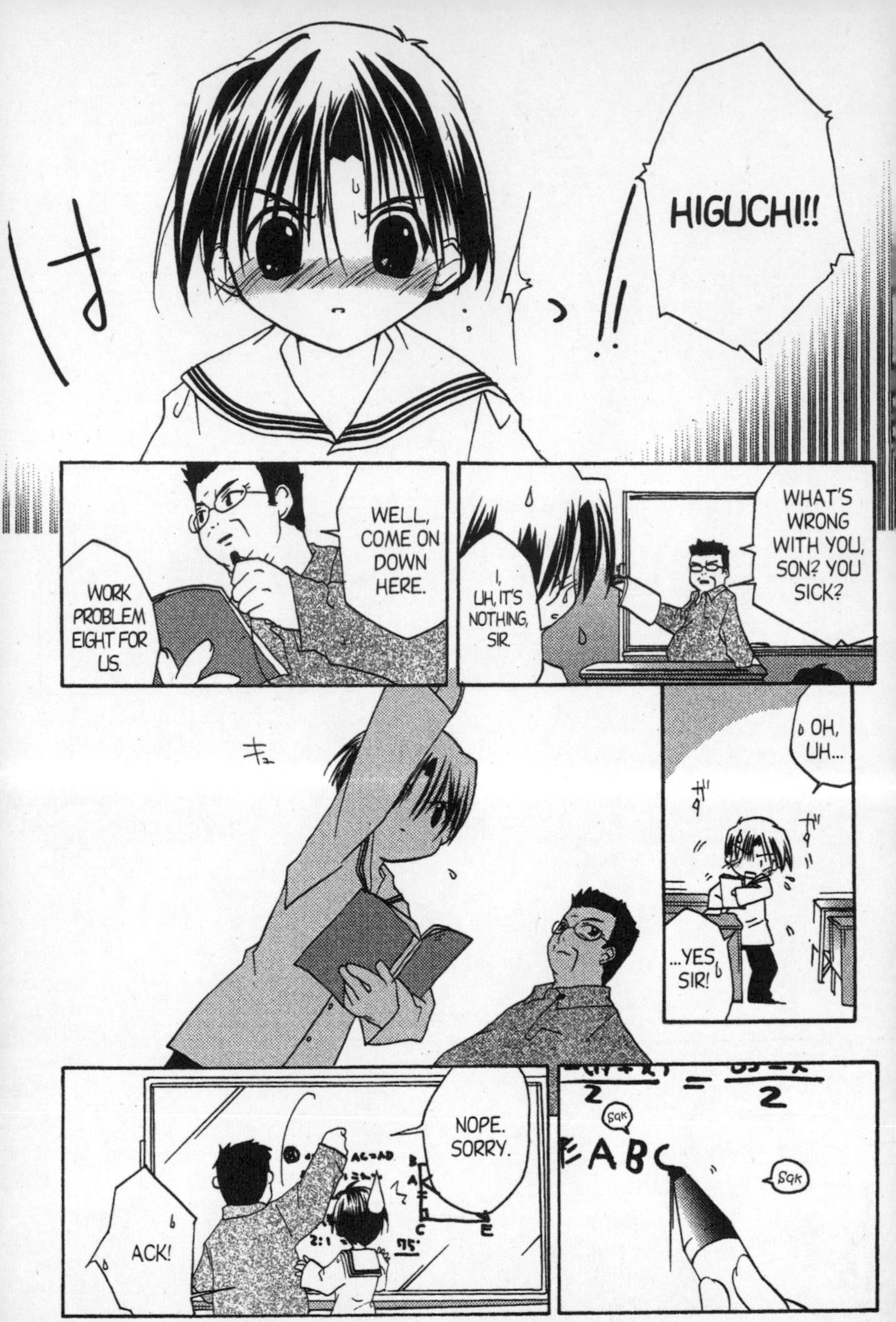
HIGUCHI!!!
は
WHAT'S WRONG WITH YOU, SON? YOU SICK?
I, UH, IT'S NOTHING, SIR.
WELL, COME ON DOWN HERE.
WORK PROBLEM EIGHT FOR US.
OH, UH...
...YES, SIR!
SQK
SQK
NOPE. SORRY.
ACK!

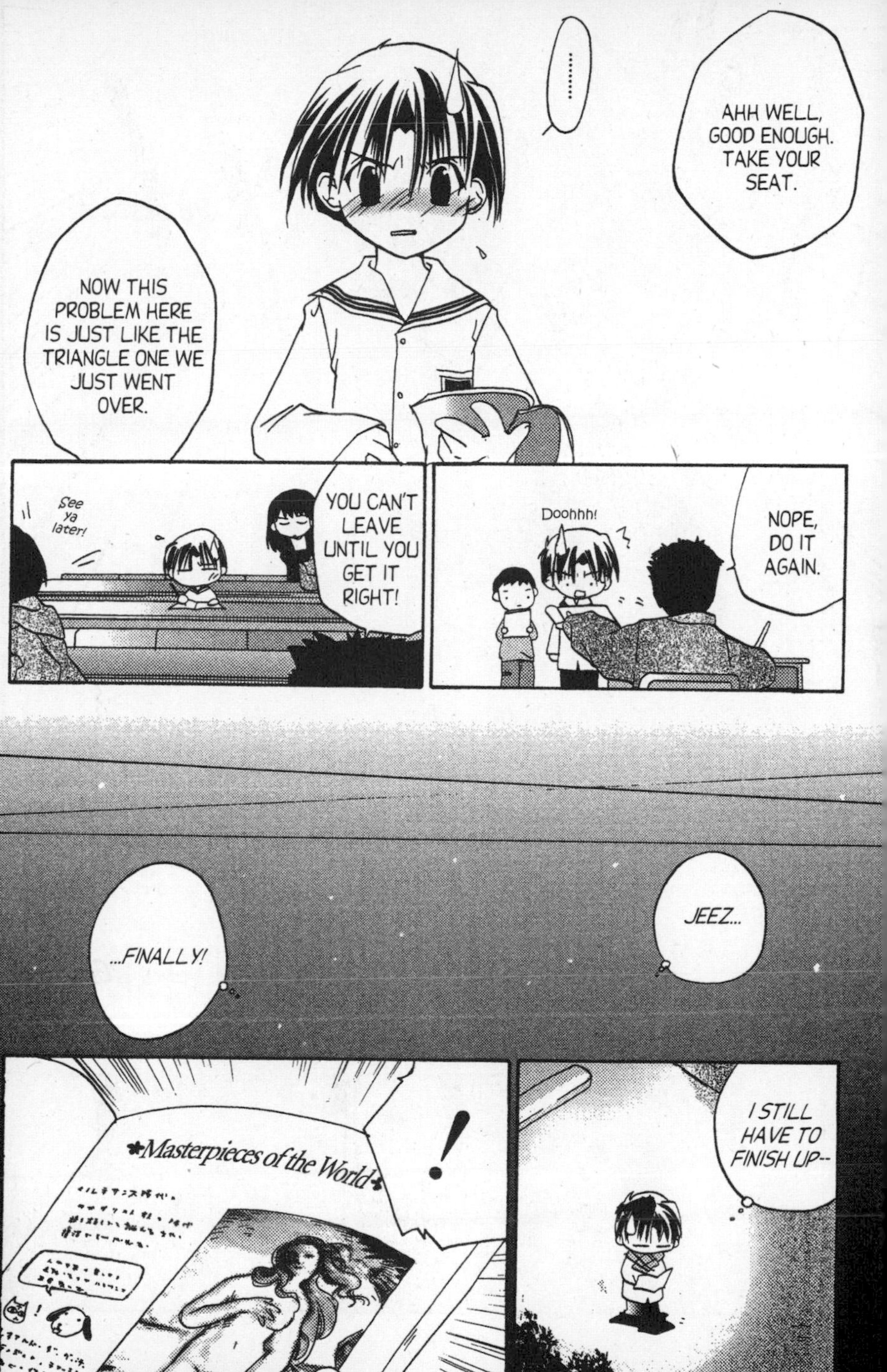
AHH WELL, GOOD ENOUGH. TAKE YOUR SEAT.
......
NOW THIS PROBLEM HERE IS JUST LIKE THE TRIANGLE ONE WE JUST WENT OVER.
NOPE, DO IT AGAIN.
Doohhh!
YOU CAN'T LEAVE UNTIL YOU GET IT RIGHT!
See ya later!
JEEZ...
...FINALLY!
I STILL HAVE TO FINISH UP--
Masterpieces of the World
!

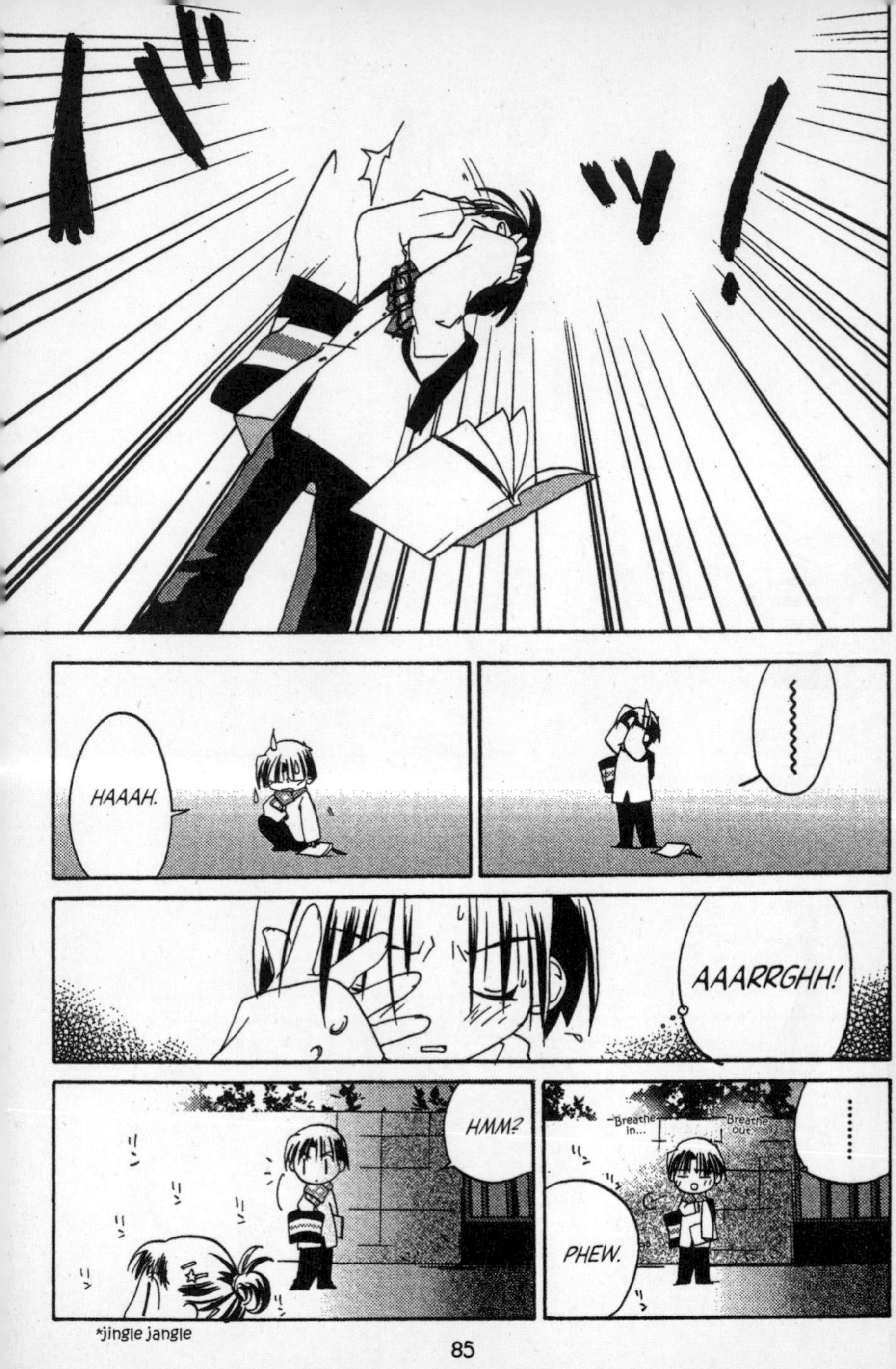

バッ!
HAAAH.
AAARRGHH!
......
Breathe in...
Breathe out.
PHEW.
HMM?

*jingle jangle

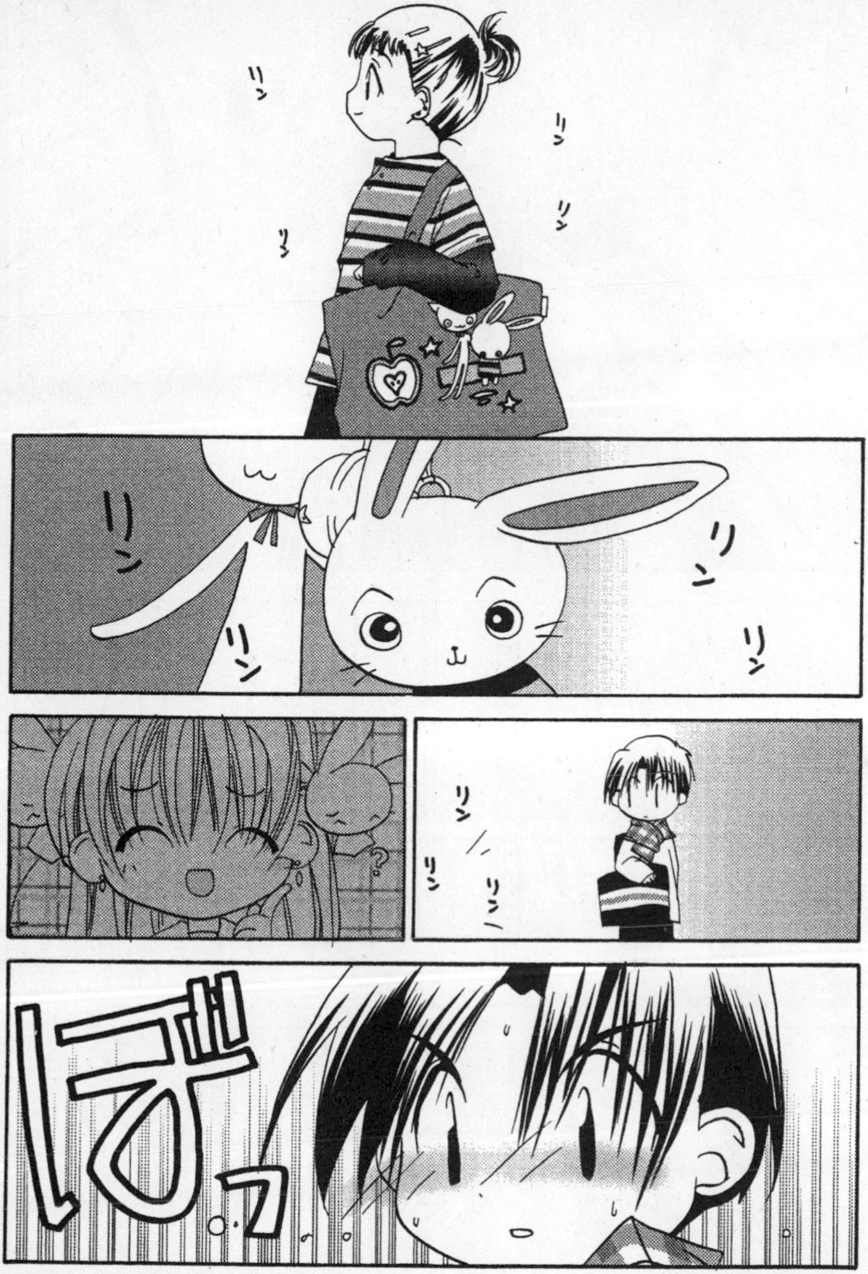
リン
リン
リン
リン
リン
リン
リン
リン
リン
リン
リン
ぼっ

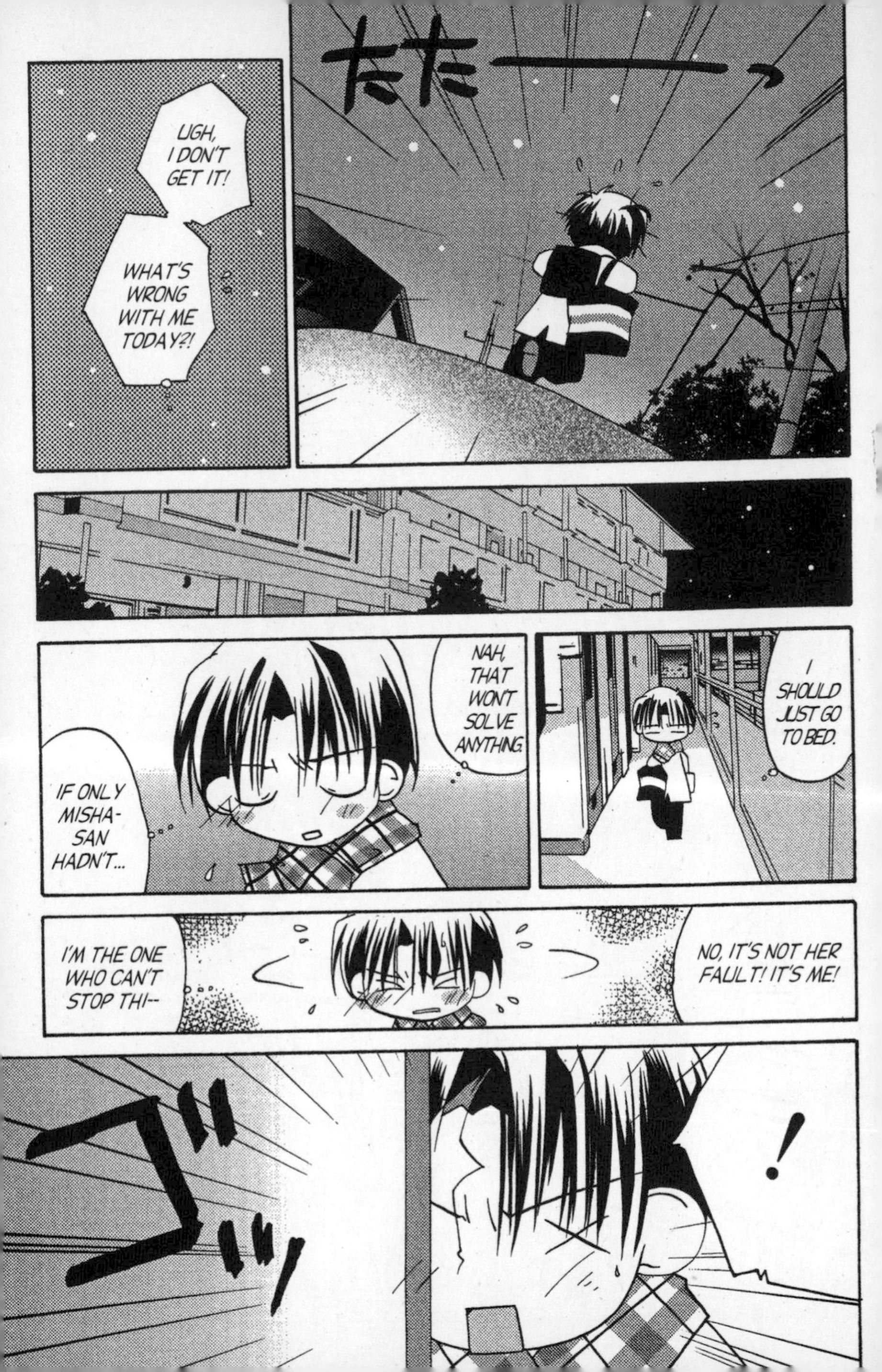
たたーーっ
UGH, I DON'T GET IT!
WHAT'S WRONG WITH ME TODAY?!
I SHOULD JUST GO TO BED.
NAH, THAT WON'T SOLVE ANYTHING.
IF ONLY MISHA-SAN HADN'T...
NO, IT'S NOT HER FAULT! IT'S ME!
I'M THE ONE WHO CAN'T STOP THI--
!
ゴッ

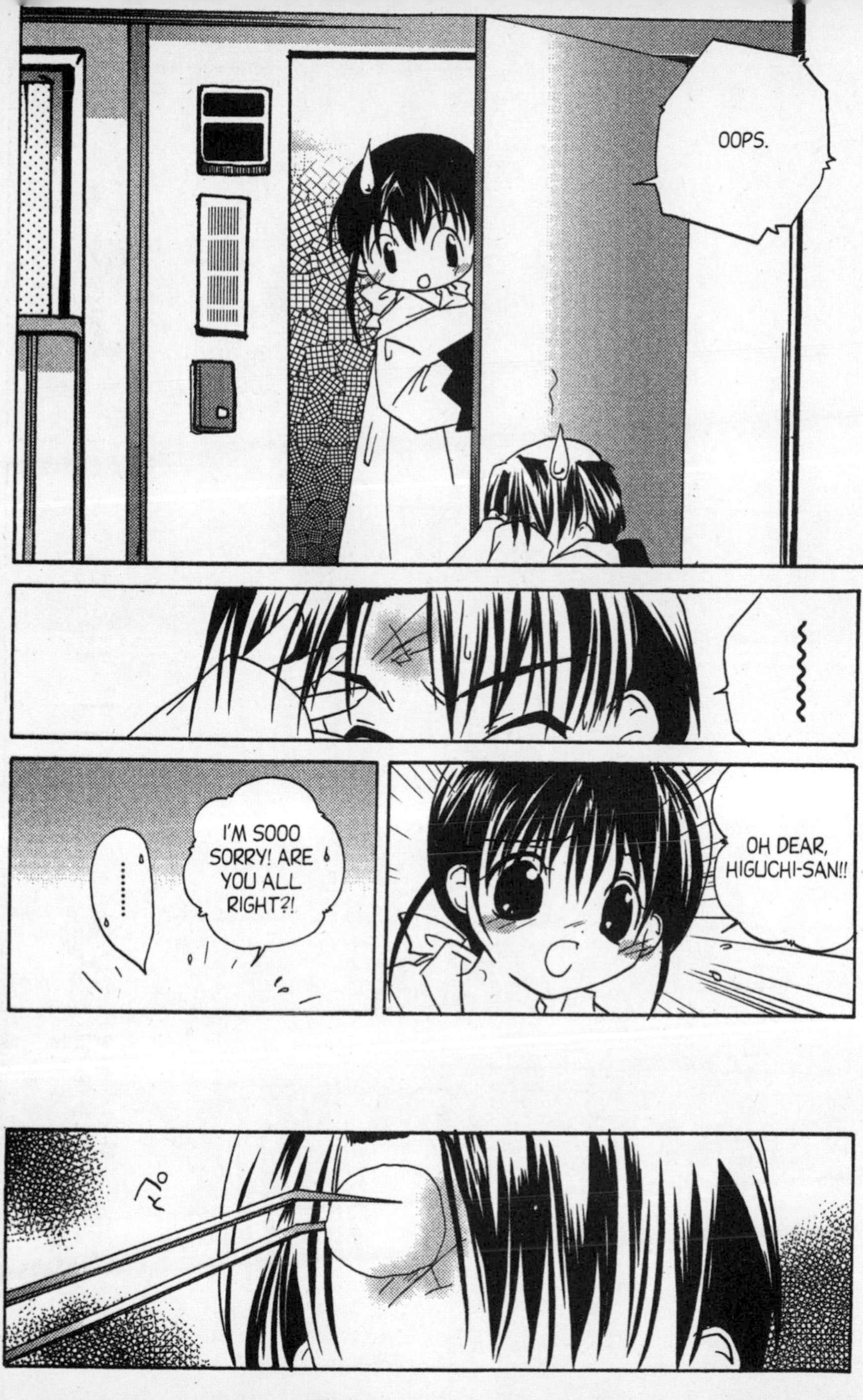
OOPS.
OH DEAR, HIGUCHI-SAN!!
I'M SOOO SORRY! ARE YOU ALL RIGHT?!
......

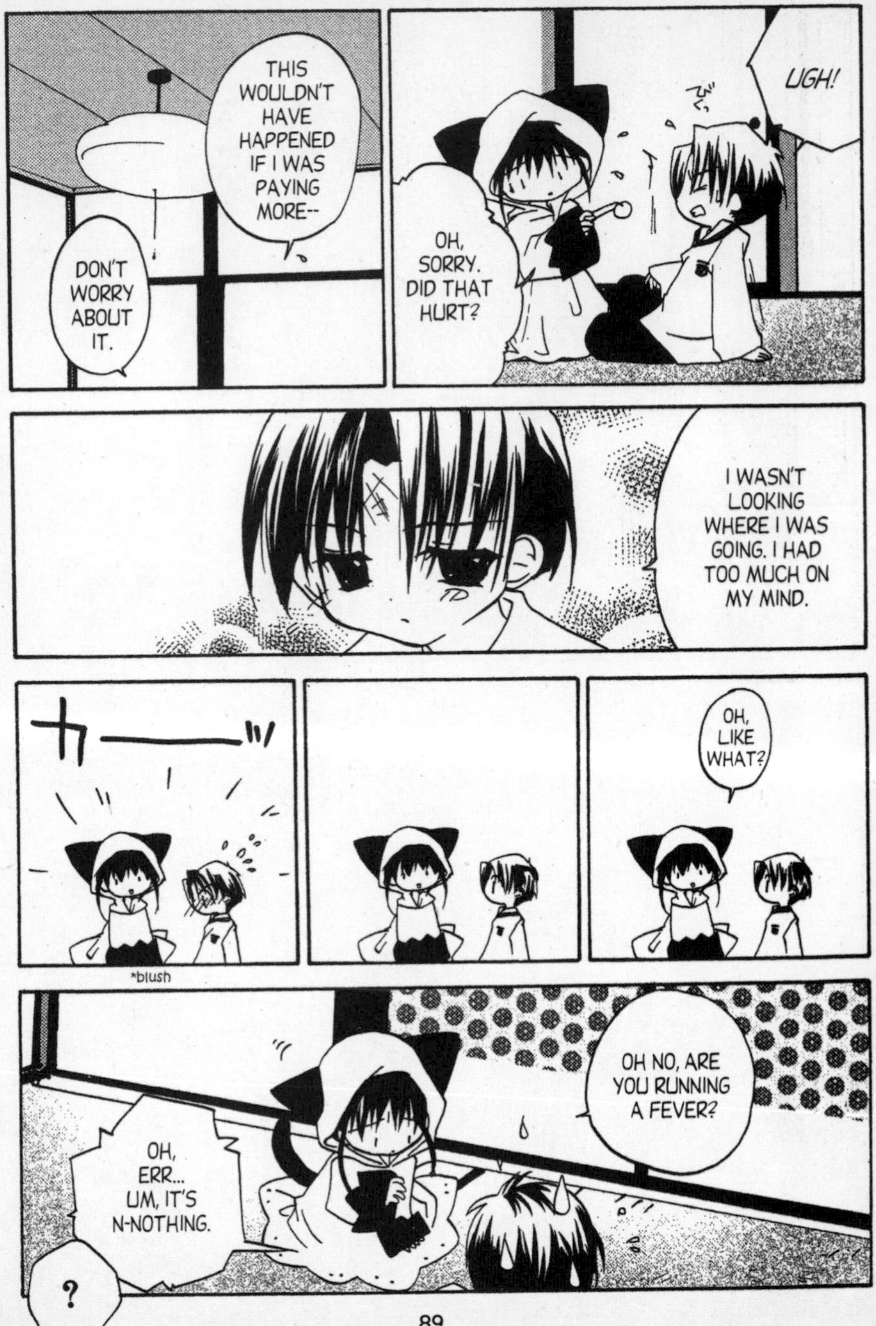
UGH!
OH, SORRY. DID THAT HURT?
THIS WOULDN'T HAVE HAPPENED IF I WAS PAYING MORE--
DON'T WORRY ABOUT IT.
I WASN'T LOOKING WHERE I WAS GOING. I HAD TOO MUCH ON MY MIND.
OH, LIKE WHAT?
カーーッ
*blush
OH NO, ARE YOU RUNNING A FEVER?
OH, ERR... UM, IT'S N-NOTHING.
?

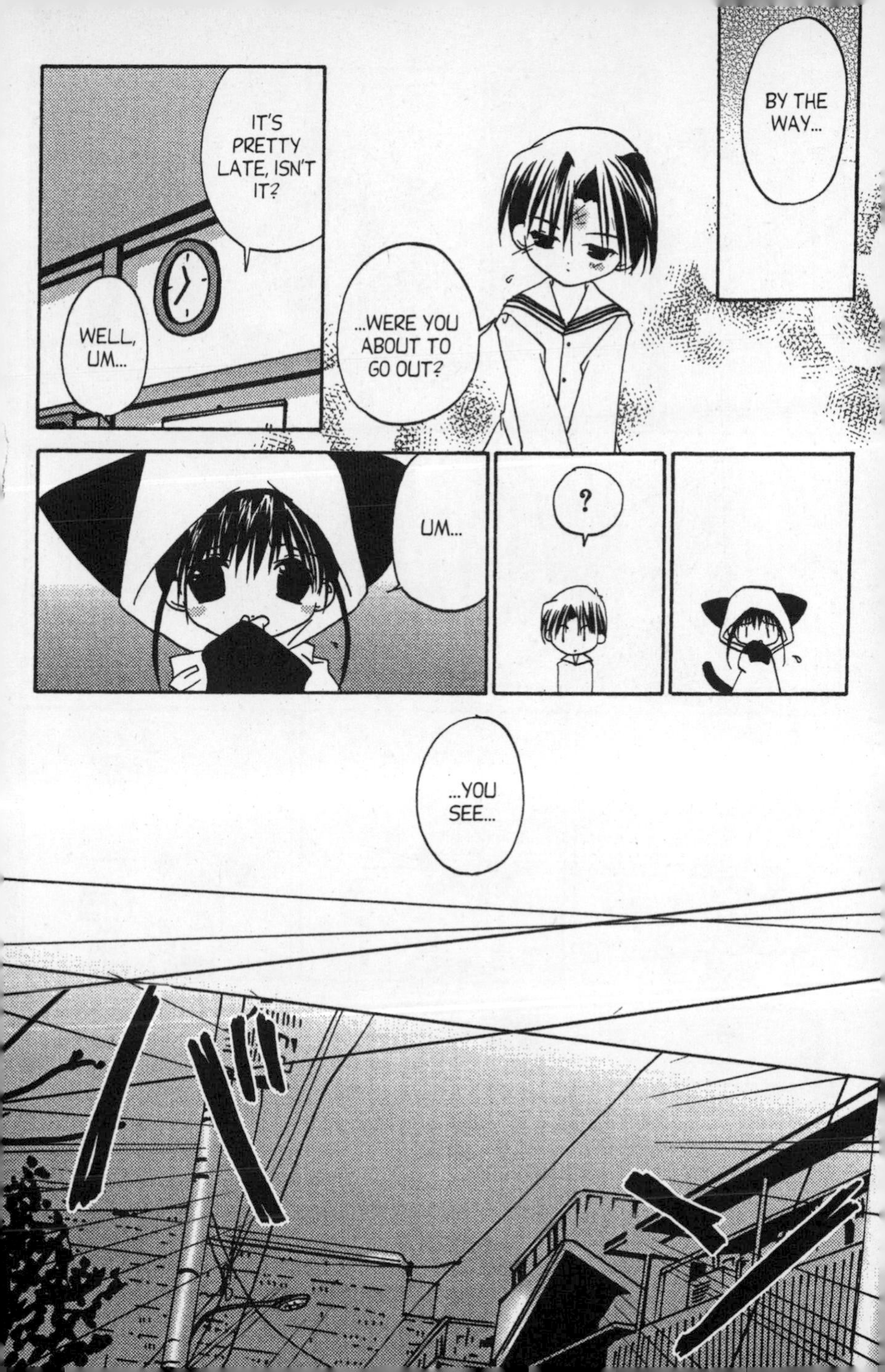
BY THE WAY...
...WERE YOU ABOUT TO GO OUT?
IT'S PRETTY LATE, ISN'T IT?
WELL, UM...
?
UM...
...YOU SEE...

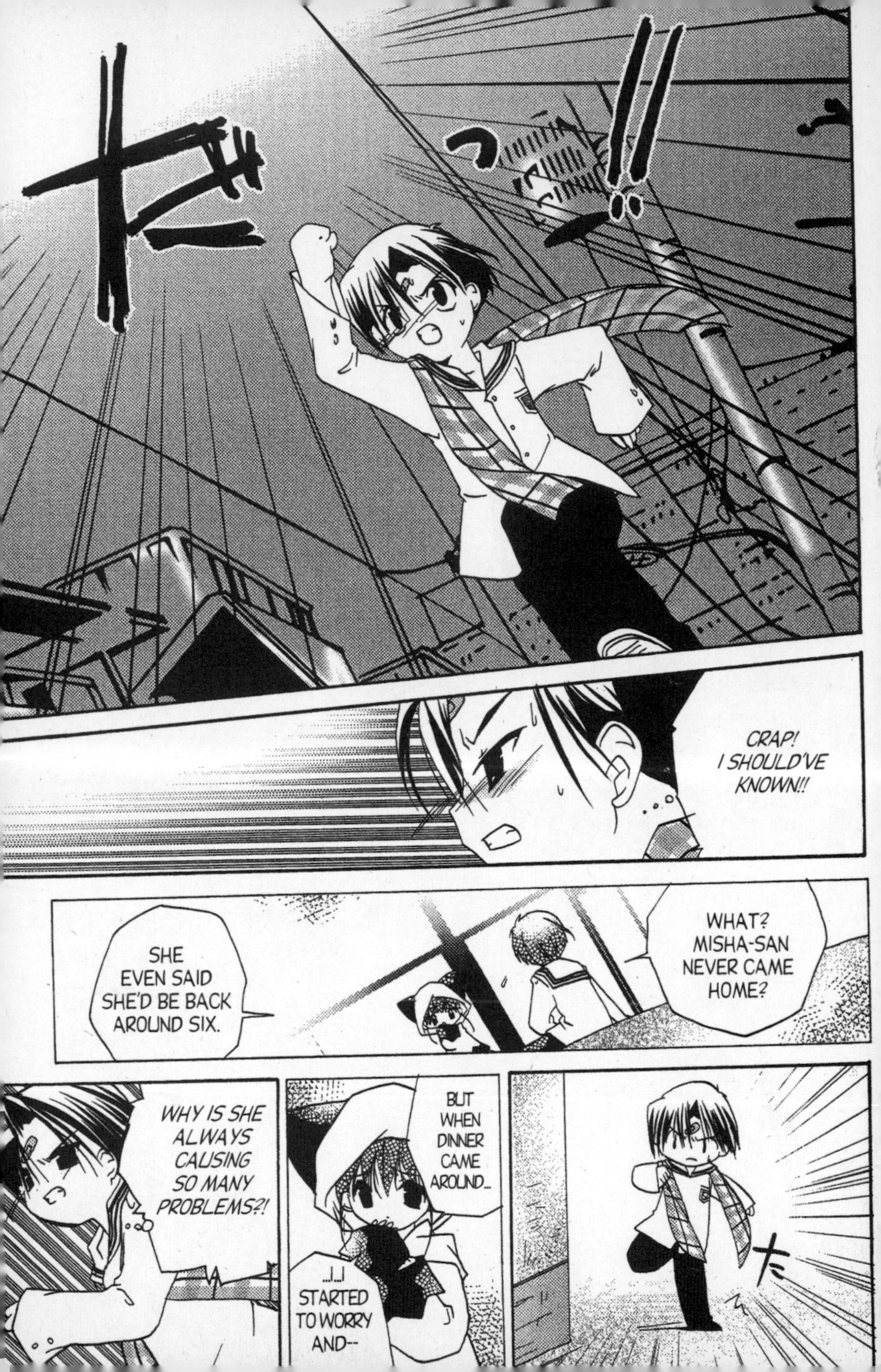
CRAP! I SHOULD'VE KNOWN!!
WHAT? MISHA-SAN NEVER CAME HOME?
SHE EVEN SAID SHE'D BE BACK AROUND SIX.
BUT WHEN DINNER CAME AROUND...
...I...I STARTED TO WORRY AND--
WHY IS SHE ALWAYS CAUSING SO MANY PROBLEMS?!

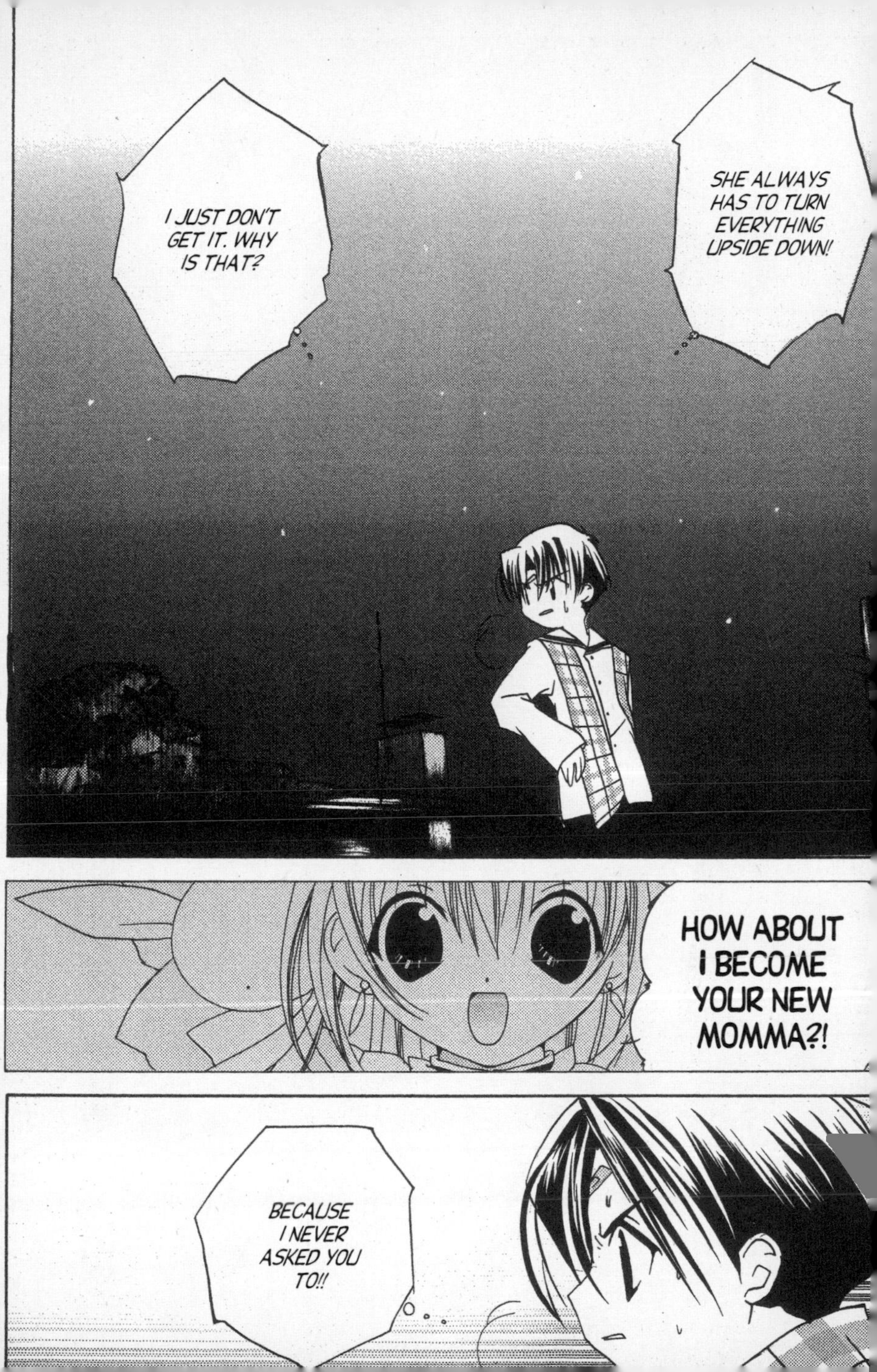
SHE ALWAYS HAS TO TURN EVERYTHING UPSIDE DOWN!
I JUST DON'T GET IT. WHY IS THAT?
HOW ABOUT I BECOME YOUR NEW MOMMA?!
BECAUSE I NEVER ASKED YOU TO!!

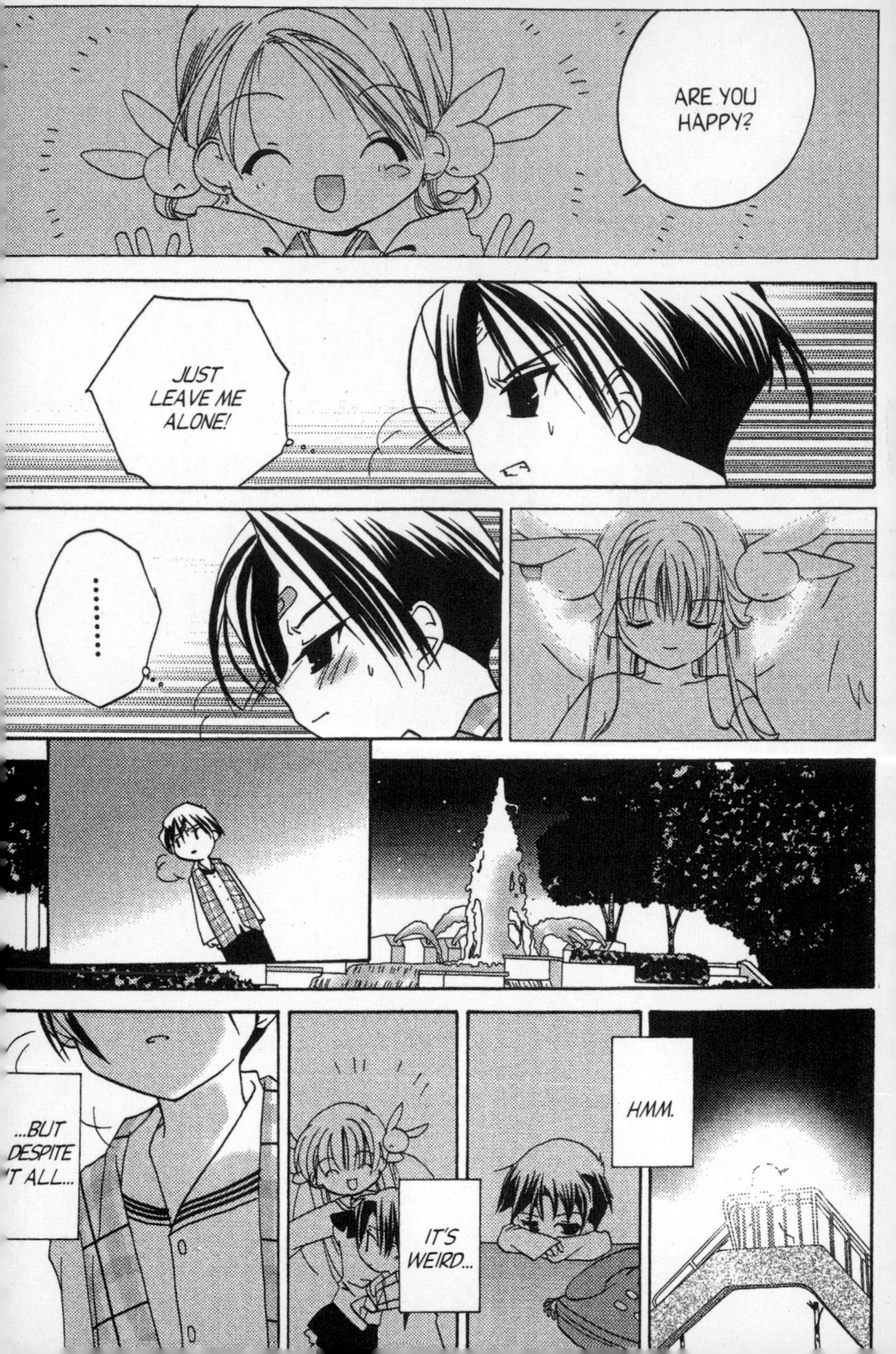
ARE YOU HAPPY?
JUST LEAVE ME ALONE!
....
HMM.
IT'S WEIRD...
...BUT DESPITE T ALL...

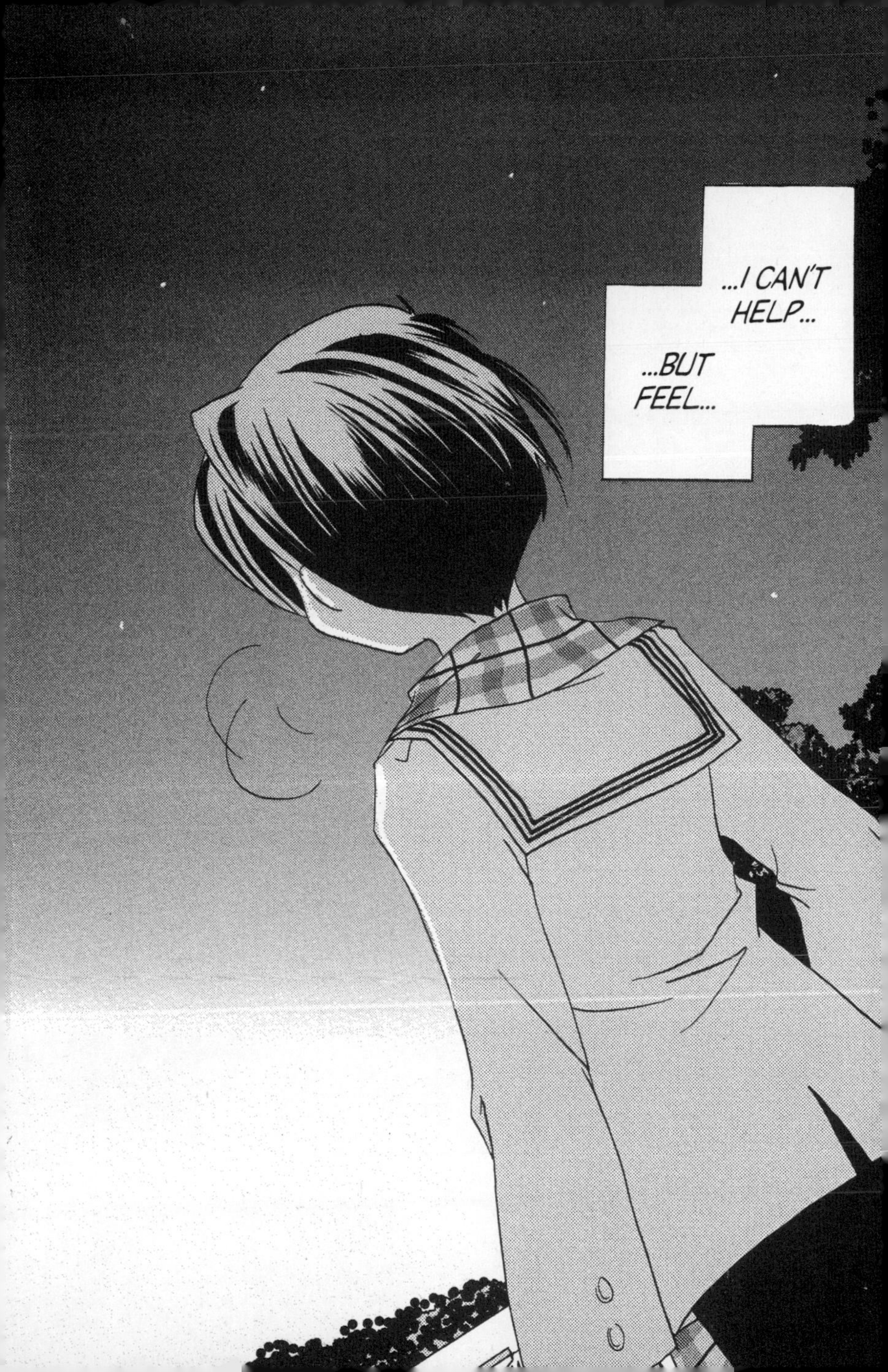
...I CAN'T HELP...
...BUT FEEL...

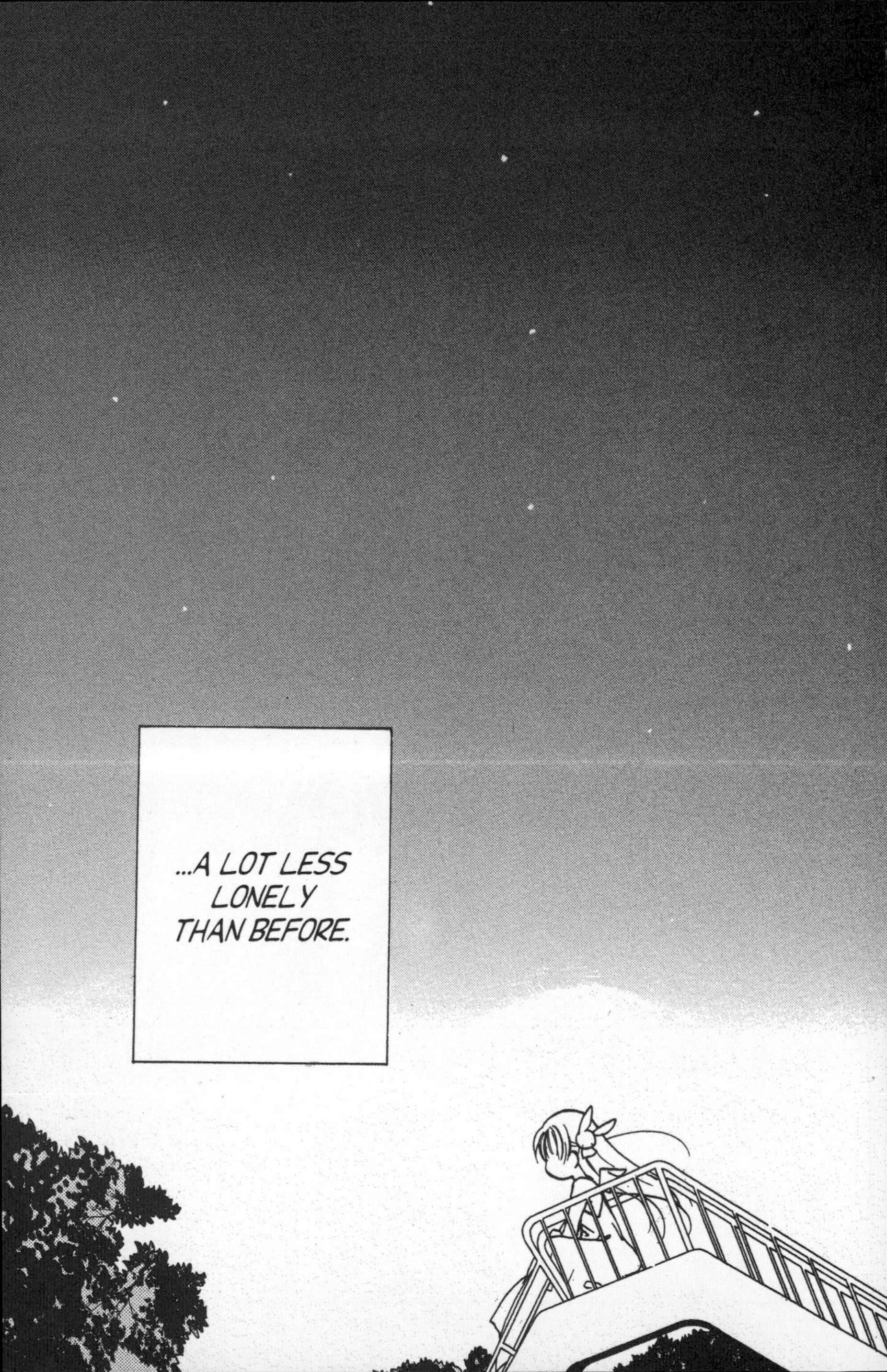
...A LOT LESS LONELY THAN BEFORE.

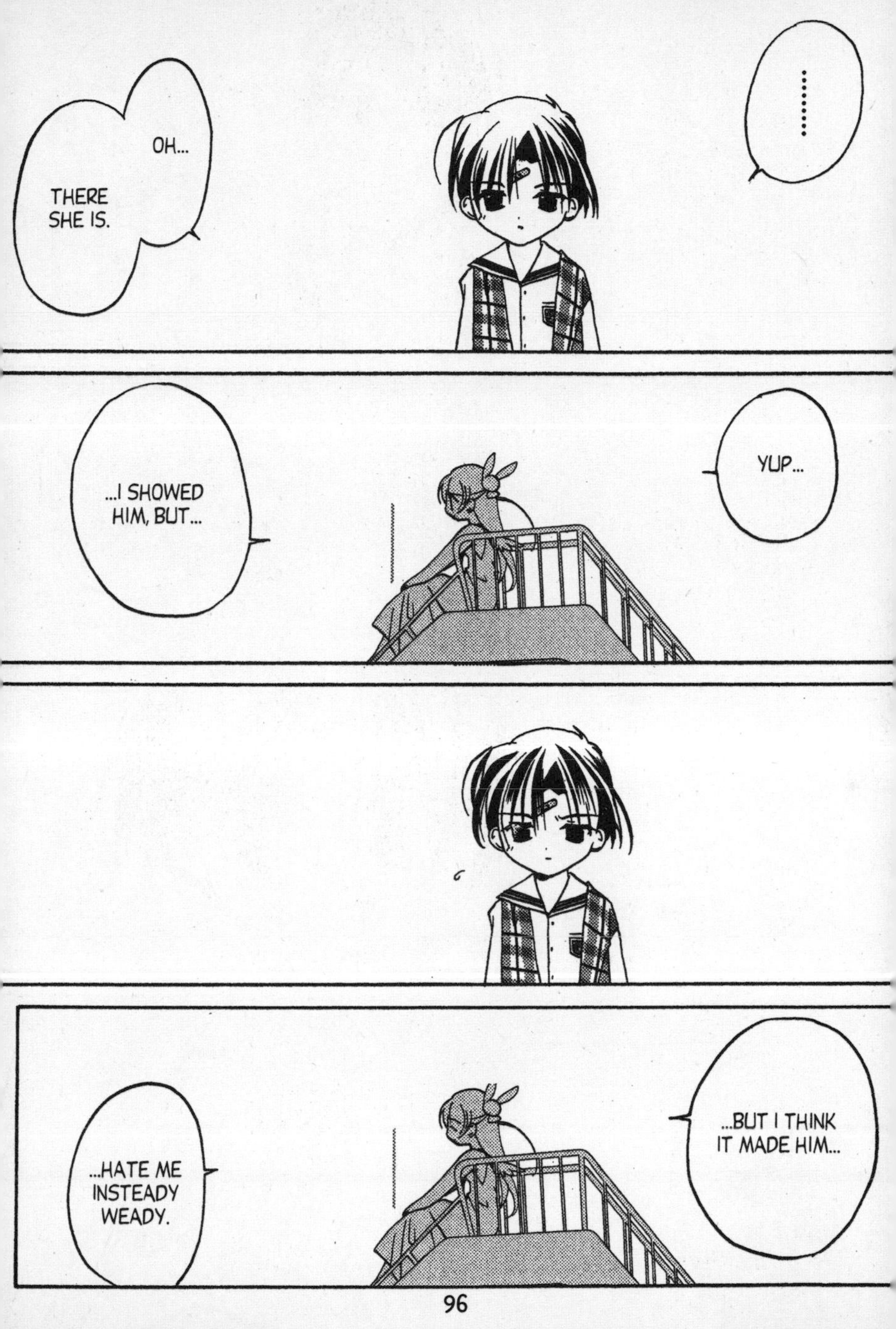
......
OH... THERE SHE IS.
YUP...
...I SHOWED HIM, BUT...
...BUT I THINK IT MADE HIM...
...HATE ME INSTEADY WEADY.

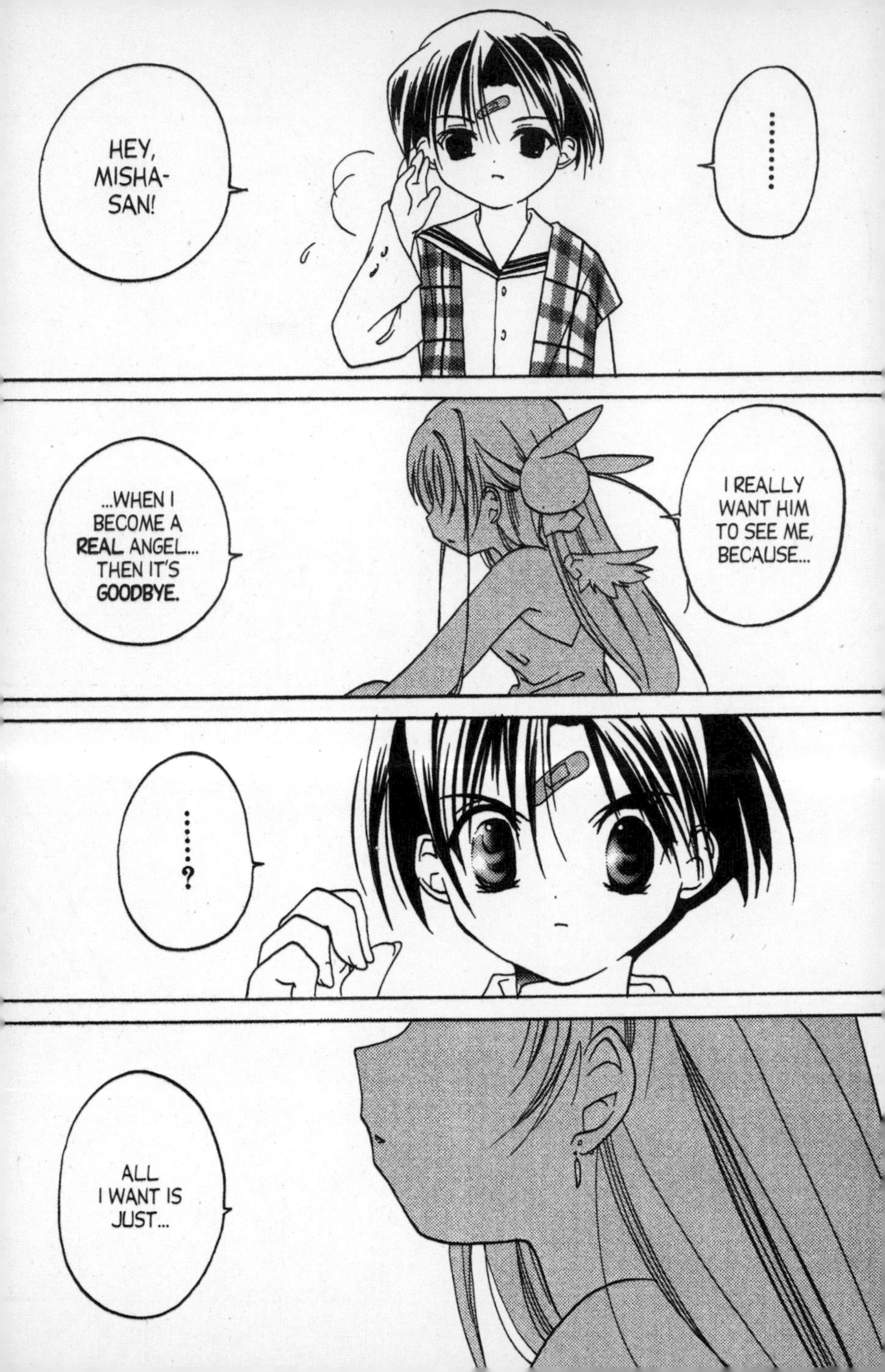
......
HEY, MISHA-SAN!
I REALLY WANT HIM TO SEE ME, BECAUSE...
...WHEN I BECOME A REAL ANGEL... THEN IT'S GOODBYE.
......?
ALL I WANT IS JUST...

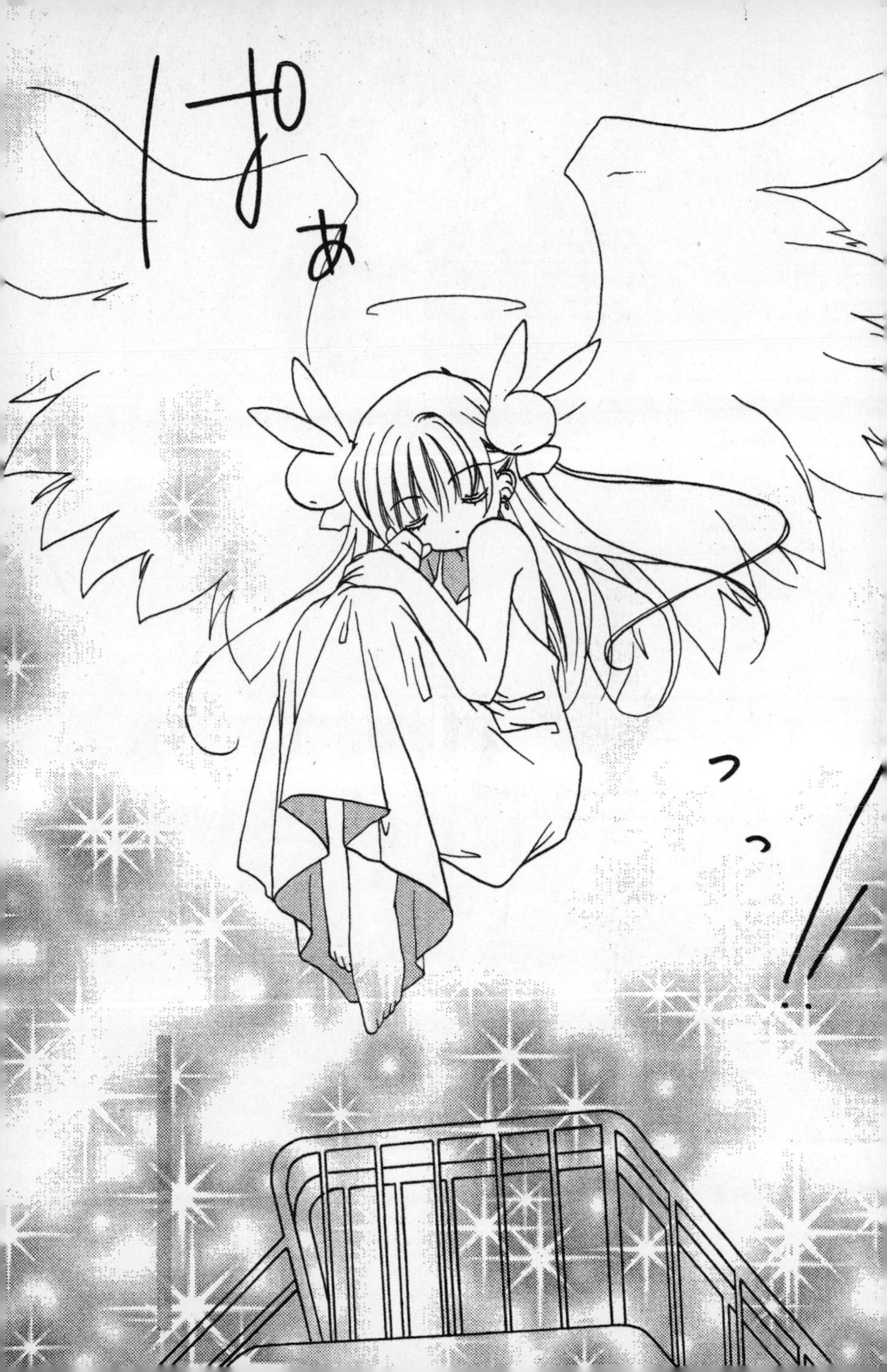
ぱぁ
っっ!!

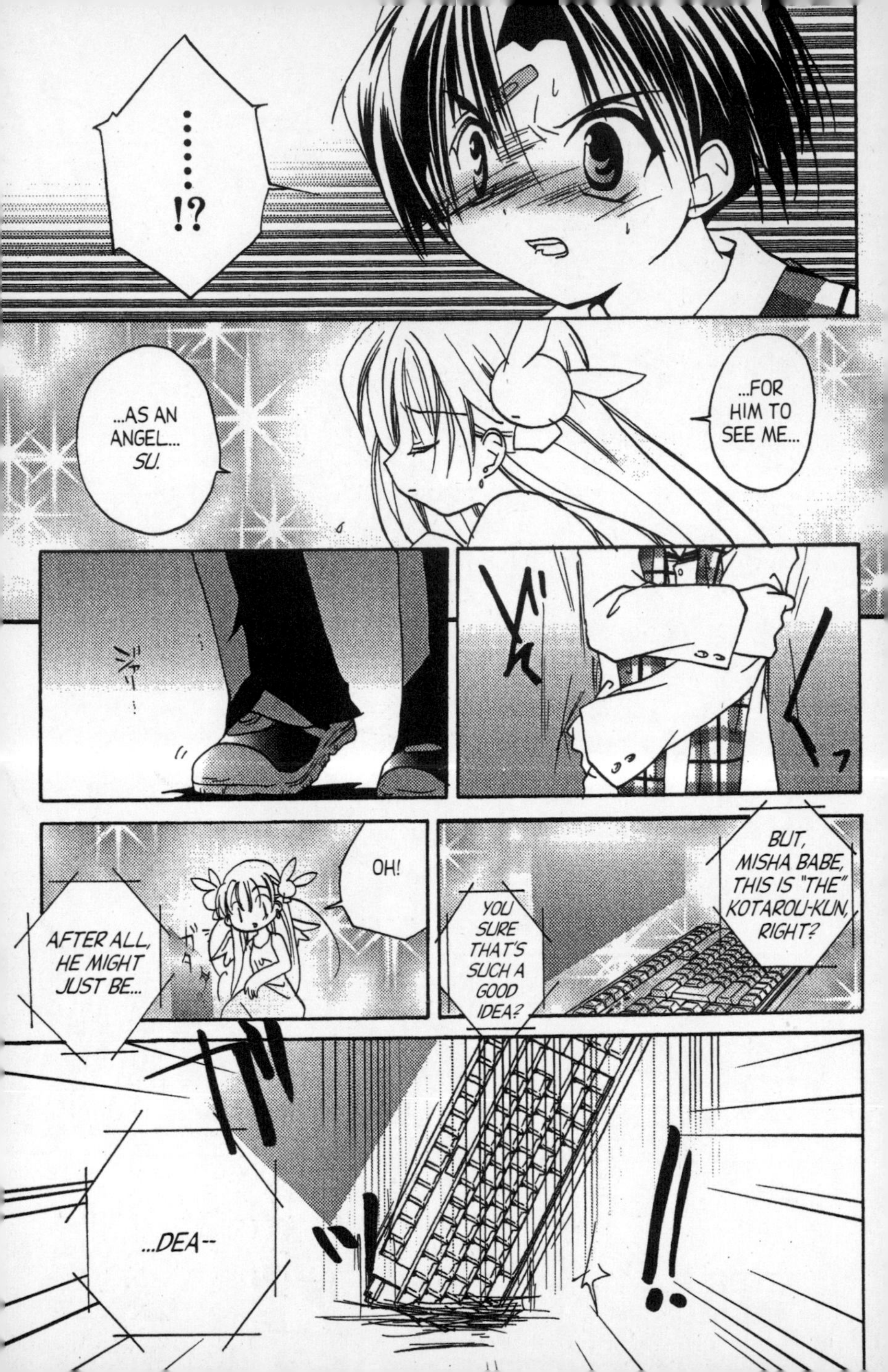
......
!?
...FOR HIM TO SEE ME...
...AS AN ANGEL... SU.
BUT, MISHA BABE, THIS IS "THE" KOTAROU-KUN, RIGHT?
YOU SURE THAT'S SUCH A GOOD IDEA?
OH!
AFTER ALL, HE MIGHT JUST BE...
...DEA--

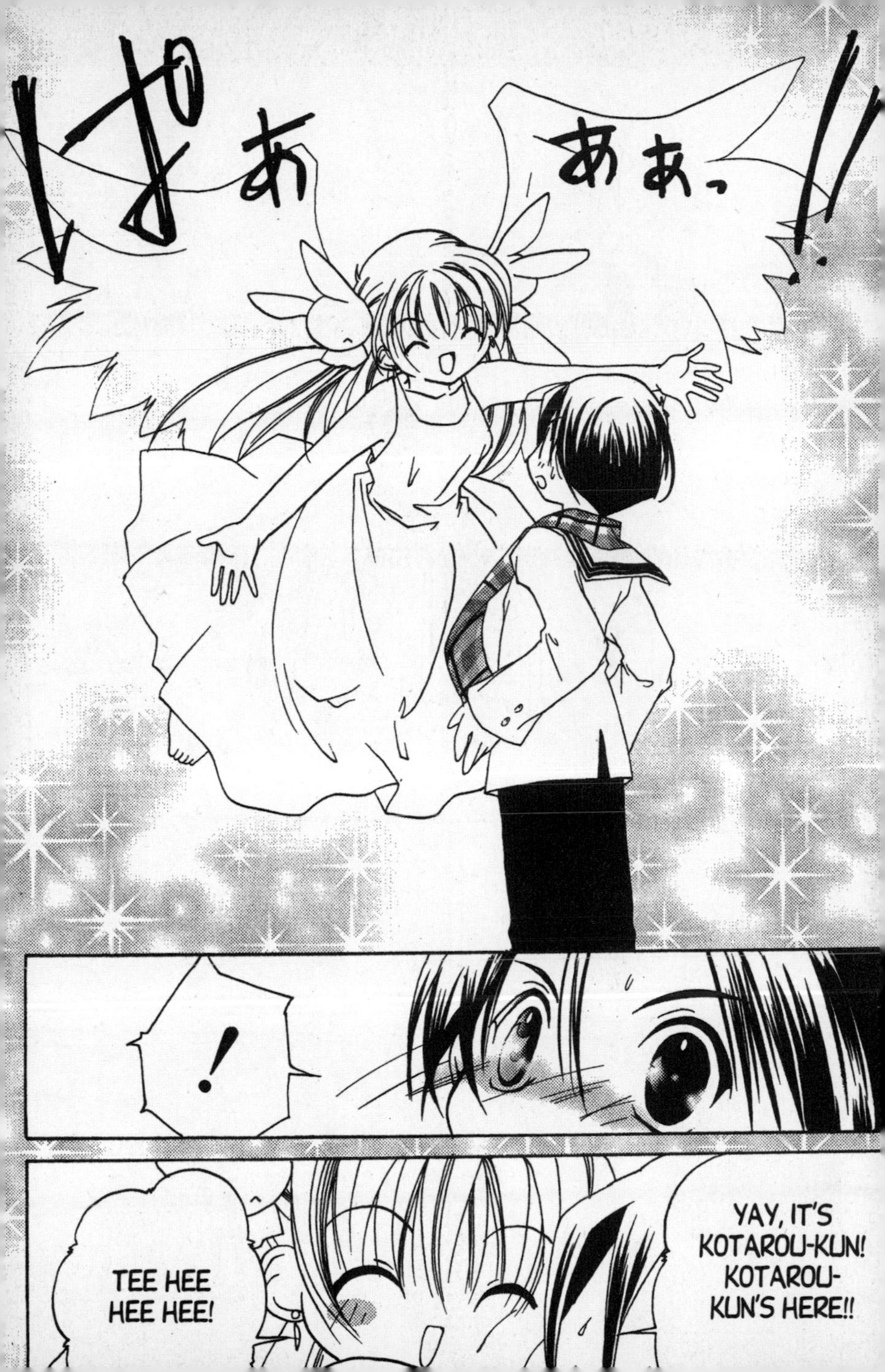
ぱあ
ああっ!!
!
YAY, IT'S KOTAROU-KUN! KOTAROU-KUN'S HERE!!
TEE HEE HEE HEE!

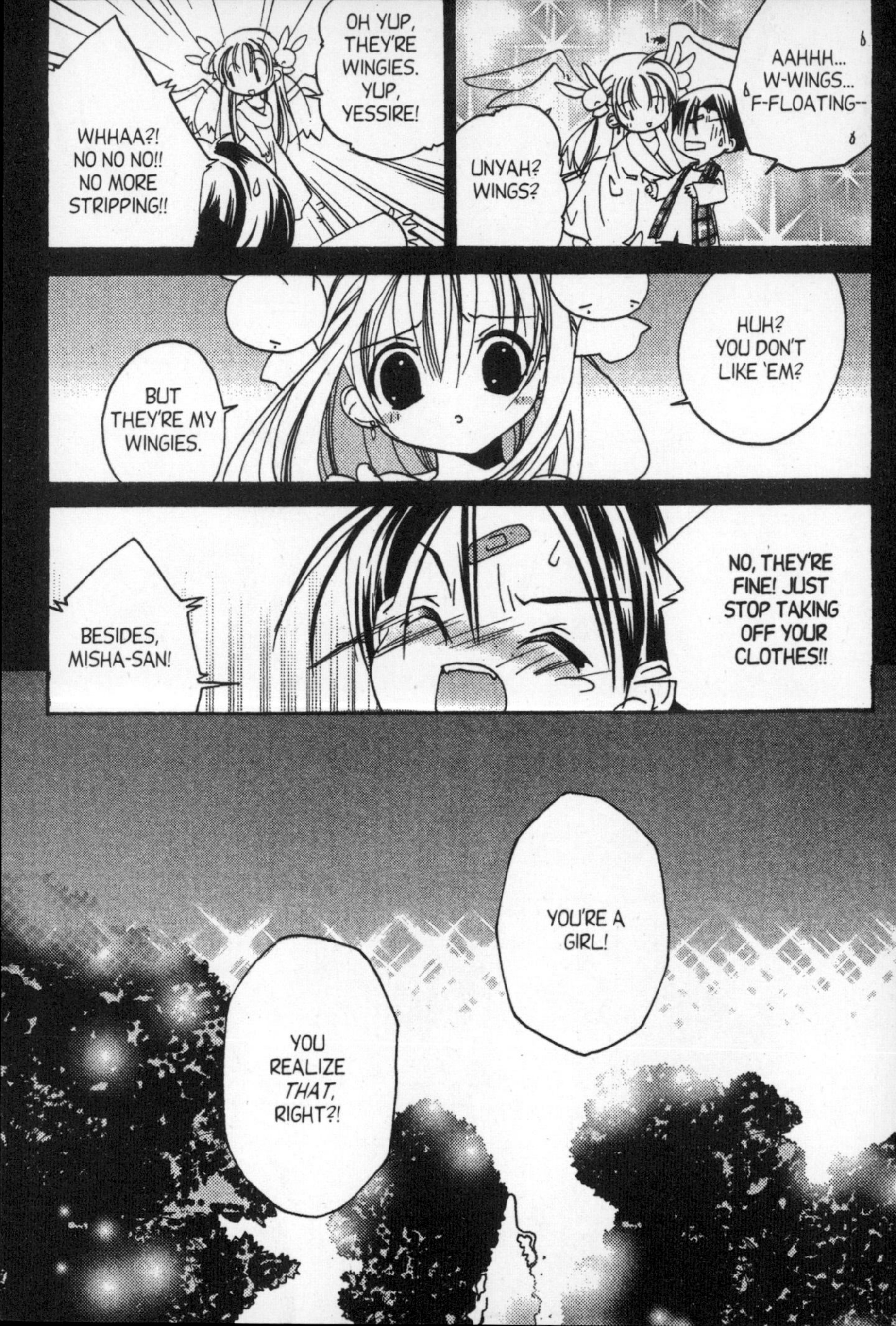
AAHHH... W-WINGS... F-FLOATING--
UNYAH? WINGS?
OH YUP, THEY'RE WINGIES. YUP, YESSIRE!
WHHAA?! NO NO NO!! NO MORE STRIPPING!!
HUH? YOU DON'T LIKE 'EM?
BUT THEY'RE MY WINGIES.
NO, THEY'RE FINE! JUST STOP TAKING OFF YOUR CLOTHES!!
BESIDES, MISHA-SAN!
YOU'RE A GIRL!
YOU REALIZE *THAT*, RIGHT?!

Lesson 23
How to Find a Lost Child

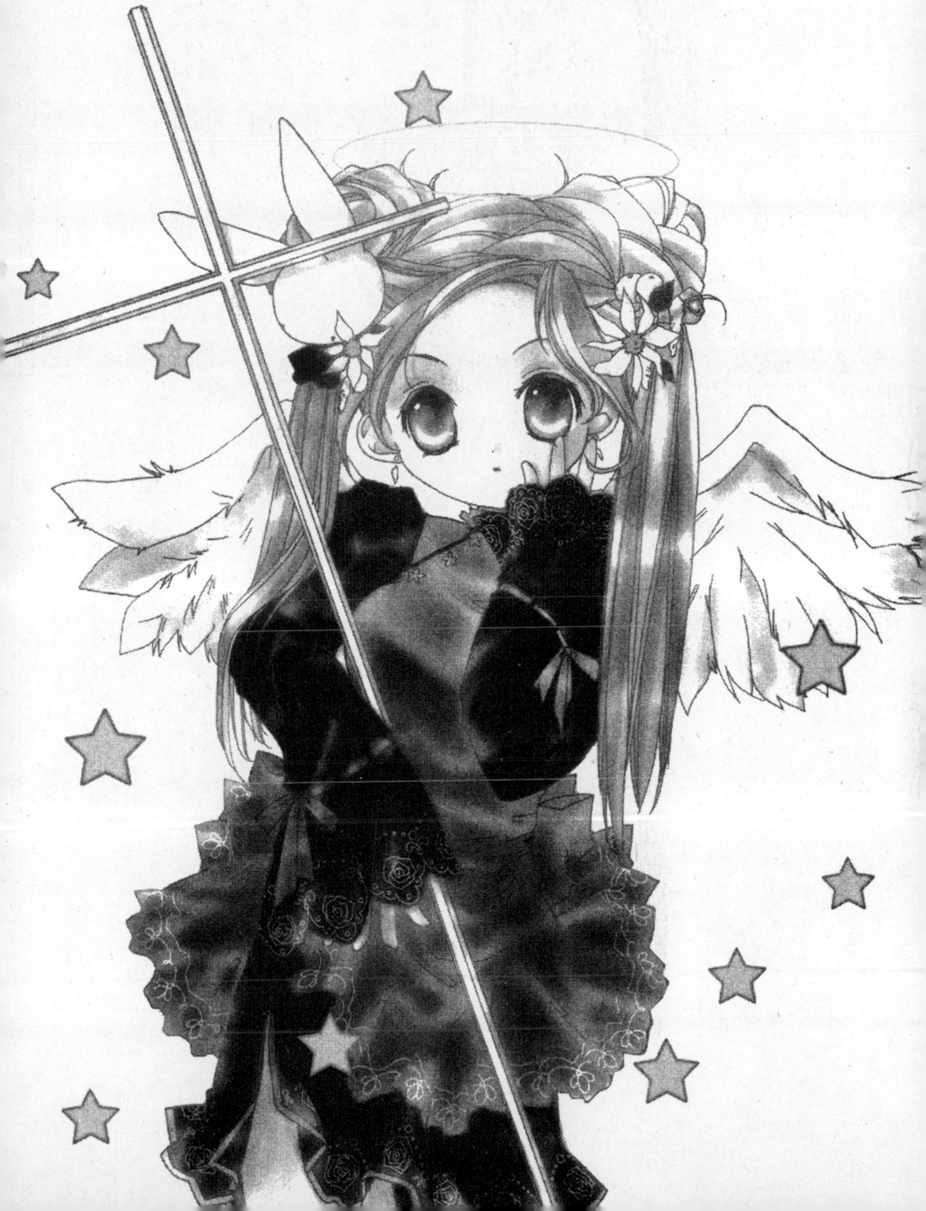

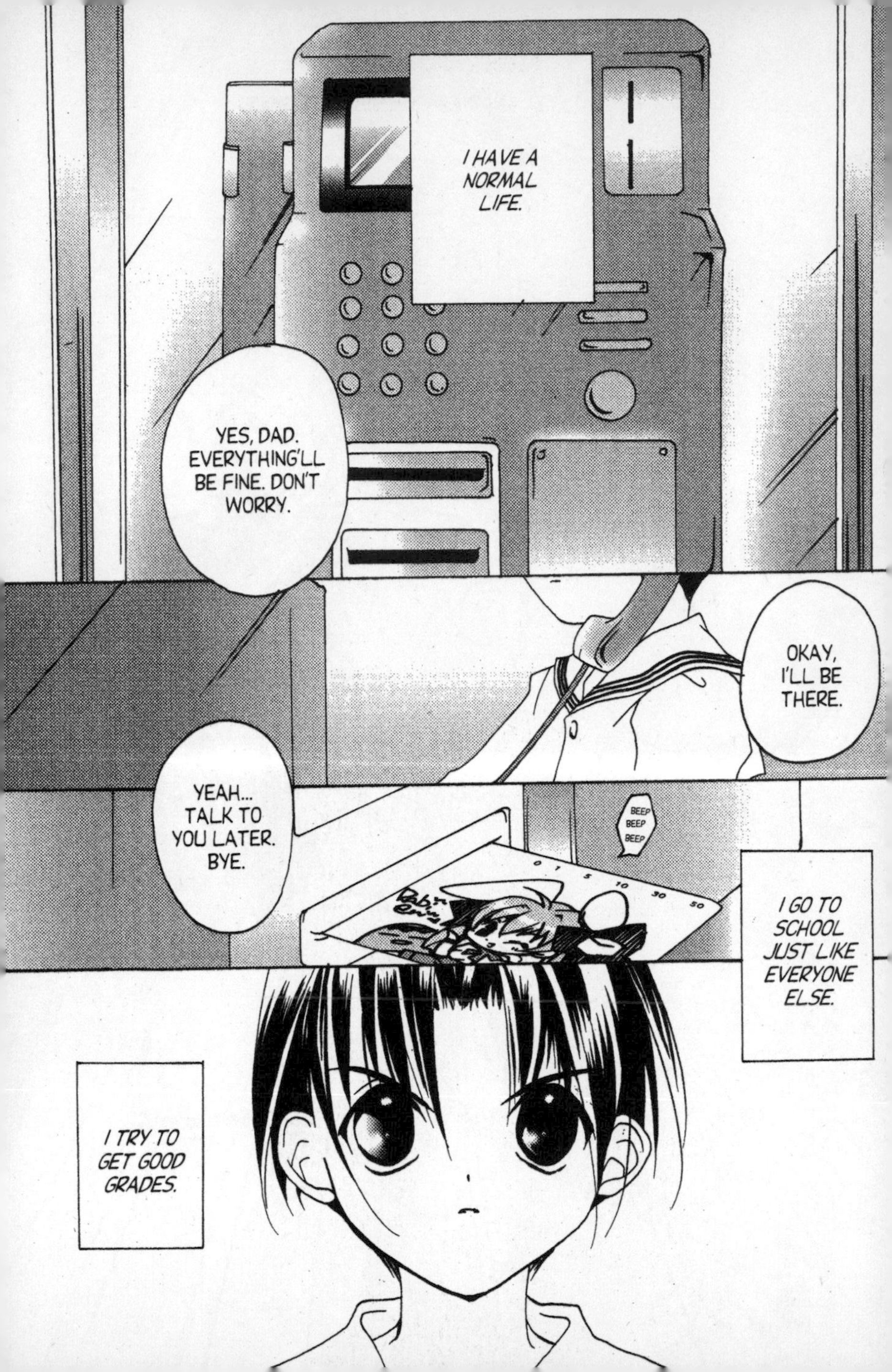
I HAVE A NORMAL LIFE.
YES, DAD. EVERYTHING'LL BE FINE. DON'T WORRY.
OKAY, I'LL BE THERE.
YEAH... TALK TO YOU LATER. BYE.
BEEP BEEP BEEP
I GO TO SCHOOL JUST LIKE EVERYONE ELSE.
I TRY TO GET GOOD GRADES.

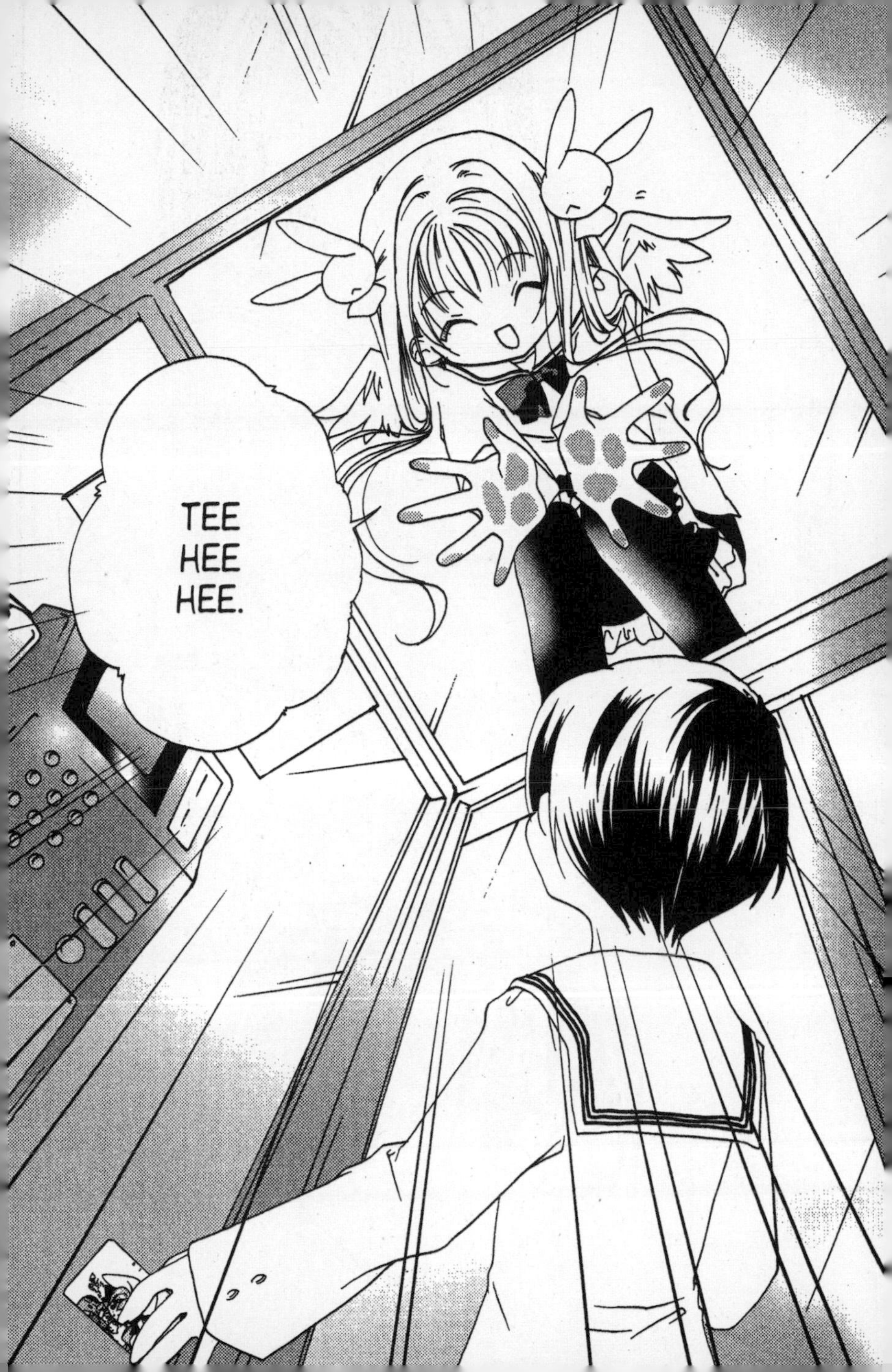
TEE HEE HEE.

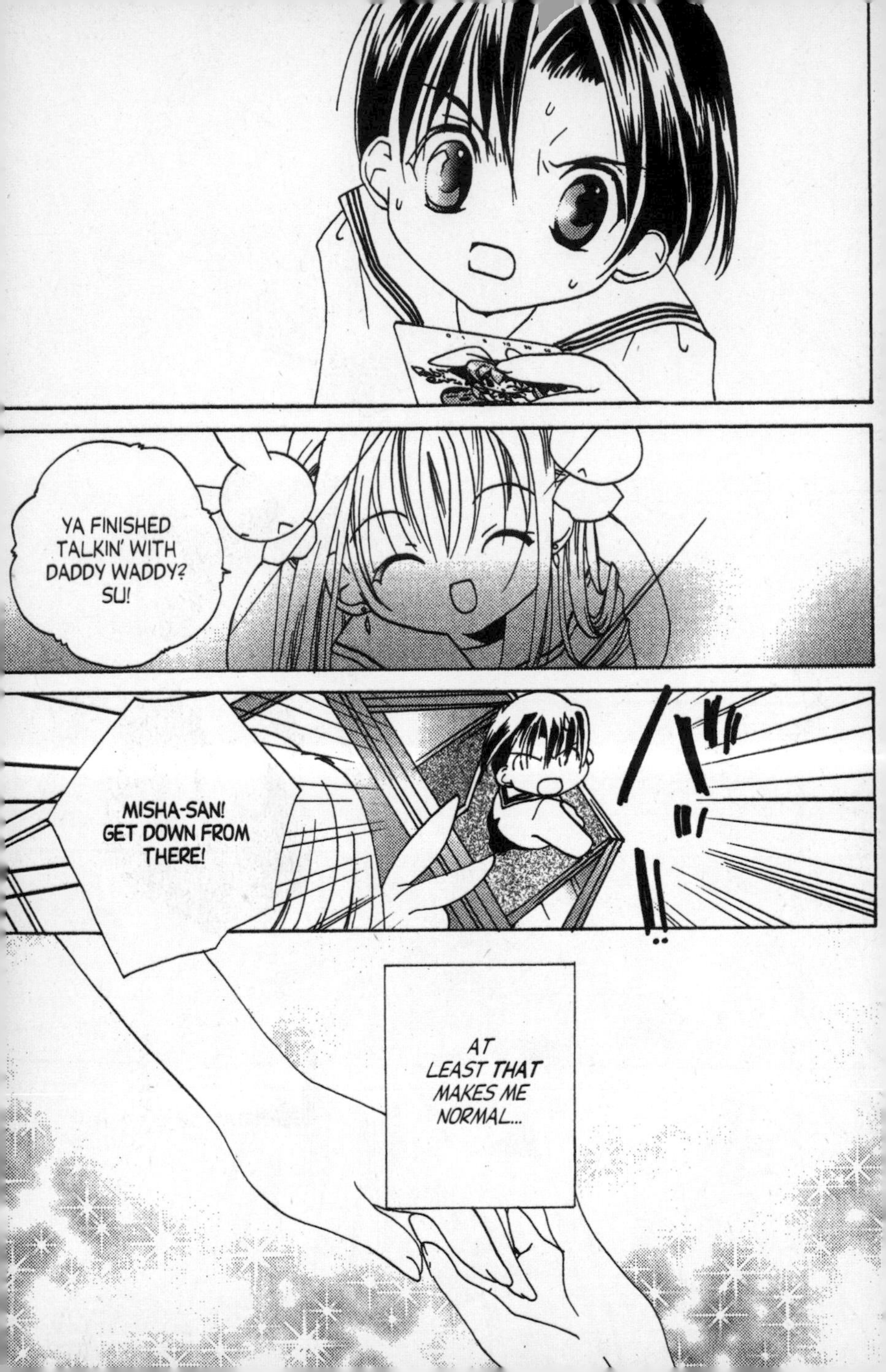
YA FINISHED TALKIN' WITH DADDY WADDY? SU!
MISHA-SAN! GET DOWN FROM THERE!
AT LEAST THAT MAKES ME NORMAL...

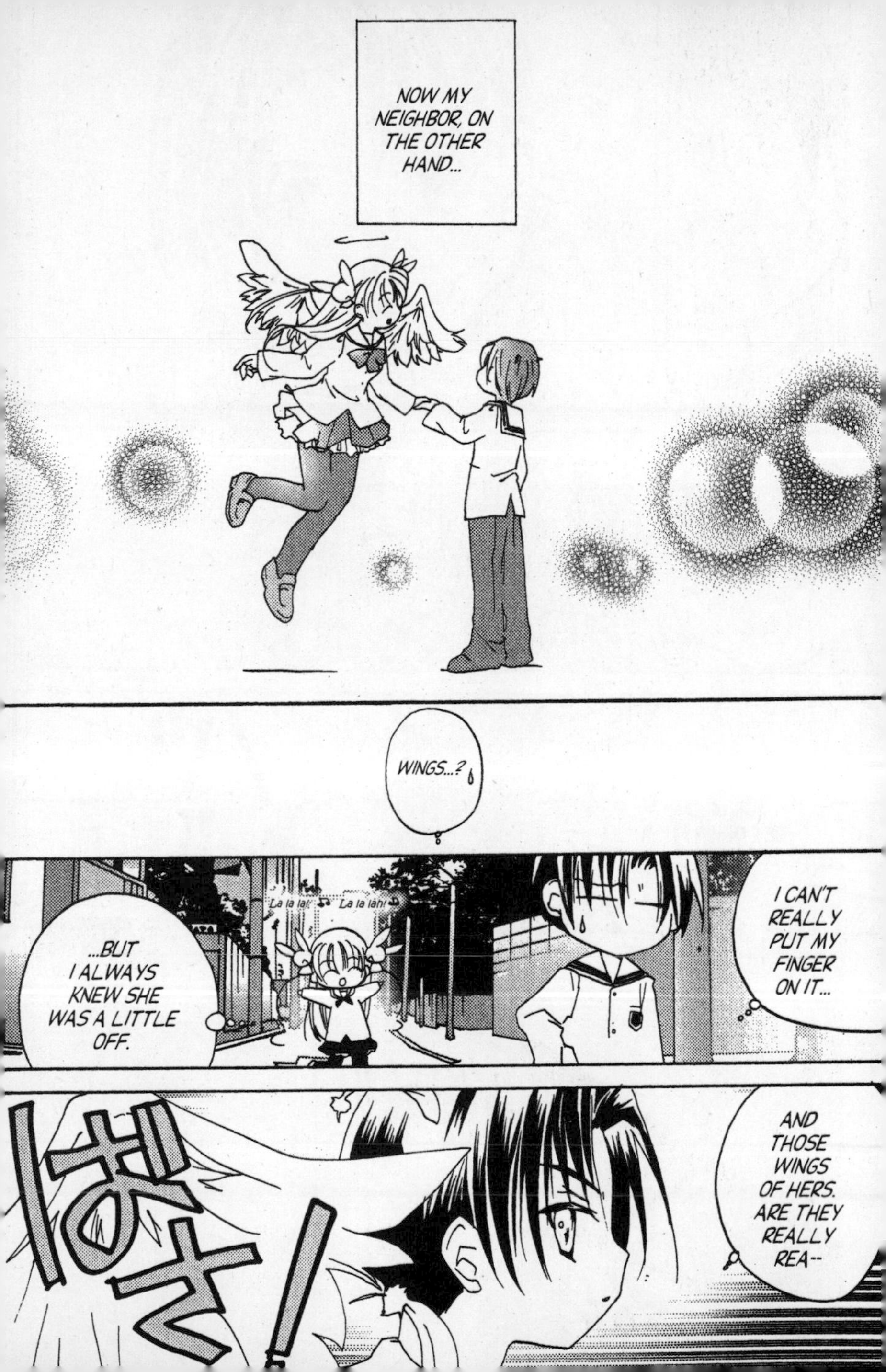
NOW MY NEIGHBOR, ON THE OTHER HAND...
WINGS...?
I CAN'T REALLY PUT MY FINGER ON IT...
La la la! La la lah!
...BUT I ALWAYS KNEW SHE WAS A LITTLE OFF.
AND THOSE WINGS OF HERS. ARE THEY REALLY REA--
ぼさ!

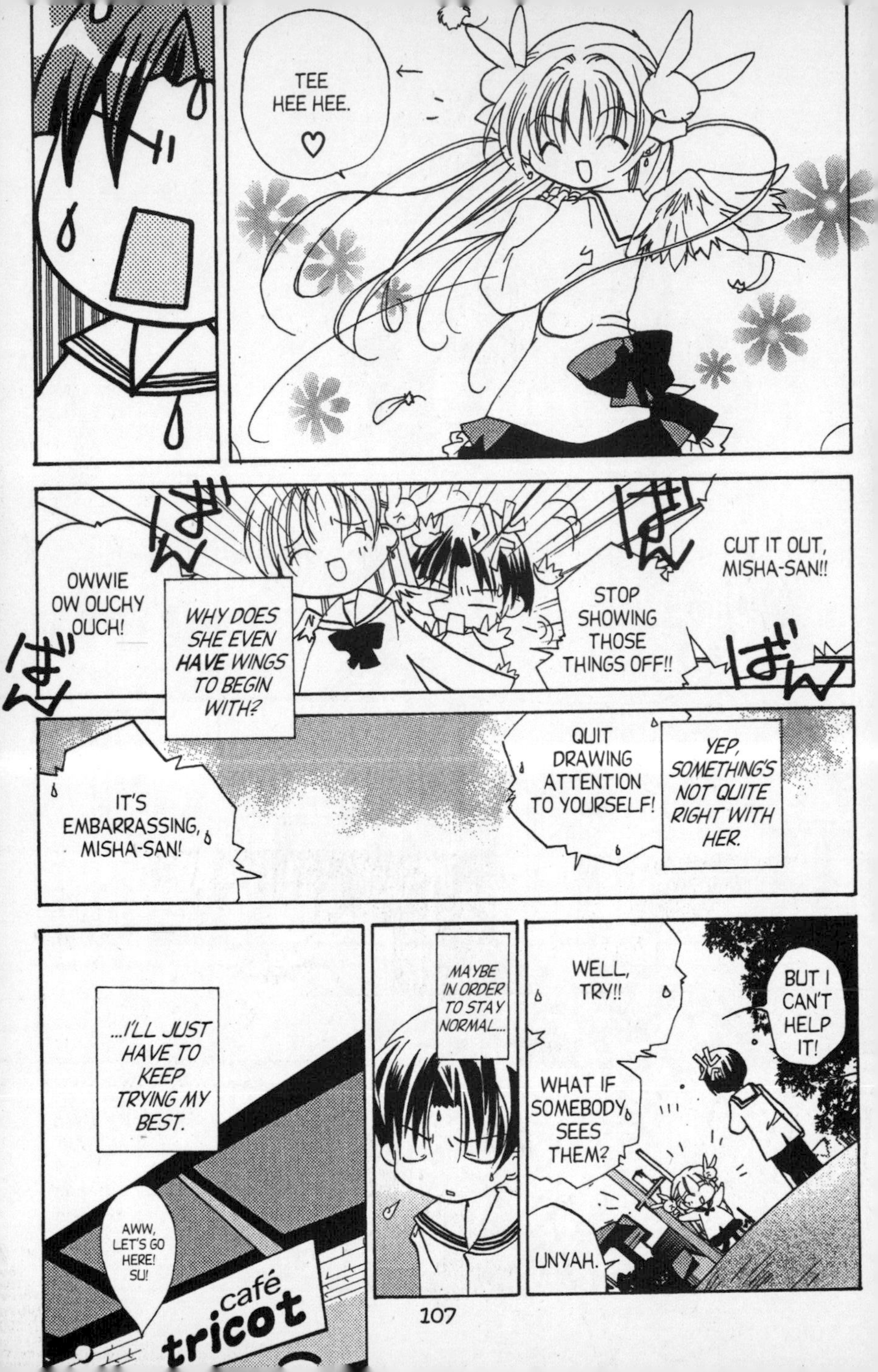
TEE HEE HEE. ♡
CUT IT OUT, MISHA-SAN!!
ばん
ばん
STOP SHOWING THOSE THINGS OFF!!
ばん
WHY DOES SHE EVEN **HAVE** WINGS TO BEGIN WITH?
OWWIE OW OUCHY OUCH!
ばん
YEP, SOMETHING'S NOT QUITE RIGHT WITH HER.
QUIT DRAWING ATTENTION TO YOURSELF!
IT'S EMBARRASSING, MISHA-SAN!
BUT I CAN'T HELP IT!
WELL, TRY!!
WHAT IF SOMEBODY SEES THEM?
UNYAH.
MAYBE IN ORDER TO STAY NORMAL...
...I'LL JUST HAVE TO KEEP TRYING MY BEST.
AWW, LET'S GO HERE! SU!
café tricot

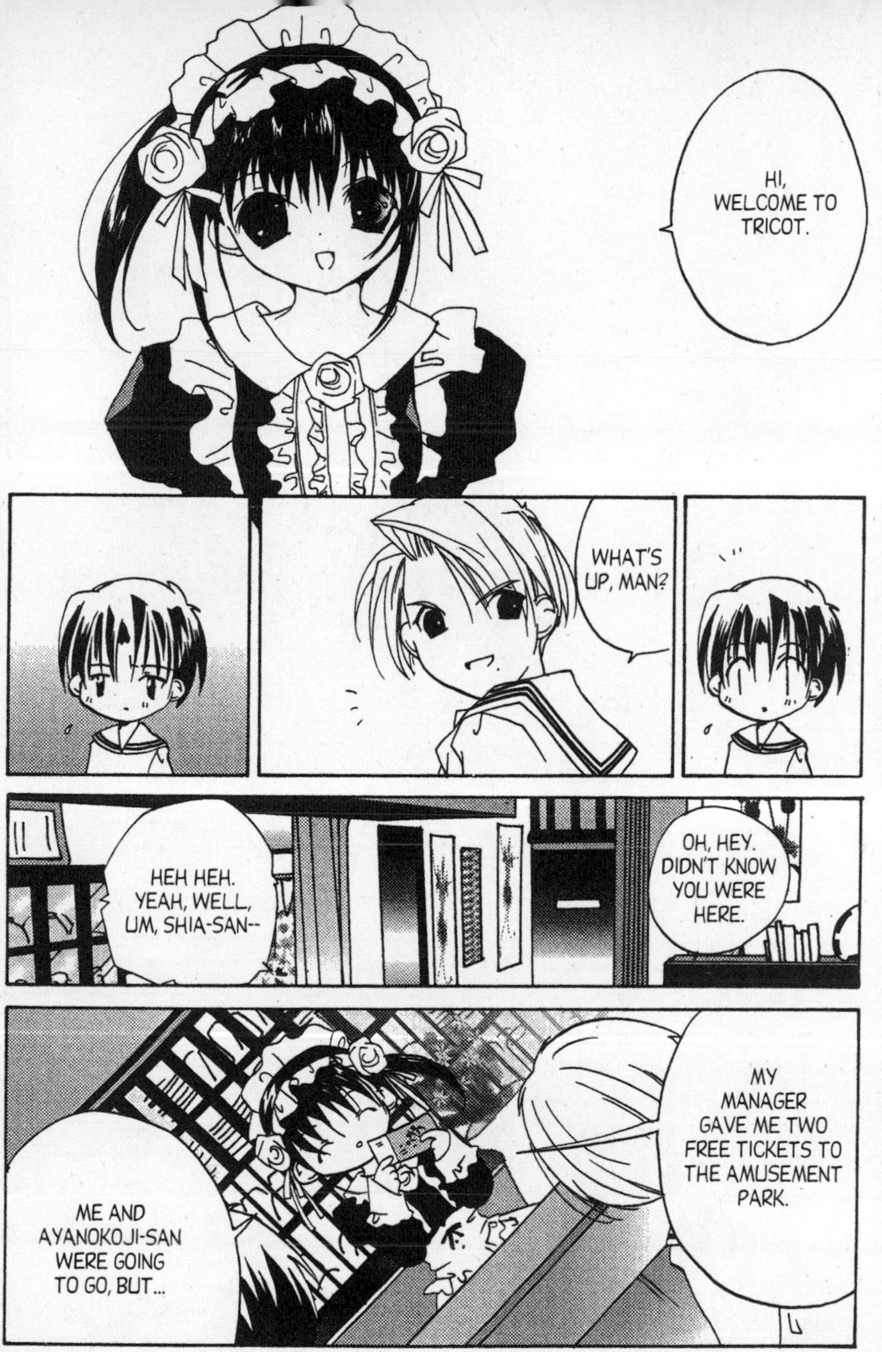
HI, WELCOME TO TRICOT.
WHAT'S UP, MAN?
OH, HEY. DIDN'T KNOW YOU WERE HERE.
HEH HEH. YEAH, WELL, UM, SHIA-SAN--
MY MANAGER GAVE ME TWO FREE TICKETS TO THE AMUSEMENT PARK.
ME AND AYANOKOJI-SAN WERE GOING TO GO, BUT...

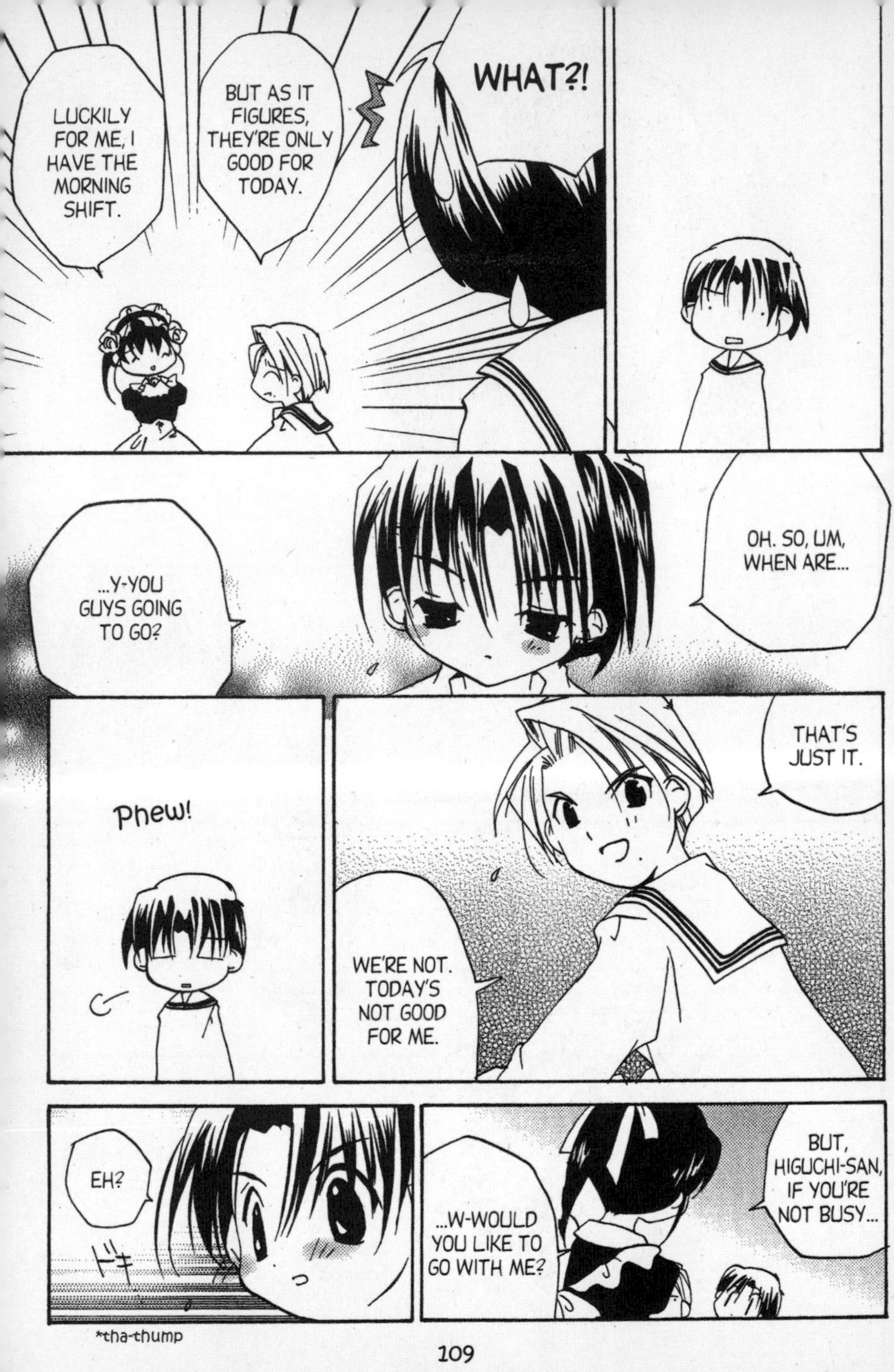
WHAT?!
BUT AS IT FIGURES, THEY'RE ONLY GOOD FOR TODAY.
LUCKILY FOR ME, I HAVE THE MORNING SHIFT.
OH. SO, UM, WHEN ARE...
...Y-YOU GUYS GOING TO GO?
THAT'S JUST IT.
WE'RE NOT. TODAY'S NOT GOOD FOR ME.
Phew!
BUT, HIGUCHI-SAN, IF YOU'RE NOT BUSY...
...W-WOULD YOU LIKE TO GO WITH ME?
EH?
ドキ

*tha-thump

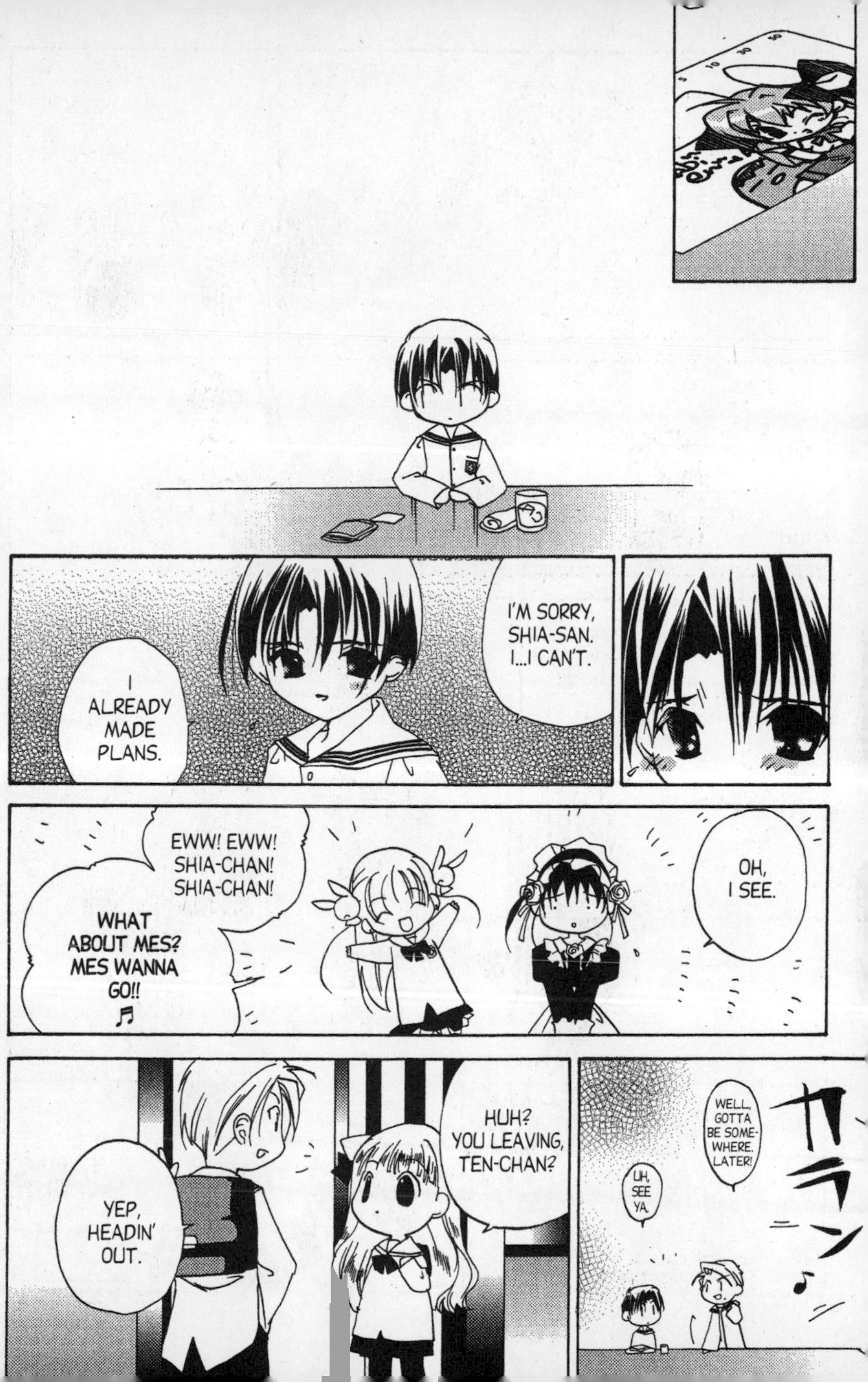
I'M SORRY, SHIA-SAN. I...I CAN'T.
I ALREADY MADE PLANS.
OH, I SEE.
EWW! EWW! SHIA-CHAN! SHIA-CHAN!
WHAT ABOUT MES? MES WANNA GO!! ♬
WELL, GOTTA BE SOME-WHERE. LATER!
UH, SEE YA.
HUH? YOU LEAVING, TEN-CHAN?
YEP, HEADIN' OUT.

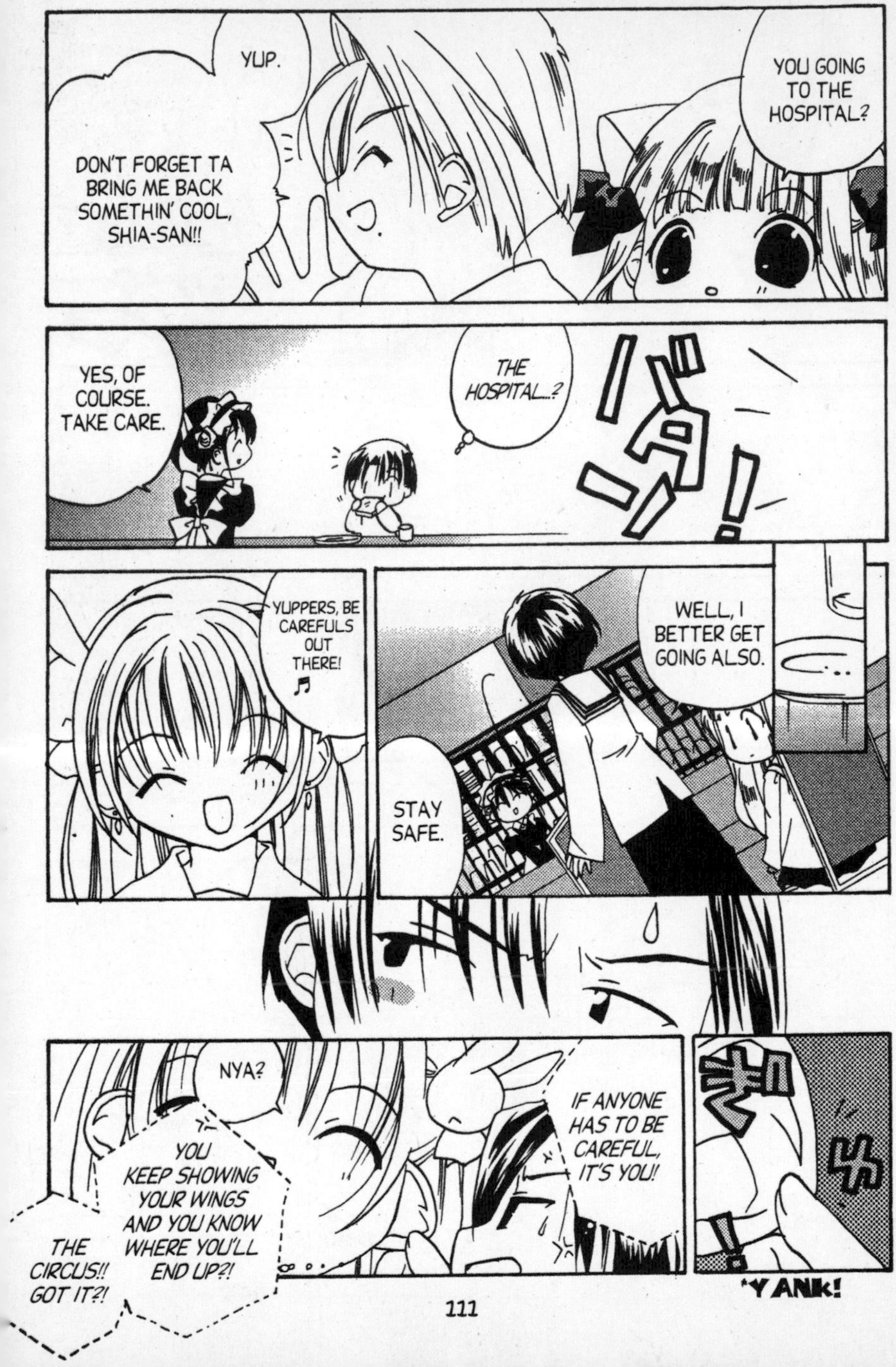
YOU GOING TO THE HOSPITAL?
YUP.
DON'T FORGET TA BRING ME BACK SOMETHIN' COOL, SHIA-SAN!!
バターン!
THE HOSPITAL...?
YES, OF COURSE. TAKE CARE.
WELL, I BETTER GET GOING ALSO.
STAY SAFE.
YUPPERS, BE CAREFULS OUT THERE! ♪
ぎゅ
*YANK!
IF ANYONE HAS TO BE CAREFUL, IT'S YOU!
NYA?
YOU KEEP SHOWING YOUR WINGS AND YOU KNOW WHERE YOU'LL END UP?!
THE CIRCUS!! GOT IT?!

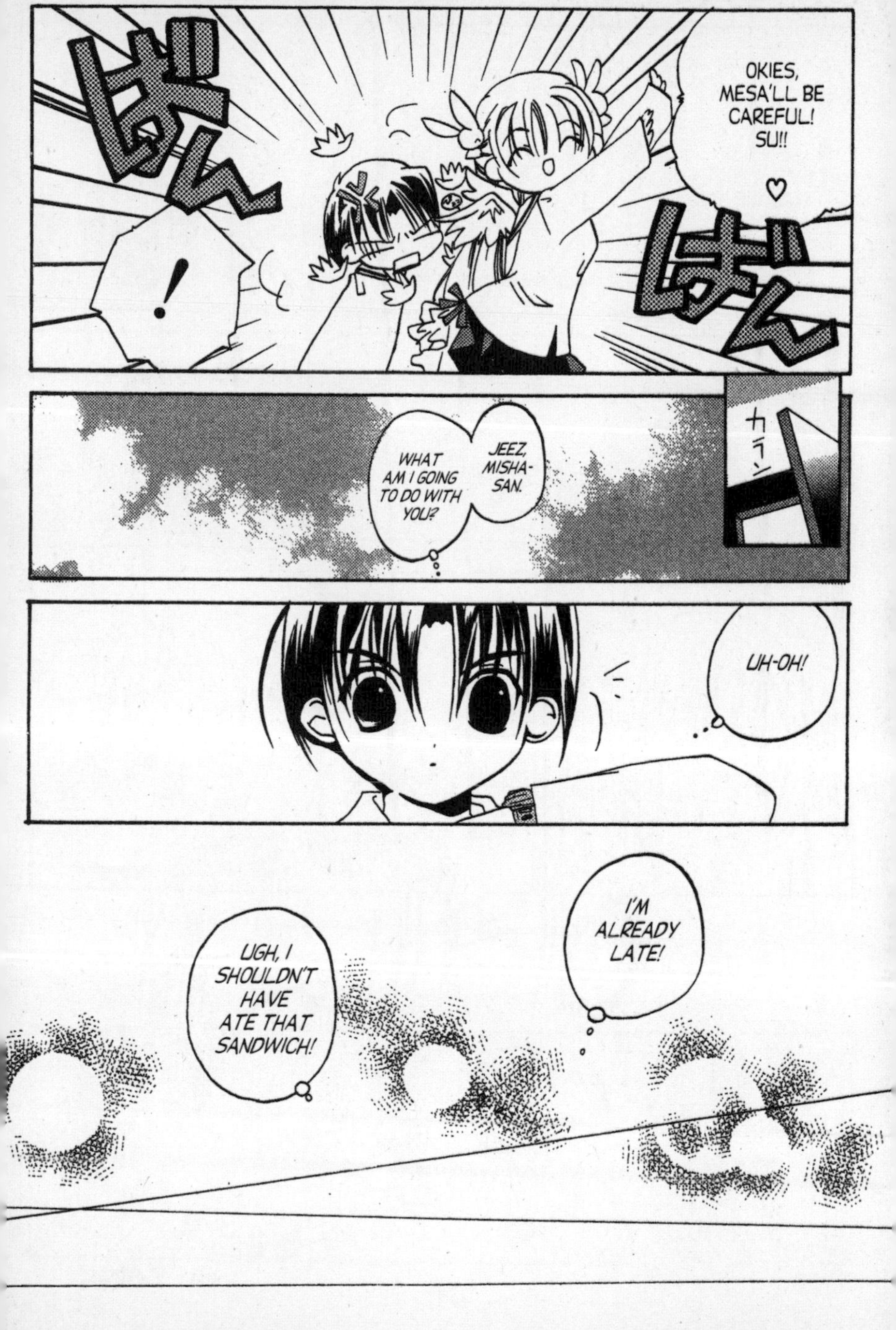
OKIES, MESA'LL BE CAREFUL! SU!! ♡
ばん
!
ばん
カラン
JEEZ, MISHA-SAN.
WHAT AM I GOING TO DO WITH YOU?
UH-OH!
I'M ALREADY LATE!
UGH, I SHOULDN'T HAVE ATE THAT SANDWICH!

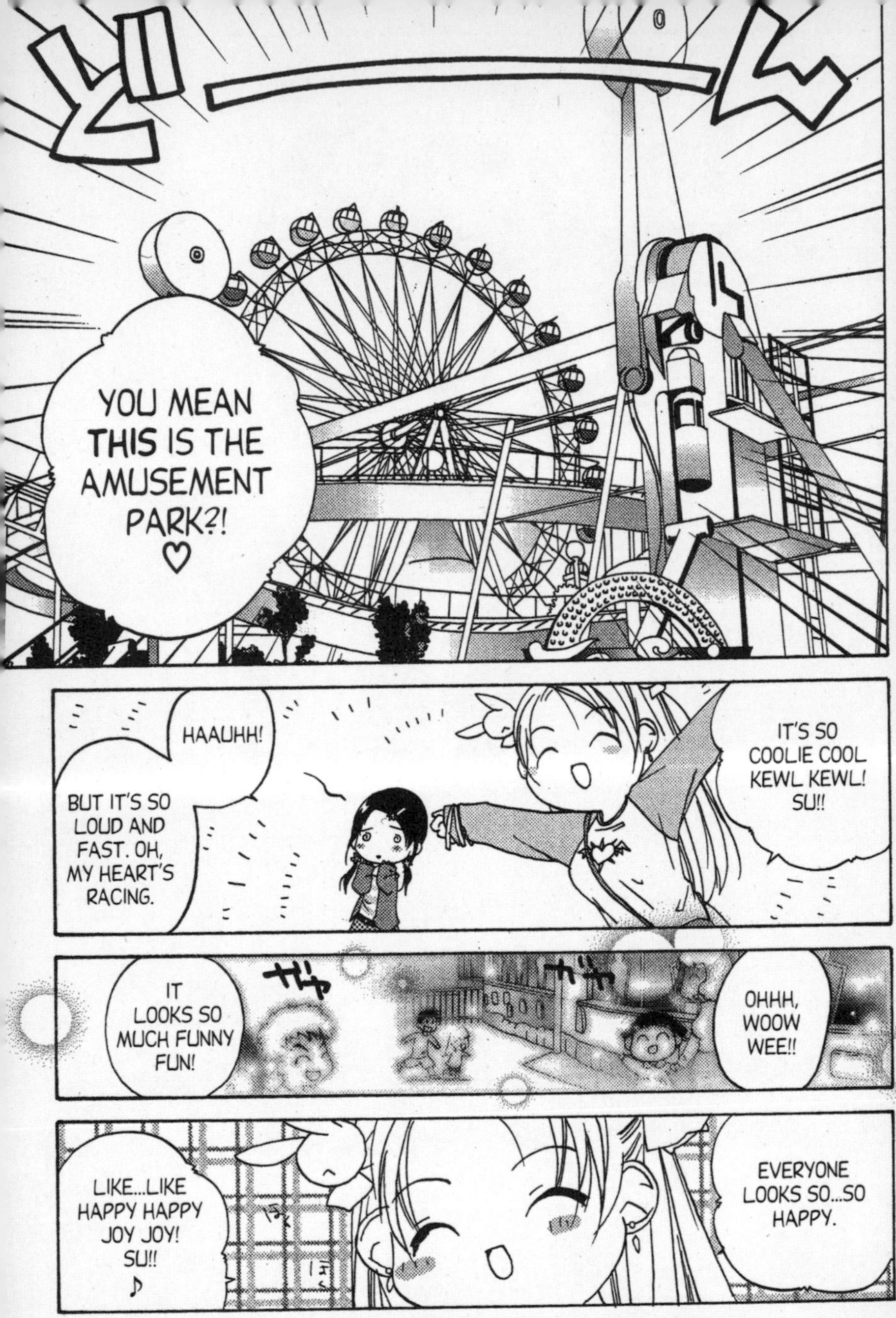
ドーン
YOU MEAN THIS IS THE AMUSEMENT PARK?! ♡
IT'S SO COOLIE COOL KEWL KEWL! SU!!
HAAUHH!
BUT IT'S SO LOUD AND FAST. OH, MY HEART'S RACING.
OHHH, WOOW WEE!!
IT LOOKS SO MUCH FUNNY FUN!
EVERYONE LOOKS SO...SO HAPPY.
LIKE...LIKE HAPPY HAPPY JOY JOY! SU!! ♪

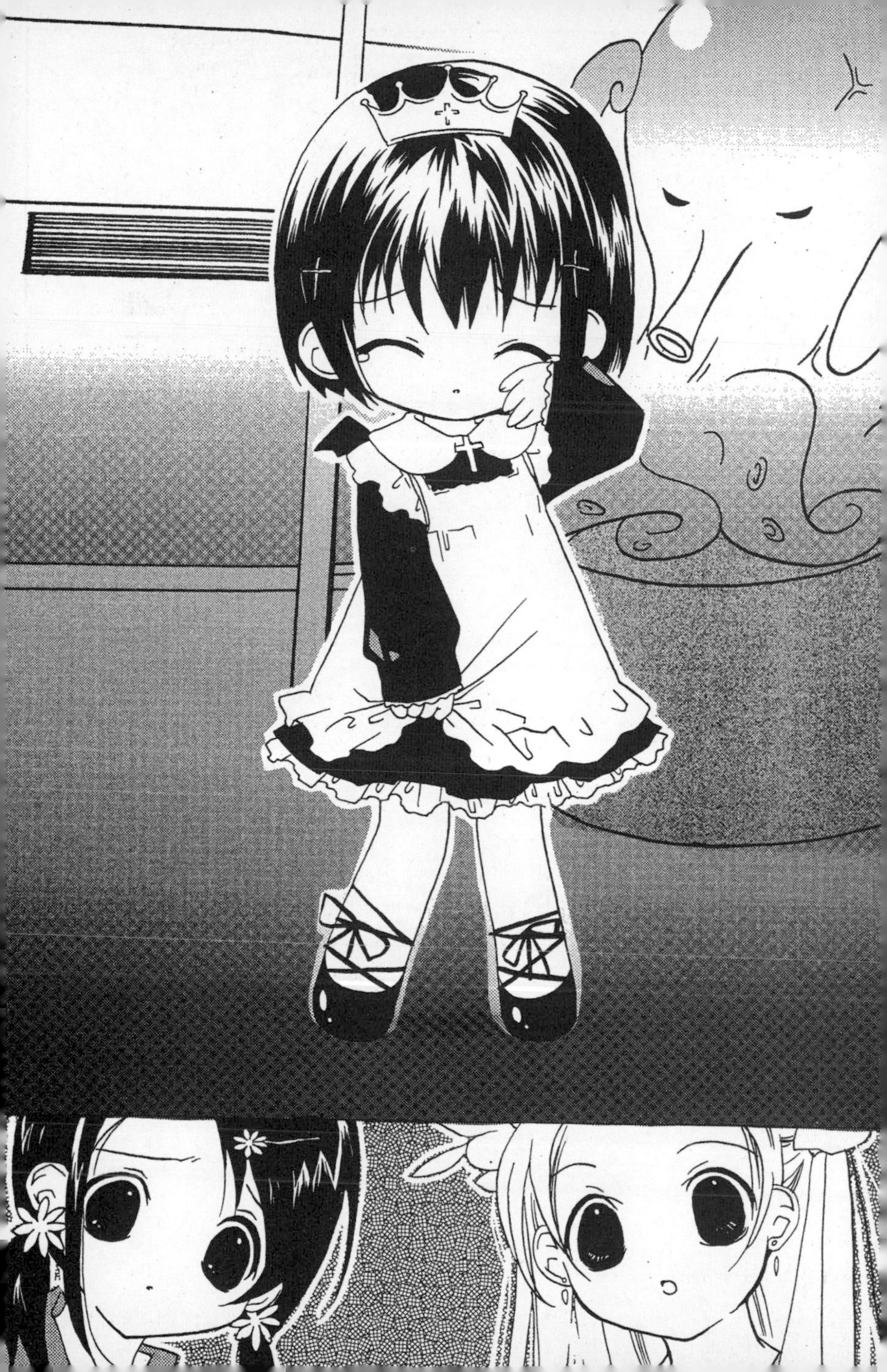

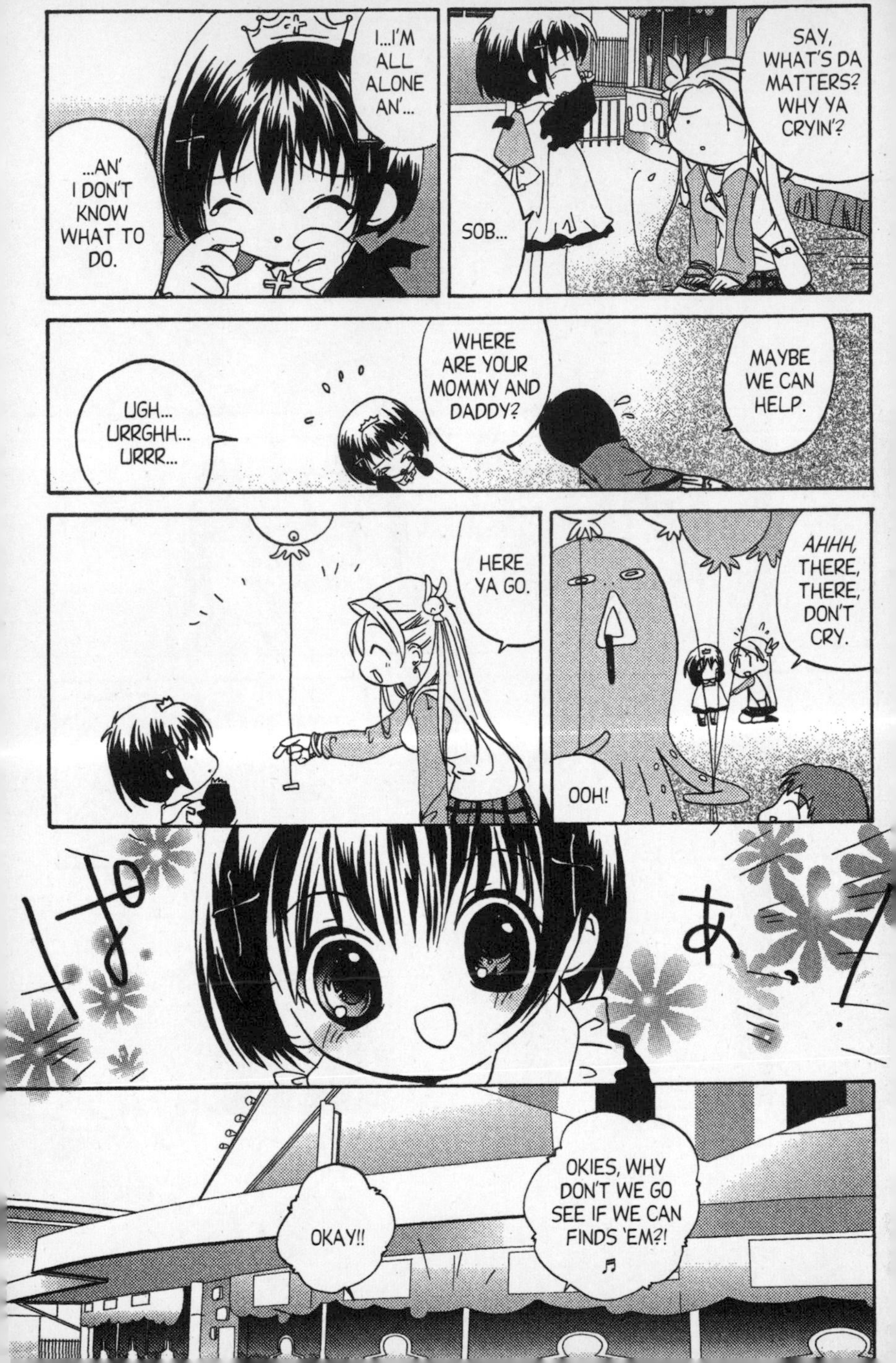
SAY, WHAT'S DA MATTERS? WHY YA CRYIN'?
SOB...
I...I'M ALL ALONE AN'...
...AN' I DON'T KNOW WHAT TO DO.
MAYBE WE CAN HELP.
WHERE ARE YOUR MOMMY AND DADDY?
UGH... URRGHH... URRR...
AHHH, THERE, THERE, DON'T CRY.
OOH!
HERE YA GO.
OKIES, WHY DON'T WE GO SEE IF WE CAN FINDS 'EM?! ♬
OKAY!!

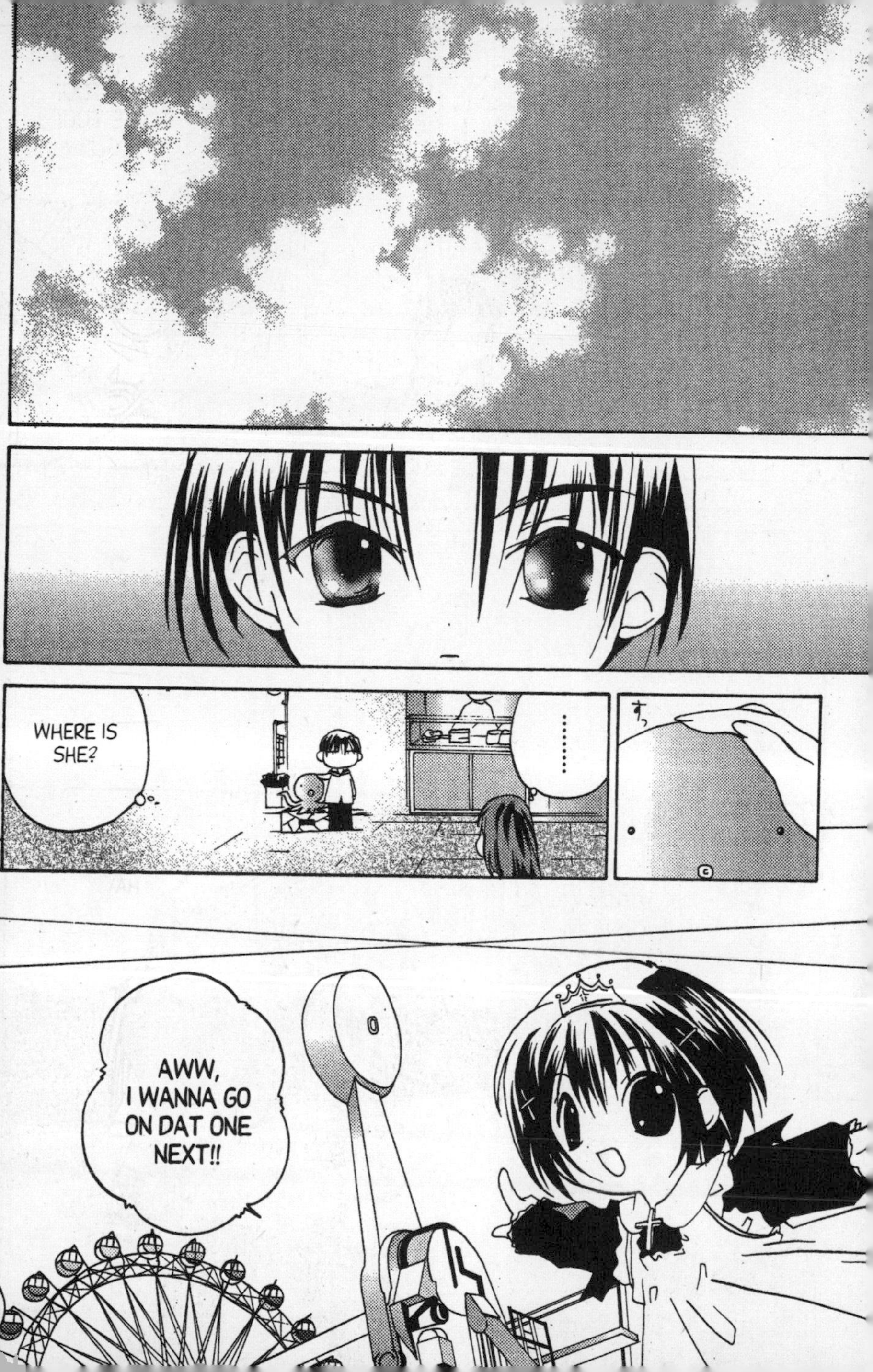

すっ
......
WHERE IS SHE?
AWW, I WANNA GO ON DAT ONE NEXT!!

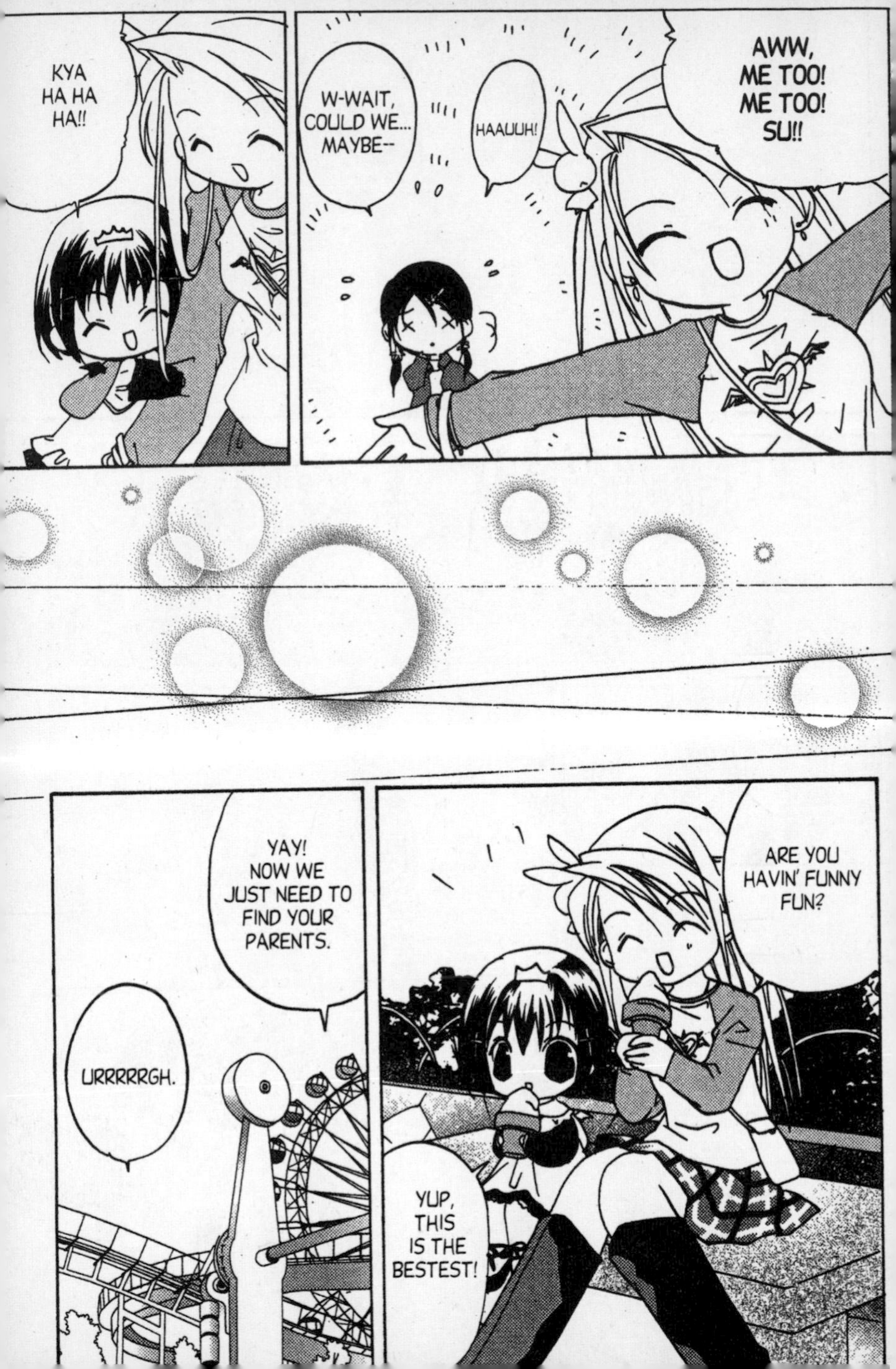
AWW, ME TOO! ME TOO! SU!!
HAAUUH!
W-WAIT, COULD WE... MAYBE--
KYA HA HA HA!!
ARE YOU HAVIN' FUNNY FUN?
YUP, THIS IS THE BESTEST!
YAY! NOW WE JUST NEED TO FIND YOUR PARENTS.
URRRRRGH.

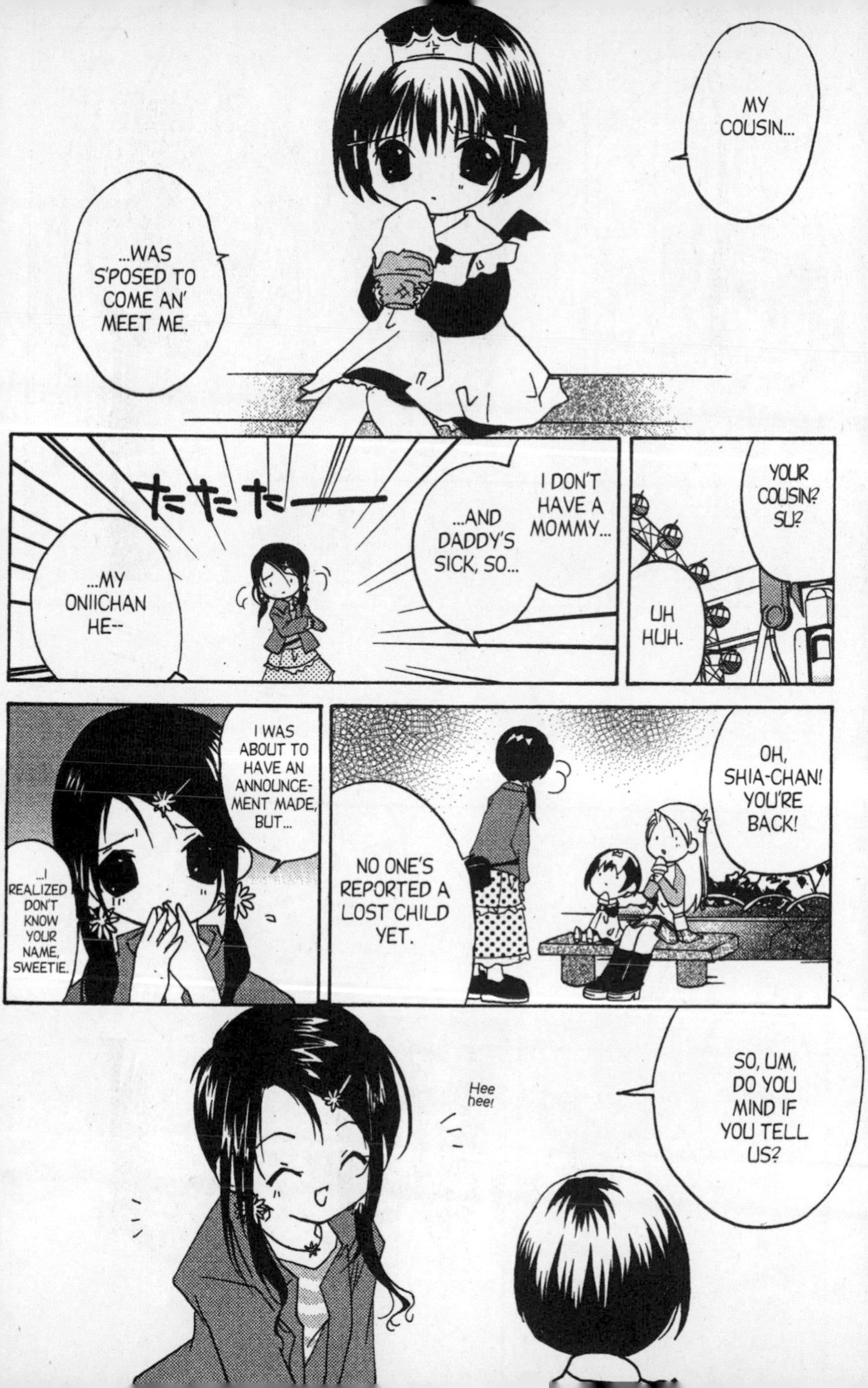
MY COUSIN...
...WAS S'POSED TO COME AN' MEET ME.
YOUR COUSIN? SU?
UH HUH.
I DON'T HAVE A MOMMY...
...AND DADDY'S SICK, SO...
たたたー
...MY ONIICHAN HE--
OH, SHIA-CHAN! YOU'RE BACK!
NO ONE'S REPORTED A LOST CHILD YET.
I WAS ABOUT TO HAVE AN ANNOUNCEMENT MADE, BUT...
...I REALIZED DON'T KNOW YOUR NAME, SWEETIE.
SO, UM, DO YOU MIND IF YOU TELL US?
Hee hee!

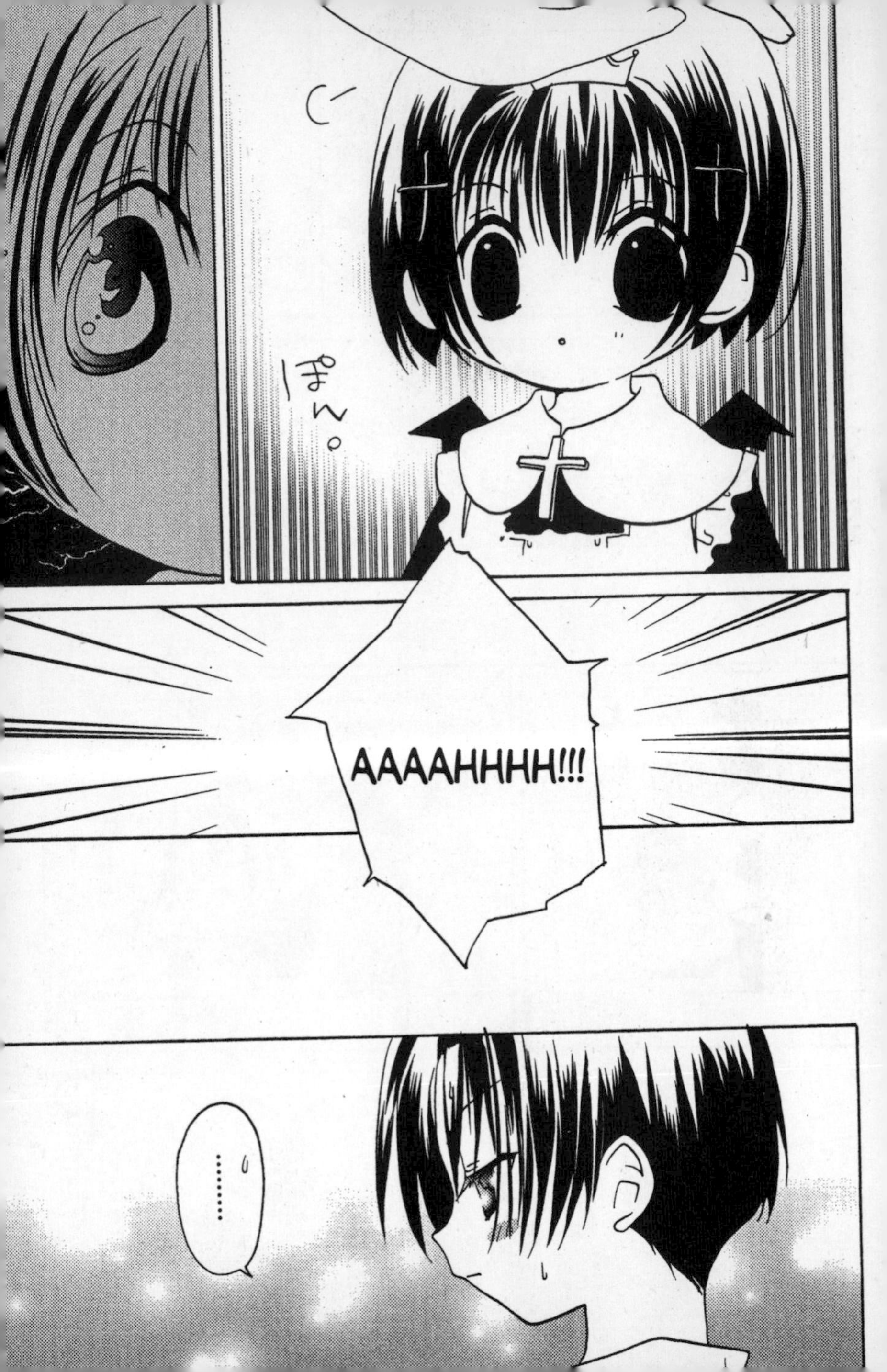

ぽん。
AAAAHHHH!!!
......

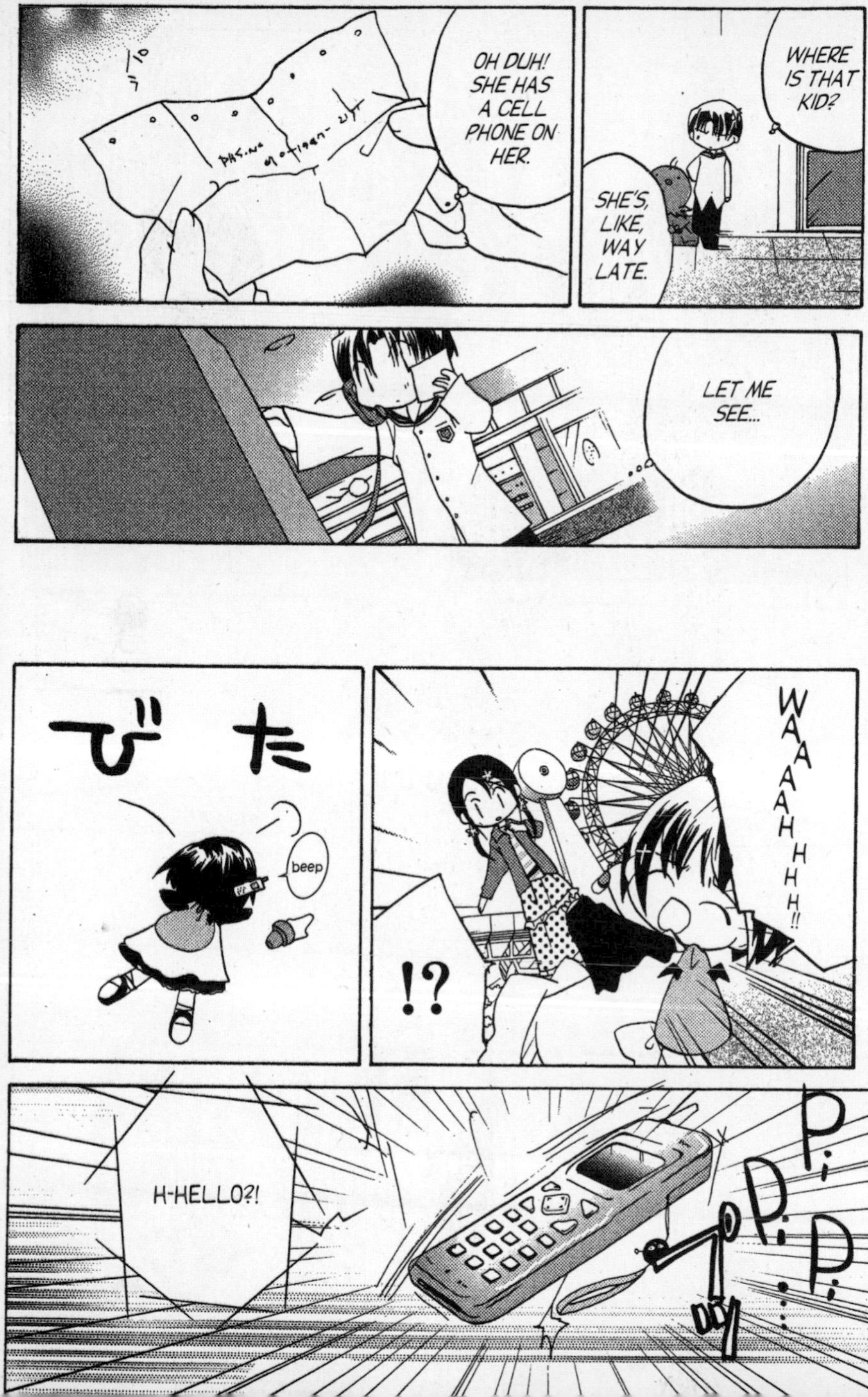
WHERE IS THAT KID?
SHE'S, LIKE, WAY LATE.
OH DUH! SHE HAS A CELL PHONE ON HER.
LET ME SEE...
WAAAAHHHH!!
!?
びた
beep
Pi
Pi
Pi
H-HELLO?!

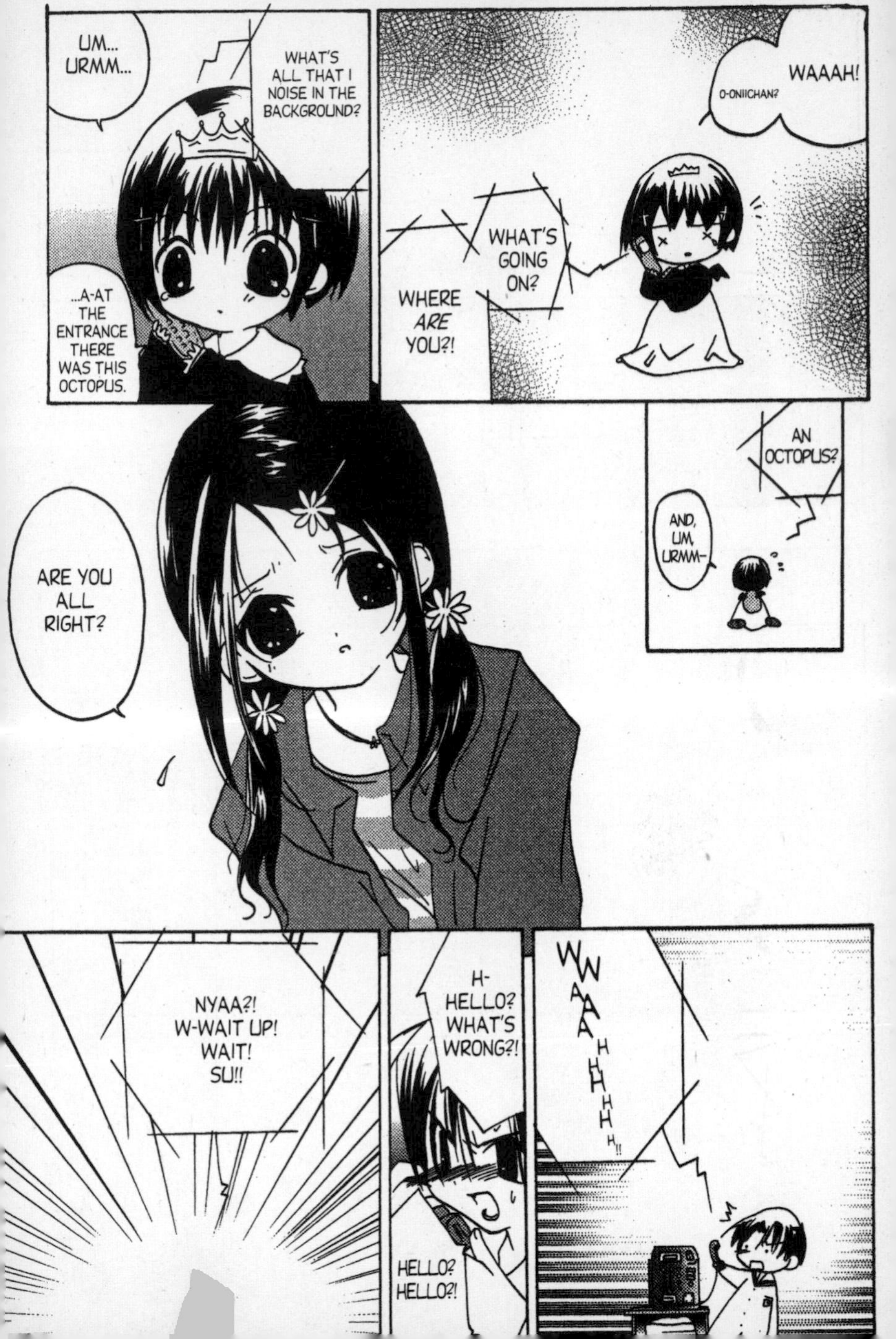
WAAAH!
O-ONIICHAN?
WHAT'S GOING ON?
WHERE *ARE* YOU?!
WHAT'S ALL THAT NOISE IN THE BACKGROUND?
UM... URMM...
...A-AT THE ENTRANCE THERE WAS THIS OCTOPUS.
AN OCTOPUS?
AND, UM, URMM-
ARE YOU ALL RIGHT?
WWAAAHHHHHH!!
H-HELLO? WHAT'S WRONG?!
HELLO? HELLO?!
NYAA?! W-WAIT UP! WAIT! SU!!

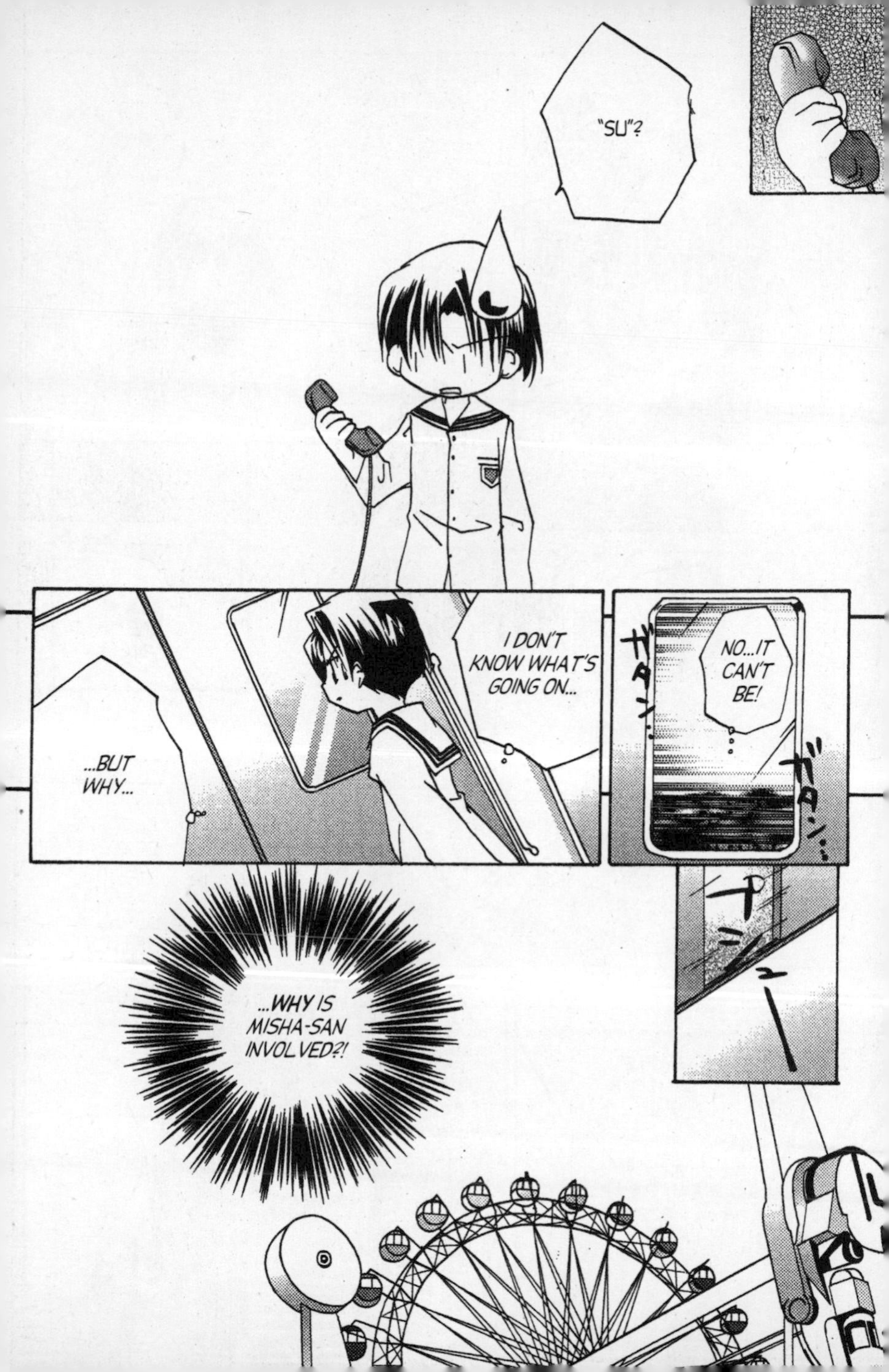
"SU"?
NO...IT CAN'T BE!
I DON'T KNOW WHAT'S GOING ON...
...BUT WHY...
...WHY IS MISHA-SAN INVOLVED?!

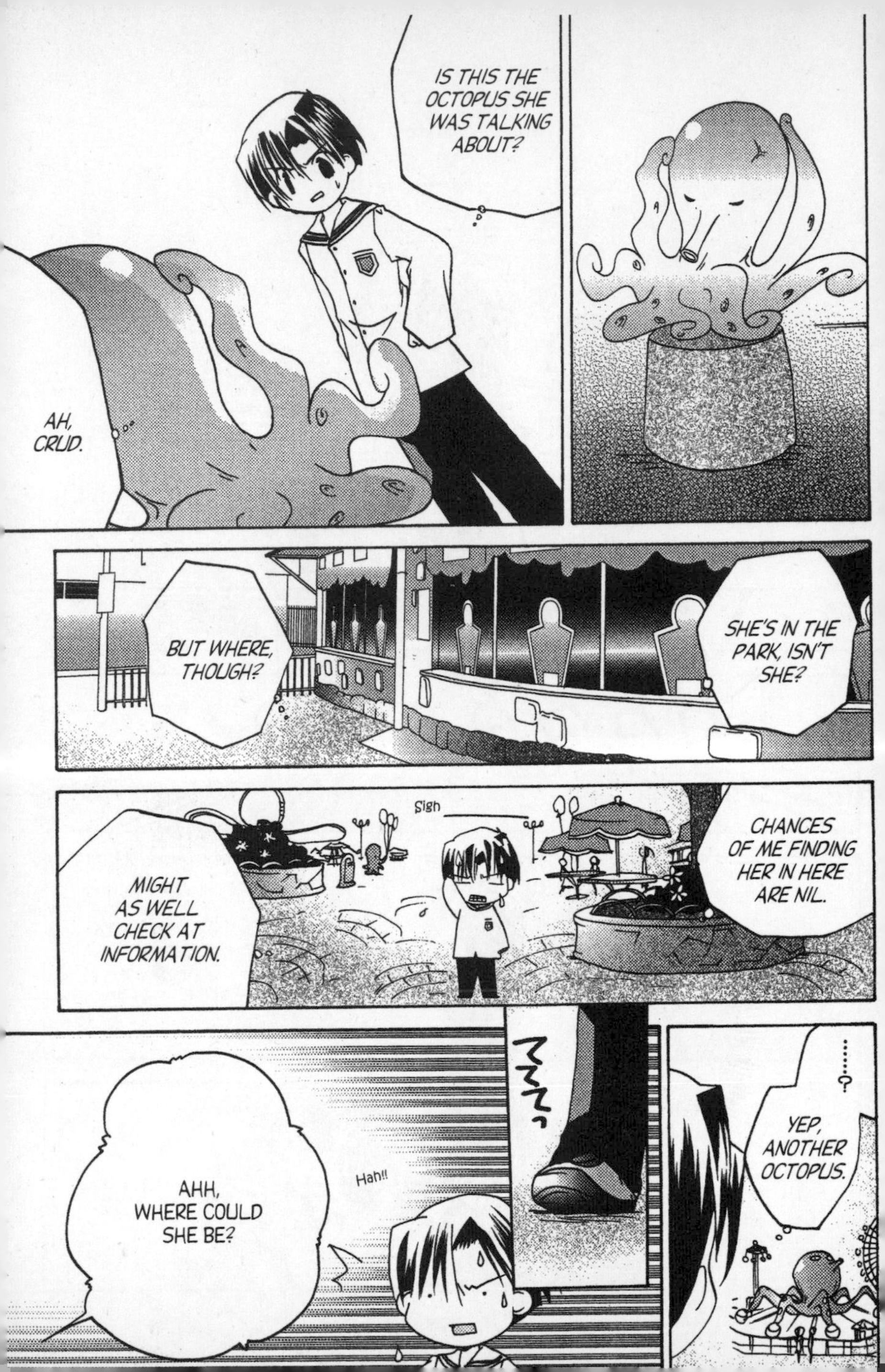
IS THIS THE OCTOPUS SHE WAS TALKING ABOUT?
AH, CRUD.
SHE'S IN THE PARK, ISN'T SHE?
BUT WHERE, THOUGH?
CHANCES OF ME FINDING HER IN HERE ARE NIL.
Sigh
MIGHT AS WELL CHECK AT INFORMATION.
......?
YEP, ANOTHER OCTOPUS.
Hah!!
AHH, WHERE COULD SHE BE?

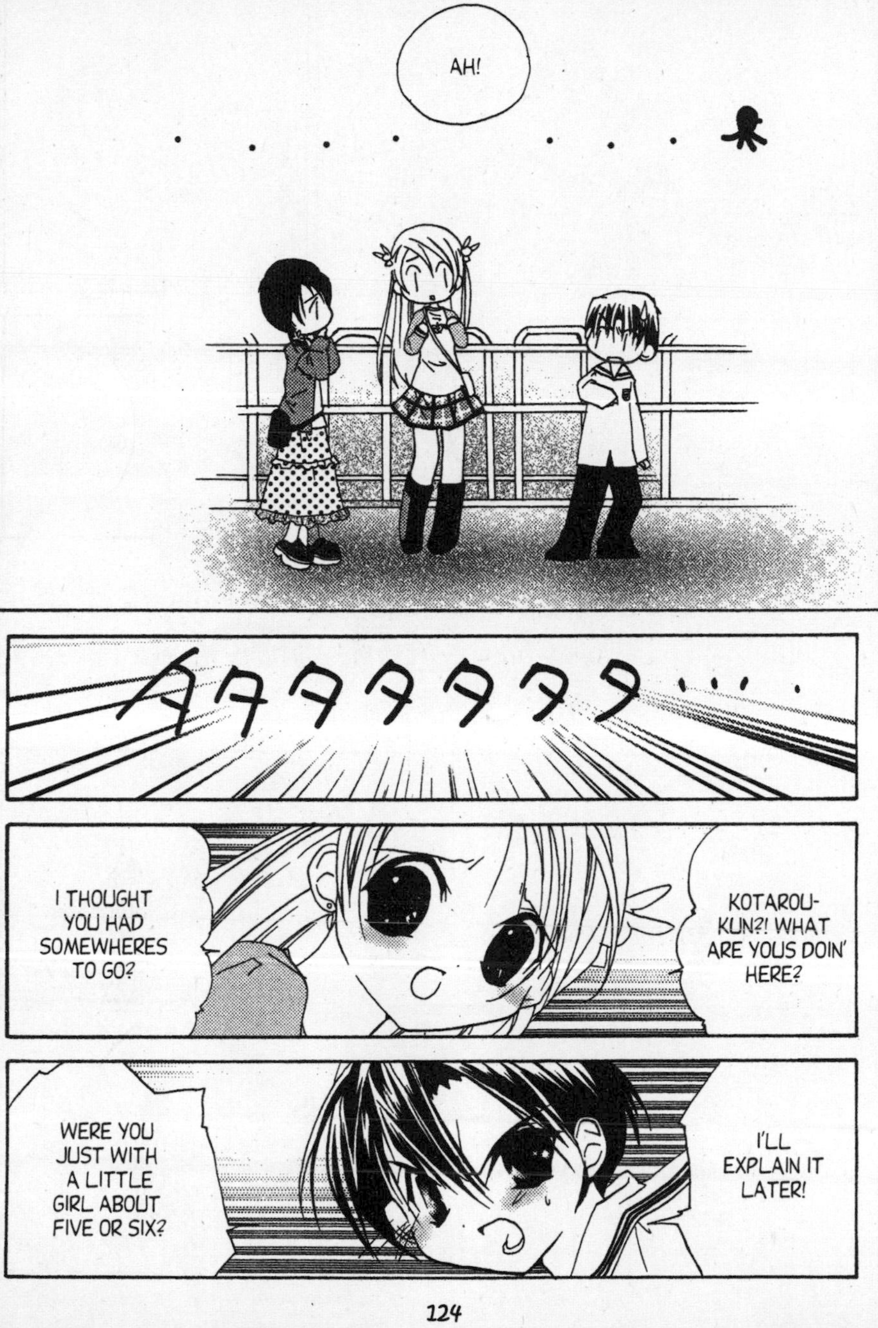
AH!
タタタタタタタ・・・
KOTAROU-KUN?! WHAT ARE YOUS DOIN' HERE?
I THOUGHT YOU HAD SOMEWHERES TO GO?
I'LL EXPLAIN IT LATER!
WERE YOU JUST WITH A LITTLE GIRL ABOUT FIVE OR SIX?

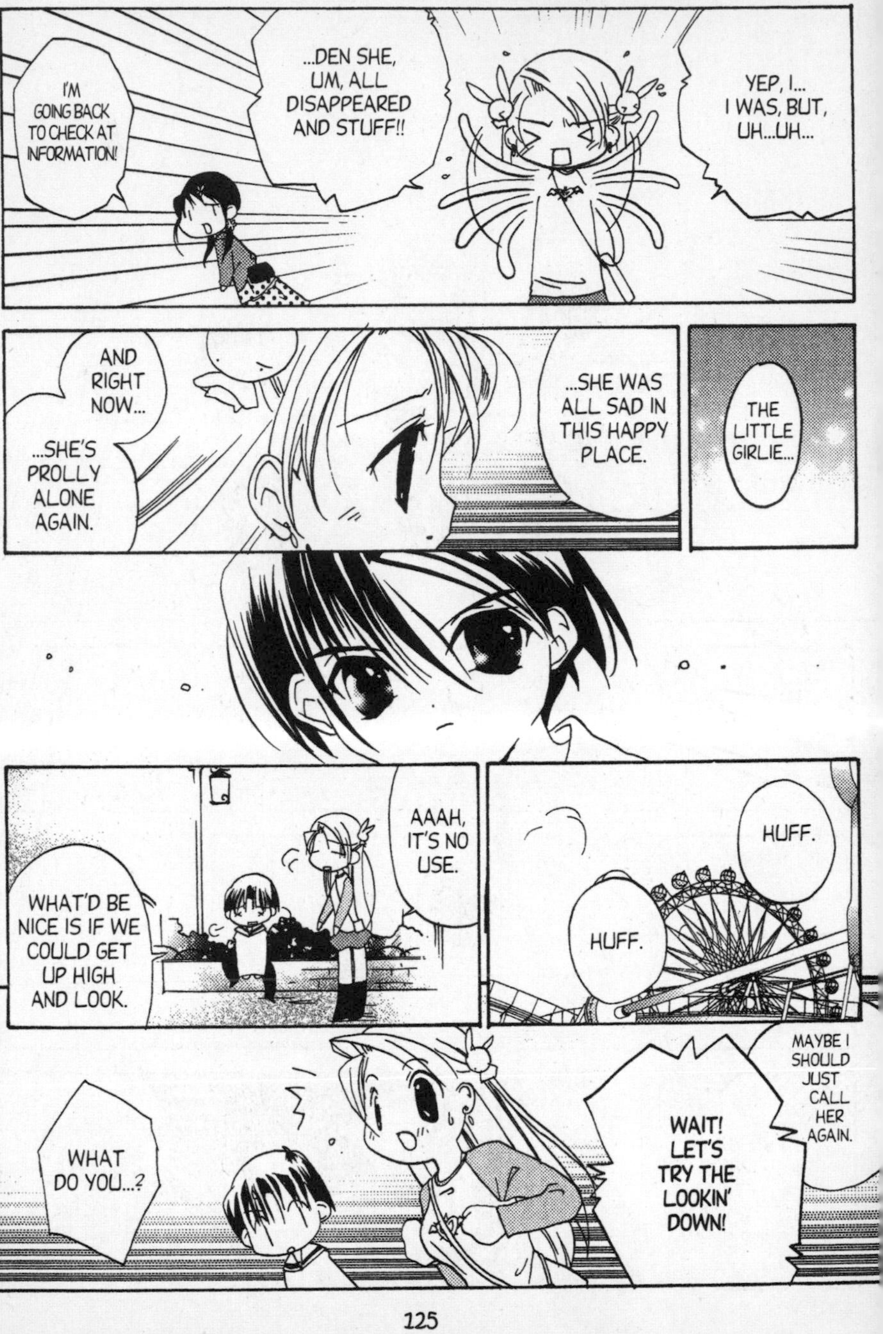
YEP, I... I WAS, BUT, UH...UH...
...DEN SHE, UM, ALL DISAPPEARED AND STUFF!!
I'M GOING BACK TO CHECK AT INFORMATION!
THE LITTLE GIRLIE...
...SHE WAS ALL SAD IN THIS HAPPY PLACE.
AND RIGHT NOW...
...SHE'S PROLLY ALONE AGAIN.
HUFF.
HUFF.
AAAH, IT'S NO USE.
WHAT'D BE NICE IS IF WE COULD GET UP HIGH AND LOOK.
MAYBE I SHOULD JUST CALL HER AGAIN.
WAIT! LET'S TRY THE LOOKIN' DOWN!
WHAT DO YOU...?

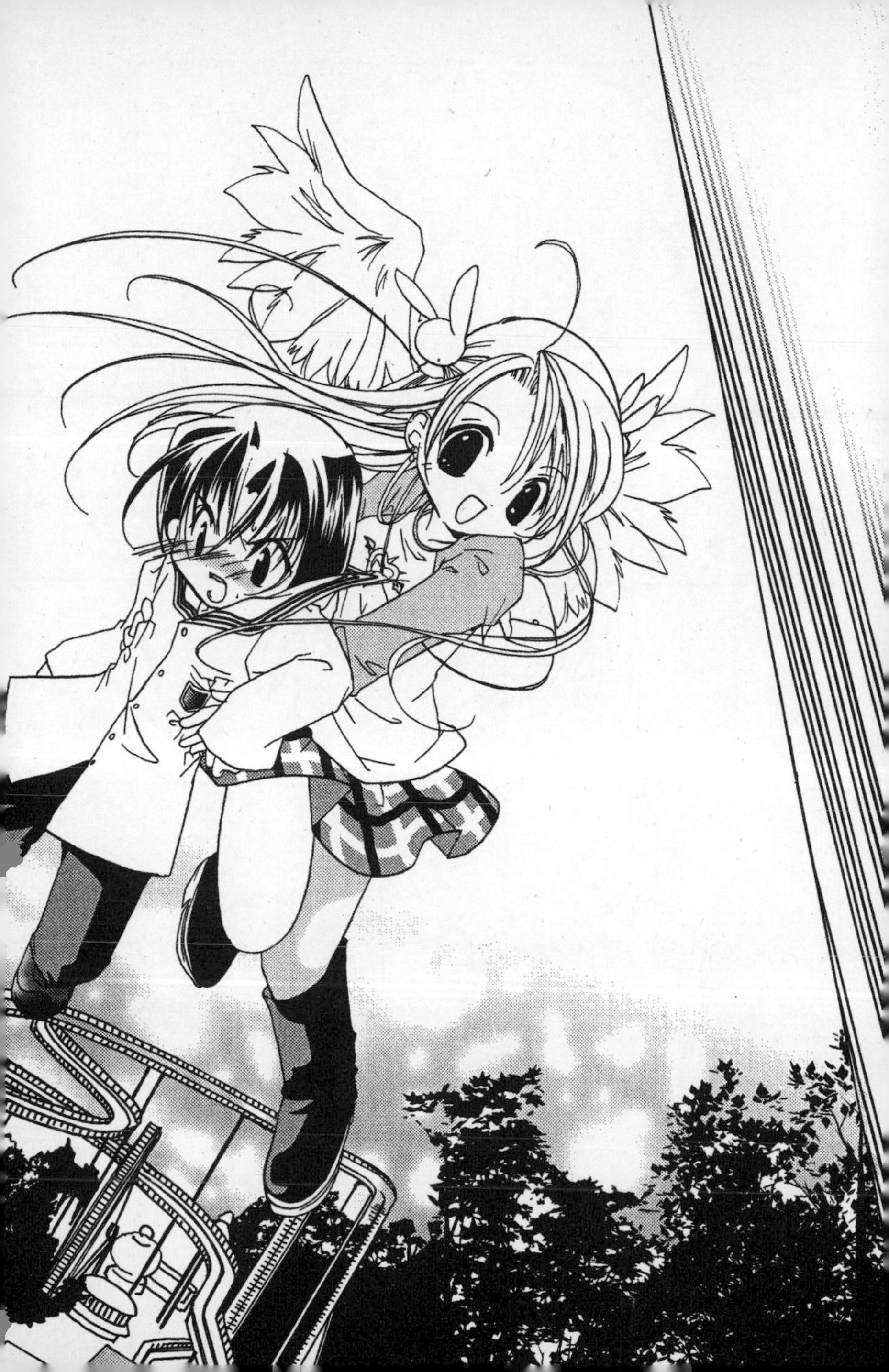

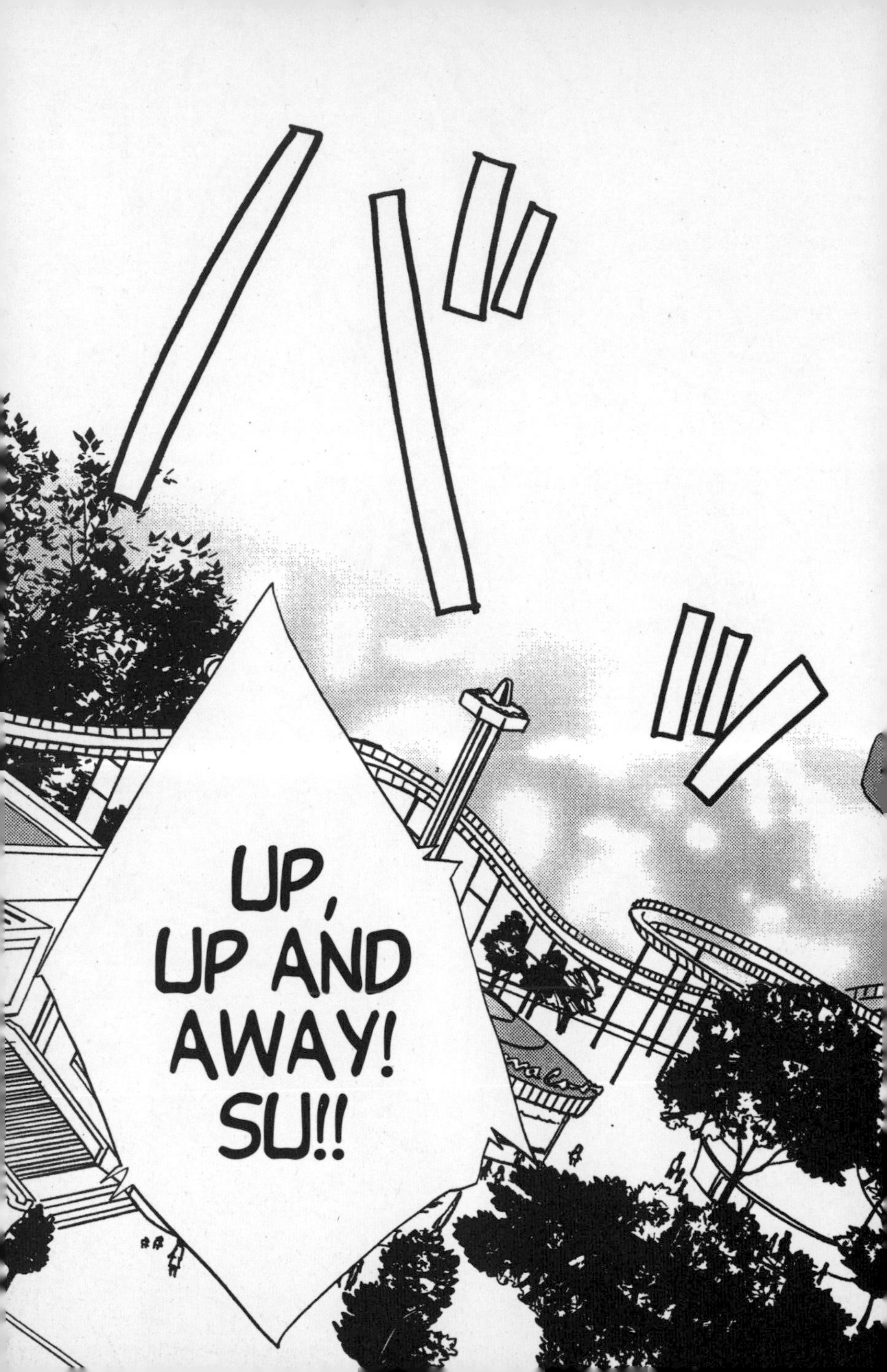
UP, UP AND AWAY! SU!!

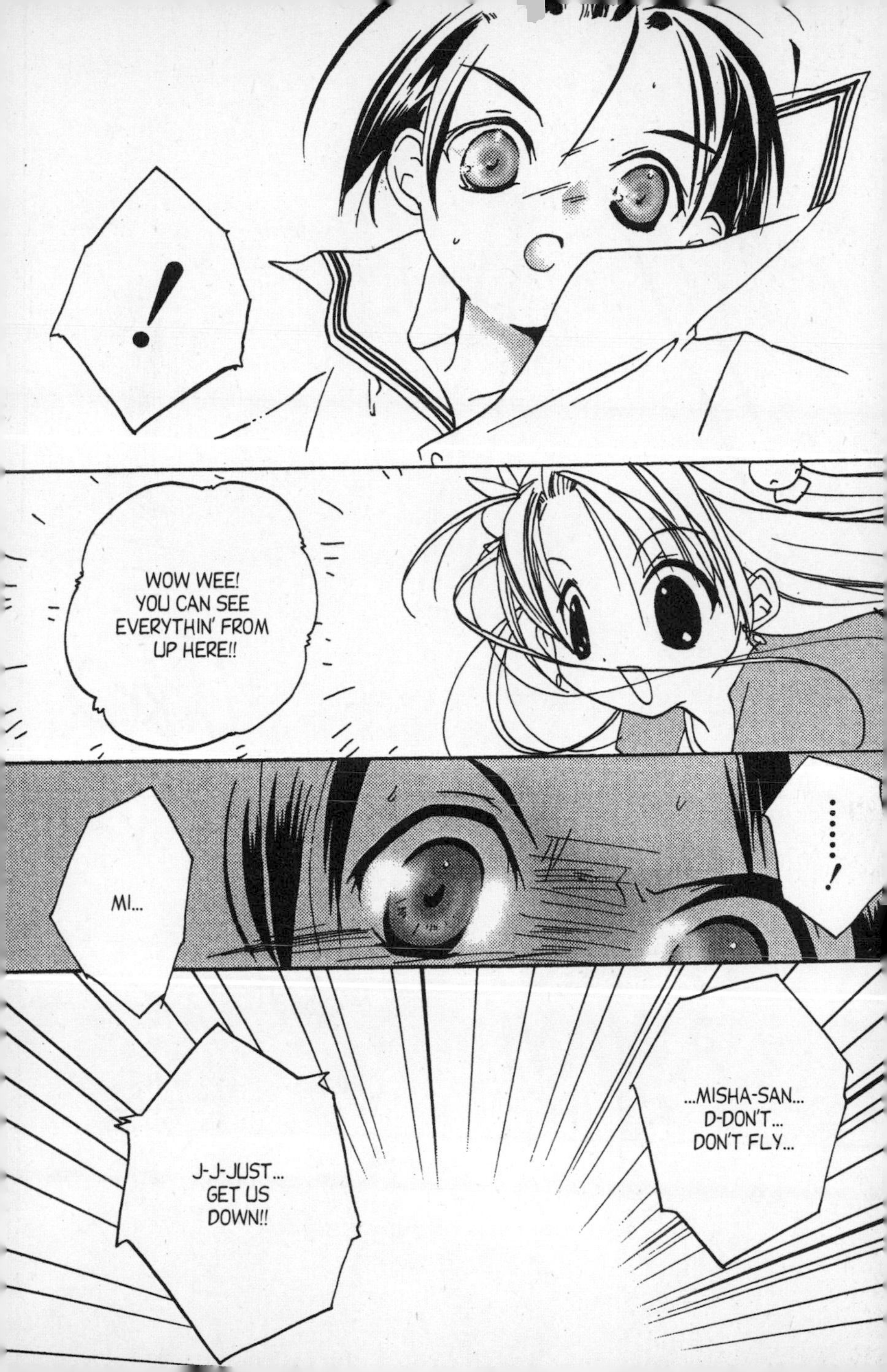
!
WOW WEE! YOU CAN SEE EVERYTHIN' FROM UP HERE!!
......!
MI...
...MISHA-SAN... D-DON'T... DON'T FLY...
J-J-JUST... GET US DOWN!!

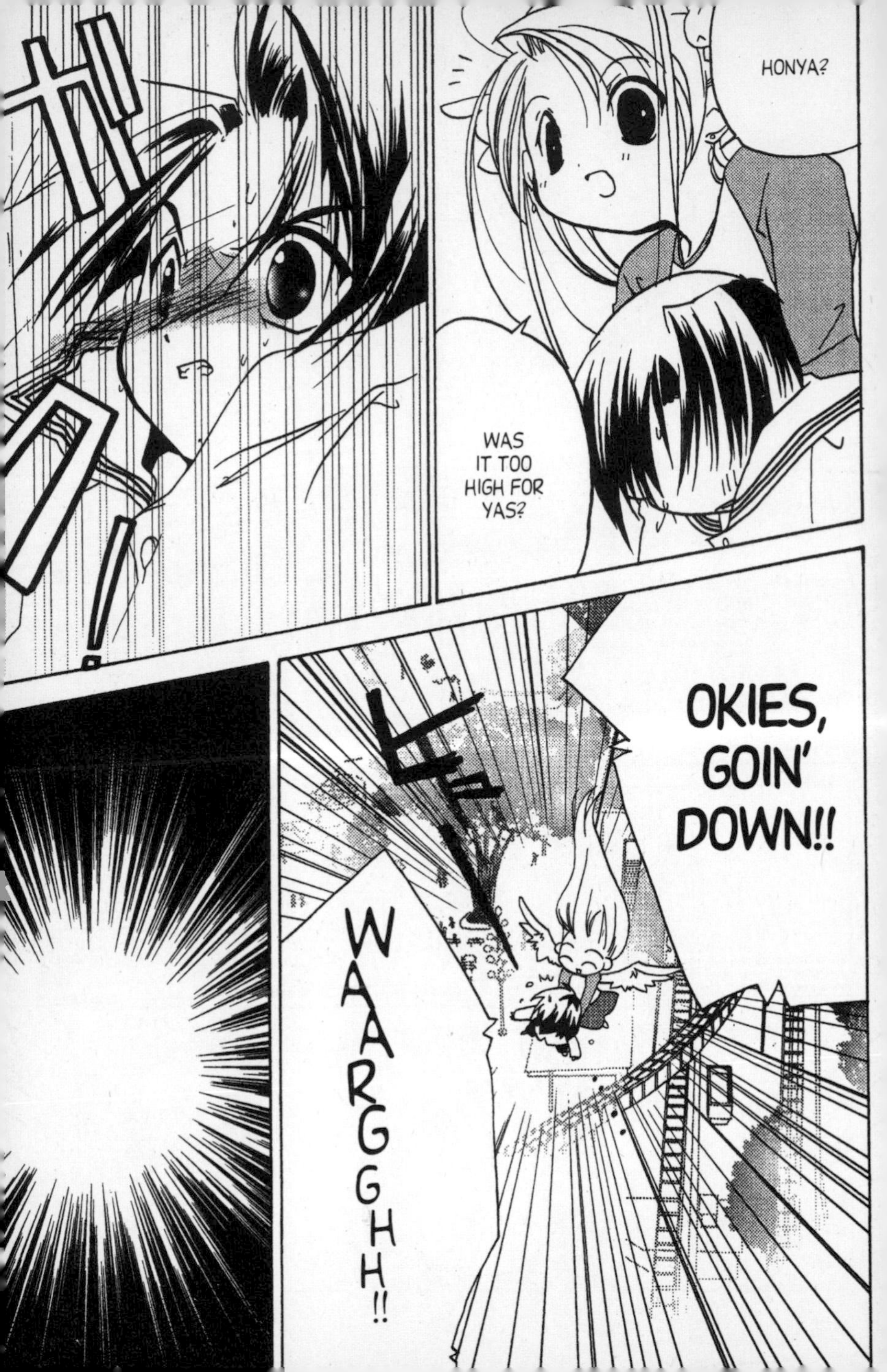
HONYA?
WAS IT TOO HIGH FOR YAS?
OKIES, GOIN' DOWN!!
WAARGGHH!!

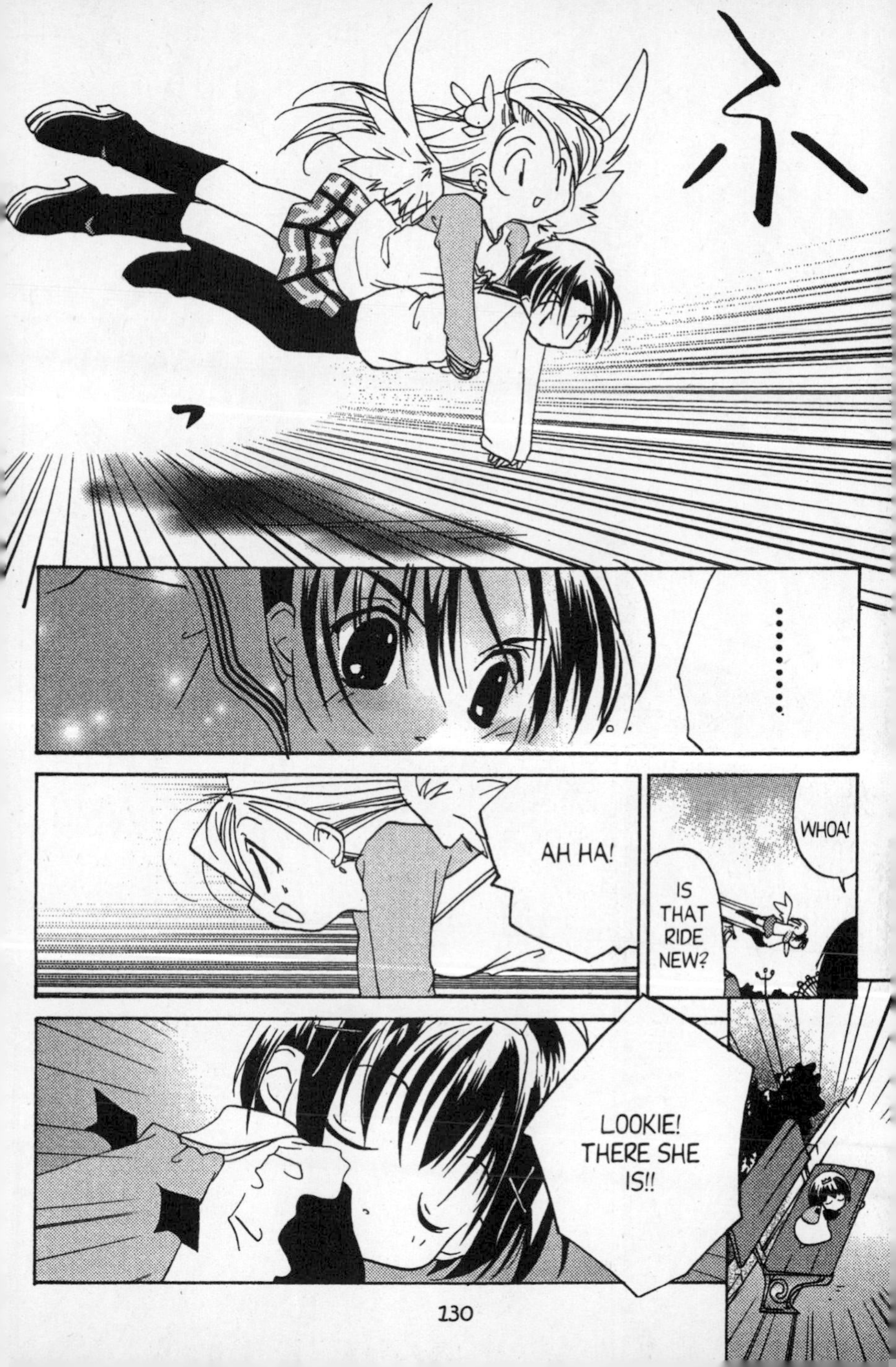
ふ
……
WHOA!
IS THAT RIDE NEW?
AH HA!
LOOKIE! THERE SHE IS!!

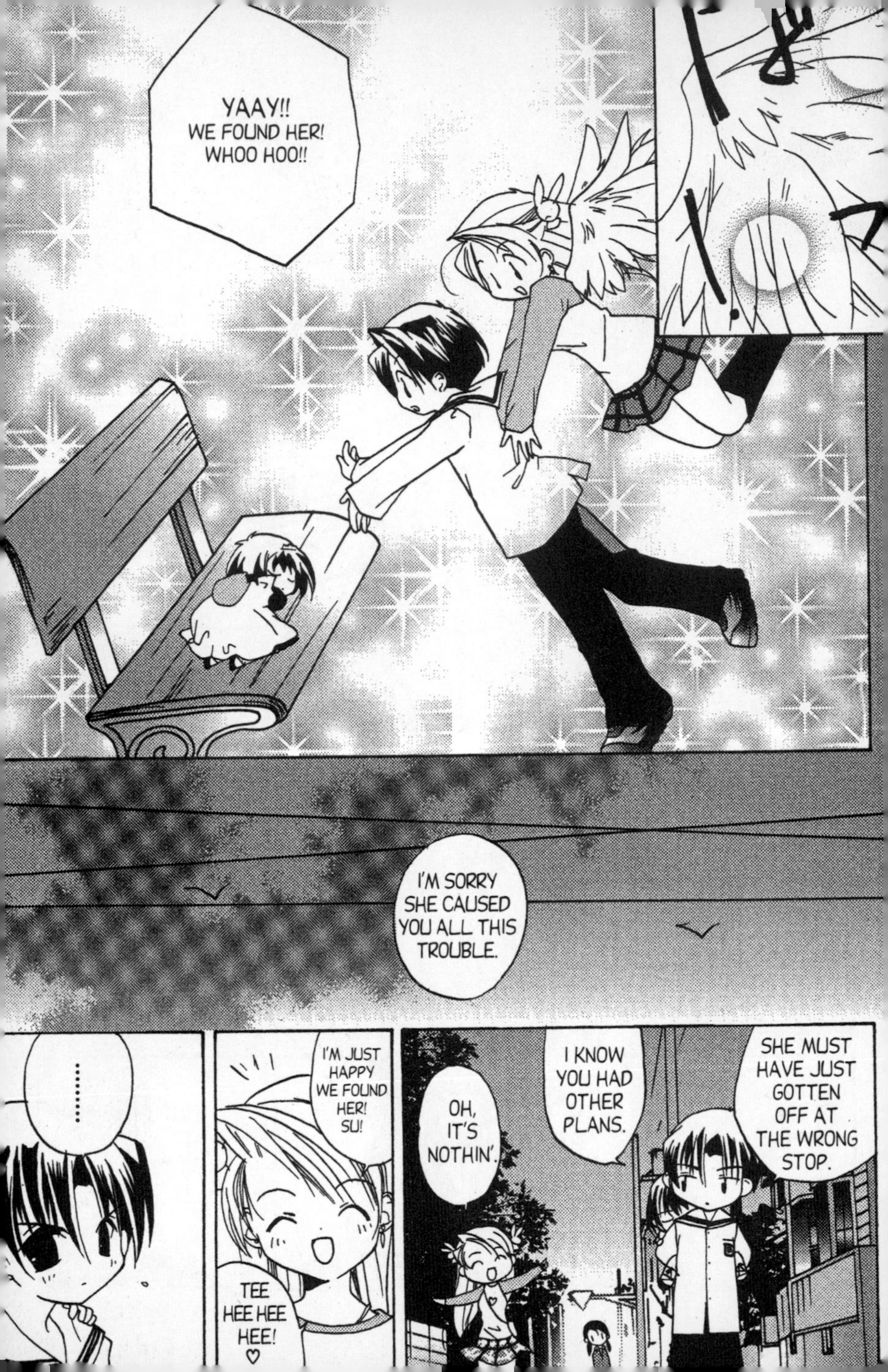
YAAY!! WE FOUND HER! WHOO HOO!!
I'M SORRY SHE CAUSED YOU ALL THIS TROUBLE.
SHE MUST HAVE JUST GOTTEN OFF AT THE WRONG STOP.
I KNOW YOU HAD OTHER PLANS.
OH, IT'S NOTHIN'.
I'M JUST HAPPY WE FOUND HER! SU!
TEE HEE HEE HEE! ♡
......

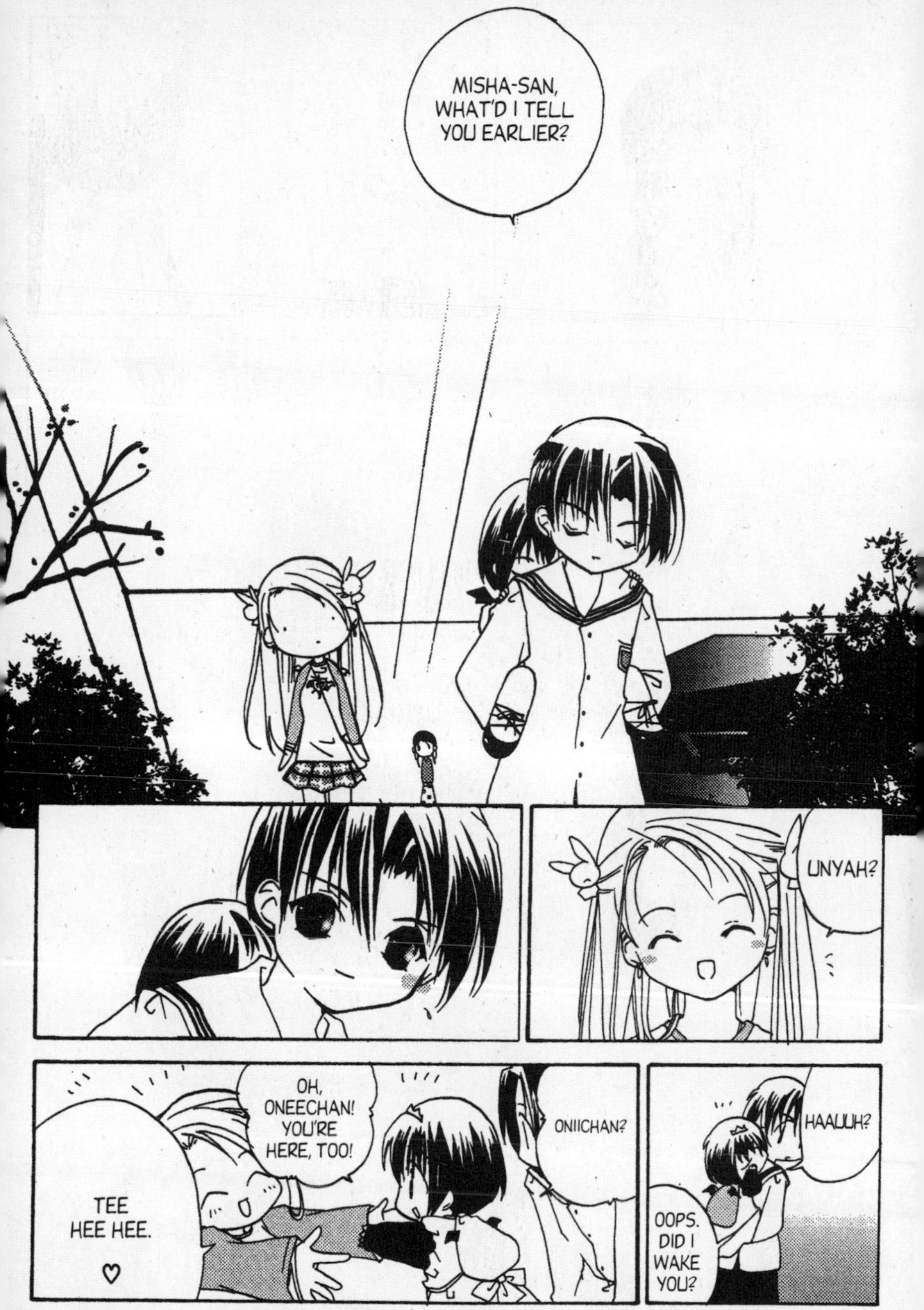
MISHA-SAN, WHAT'D I TELL YOU EARLIER?
UNYAH?
HAAUUH?
OOPS. DID I WAKE YOU?
ONIICHAN?
OH, ONEECHAN! YOU'RE HERE, TOO!
TEE HEE HEE. ♡

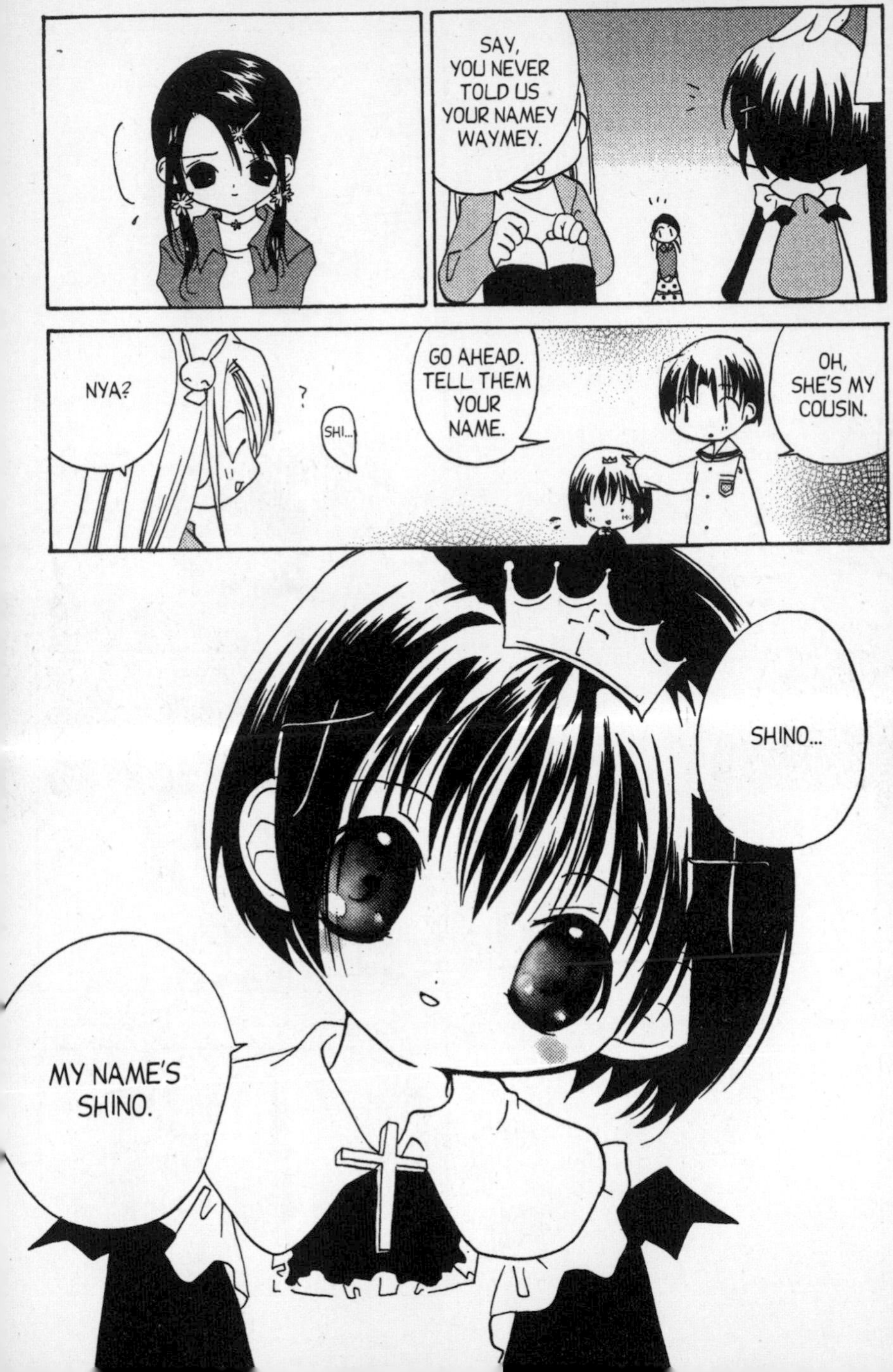
SAY, YOU NEVER TOLD US YOUR NAMEY WAYMEY.
OH, SHE'S MY COUSIN.
GO AHEAD. TELL THEM YOUR NAME.
SHI...
NYA?
SHINO...
MY NAME'S SHINO.

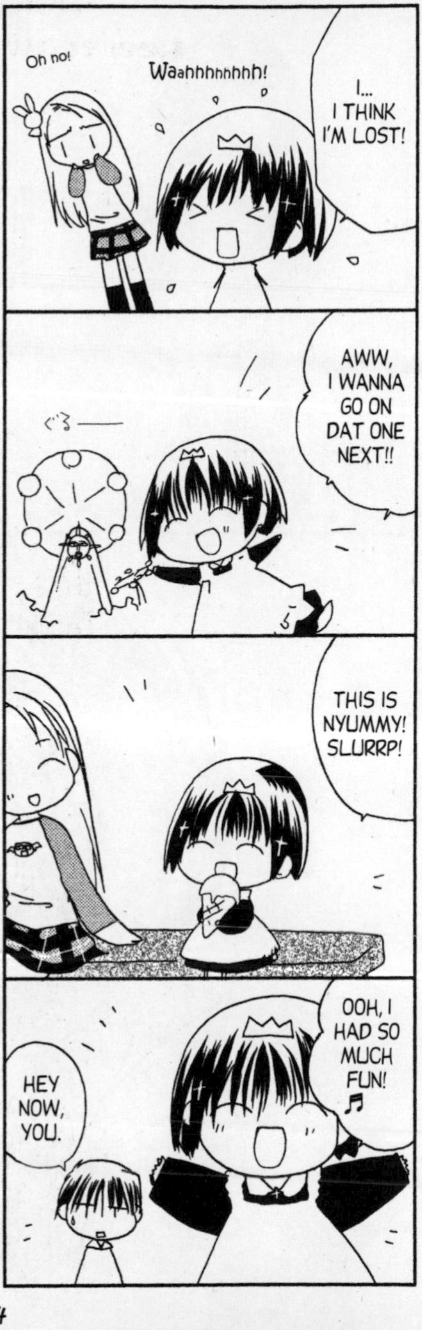
I... I THINK I'M LOST!
Waahhhhhhhh!
Oh no!
AWW, I WANNA GO ON DAT ONE NEXT!!
THIS IS NYUMMY! SLURRP!
OOH, I HAD SO MUCH FUN! ♬
HEY NOW, YOU.

Lesson 24
How to Walk to School

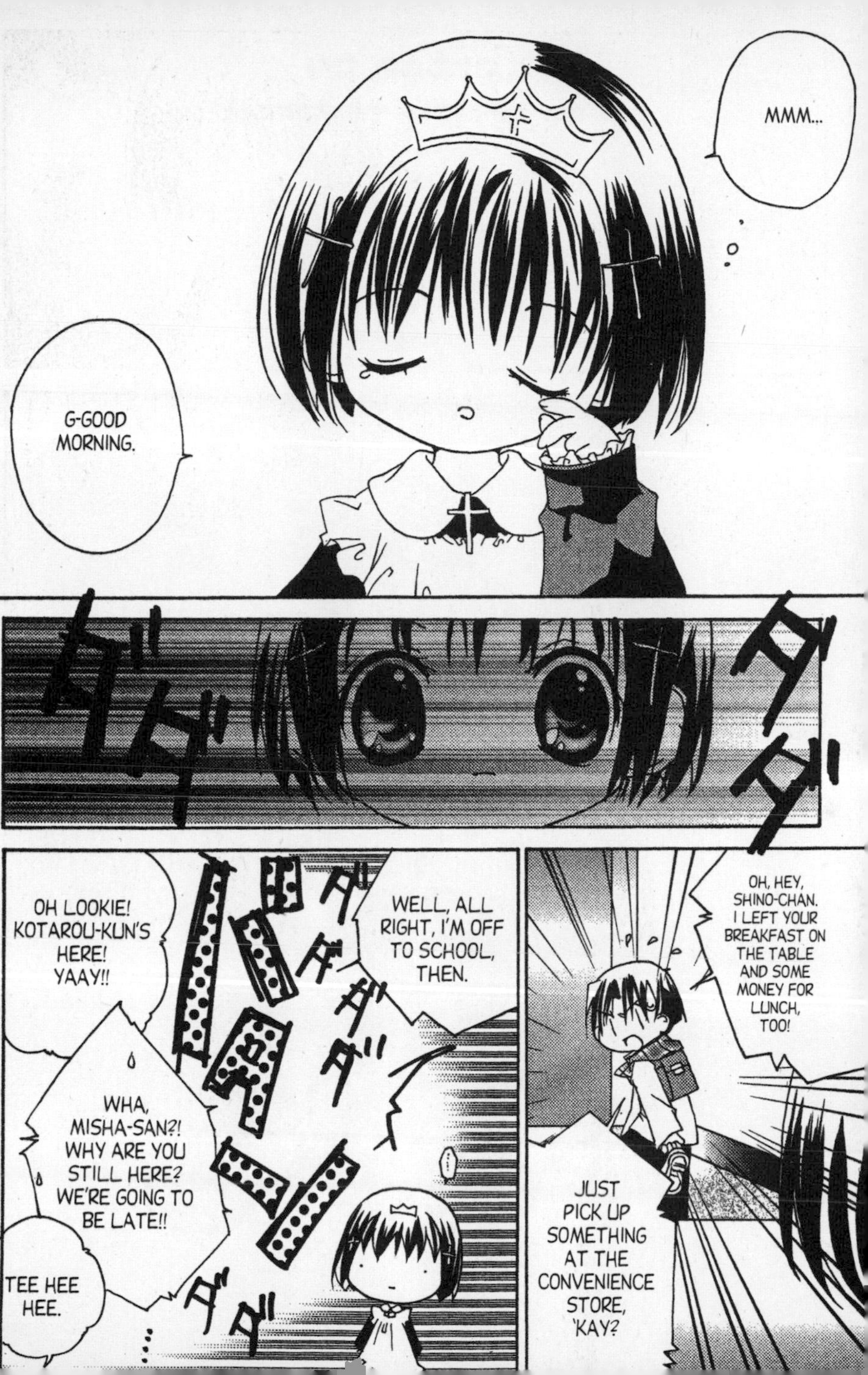
MMM...
G-GOOD MORNING.
OH, HEY, SHINO-CHAN. I LEFT YOUR BREAKFAST ON THE TABLE AND SOME MONEY FOR LUNCH, TOO!
JUST PICK UP SOMETHING AT THE CONVENIENCE STORE, 'KAY?
WELL, ALL RIGHT, I'M OFF TO SCHOOL, THEN.
OH LOOKIE! KOTAROU-KUN'S HERE! YAAY!!
WHA, MISHA-SAN?! WHY ARE YOU STILL HERE? WE'RE GOING TO BE LATE!!
TEE HEE HEE.

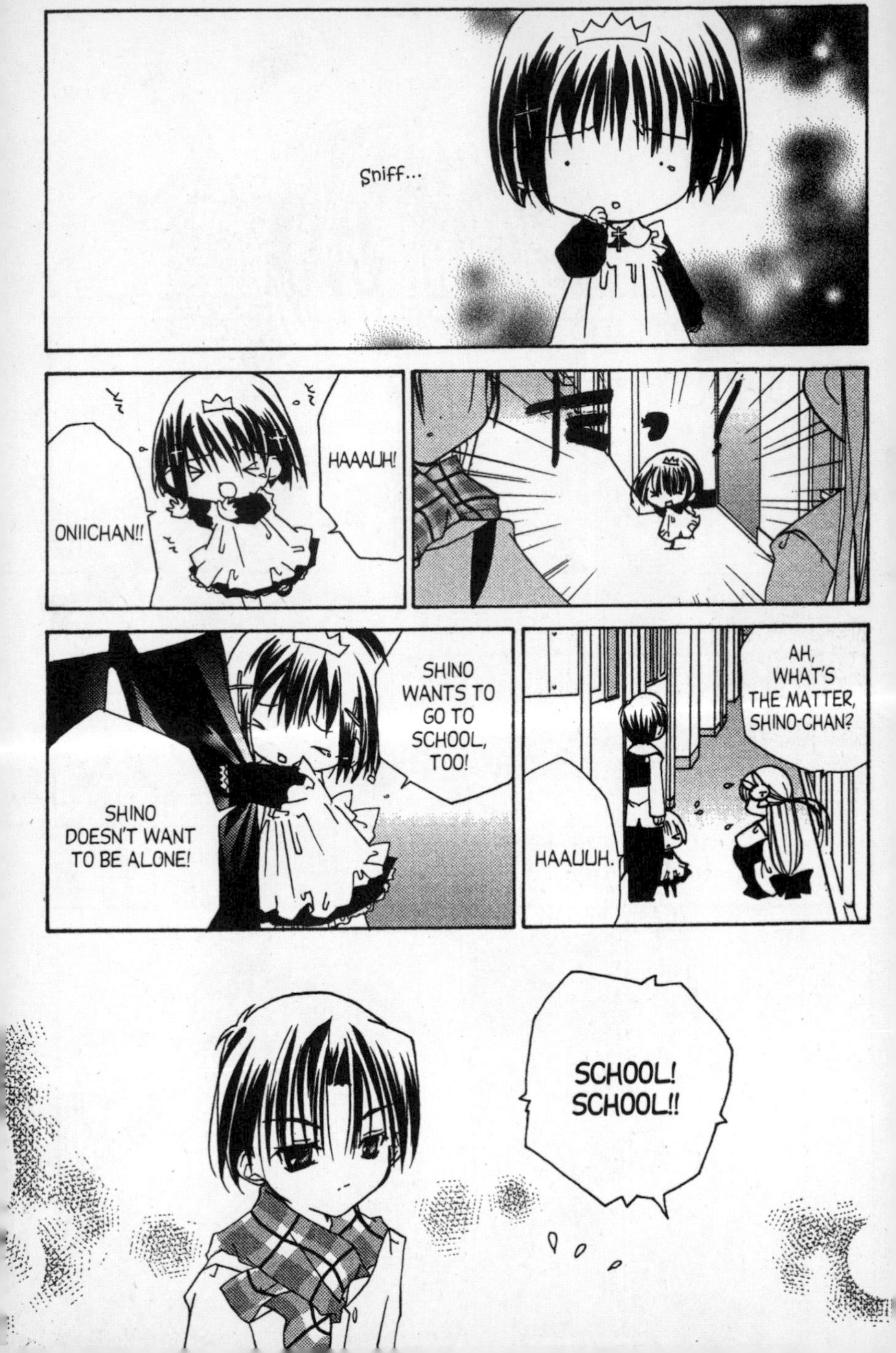
Sniff...
HAAAUH!
ONIICHAN!!
AH, WHAT'S THE MATTER, SHINO-CHAN?
HAAUUH.
SHINO WANTS TO GO TO SCHOOL, TOO!
SHINO DOESN'T WANT TO BE ALONE!
SCHOOL! SCHOOL!!

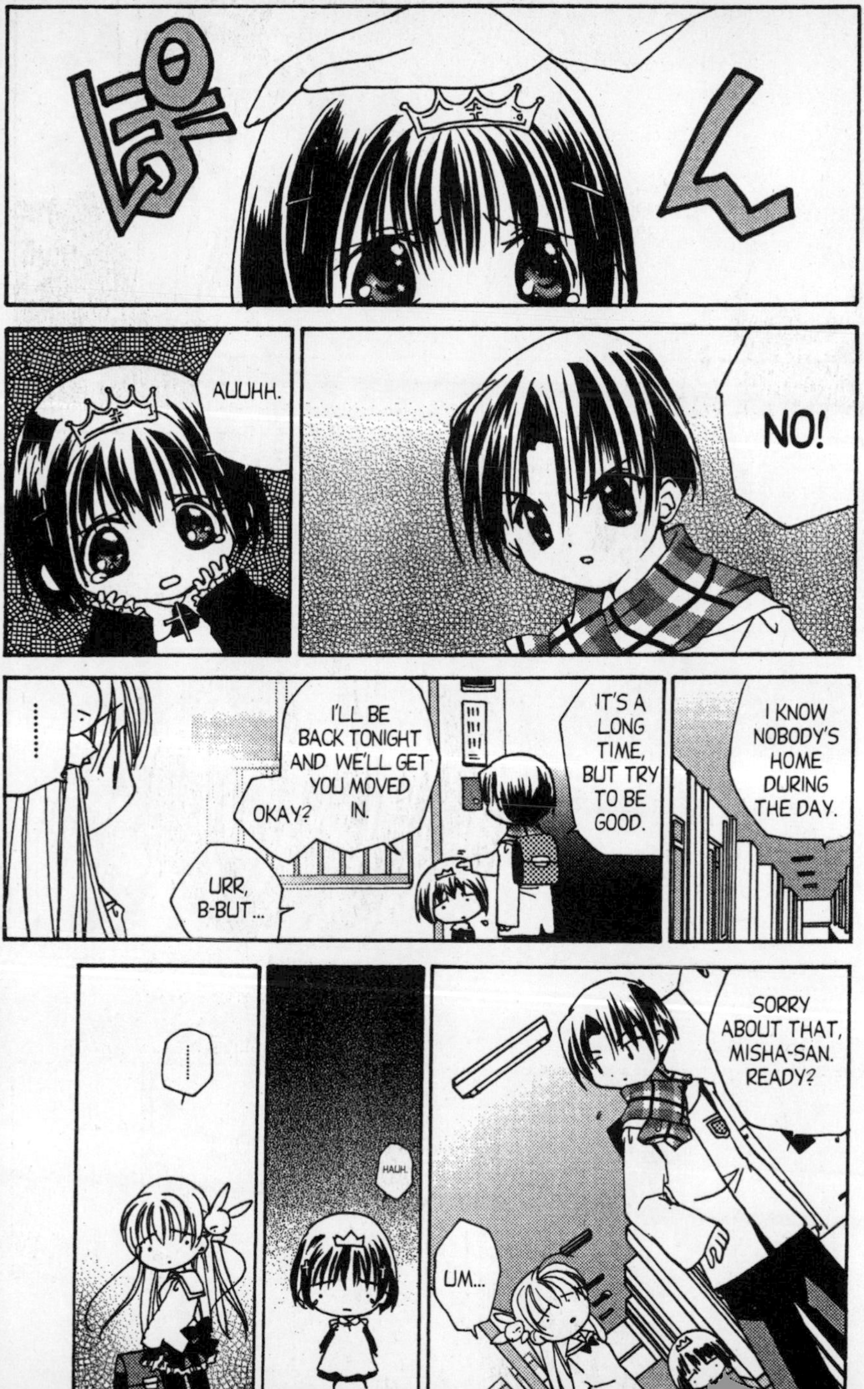
ぽん
NO!
AUUHH.
I KNOW NOBODY'S HOME DURING THE DAY.
IT'S A LONG TIME, BUT TRY TO BE GOOD.
I'LL BE BACK TONIGHT AND WE'LL GET YOU MOVED IN.
OKAY?
URR, B-BUT...
....
SORRY ABOUT THAT, MISHA-SAN. READY?
UM...
HAUH.
......

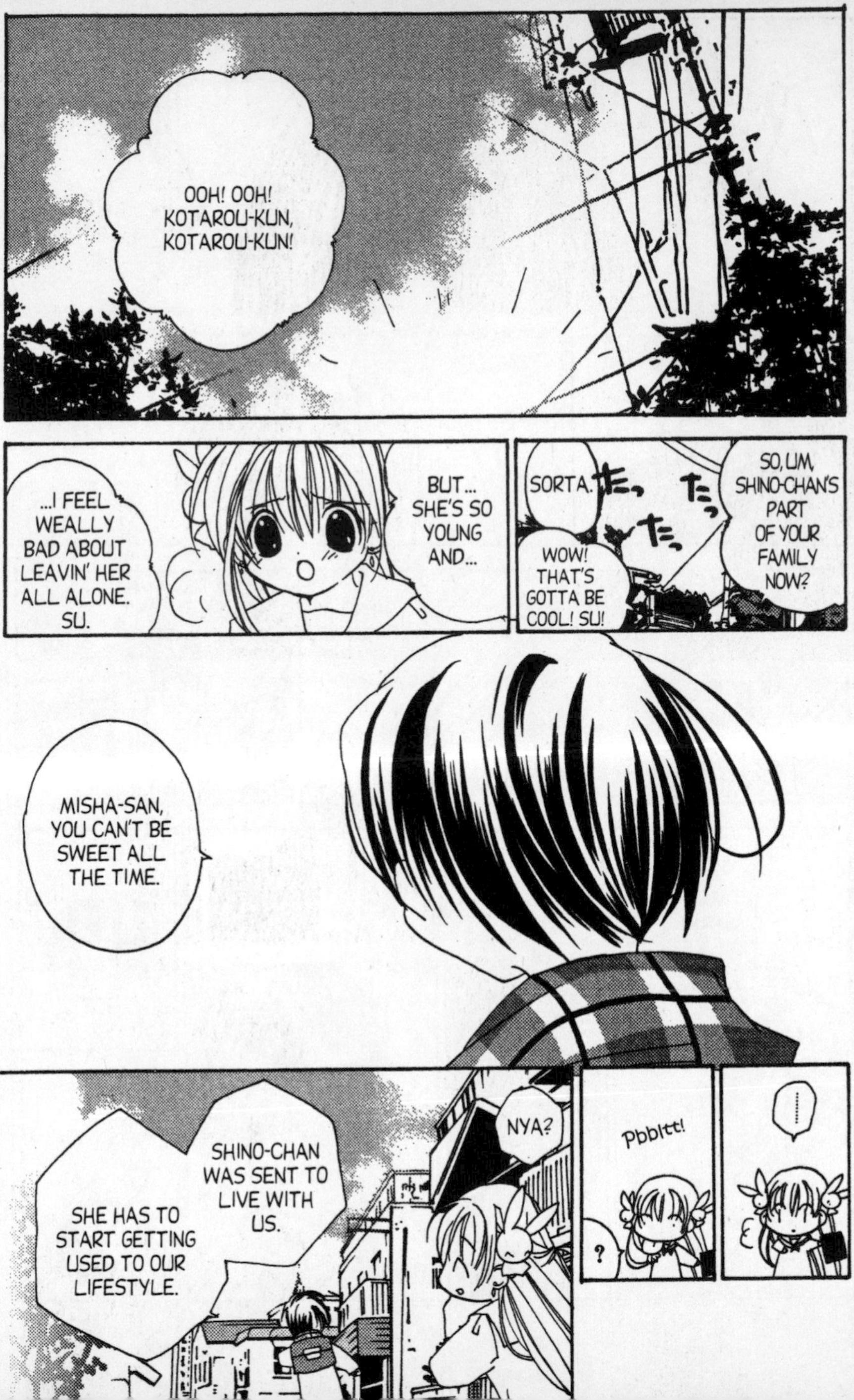
OOH! OOH! KOTAROU-KUN, KOTAROU-KUN!
SO, UM, SHINO-CHAN'S PART OF YOUR FAMILY NOW?
SORTA.
WOW! THAT'S GOTTA BE COOL! SU!
BUT... SHE'S SO YOUNG AND...
...I FEEL WEALLY BAD ABOUT LEAVIN' HER ALL ALONE. SU.
MISHA-SAN, YOU CAN'T BE SWEET ALL THE TIME.
...!
Pbbltt!
?
NYA?
SHINO-CHAN WAS SENT TO LIVE WITH US.
SHE HAS TO START GETTING USED TO OUR LIFESTYLE.

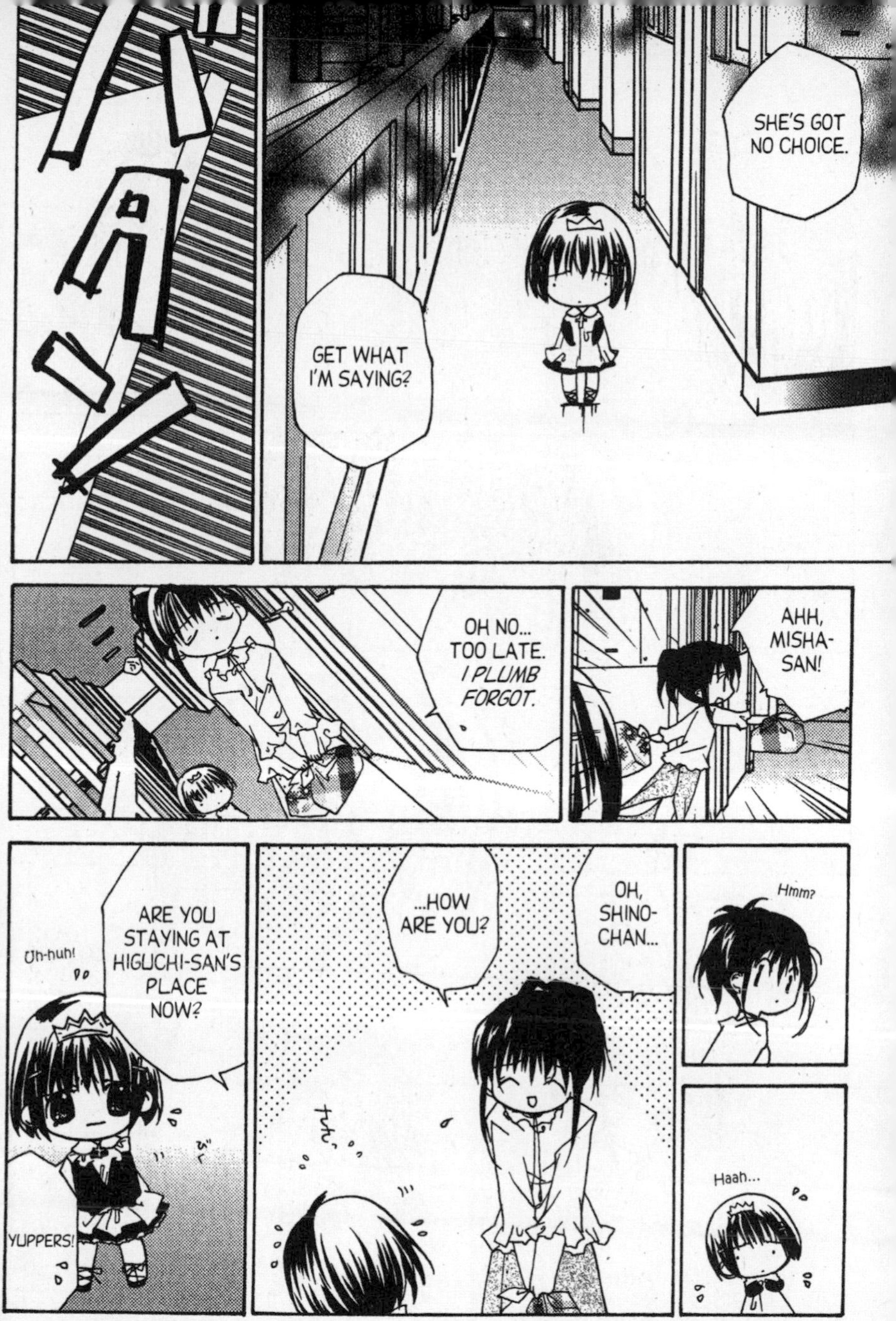

SHE'S GOT NO CHOICE.
GET WHAT I'M SAYING?
AHH, MISHA-SAN!
OH NO... TOO LATE. *I PLUMB FORGOT.*
Hmm?
Haah...
OH, SHINO-CHAN...
...HOW ARE YOU?
ARE YOU STAYING AT HIGUCHI-SAN'S PLACE NOW?
Uh-huh!
YUPPERS!

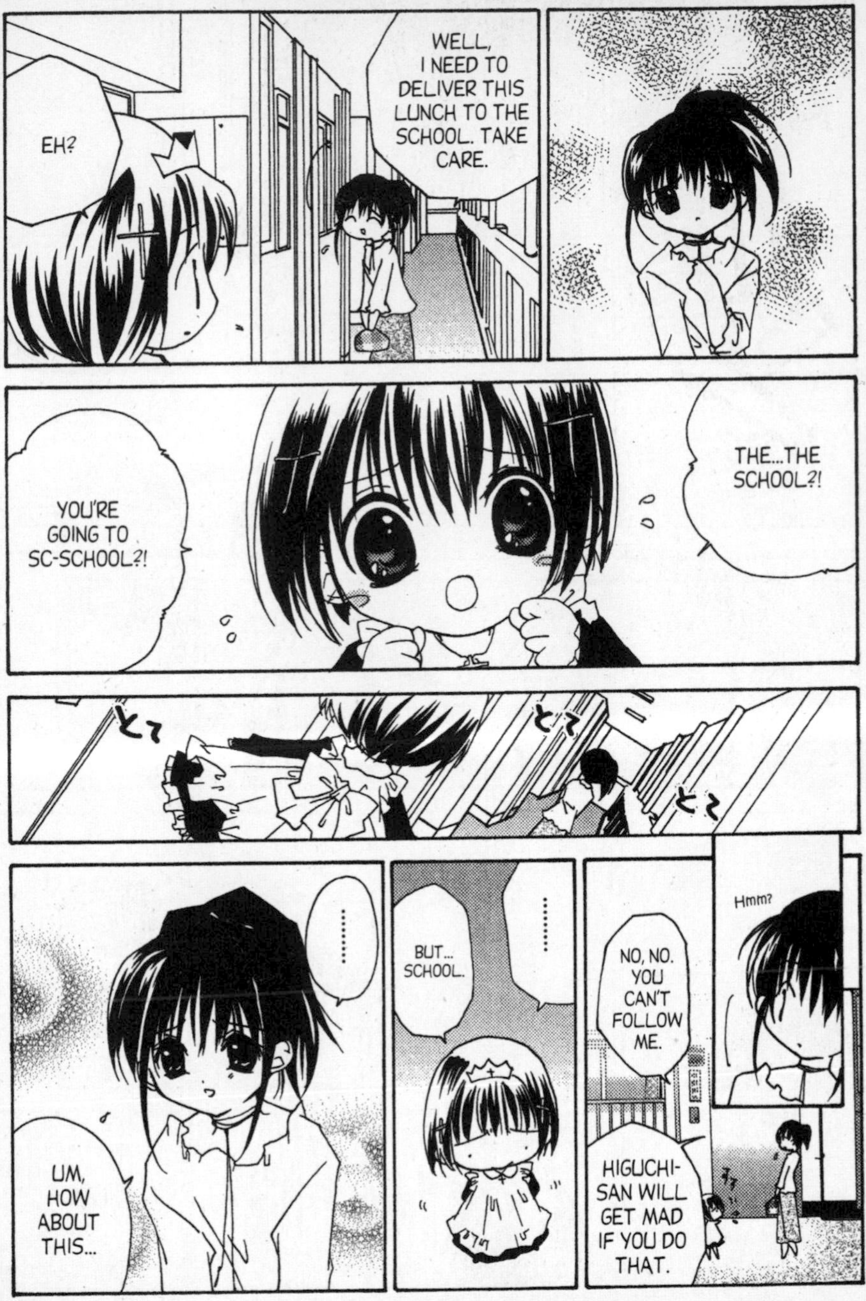
WELL, I NEED TO DELIVER THIS LUNCH TO THE SCHOOL. TAKE CARE.
EH?
THE...THE SCHOOL?!
YOU'RE GOING TO SC-SCHOOL?!
とて
とて
とて
Hmm?
NO, NO. YOU CAN'T FOLLOW ME.
HIGUCHI-SAN WILL GET MAD IF YOU DO THAT.
....
BUT... SCHOOL.
....
UM, HOW ABOUT THIS...

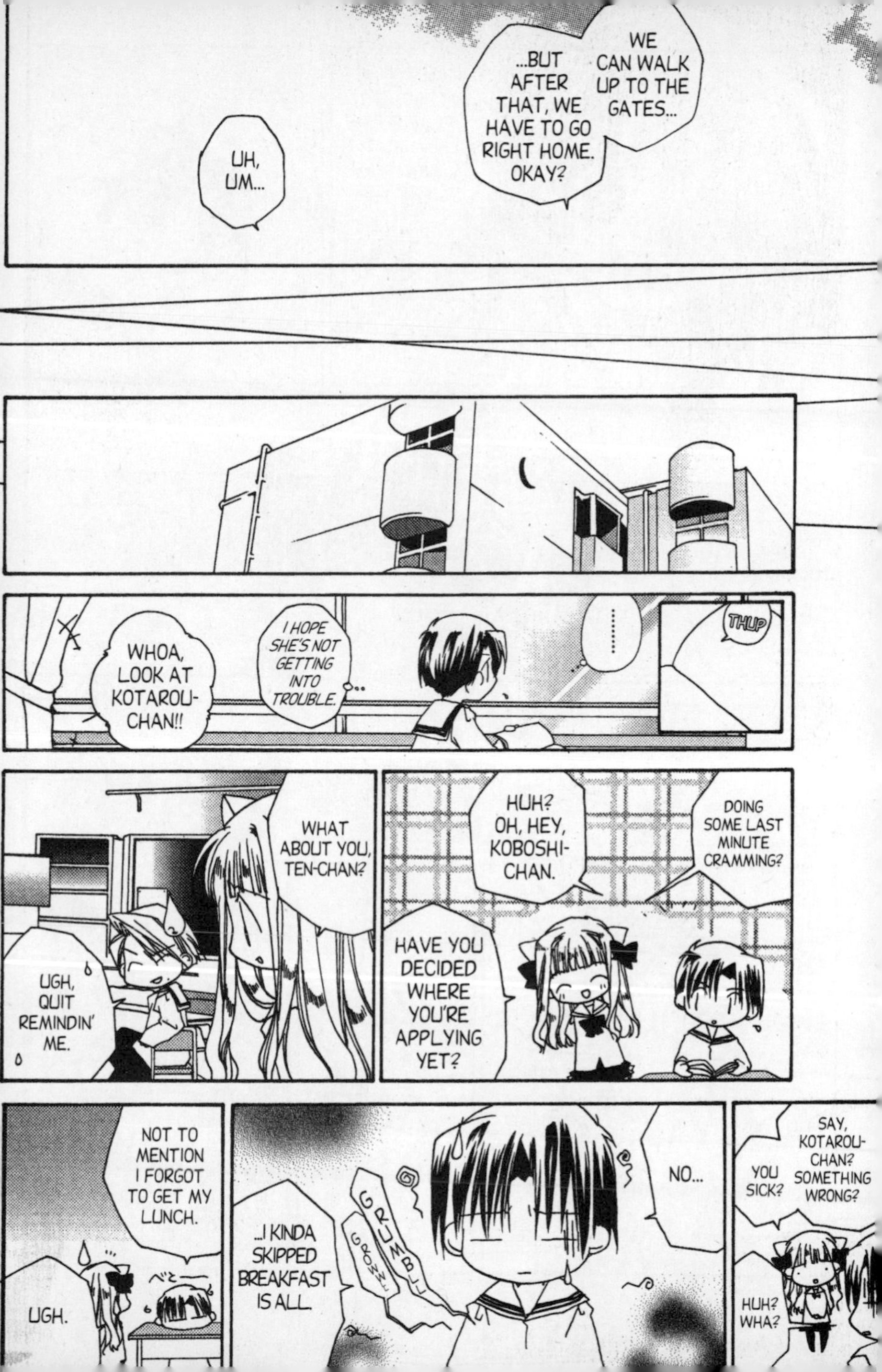
WE CAN WALK UP TO THE GATES...
...BUT AFTER THAT, WE HAVE TO GO RIGHT HOME. OKAY?
UH, UM...
THUP
......
I HOPE SHE'S NOT GETTING INTO TROUBLE.
WHOA, LOOK AT KOTAROU-CHAN!!
DOING SOME LAST MINUTE CRAMMING?
HUH? OH, HEY, KOBOSHI-CHAN.
HAVE YOU DECIDED WHERE YOU'RE APPLYING YET?
WHAT ABOUT YOU, TEN-CHAN?
UGH, QUIT REMINDIN' ME.
SAY, KOTAROU-CHAN? SOMETHING WRONG?
YOU SICK?
HUH? WHA?
NO...
GRUMBLL
GROWLL
...I KINDA SKIPPED BREAKFAST IS ALL.
NOT TO MENTION I FORGOT TO GET MY LUNCH.
UGH.

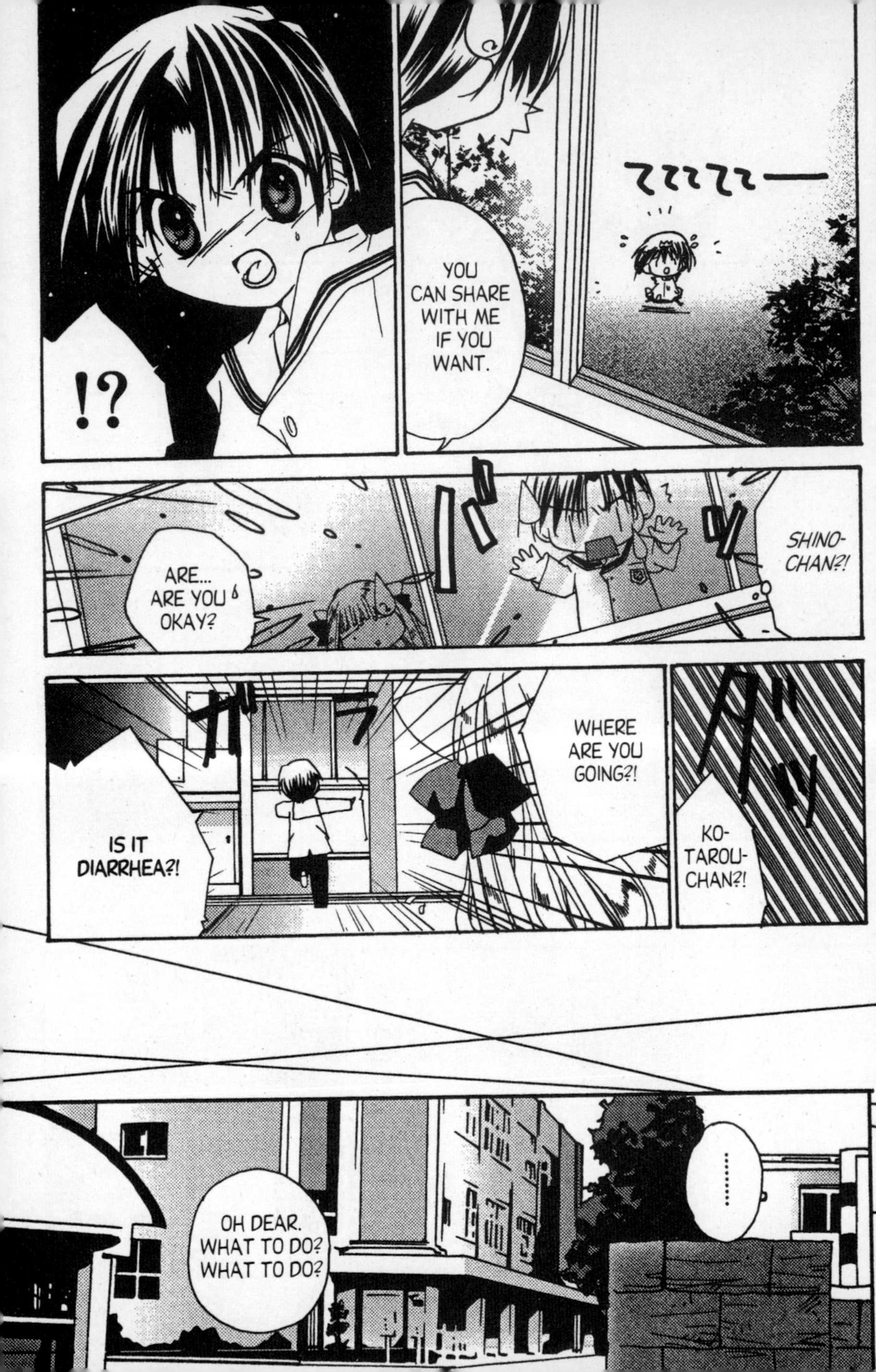
てててててー
YOU CAN SHARE WITH ME IF YOU WANT.
!?
SHINO-CHAN?!
ARE... ARE YOU OKAY?
KO-TAROU-CHAN?!
WHERE ARE YOU GOING?!
IS IT DIARRHEA?!
....
OH DEAR. WHAT TO DO? WHAT TO DO?

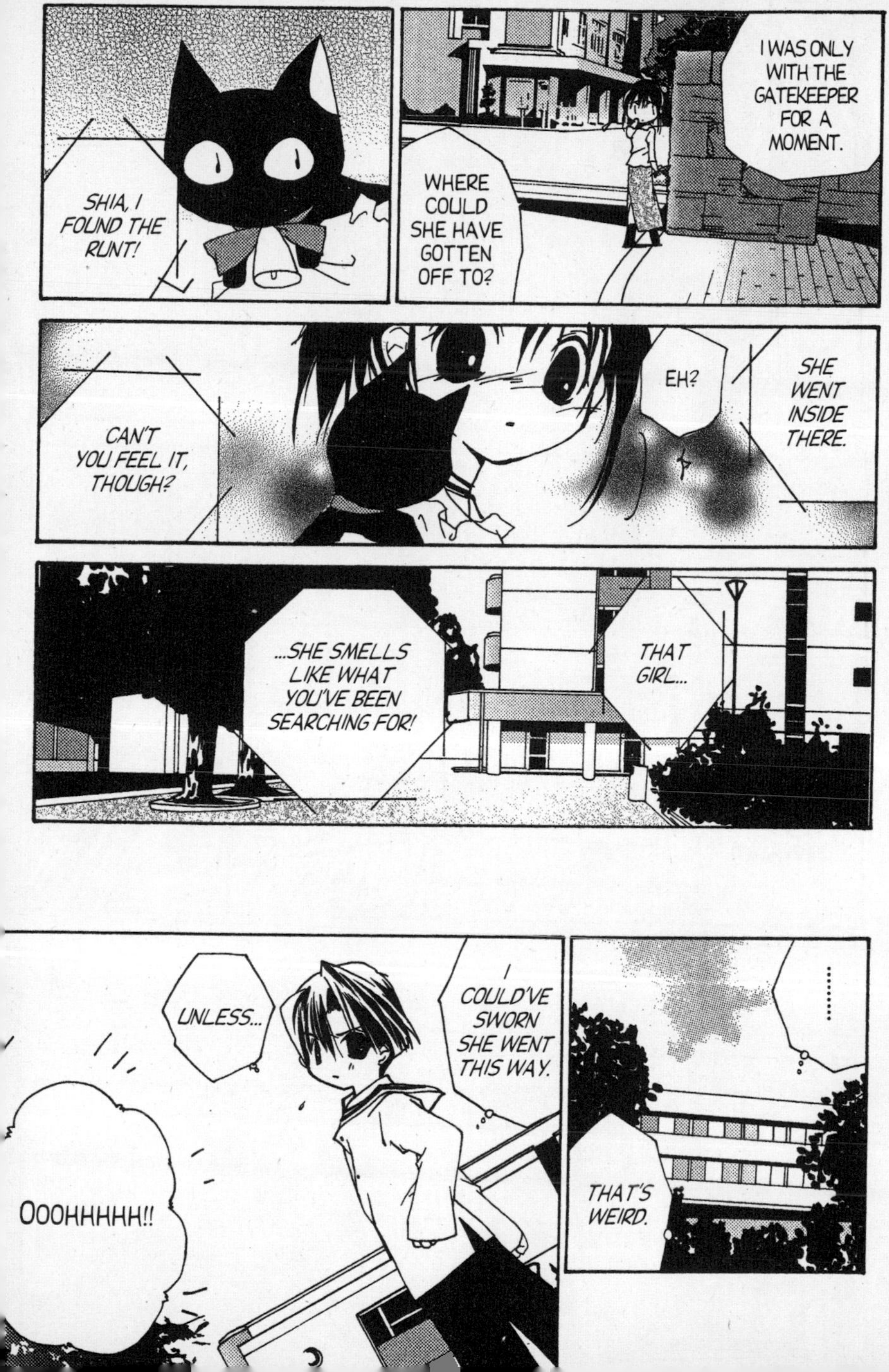
I WAS ONLY WITH THE GATEKEEPER FOR A MOMENT.
WHERE COULD SHE HAVE GOTTEN OFF TO?
SHIA, I FOUND THE RUNT!
SHE WENT INSIDE THERE.
EH?
CAN'T YOU FEEL IT, THOUGH?
THAT GIRL...
...SHE SMELLS LIKE WHAT YOU'VE BEEN SEARCHING FOR!
....
THAT'S WEIRD.
I COULD'VE SWORN SHE WENT THIS WAY.
UNLESS...
OOOHHHHH!!

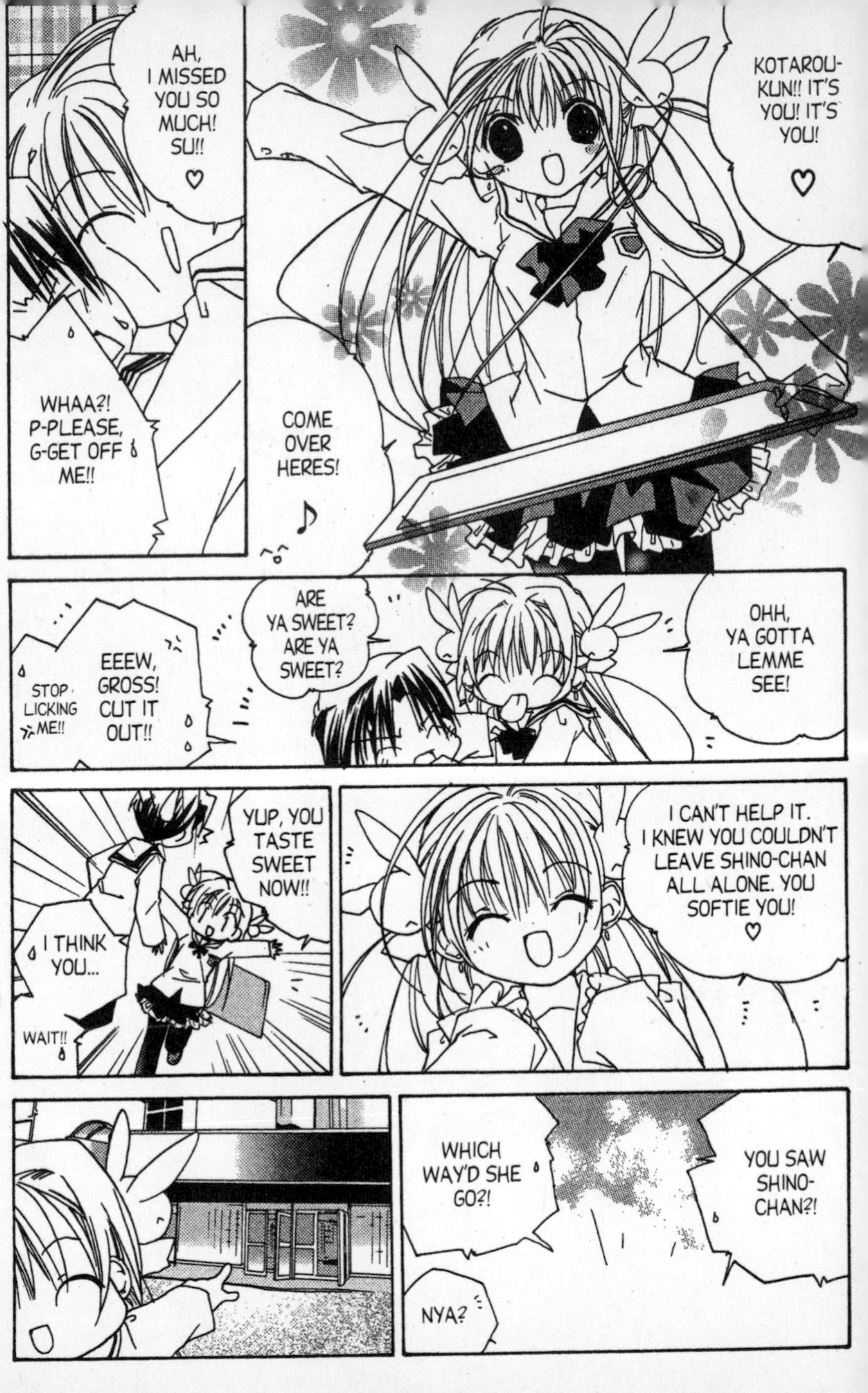
KOTAROU-KUN!! IT'S YOU! IT'S YOU! ♡
COME OVER HERES! ♪
AH, I MISSED YOU SO MUCH! SU!! ♡
WHAA?! P-PLEASE, G-GET OFF ME!!
OHH, YA GOTTA LEMME SEE!
ARE YA SWEET? ARE YA SWEET?
EEEW, GROSS! CUT IT OUT!!
STOP LICKING ME!!
I CAN'T HELP IT. I KNEW YOU COULDN'T LEAVE SHINO-CHAN ALL ALONE. YOU SOFTIE YOU! ♡
YUP, YOU TASTE SWEET NOW!!
I THINK YOU...
WAIT!!
YOU SAW SHINO-CHAN?!
WHICH WAY'D SHE GO?!
NYA?

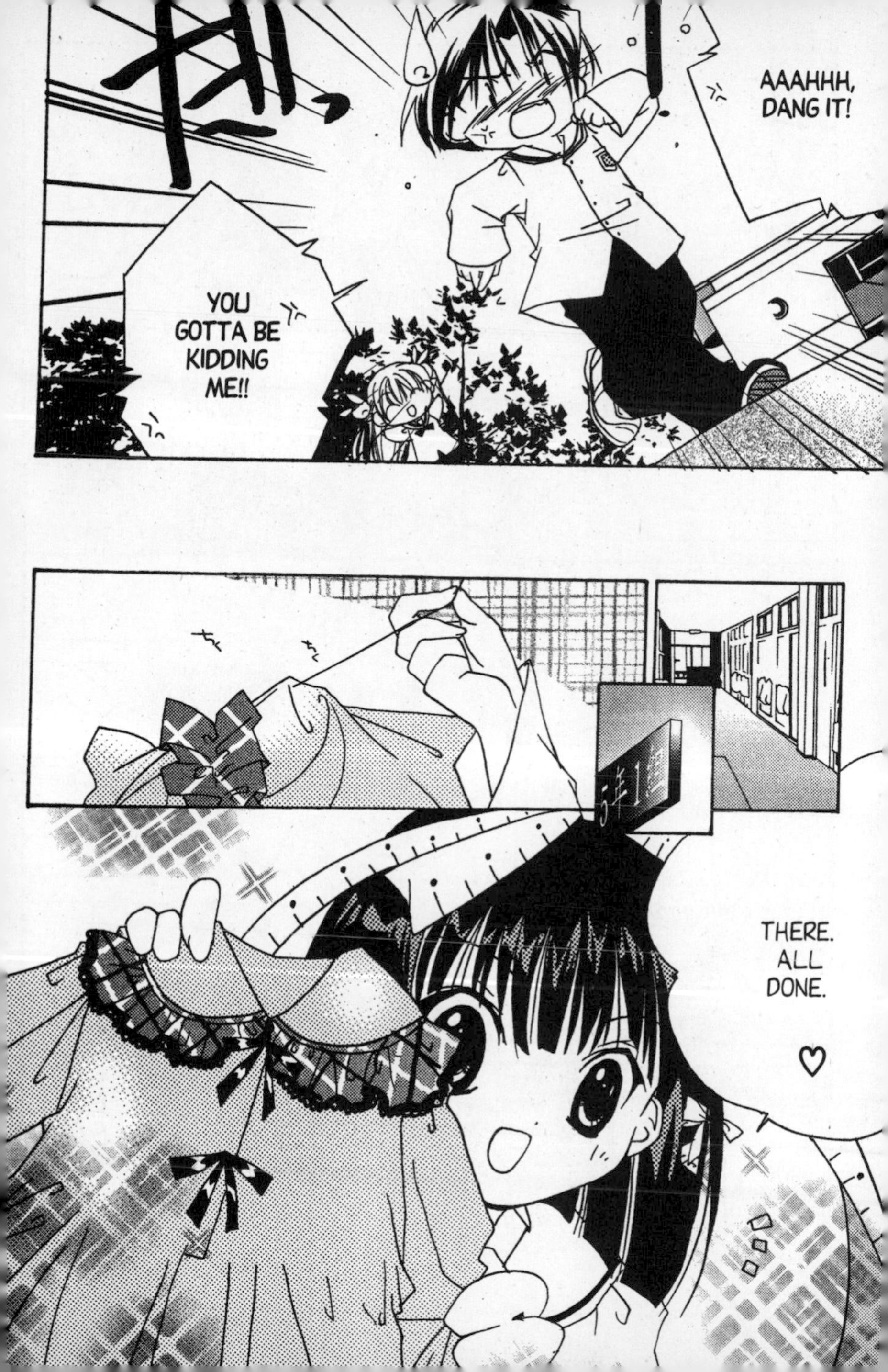
AAAHHH, DANG IT!
YOU GOTTA BE KIDDING ME!!
THERE. ALL DONE. ♥

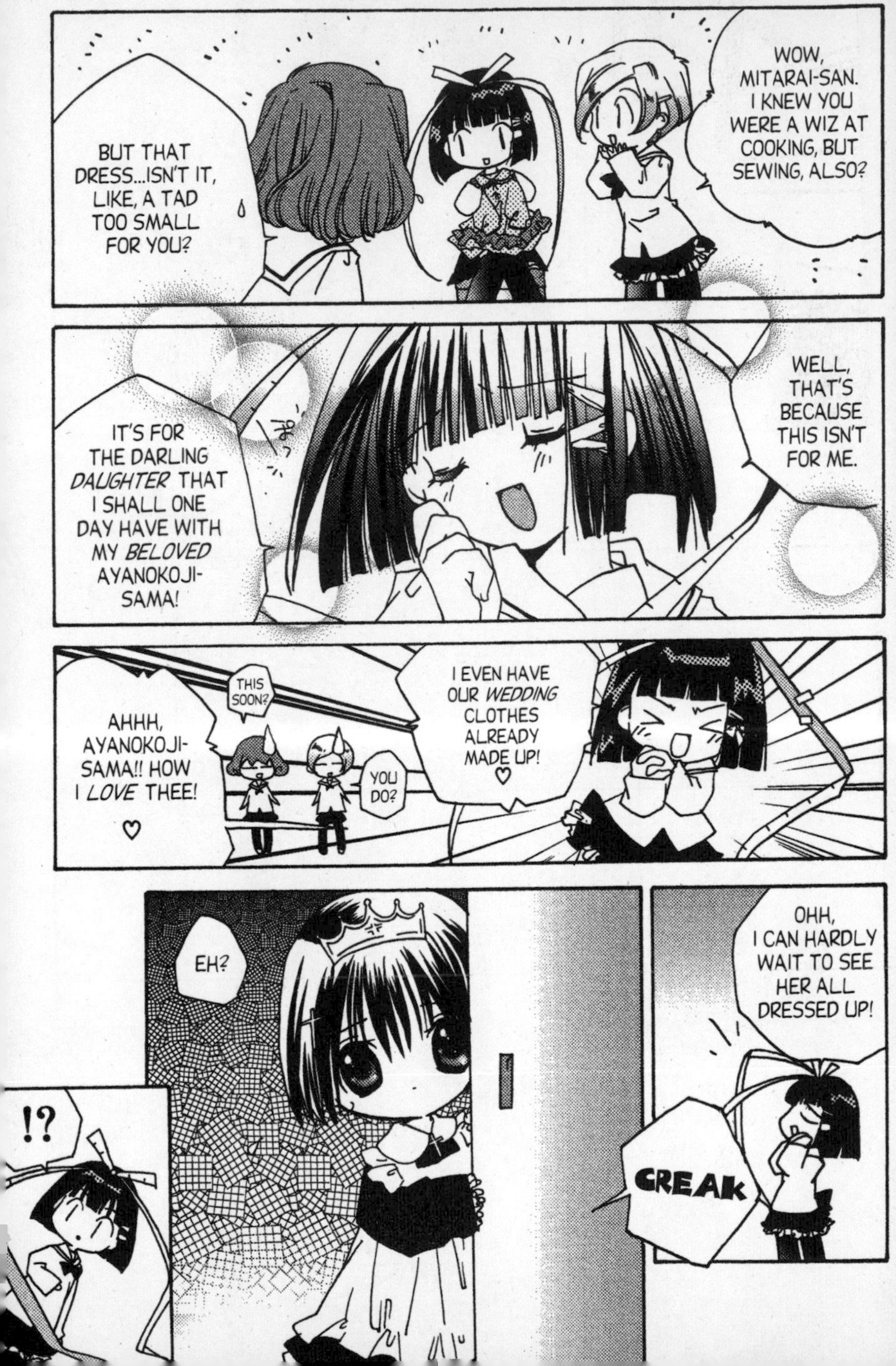
WOW, MITARAI-SAN. I KNEW YOU WERE A WIZ AT COOKING, BUT SEWING, ALSO?
BUT THAT DRESS...ISN'T IT, LIKE, A TAD TOO SMALL FOR YOU?
WELL, THAT'S BECAUSE THIS ISN'T FOR ME.
IT'S FOR THE DARLING *DAUGHTER* THAT I SHALL ONE DAY HAVE WITH MY *BELOVED* AYANOKOJI-SAMA!
I EVEN HAVE OUR *WEDDING* CLOTHES ALREADY MADE UP! ♡
YOU DO?
THIS SOON?
AHHH, AYANOKOJI-SAMA!! HOW I *LOVE* THEE! ♡
OHH, I CAN HARDLY WAIT TO SEE HER ALL DRESSED UP!
CREAK
EH?
!?

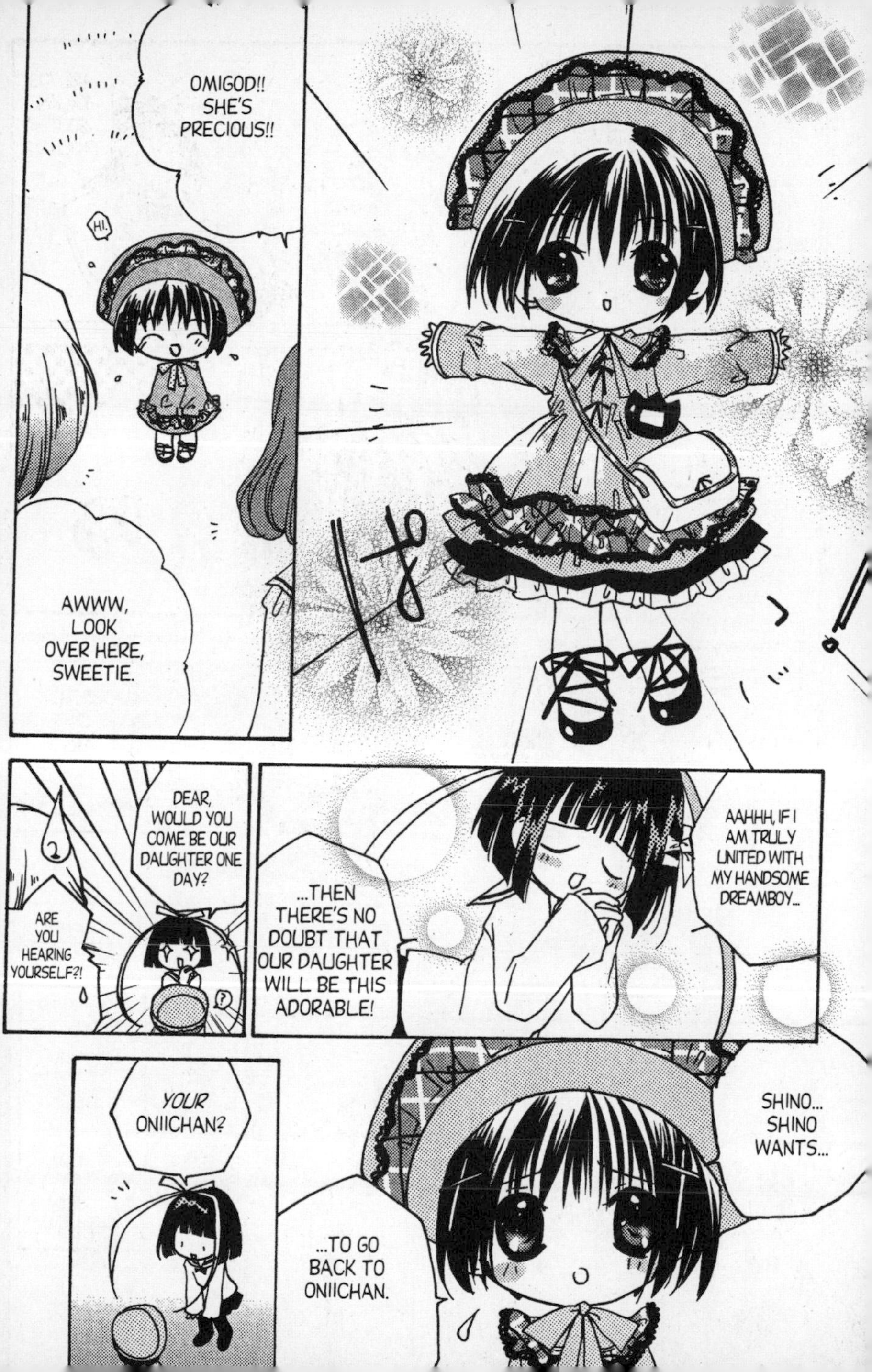
OMIGOD!! SHE'S PRECIOUS!!
HI!
AWWW, LOOK OVER HERE, SWEETIE.
AAHHH, IF I AM TRULY UNITED WITH MY HANDSOME DREAMBOY...
...THEN THERE'S NO DOUBT THAT OUR DAUGHTER WILL BE THIS ADORABLE!
DEAR, WOULD YOU COME BE OUR DAUGHTER ONE DAY?
ARE YOU HEARING YOURSELF?!
?
SHINO... SHINO WANTS...
...TO GO BACK TO ONIICHAN.
YOUR ONIICHAN?

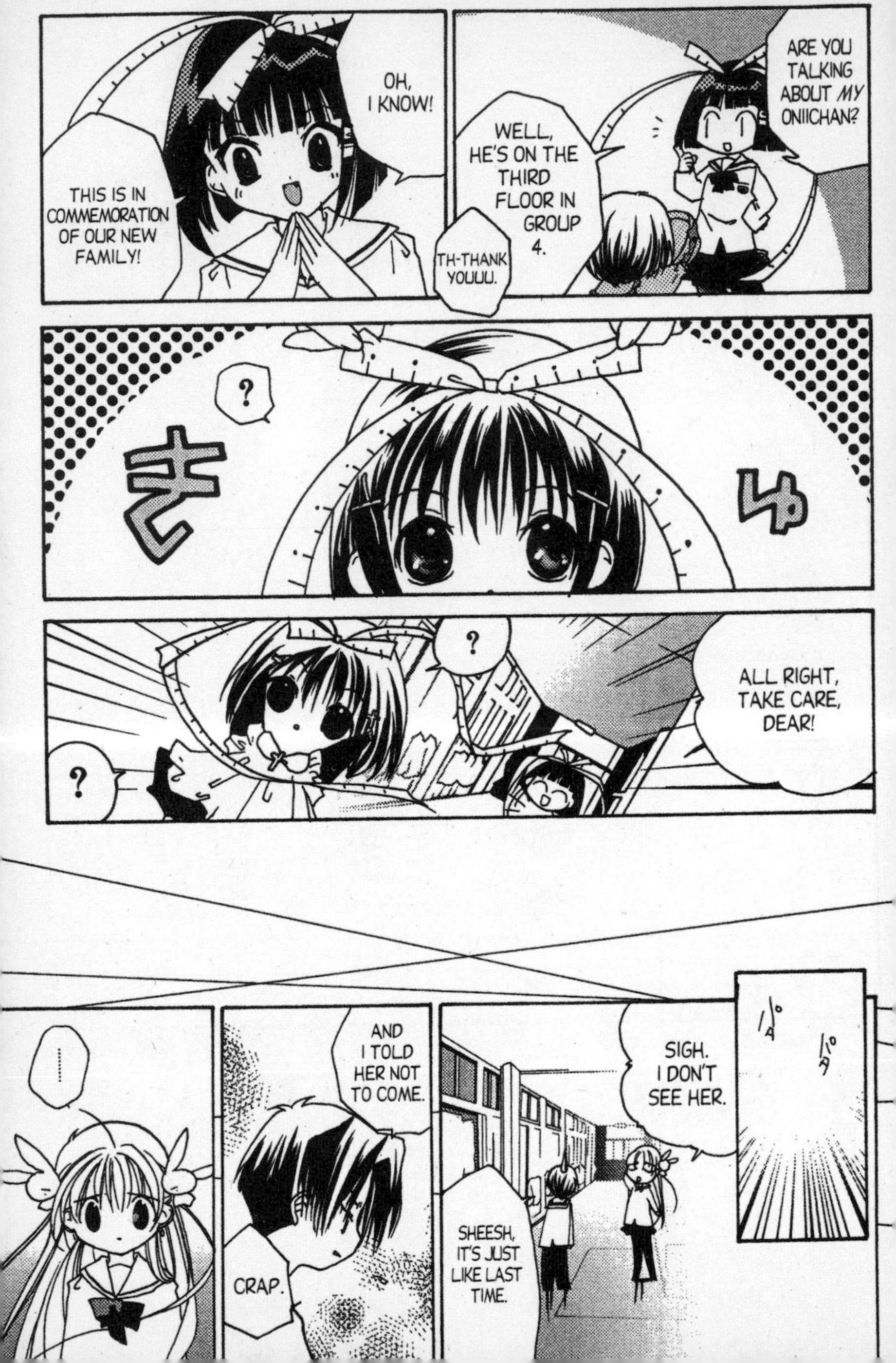
ARE YOU TALKING ABOUT *MY* ONIICHAN?
WELL, HE'S ON THE THIRD FLOOR IN GROUP 4.
TH-THANK YOUUU.
OH, I KNOW!
THIS IS IN COMMEMORATION OF OUR NEW FAMILY!
?
きゅ
ALL RIGHT, TAKE CARE, DEAR!
?
?
SIGH. I DON'T SEE HER.
SHEESH, IT'S JUST LIKE LAST TIME.
AND I TOLD HER NOT TO COME.
CRAP.
...!

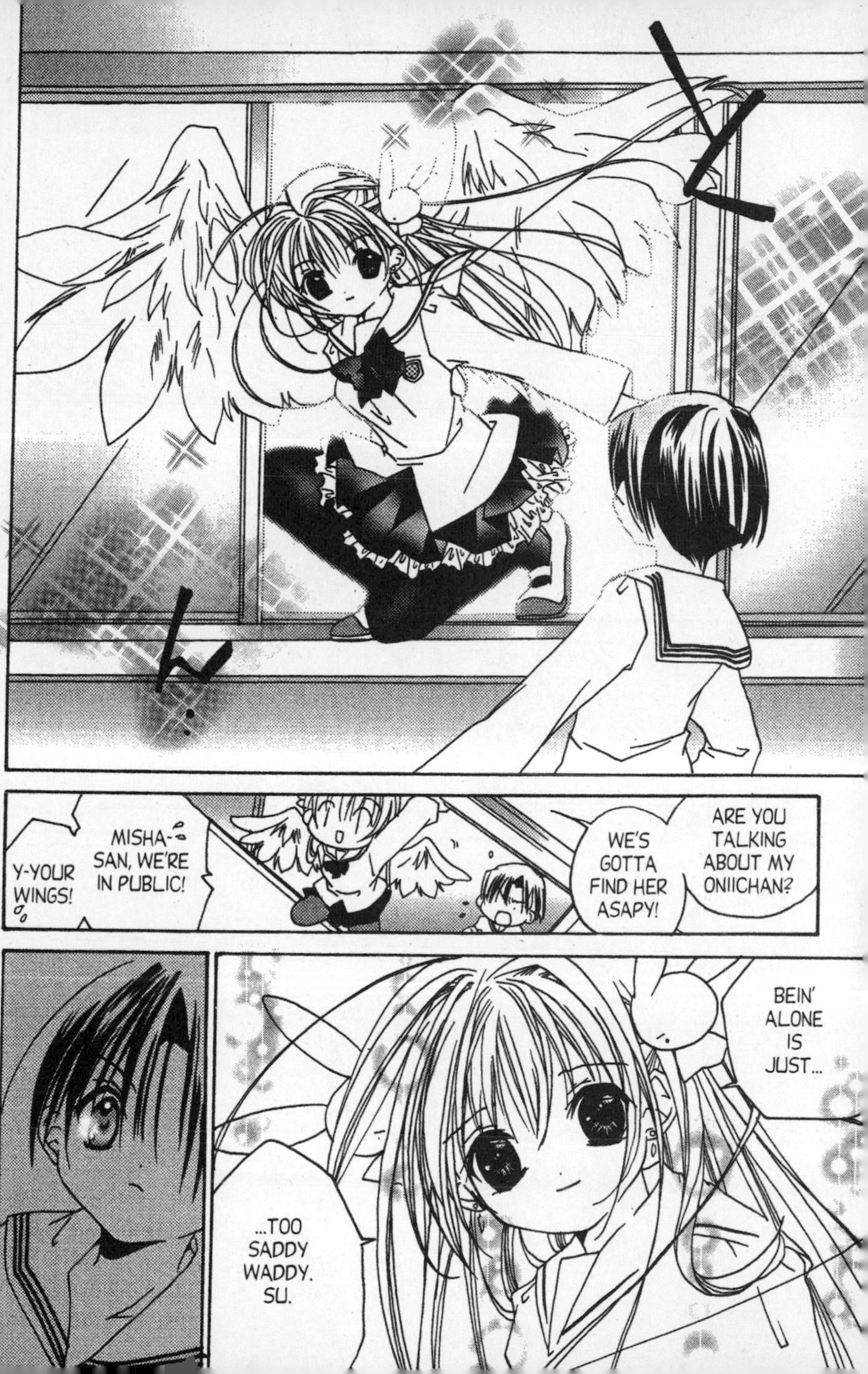
ARE YOU TALKING ABOUT MY ONIICHAN?
WE'S GOTTA FIND HER ASAPY!
MISHA-SAN, WE'RE IN PUBLIC!
Y-YOUR WINGS!
BEIN' ALONE IS JUST...
...TOO SADDY WADDY. SU.

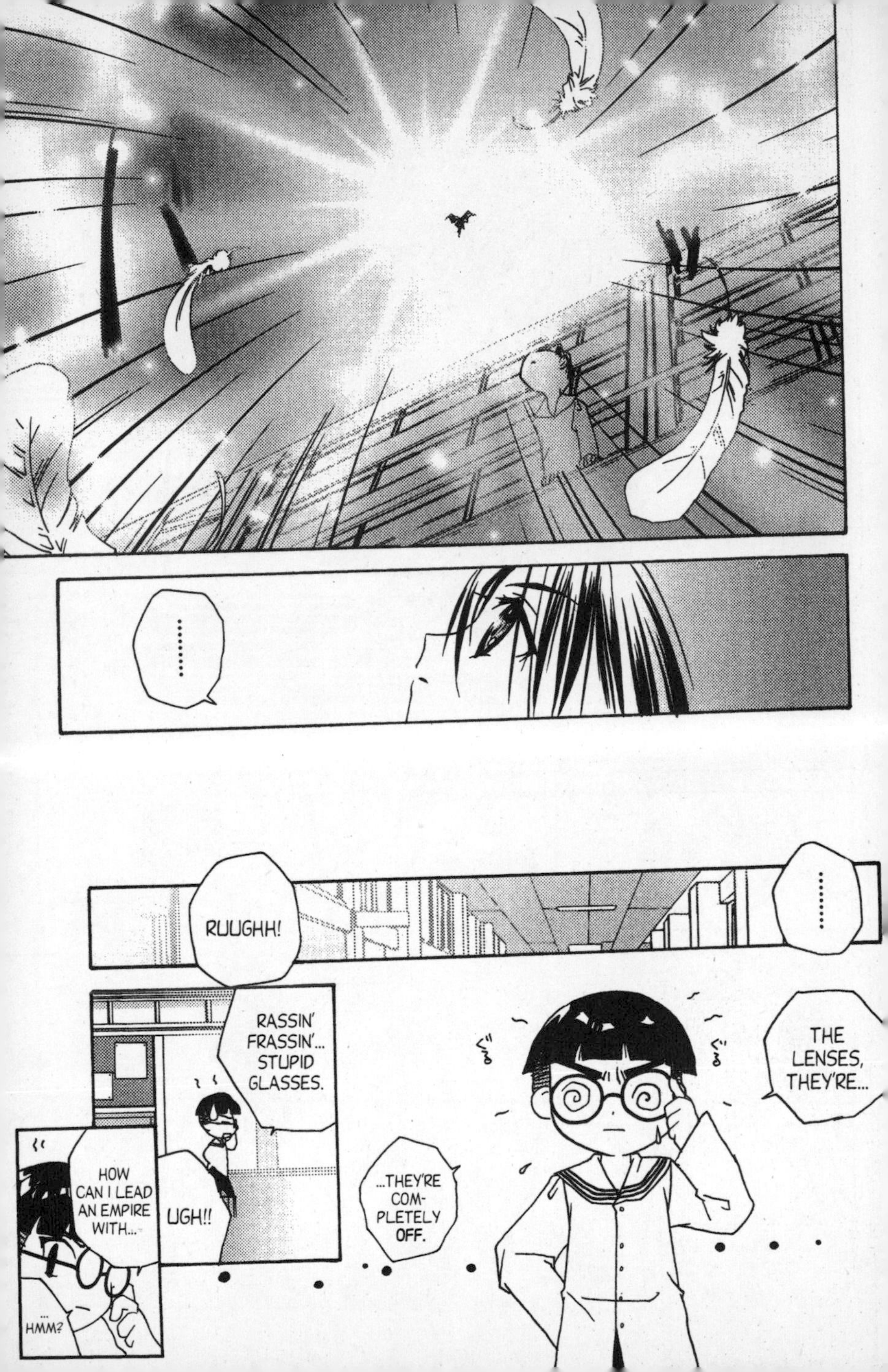
....
......
RUUGHH!
THE LENSES, THEY'RE...
...THEY'RE COM-PLETELY OFF.
RASSIN' FRASSIN'... STUPID GLASSES.
UGH!!
HOW CAN I LEAD AN EMPIRE WITH...
... HMM?

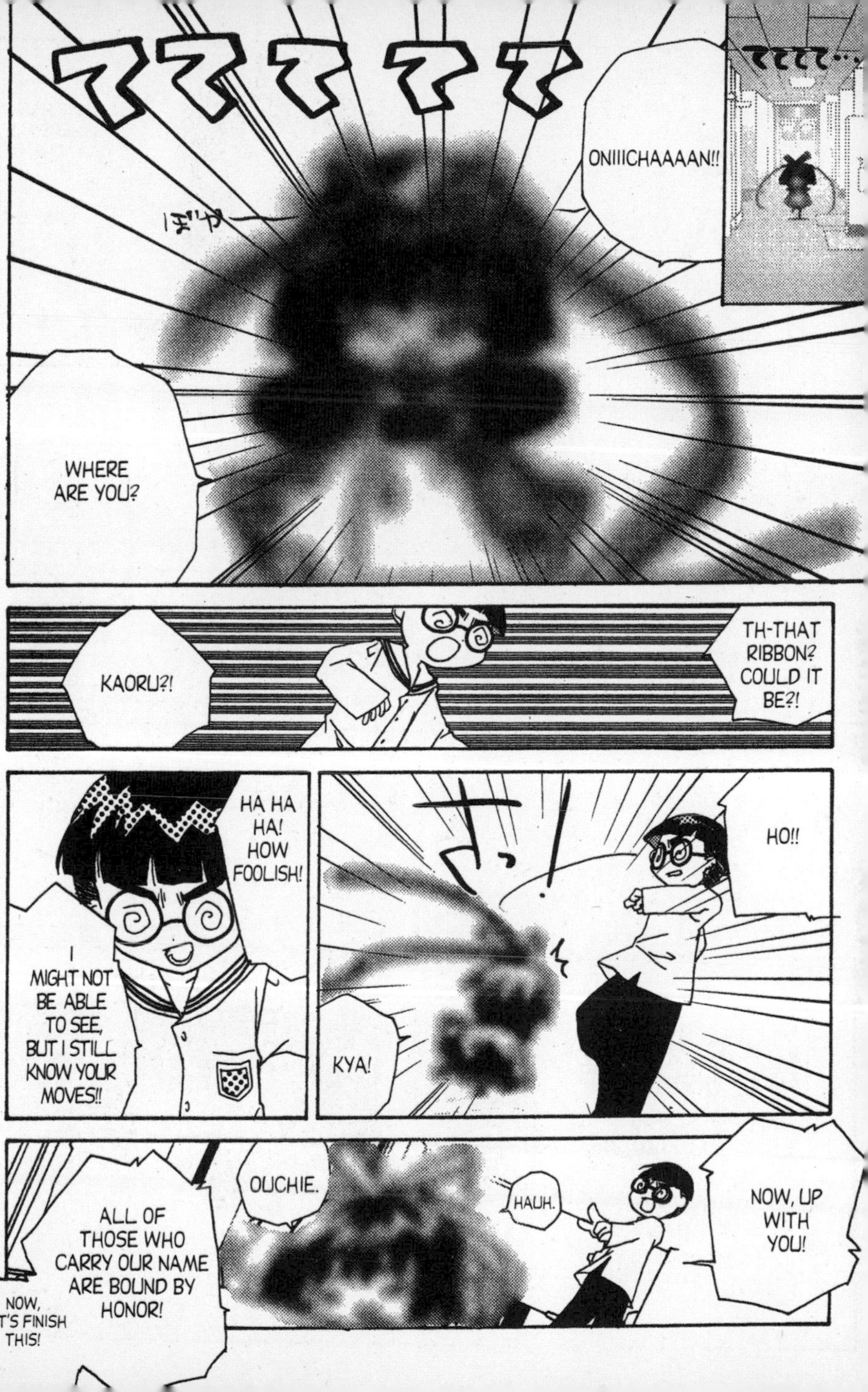

てててて…
ONIIICHAAAAN!!
WHERE ARE YOU?
TH-THAT RIBBON? COULD IT BE?!
KAORU?!
HO!!
さっ!
KYA!
HA HA HA! HOW FOOLISH!
I MIGHT NOT BE ABLE TO SEE, BUT I STILL KNOW YOUR MOVES!!
NOW, UP WITH YOU!
HAUH.
OUCHIE.
ALL OF THOSE WHO CARRY OUR NAME ARE BOUND BY HONOR!
NOW, LET'S FINISH THIS!

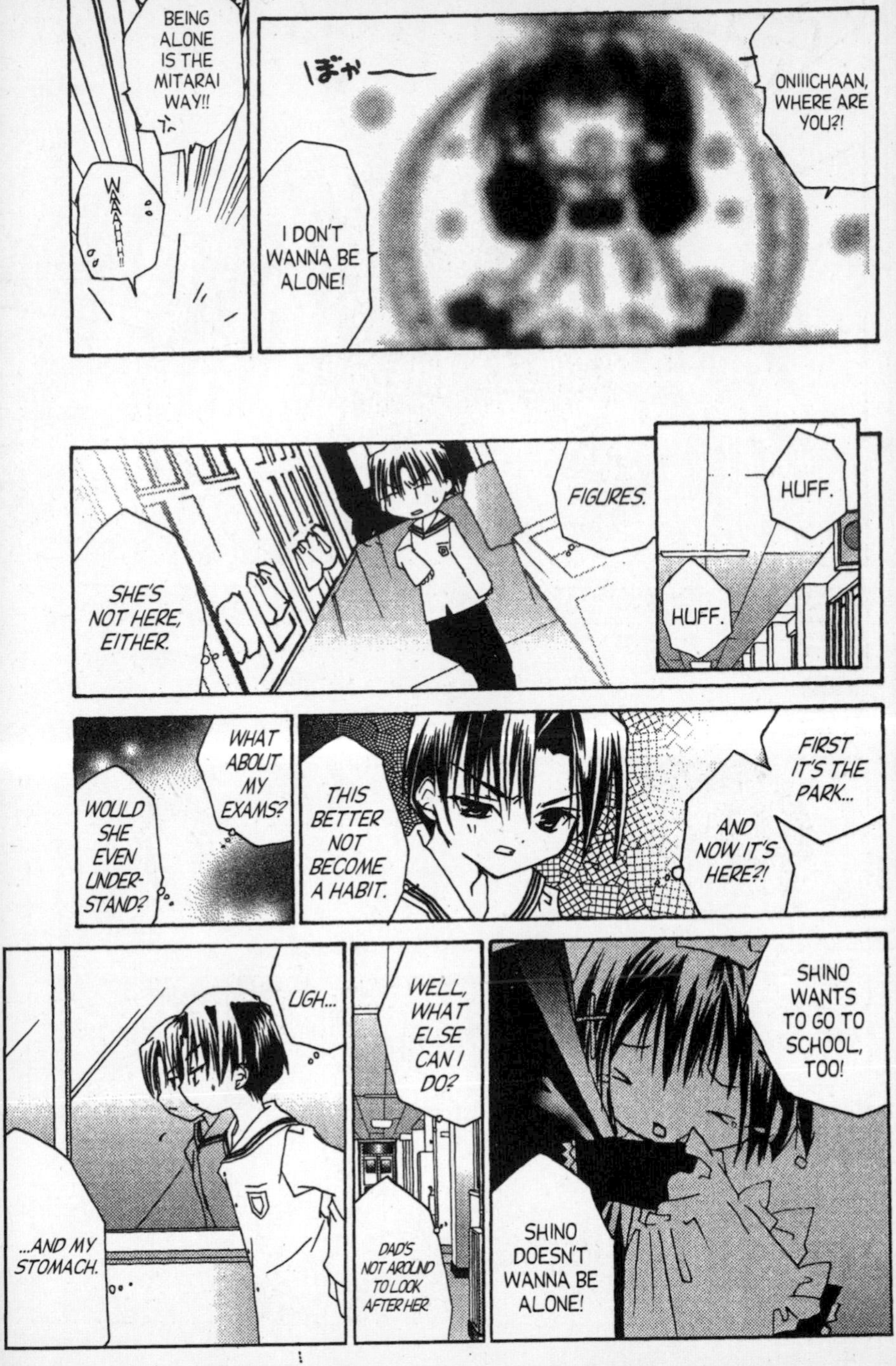
ONIIICHAAN, WHERE ARE YOU?!
ぼや——
I DON'T WANNA BE ALONE!
BEING ALONE IS THE MITARAI WAY!!
WAAAHHH!!
HUFF.
HUFF.
FIGURES.
SHE'S NOT HERE, EITHER.
FIRST IT'S THE PARK...
AND NOW IT'S HERE?!
THIS BETTER NOT BECOME A HABIT.
WHAT ABOUT MY EXAMS?
WOULD SHE EVEN UNDER-STAND?
SHINO WANTS TO GO TO SCHOOL, TOO!
SHINO DOESN'T WANNA BE ALONE!
WELL, WHAT ELSE CAN I DO?
DAD'S NOT AROUND TO LOOK AFTER HER.
UGH...
...AND MY STOMACH.

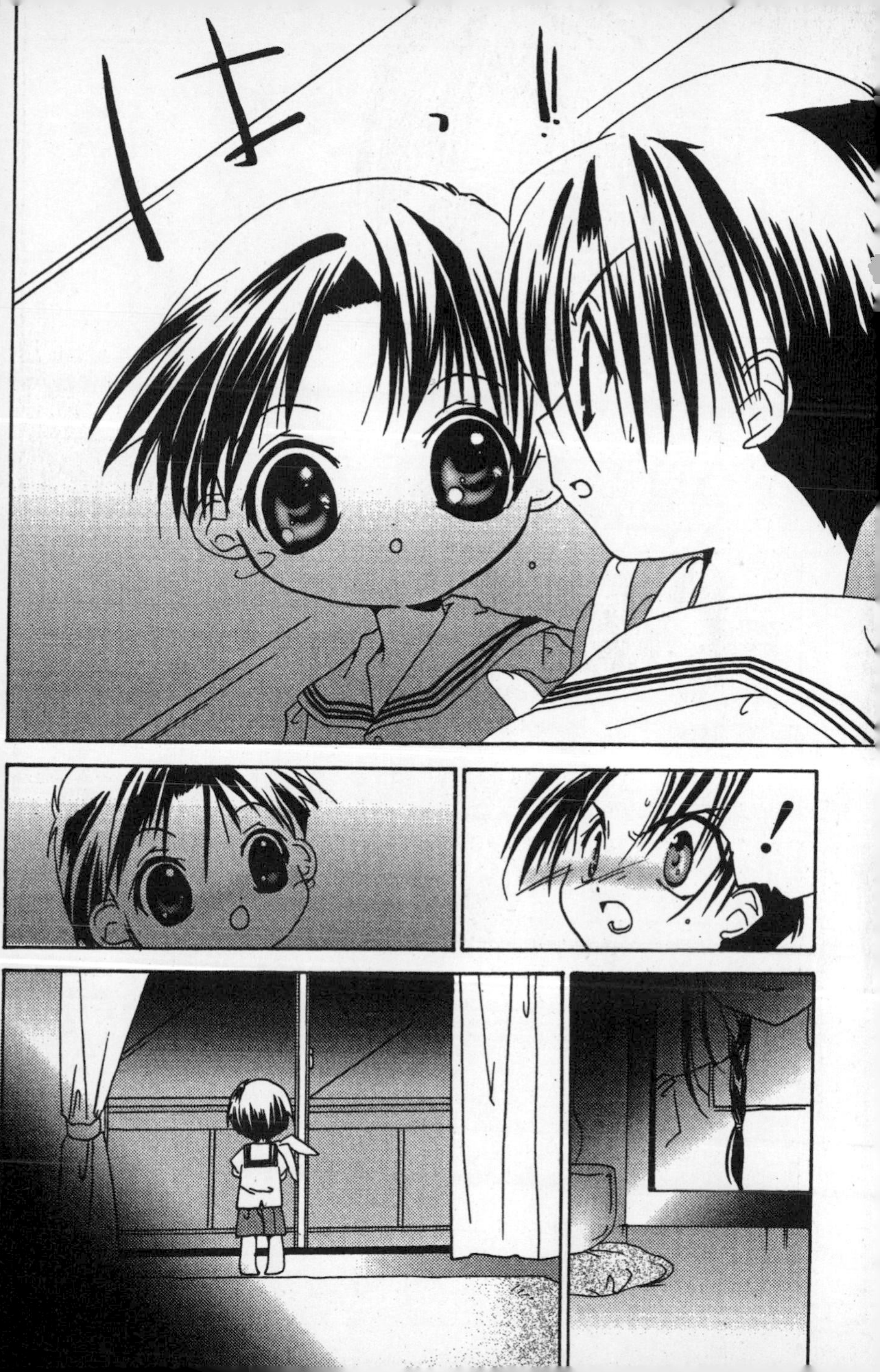
はっ!!
!

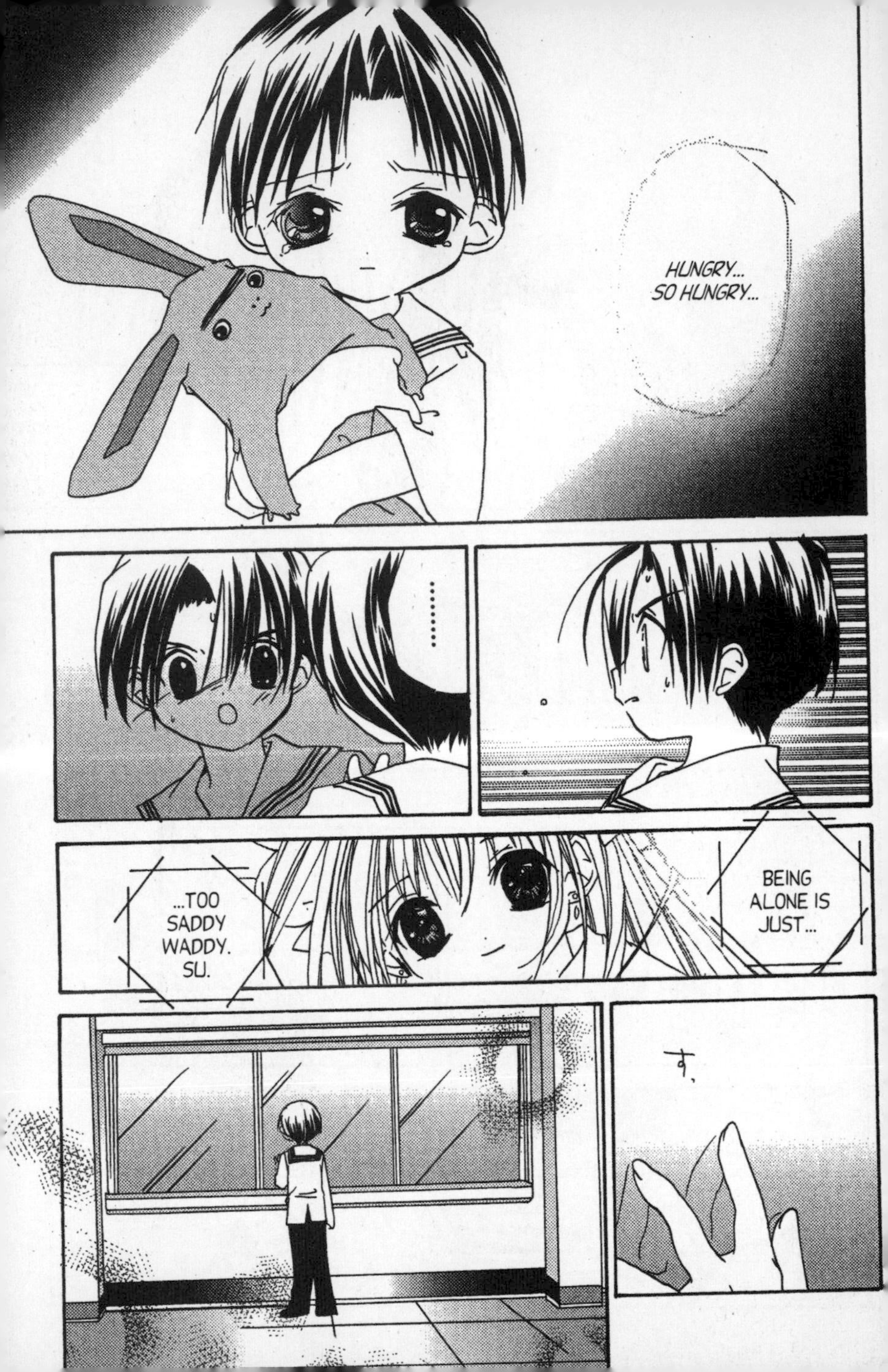
HUNGRY... SO HUNGRY...
......
BEING ALONE IS JUST...
...TOO SADDY WADDY. SU.
す、

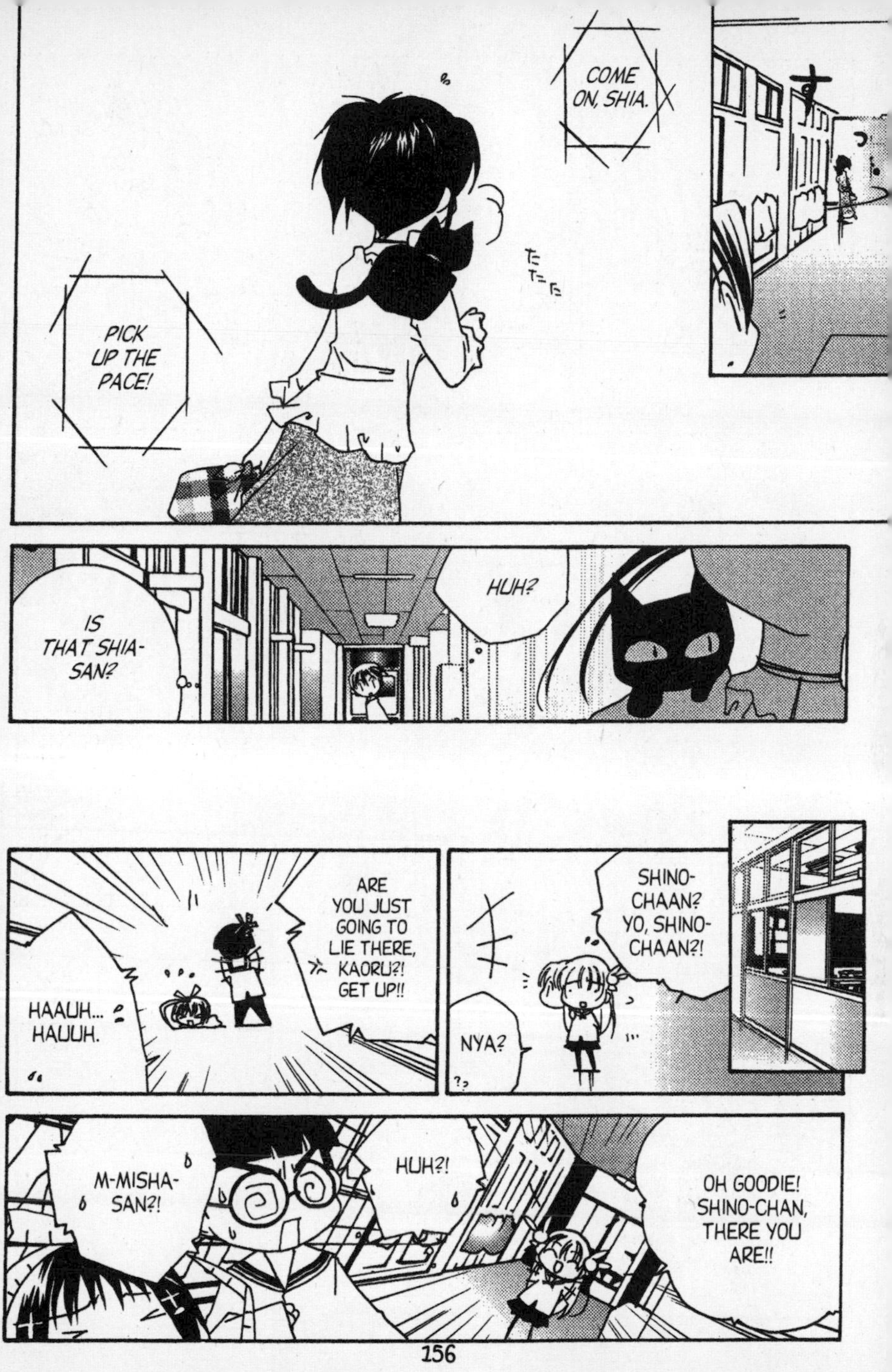
COME ON, SHIA.
PICK UP THE PACE!
HUH?
IS THAT SHIA-SAN?
SHINO-CHAAN? YO, SHINO-CHAAN?!
NYA?
ARE YOU JUST GOING TO LIE THERE, KAORU?! GET UP!!
HAAUH... HAUUH.
OH GOODIE! SHINO-CHAN, THERE YOU ARE!!
HUH?!
M-MISHA-SAN?!

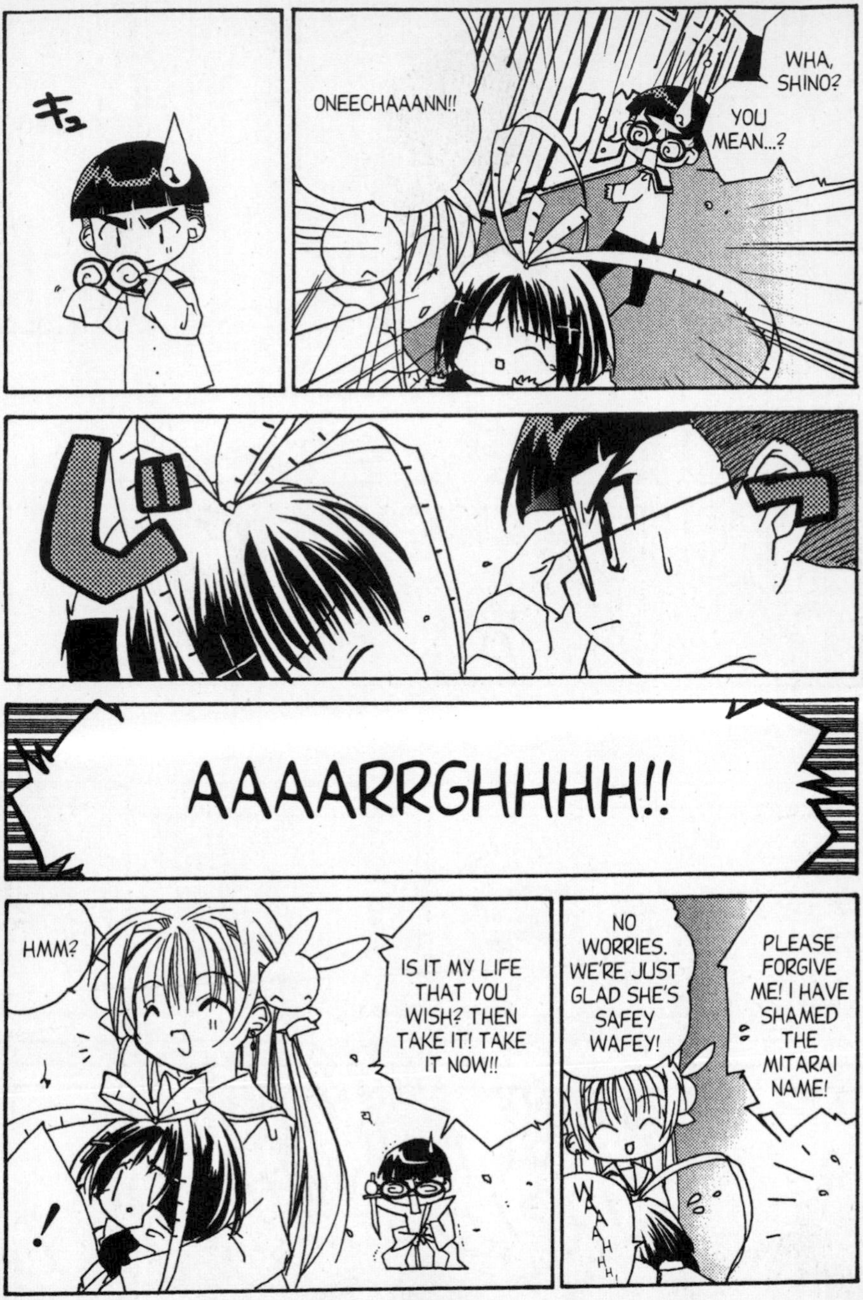

WHA, SHINO?
YOU MEAN...?
ONEECHAAANN!!
キュ
AAAARRGHHHH!!
PLEASE FORGIVE ME! I HAVE SHAMED THE MITARAI NAME!
NO WORRIES. WE'RE JUST GLAD SHE'S SAFEY WAFEY!
IS IT MY LIFE THAT YOU WISH? THEN TAKE IT! TAKE IT NOW!!
HMM?

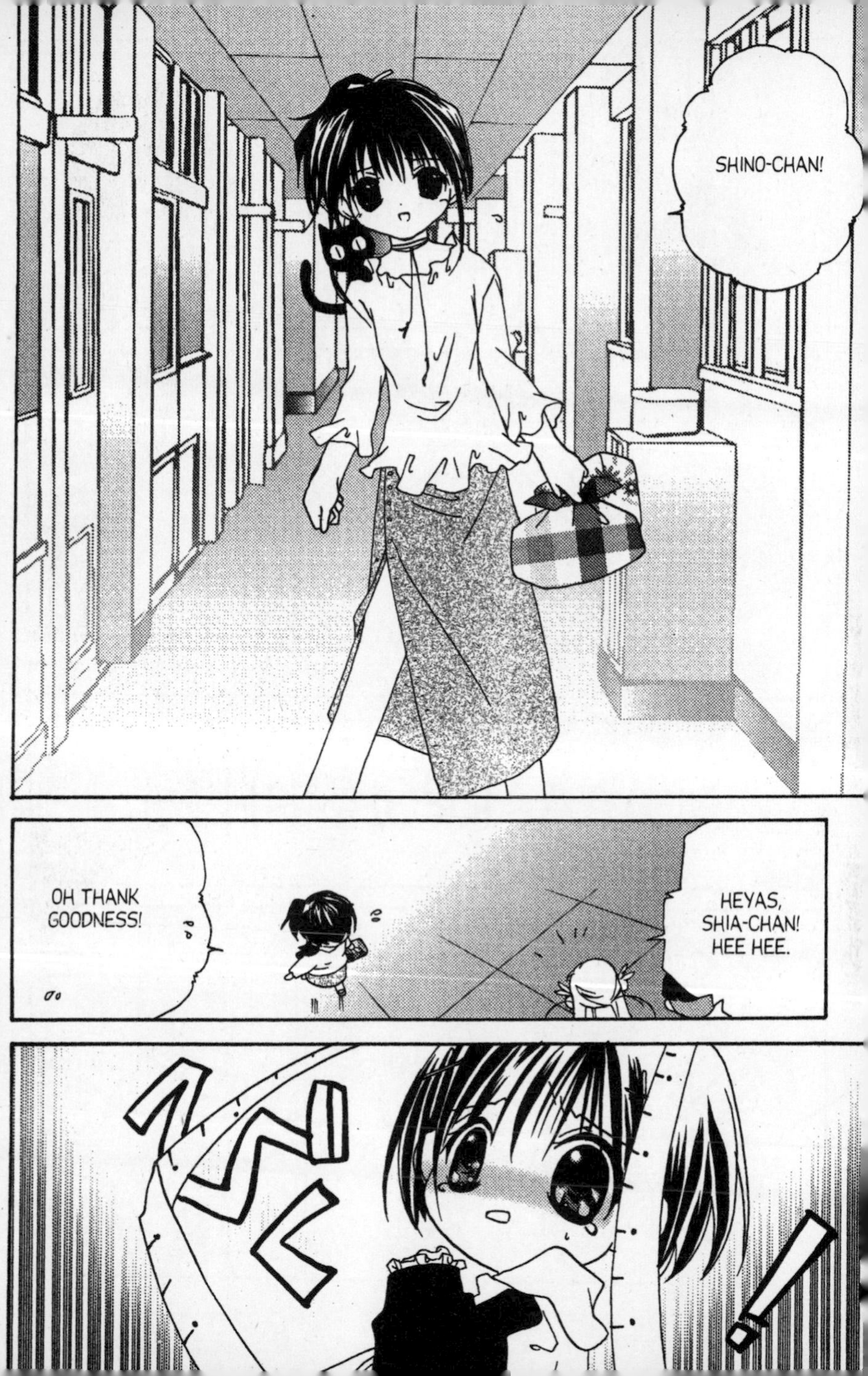
SHINO-CHAN!
HEYAS, SHIA-CHAN! HEE HEE.
OH THANK GOODNESS!

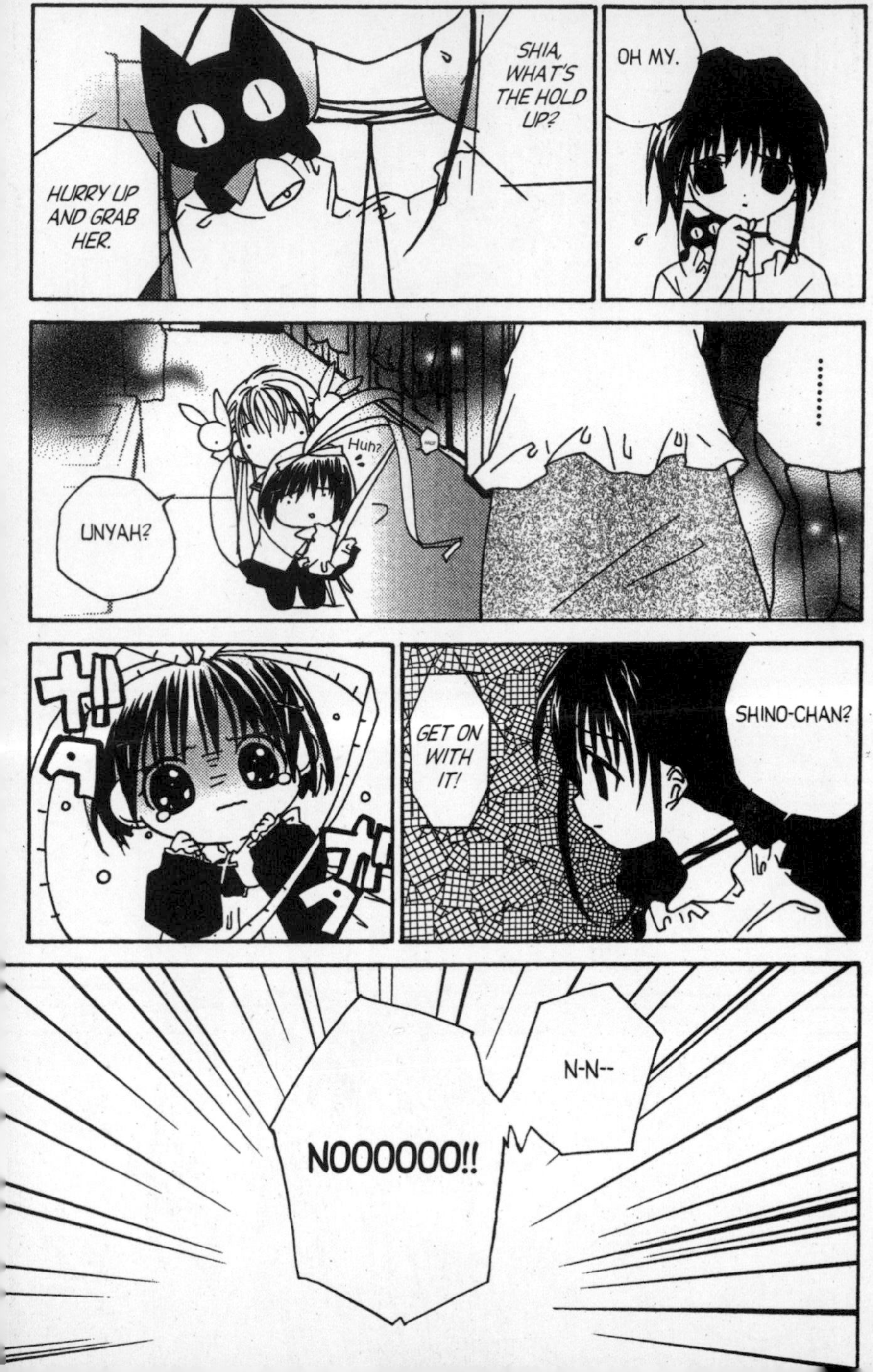
OH MY.
SHIA, WHAT'S THE HOLD UP?
HURRY UP AND GRAB HER.
....
Huh?
UNYAH?
SHINO-CHAN?
GET ON WITH IT!
N-N--
NOOOOOO!!

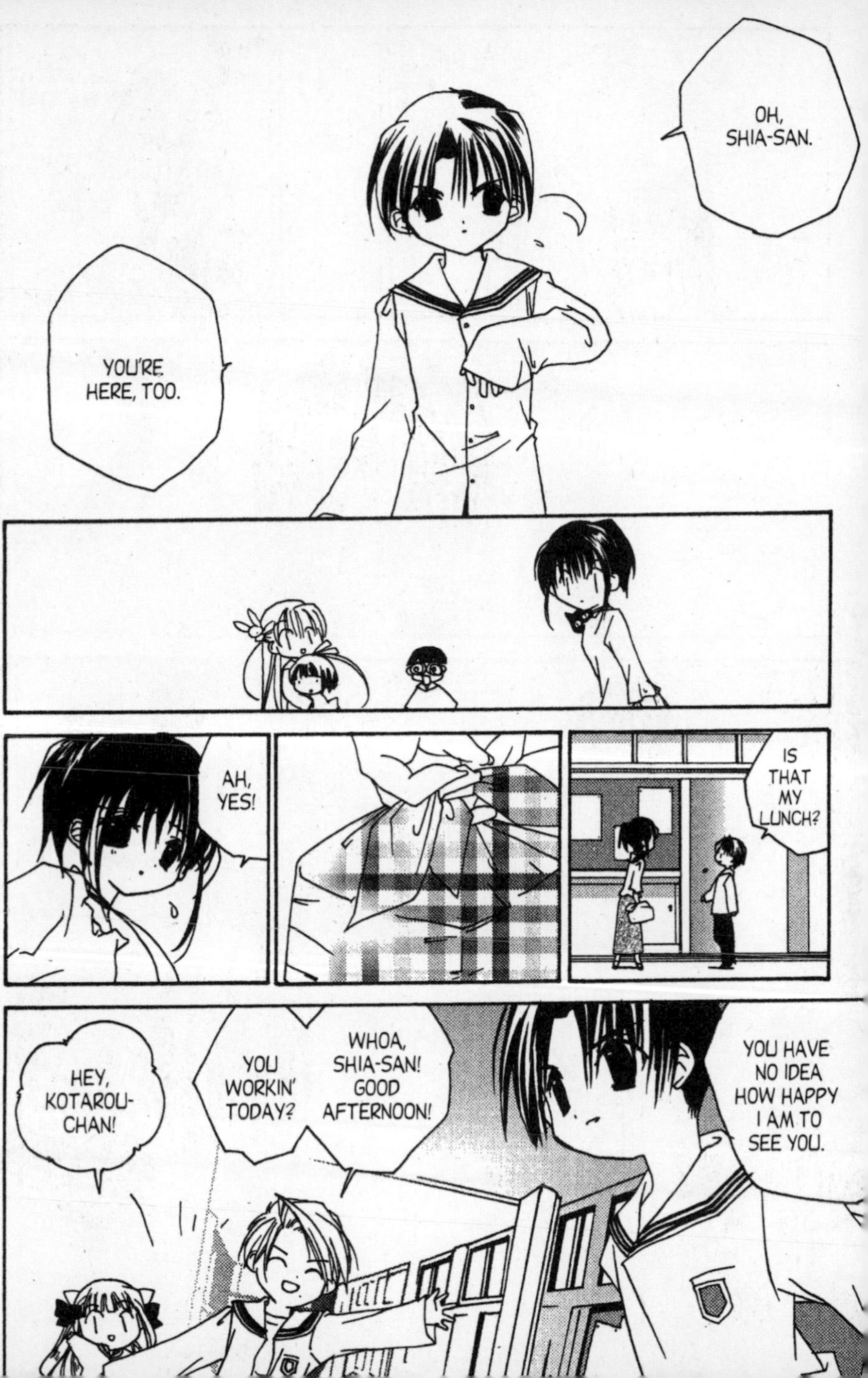
OH, SHIA-SAN.
YOU'RE HERE, TOO.
IS THAT MY LUNCH?
AH, YES!
YOU HAVE NO IDEA HOW HAPPY I AM TO SEE YOU.
WHOA, SHIA-SAN! GOOD AFTERNOON!
YOU WORKIN' TODAY?
HEY, KOTAROU-CHAN!

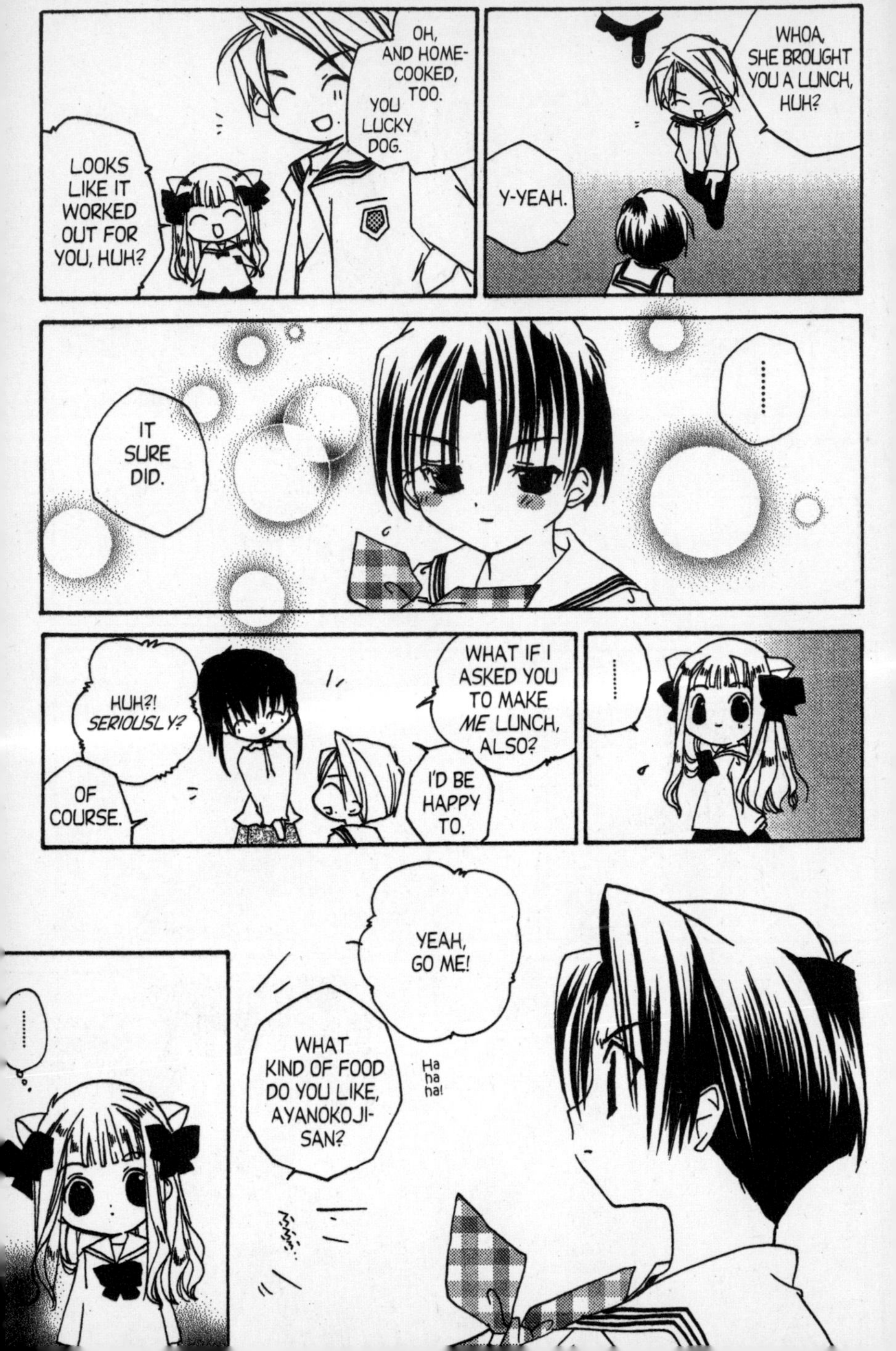
WHOA, SHE BROUGHT YOU A LUNCH, HUH?
Y-YEAH.
OH, AND HOME-COOKED, TOO.
YOU LUCKY DOG.
LOOKS LIKE IT WORKED OUT FOR YOU, HUH?
....
IT SURE DID.
....
WHAT IF I ASKED YOU TO MAKE *ME* LUNCH, ALSO?
I'D BE HAPPY TO.
HUH?! *SERIOUSLY?*
OF COURSE.
YEAH, GO ME!
Ha ha ha!
WHAT KIND OF FOOD DO YOU LIKE, AYANOKOJI-SAN?
....

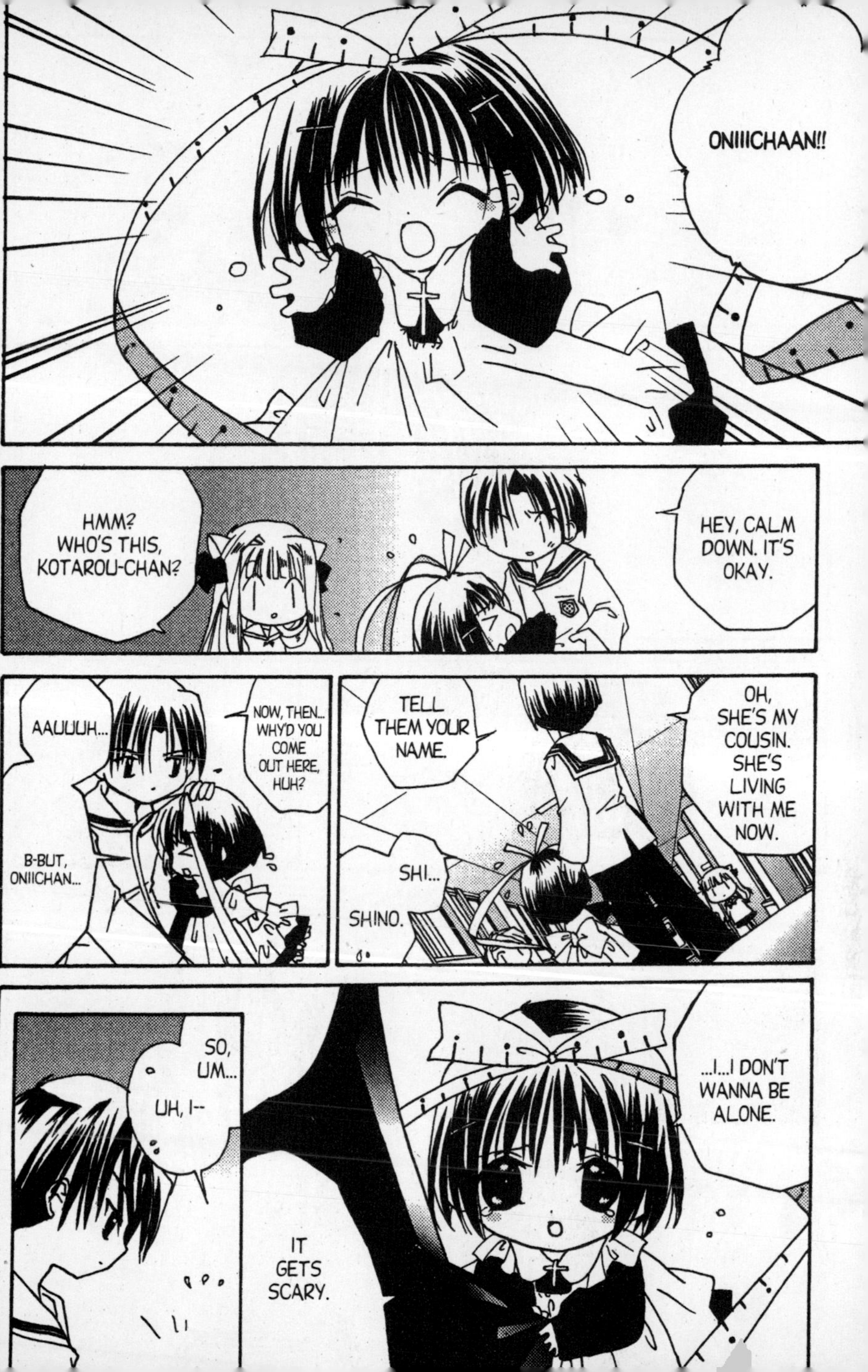
ONIIICHAAN!!
HEY, CALM DOWN. IT'S OKAY.
HMM? WHO'S THIS, KOTAROU-CHAN?
OH, SHE'S MY COUSIN. SHE'S LIVING WITH ME NOW.
TELL THEM YOUR NAME.
SHI...
SHINO.
NOW, THEN... WHY'D YOU COME OUT HERE, HUH?
AAUUUH...
B-BUT, ONIICHAN...
...I...I DON'T WANNA BE ALONE.
SO, UM...
UH, I-
IT GETS SCARY.

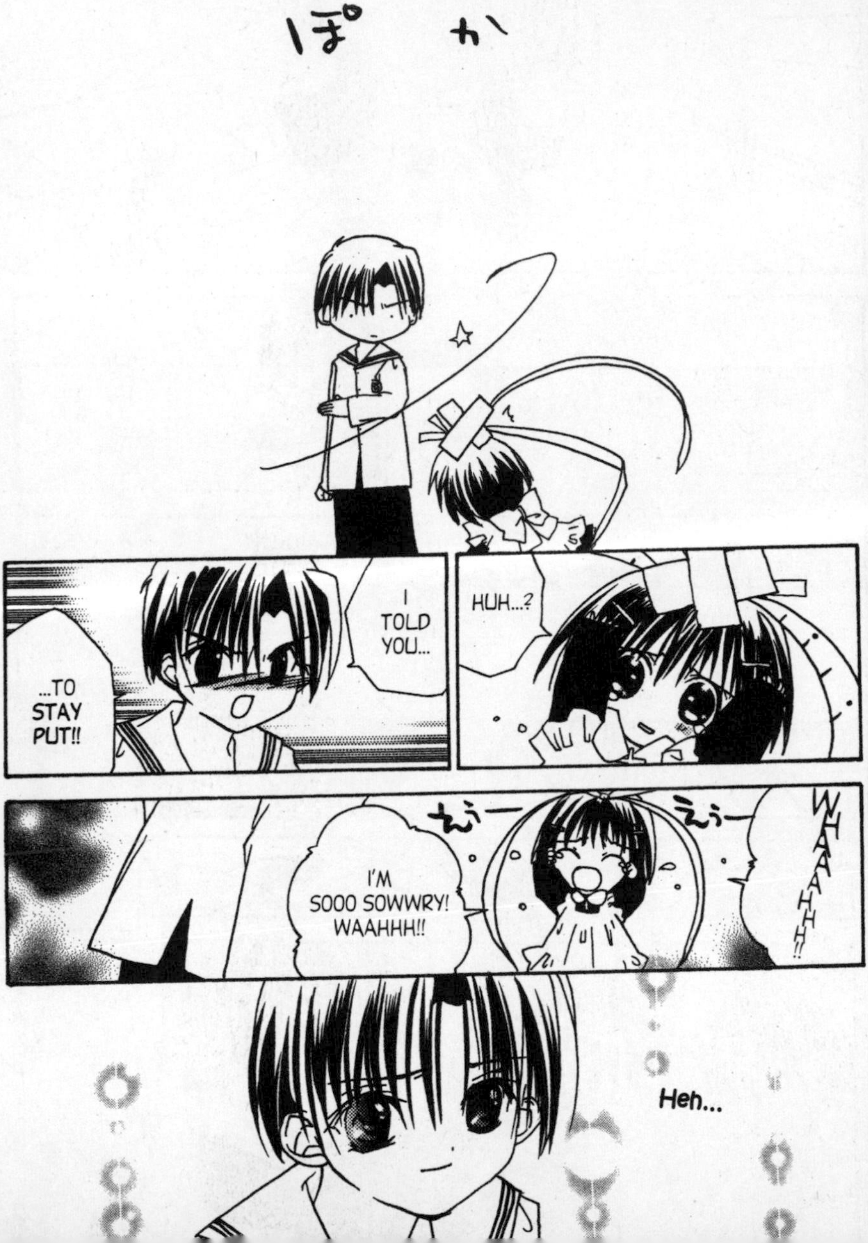

ぽか
HUH...?
I TOLD YOU...
...TO STAY PUT!!
WHAAAAHH!!
えぅー
えぅー
I'M SOOO SOWWRY! WAAHHH!!
Heh...

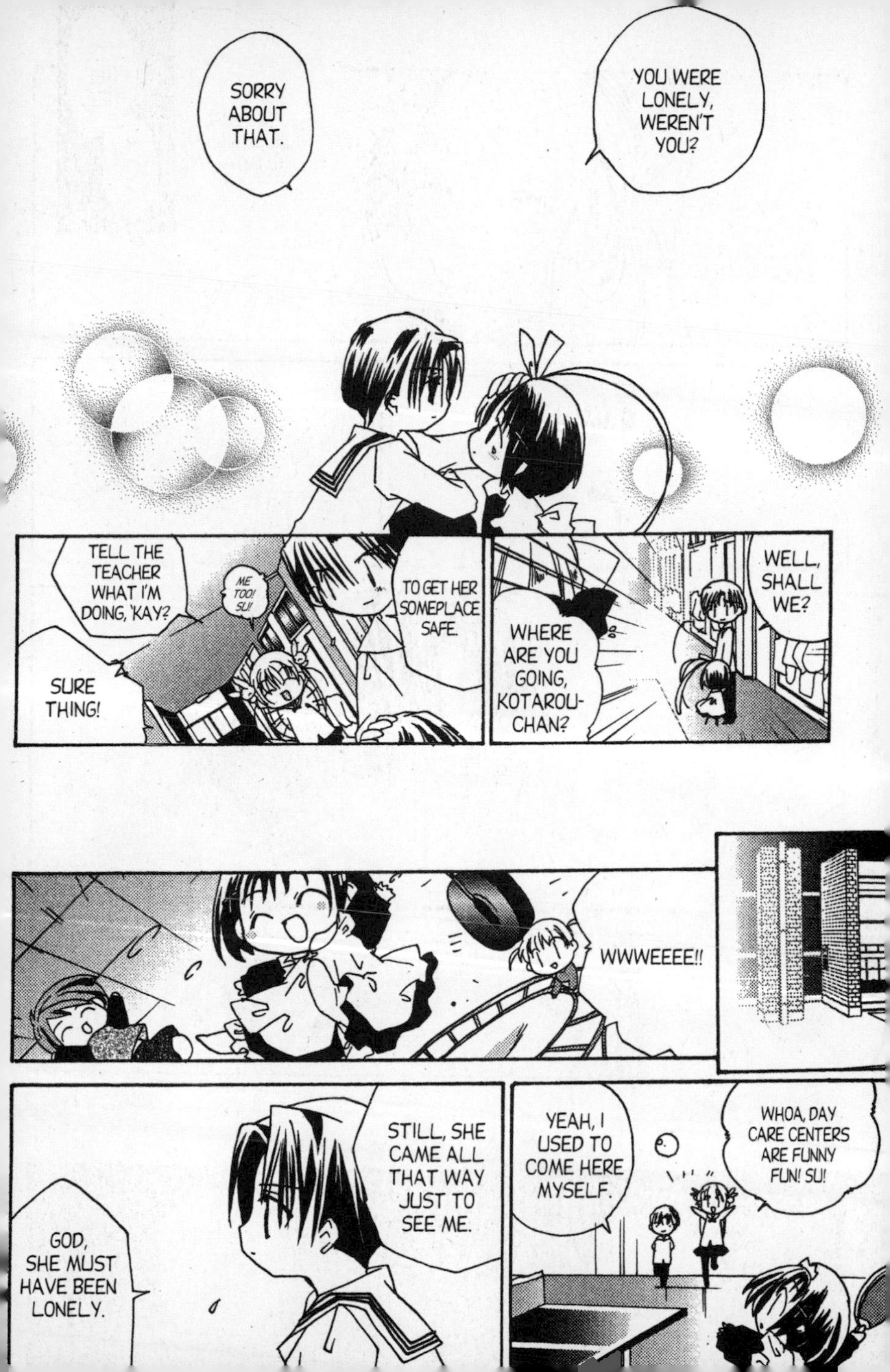
YOU WERE LONELY, WEREN'T YOU?
SORRY ABOUT THAT.
WELL, SHALL WE?
WHERE ARE YOU GOING, KOTAROU-CHAN?
TO GET HER SOMEPLACE SAFE.
TELL THE TEACHER WHAT I'M DOING, 'KAY?
ME TOO! SU!
SURE THING!
WWWEEEE!!
WHOA, DAY CARE CENTERS ARE FUNNY FUN! SU!
YEAH, I USED TO COME HERE MYSELF.
STILL, SHE CAME ALL THAT WAY JUST TO SEE ME.
GOD, SHE MUST HAVE BEEN LONELY.

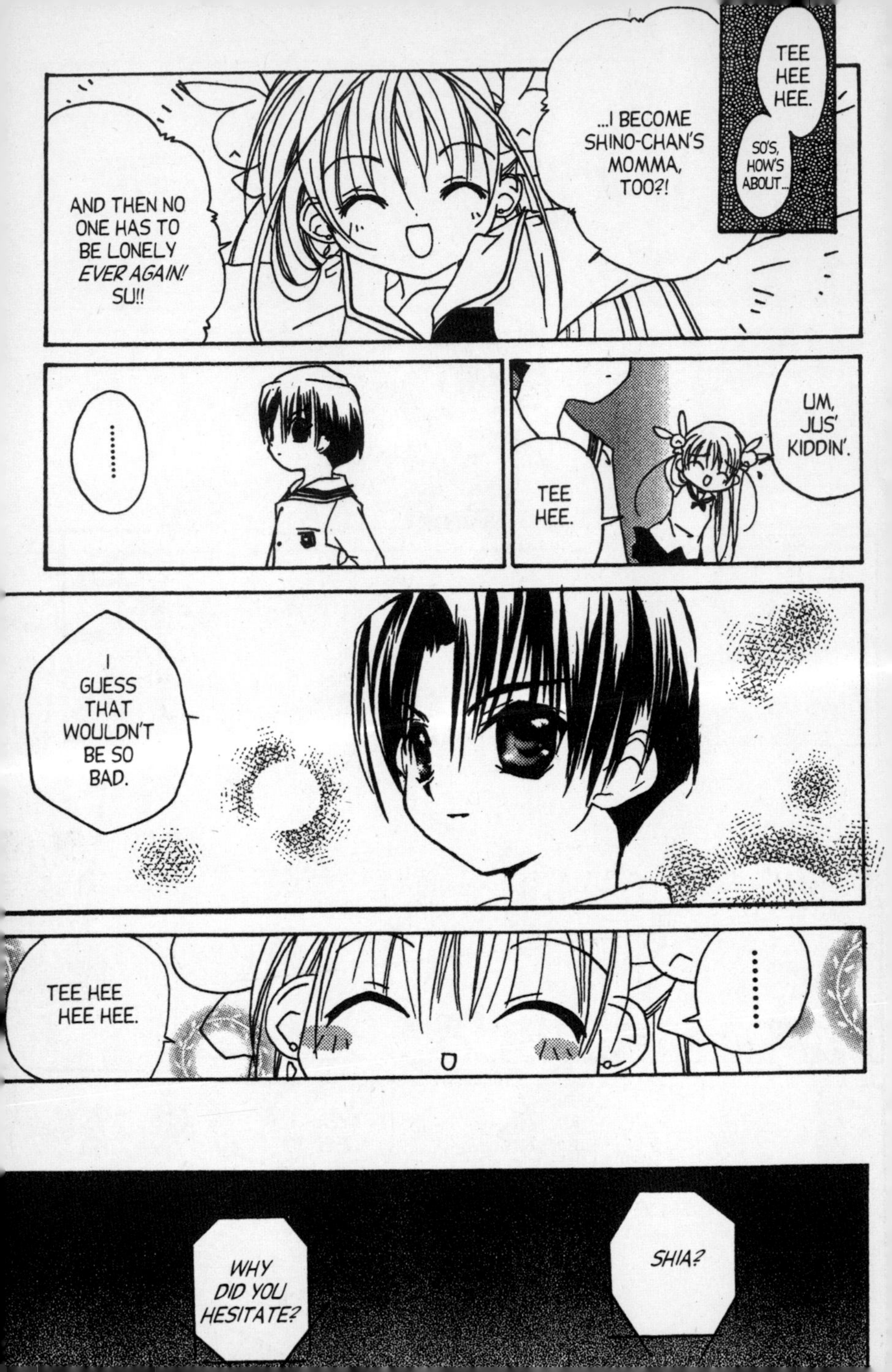
TEE HEE HEE.
SO'S, HOW'S ABOUT...
...I BECOME SHINO-CHAN'S MOMMA, TOO?!
AND THEN NO ONE HAS TO BE LONELY *EVER AGAIN!* SU!!
UM, JUS' KIDDIN'.
TEE HEE.
....
I GUESS THAT WOULDN'T BE SO BAD.
....
TEE HEE HEE HEE.
SHIA?
WHY DID YOU HESITATE?

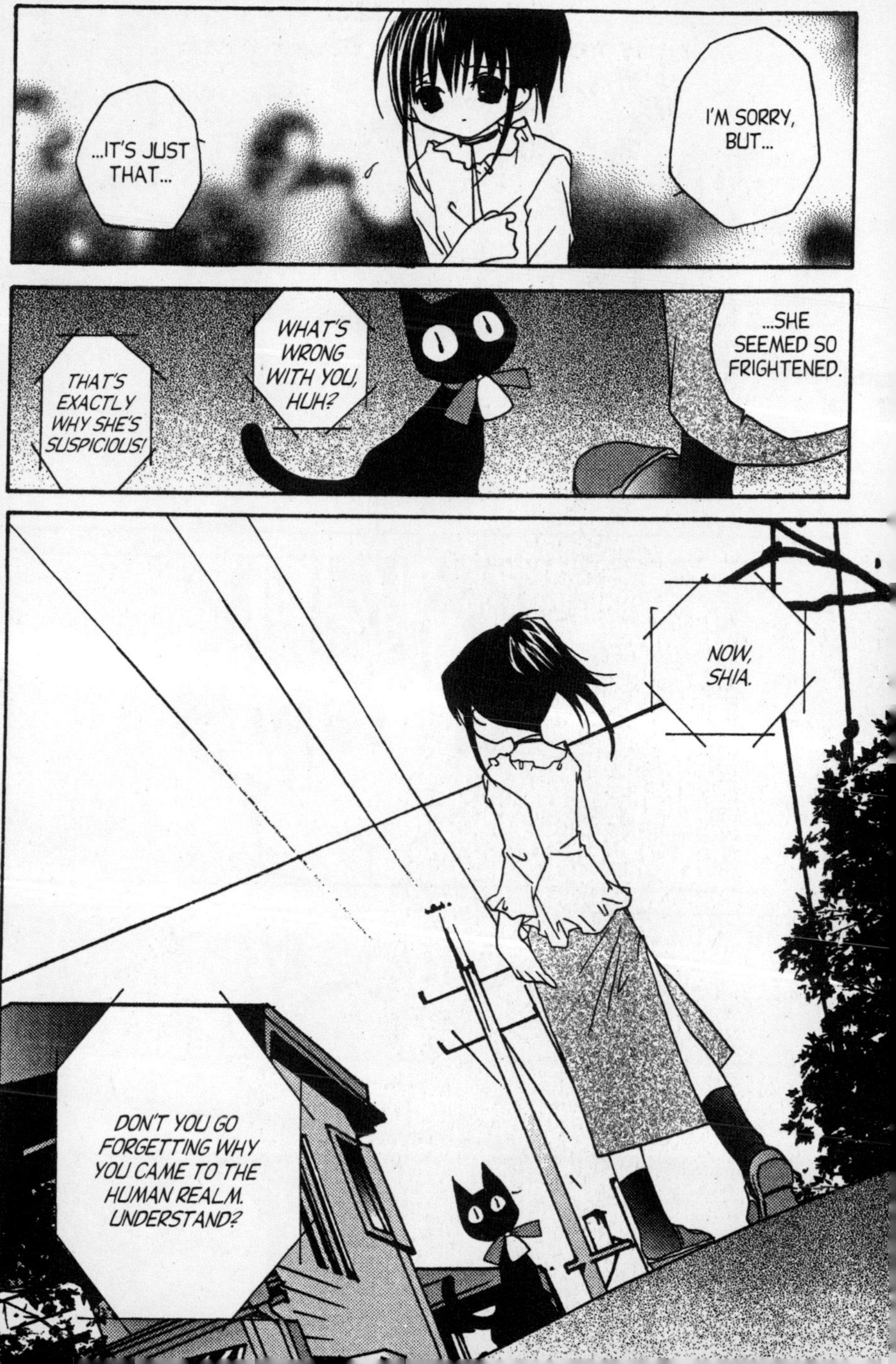
I'M SORRY, BUT...
...IT'S JUST THAT...
...SHE SEEMED SO FRIGHTENED.
WHAT'S WRONG WITH YOU, HUH?
THAT'S EXACTLY WHY SHE'S SUSPICIOUS!
NOW, SHIA.
DON'T YOU GO FORGETTING WHY YOU CAME TO THE HUMAN REALM. UNDERSTAND?

Lesson 25
How to Determine One's Path

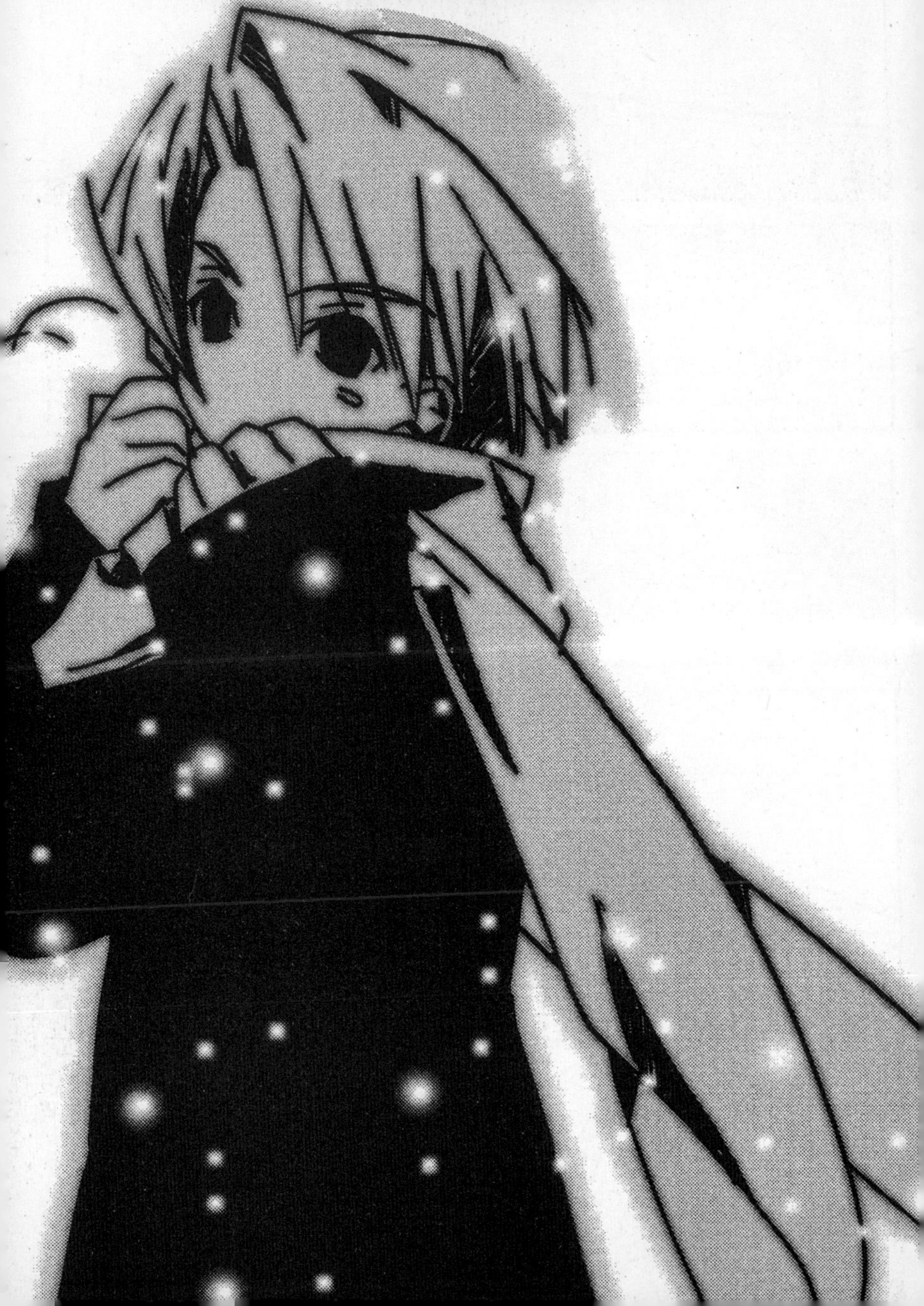

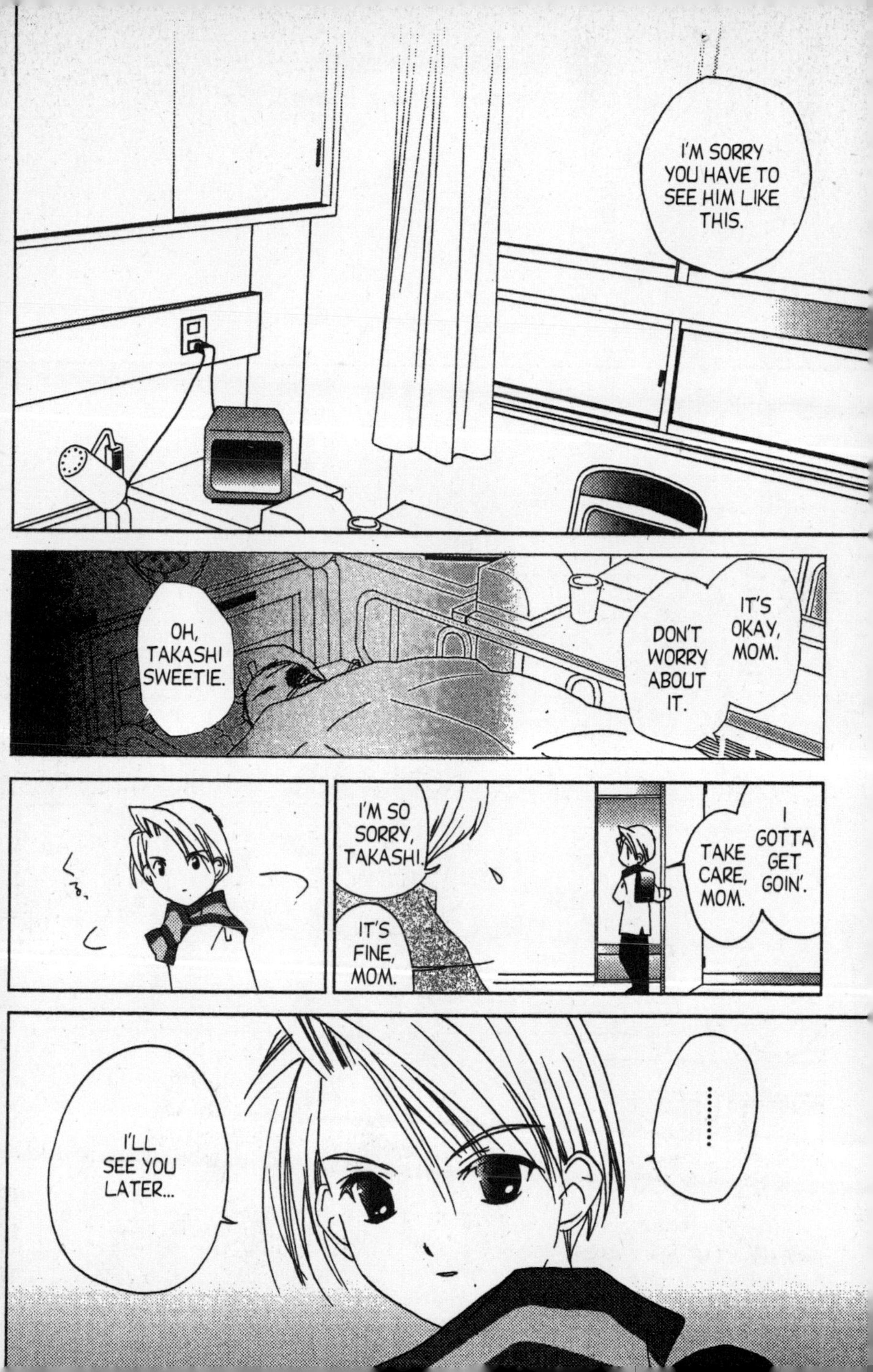
I'M SORRY YOU HAVE TO SEE HIM LIKE THIS.
IT'S OKAY, MOM.
DON'T WORRY ABOUT IT.
OH, TAKASHI SWEETIE.
I GOTTA GET GOIN'.
TAKE CARE, MOM.
I'M SO SORRY, TAKASHI.
IT'S FINE, MOM.
......
I'LL SEE YOU LATER...

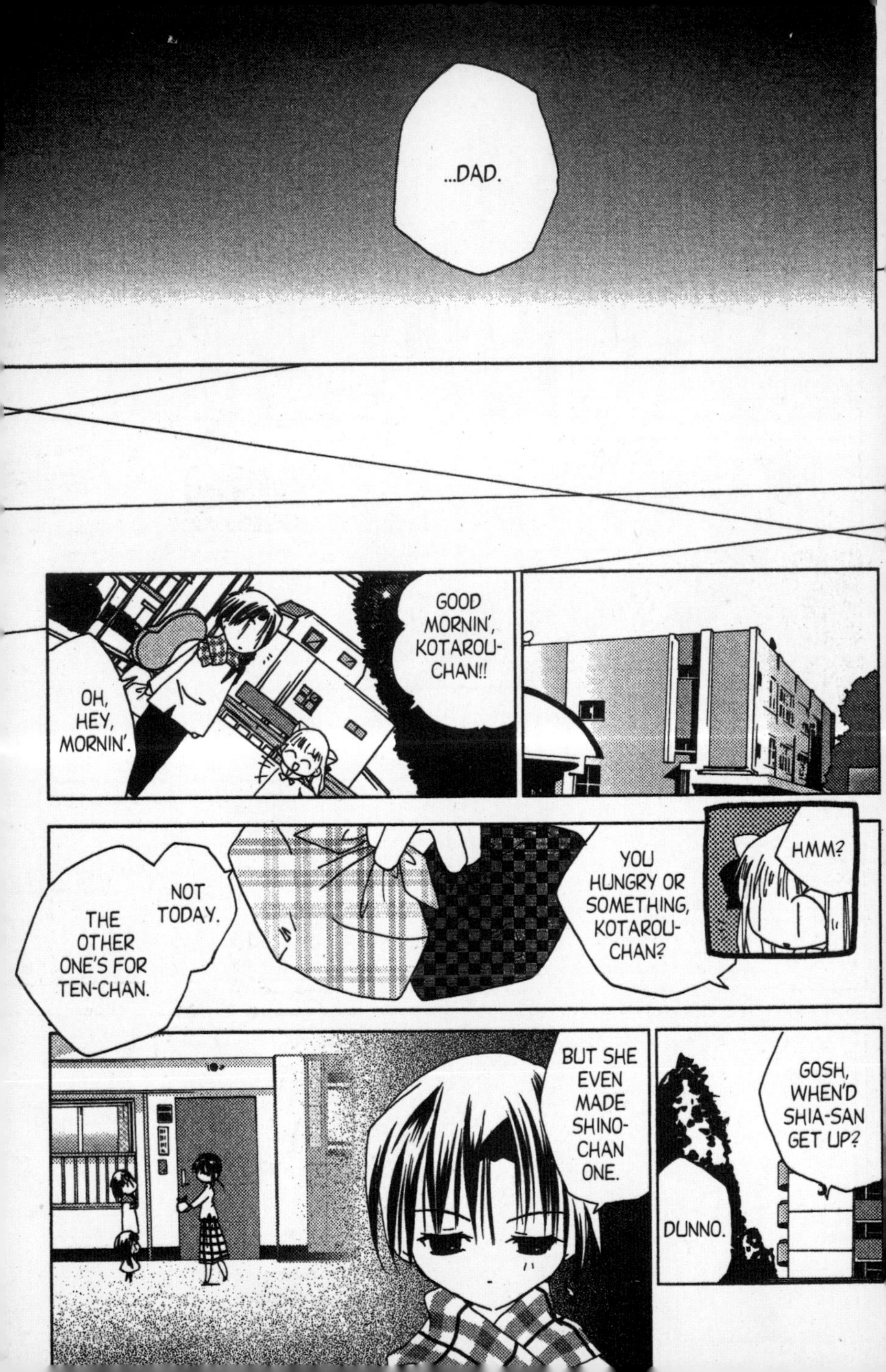
...DAD.
GOOD MORNIN', KOTAROU-CHAN!!
OH, HEY, MORNIN'.
HMM?
YOU HUNGRY OR SOMETHING, KOTAROU-CHAN?
NOT TODAY.
THE OTHER ONE'S FOR TEN-CHAN.
GOSH, WHEN'D SHIA-SAN GET UP?
DUNNO.
BUT SHE EVEN MADE SHINO-CHAN ONE.

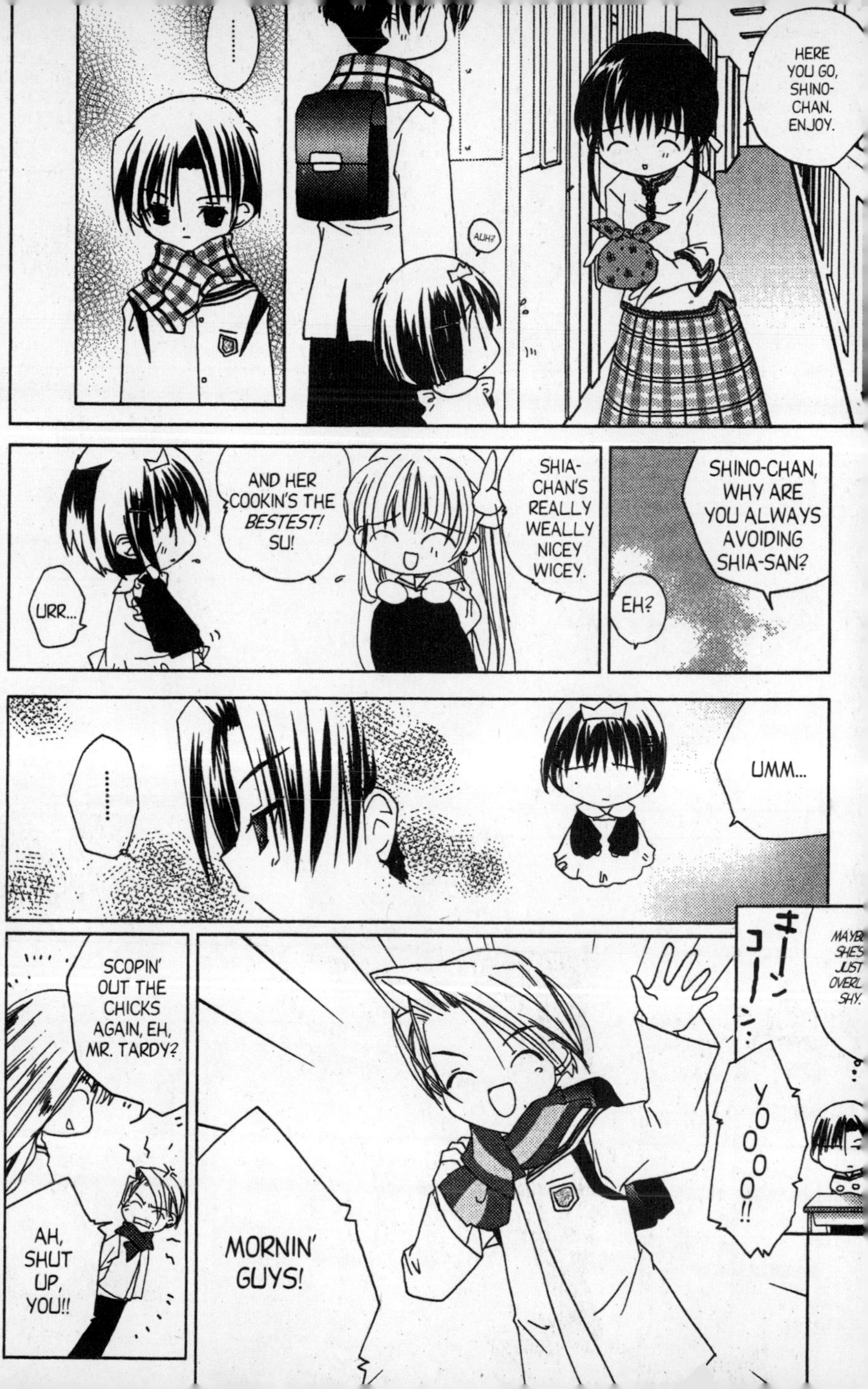
HERE YOU GO, SHINO-CHAN. ENJOY.
AUH?
......
SHINO-CHAN, WHY ARE YOU ALWAYS AVOIDING SHIA-SAN?
EH?
SHIA-CHAN'S REALLY WEALLY NICEY WICEY.
AND HER COOKIN'S THE BESTEST! SU!
URR...
UMM...
......
MAYB SHE'S JUST OVERL SHY.
キーンコーン
YOOOOO!!
MORNIN' GUYS!
SCOPIN' OUT THE CHICKS AGAIN, EH, MR. TARDY?
AH, SHUT UP, YOU!!

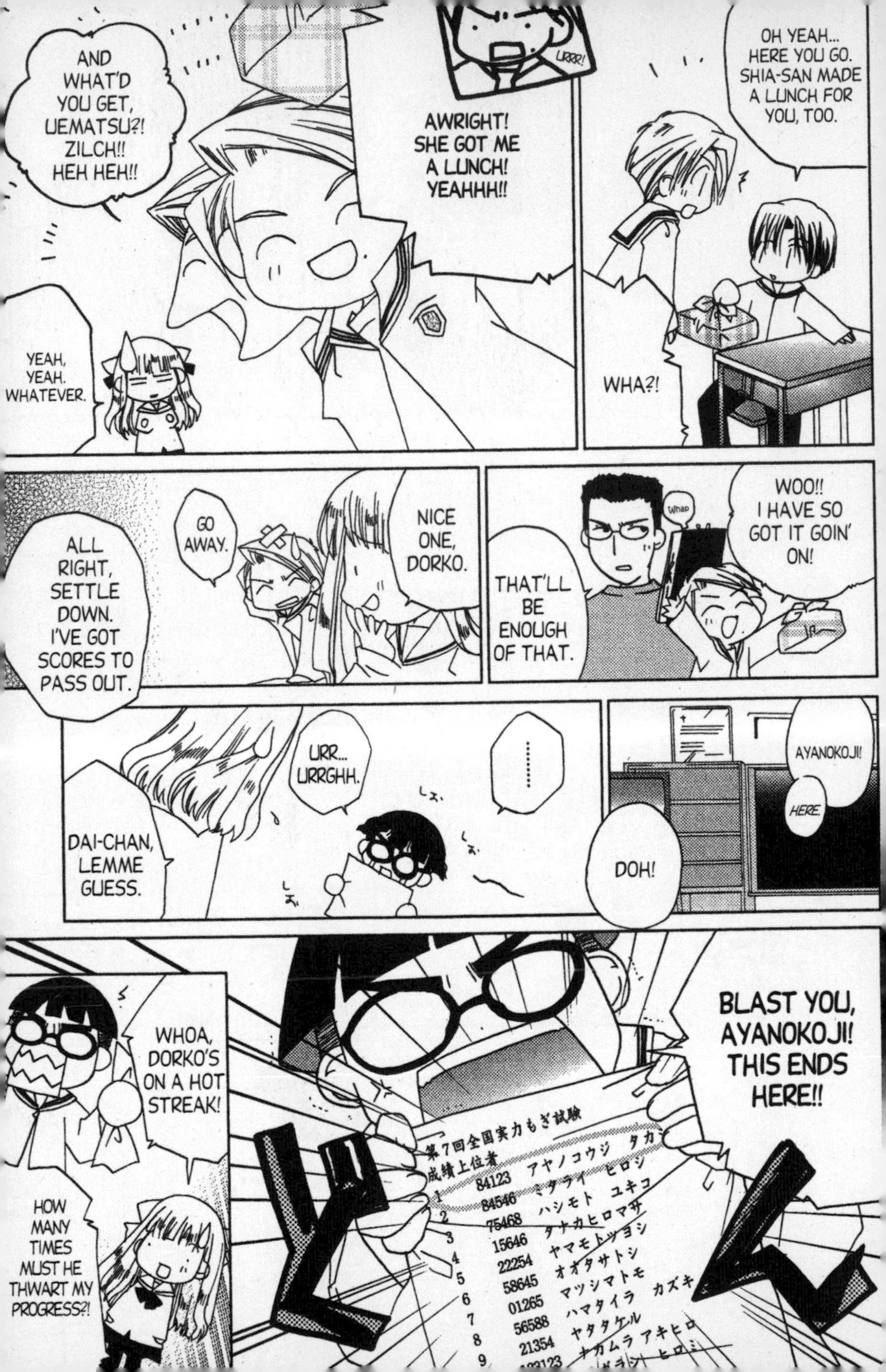
OH YEAH... HERE YOU GO. SHIA-SAN MADE A LUNCH FOR YOU, TOO.
WHA?!
URRR!
AWRIGHT! SHE GOT ME A LUNCH! YEAHHH!!
AND WHAT'D YOU GET, UEMATSU?! ZILCH!! HEH HEH!!
YEAH, YEAH. WHATEVER.
WOO!! I HAVE SO GOT IT GOIN' ON!
Whap
THAT'LL BE ENOUGH OF THAT.
NICE ONE, DORKO.
GO AWAY.
ALL RIGHT, SETTLE DOWN. I'VE GOT SCORES TO PASS OUT.
AYANOKOJI!
HERE.
DOH!
......
URR... URRGHH.
DAI-CHAN, LEMME GUESS.
BLAST YOU, AYANOKOJI! THIS ENDS HERE!!
第7回全国実力もぎ試験
成績上位者 84123 アヤノコウジ タカ
1 84546 ミタライ ヒロシ
2 75468 ハシモト ユキコ
3 15646 タナカヒロマサ
4 22254 ヤマモトツヨシ
5 58645 オオタサトシ
6 01265 マツシマトモ
7 56588 ハマタイラ カズキ
8 21354 ヤタタケル
9 ナカムラ アキヒロ
WHOA, DORKO'S ON A HOT STREAK!
HOW MANY TIMES MUST HE THWART MY PROGRESS?!

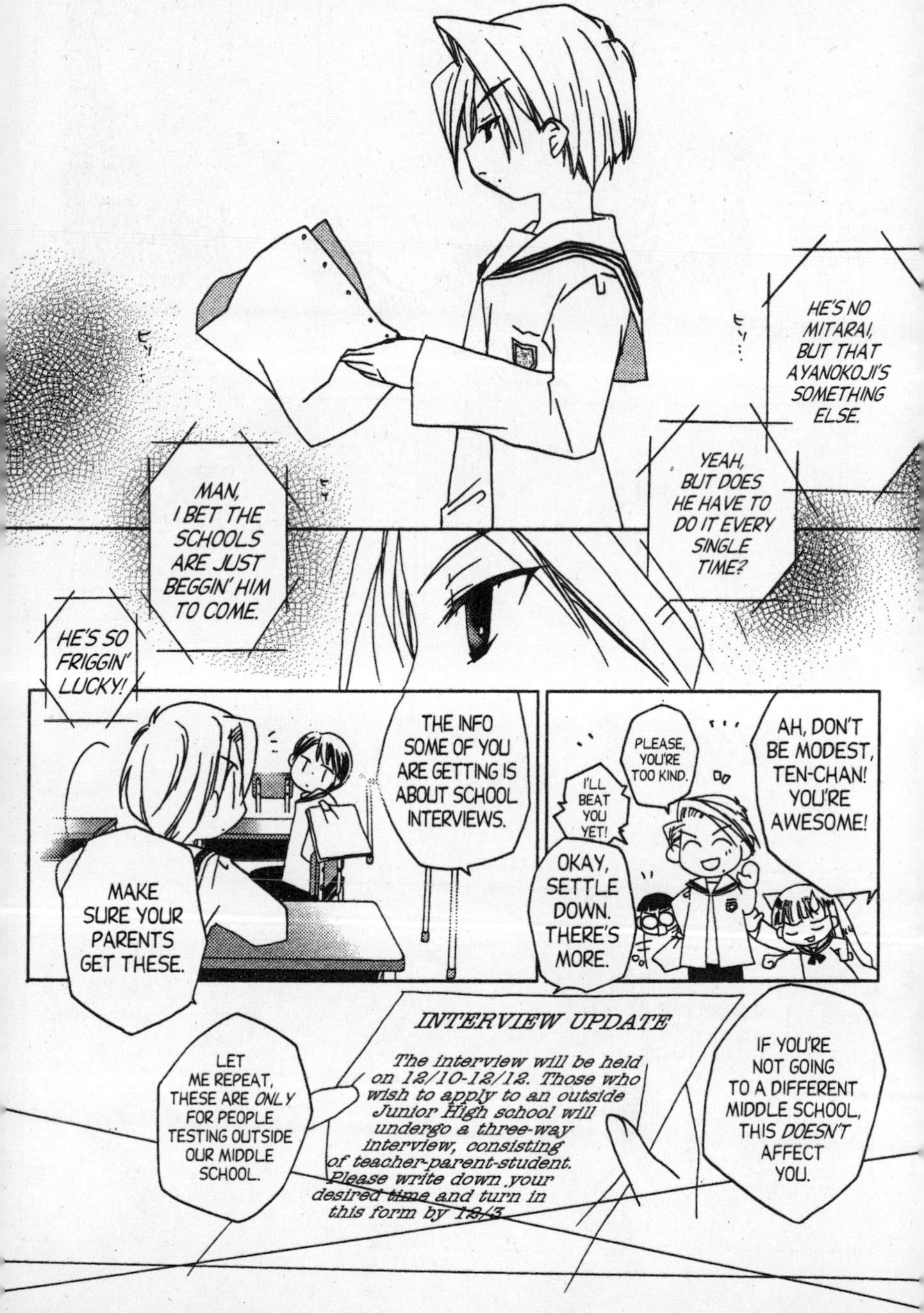
HE'S NO MITARAI, BUT THAT AYANOKOJI'S SOMETHING ELSE.
YEAH, BUT DOES HE HAVE TO DO IT EVERY SINGLE TIME?
MAN, I BET THE SCHOOLS ARE JUST BEGGIN' HIM TO COME.
HE'S SO FRIGGIN' LUCKY!
AH, DON'T BE MODEST, TEN-CHAN! YOU'RE AWESOME!
PLEASE, YOU'RE TOO KIND.
I'LL BEAT YOU YET!
OKAY, SETTLE DOWN. THERE'S MORE.
THE INFO SOME OF YOU ARE GETTING IS ABOUT SCHOOL INTERVIEWS.
MAKE SURE YOUR PARENTS GET THESE.
IF YOU'RE NOT GOING TO A DIFFERENT MIDDLE SCHOOL, THIS DOESN'T AFFECT YOU.
INTERVIEW UPDATE
The interview will be held on 12/10-12/12. Those who wish to apply to an outside Junior High school will undergo a three-way interview, consisting of teacher-parent-student. Please write down your desired time and turn in this form by 12/3
LET ME REPEAT, THESE ARE ONLY FOR PEOPLE TESTING OUTSIDE OUR MIDDLE SCHOOL.

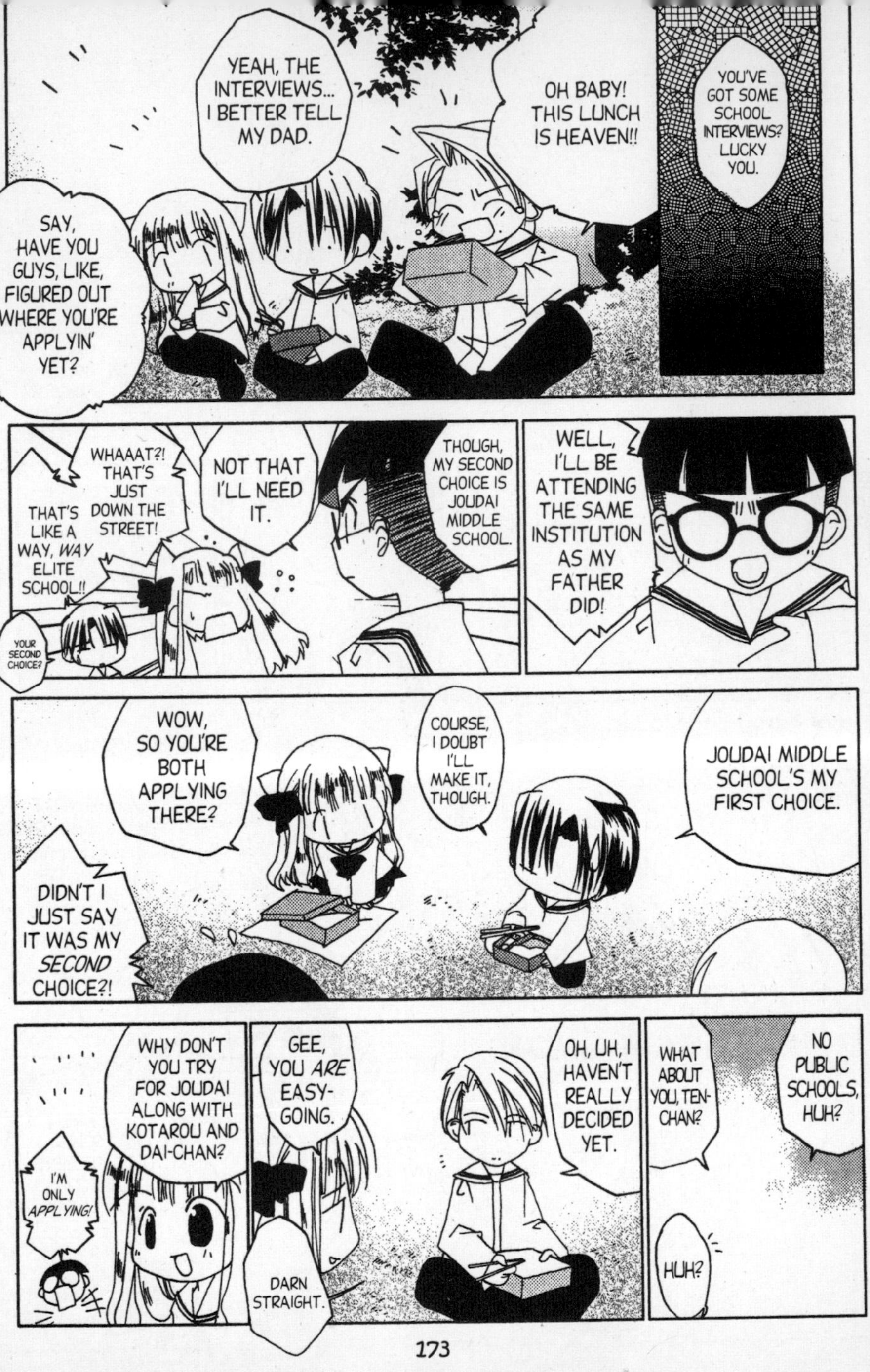
YOU'VE GOT SOME SCHOOL INTERVIEWS? LUCKY YOU.
OH BABY! THIS LUNCH IS HEAVEN!!
YEAH, THE INTERVIEWS... I BETTER TELL MY DAD.
SAY, HAVE YOU GUYS, LIKE, FIGURED OUT WHERE YOU'RE APPLYIN' YET?
WELL, I'LL BE ATTENDING THE SAME INSTITUTION AS MY FATHER DID!
THOUGH, MY SECOND CHOICE IS JOUDAI MIDDLE SCHOOL.
NOT THAT I'LL NEED IT.
WHAAAT?! THAT'S JUST DOWN THE STREET!
THAT'S LIKE A WAY, *WAY* ELITE SCHOOL!!
YOUR SECOND CHOICE?
JOUDAI MIDDLE SCHOOL'S MY FIRST CHOICE.
COURSE, I DOUBT I'LL MAKE IT, THOUGH.
WOW, SO YOU'RE BOTH APPLYING THERE?
DIDN'T I JUST SAY IT WAS MY *SECOND* CHOICE?!
NO PUBLIC SCHOOLS, HUH?
WHAT ABOUT YOU, TEN-CHAN?
HUH?
OH, UH, I HAVEN'T REALLY DECIDED YET.
GEE, YOU *ARE* EASY-GOING.
DARN STRAIGHT.
WHY DON'T YOU TRY FOR JOUDAI ALONG WITH KOTAROU AND DAI-CHAN?
I'M ONLY *APPLYING!*

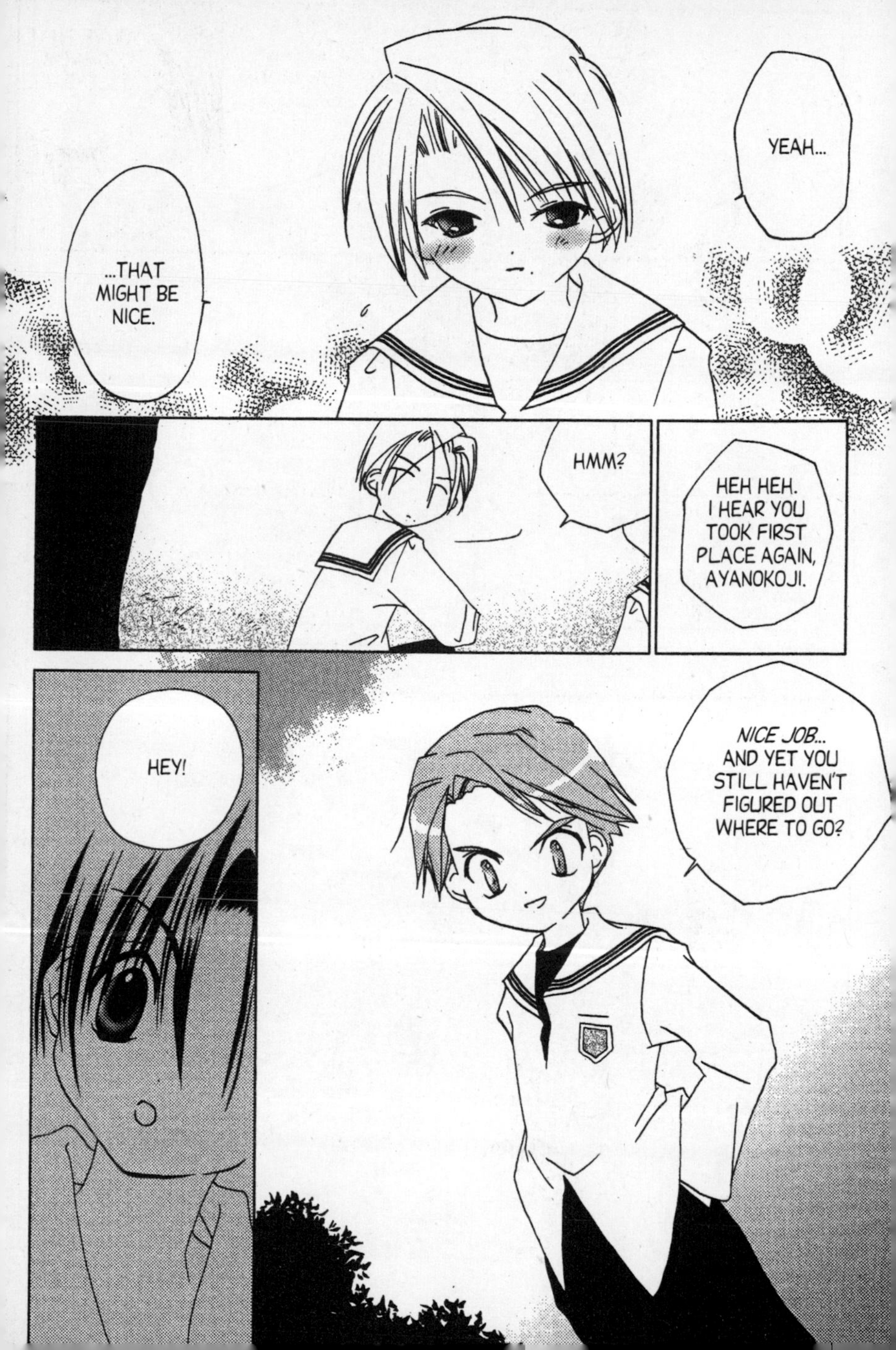
YEAH...
...THAT MIGHT BE NICE.
HEH HEH. I HEAR YOU TOOK FIRST PLACE AGAIN, AYANOKOJI.
HMM?
NICE JOB... AND YET YOU STILL HAVEN'T FIGURED OUT WHERE TO GO?
HEY!

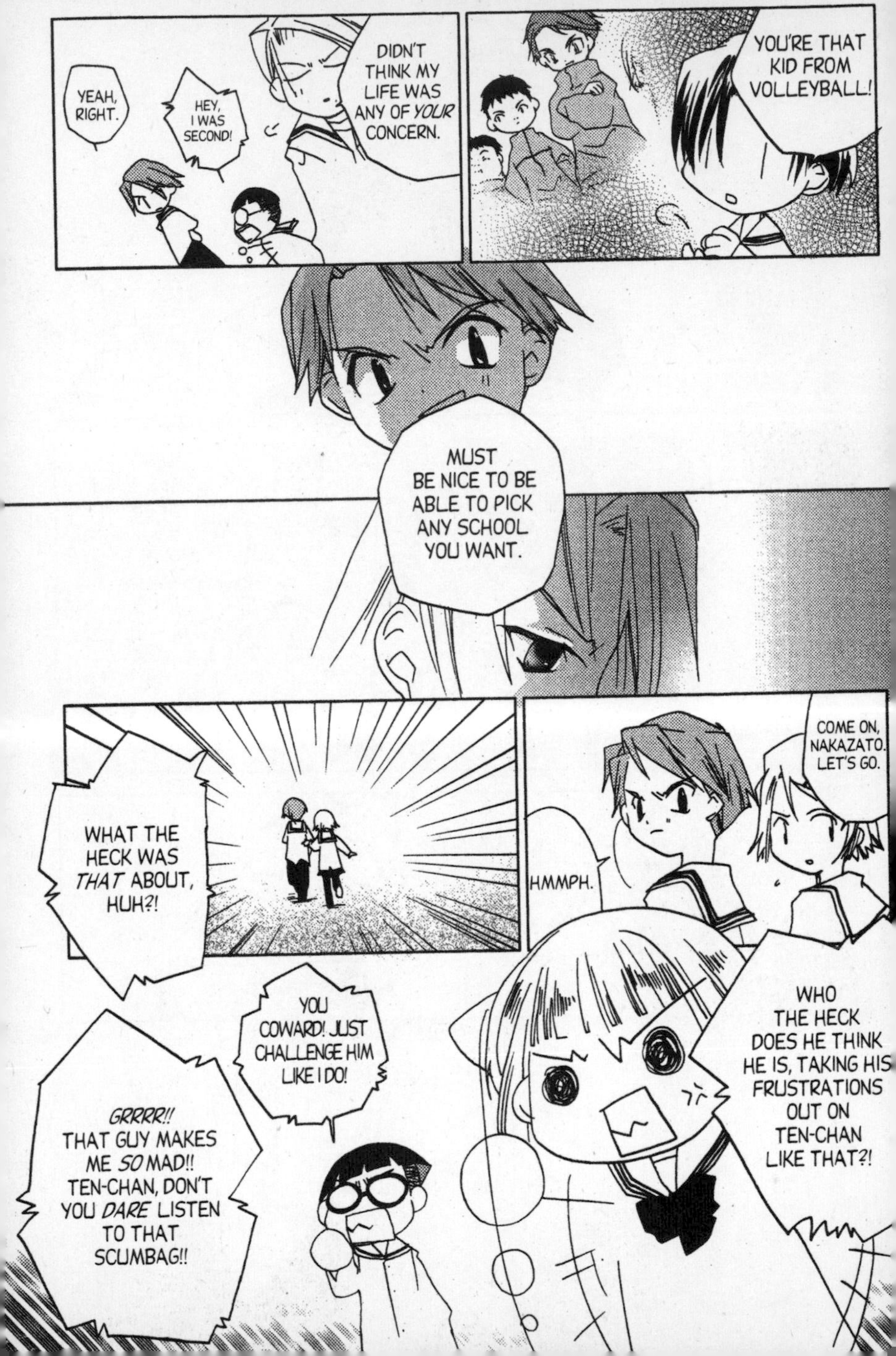
YOU'RE THAT KID FROM VOLLEYBALL!
DIDN'T THINK MY LIFE WAS ANY OF *YOUR* CONCERN.
HEY, I WAS SECOND!
YEAH, RIGHT.
MUST BE NICE TO BE ABLE TO PICK ANY SCHOOL YOU WANT.
COME ON, NAKAZATO. LET'S GO.
HMMPH.
WHAT THE HECK WAS *THAT* ABOUT, HUH?!
WHO THE HECK DOES HE THINK HE IS, TAKING HIS FRUSTRATIONS OUT ON TEN-CHAN LIKE THAT?!
YOU COWARD! JUST CHALLENGE HIM LIKE I DO!
GRRRR!! THAT GUY MAKES ME *SO* MAD!! TEN-CHAN, DON'T YOU *DARE* LISTEN TO THAT SCUMBAG!!

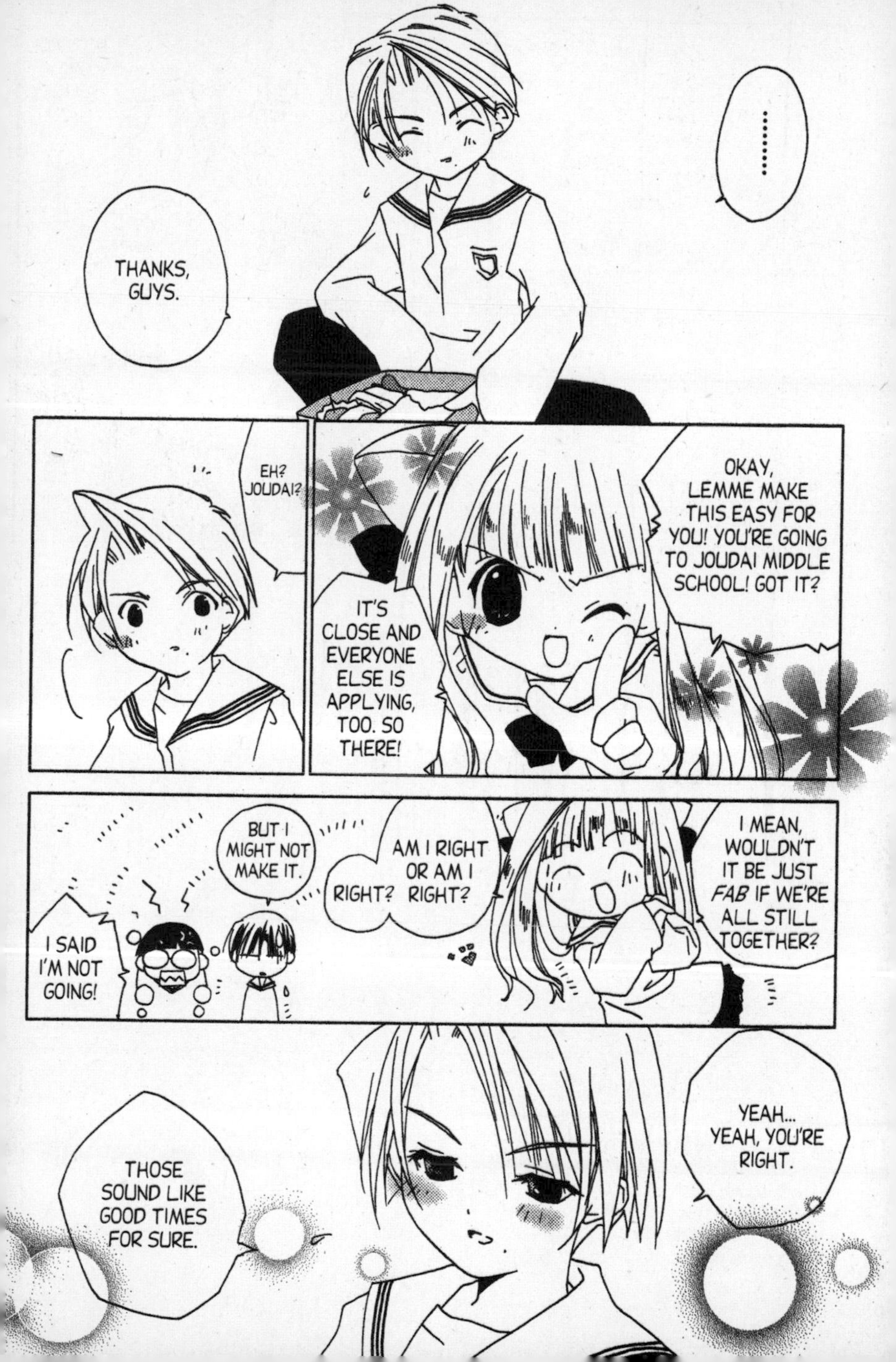
......
THANKS, GUYS.
OKAY, LEMME MAKE THIS EASY FOR YOU! YOU'RE GOING TO JOUDAI MIDDLE SCHOOL! GOT IT?
IT'S CLOSE AND EVERYONE ELSE IS APPLYING, TOO. SO THERE!
EH? JOUDAI?
I MEAN, WOULDN'T IT BE JUST *FAB* IF WE'RE ALL STILL TOGETHER?
AM I RIGHT OR AM I RIGHT? RIGHT?
BUT I MIGHT NOT MAKE IT.
I SAID I'M NOT GOING!
YEAH... YEAH, YOU'RE RIGHT.
THOSE SOUND LIKE GOOD TIMES FOR SURE.

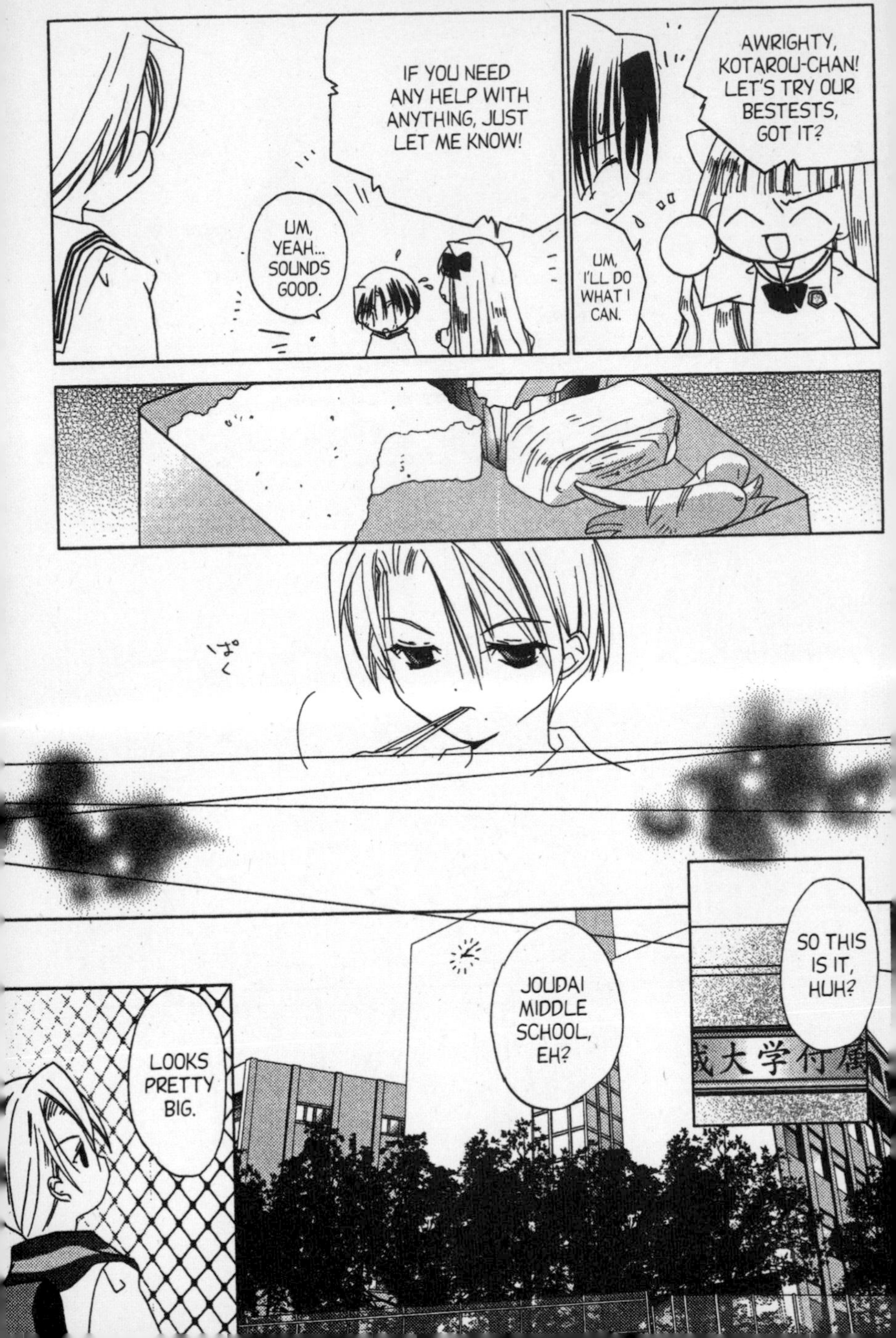
AWRIGHTY, KOTAROU-CHAN! LET'S TRY OUR BESTESTS, GOT IT?
UM, I'LL DO WHAT I CAN.
IF YOU NEED ANY HELP WITH ANYTHING, JUST LET ME KNOW!
UM, YEAH... SOUNDS GOOD.
ぱく
SO THIS IS IT, HUH?
JOUDAI MIDDLE SCHOOL, EH?
LOOKS PRETTY BIG.

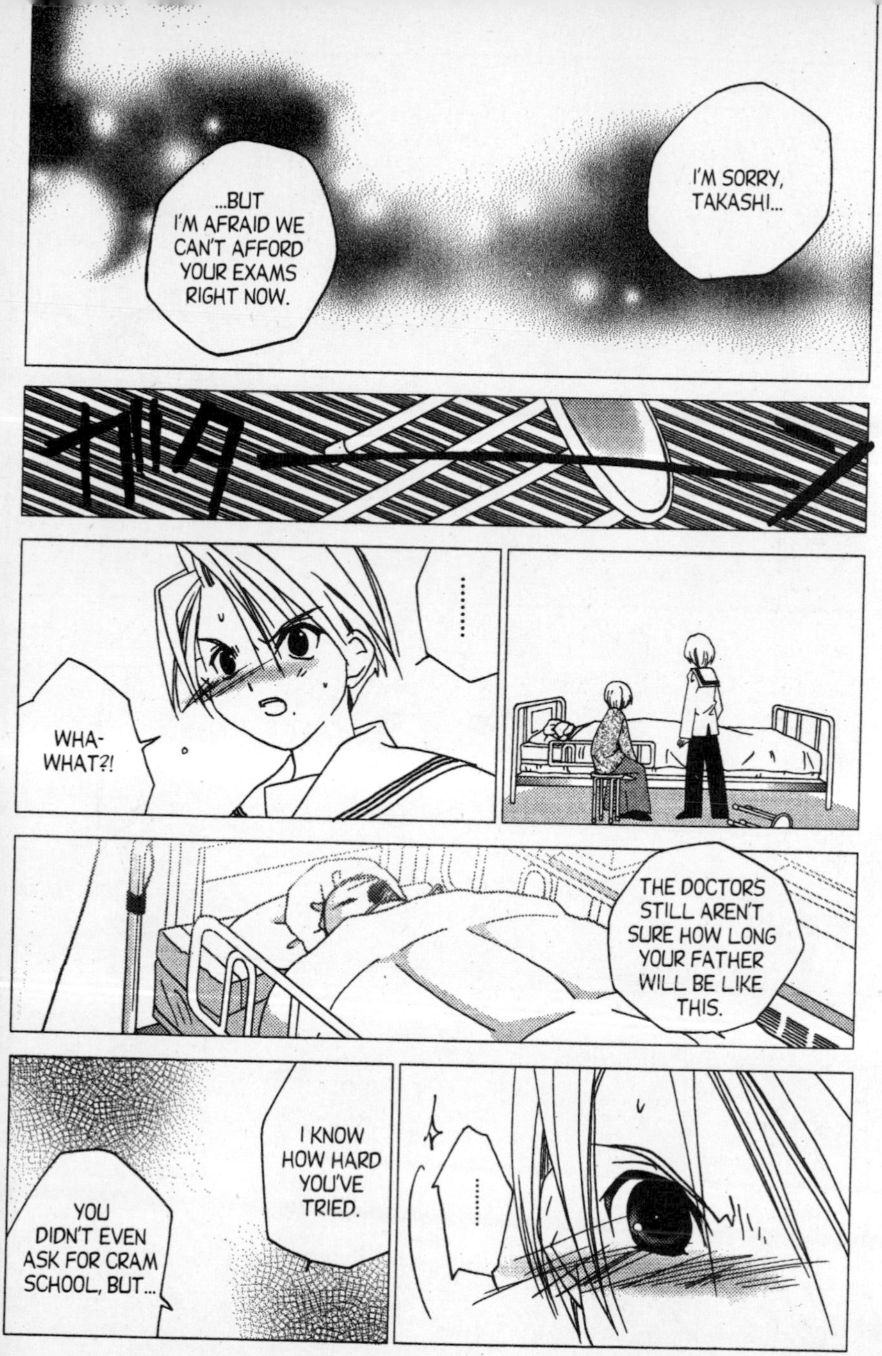
I'M SORRY, TAKASHI...
...BUT I'M AFRAID WE CAN'T AFFORD YOUR EXAMS RIGHT NOW.
......
WHA- WHAT?!
THE DOCTORS STILL AREN'T SURE HOW LONG YOUR FATHER WILL BE LIKE THIS.
......
I KNOW HOW HARD YOU'VE TRIED.
YOU DIDN'T EVEN ASK FOR CRAM SCHOOL, BUT...

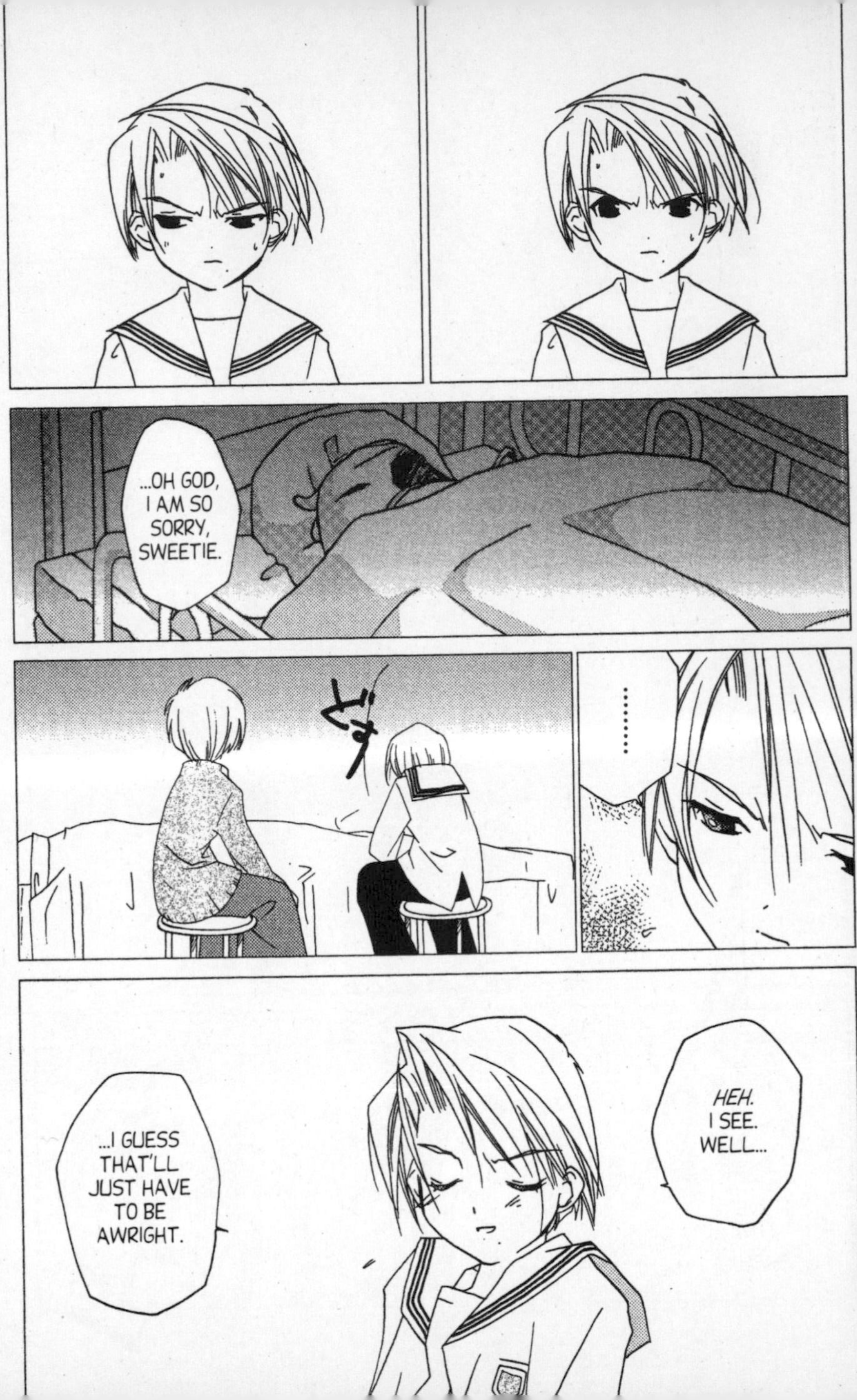
...OH GOD, I AM SO SORRY, SWEETIE.
......
どす
HEH. I SEE. WELL...
...I GUESS THAT'LL JUST HAVE TO BE AWRIGHT.

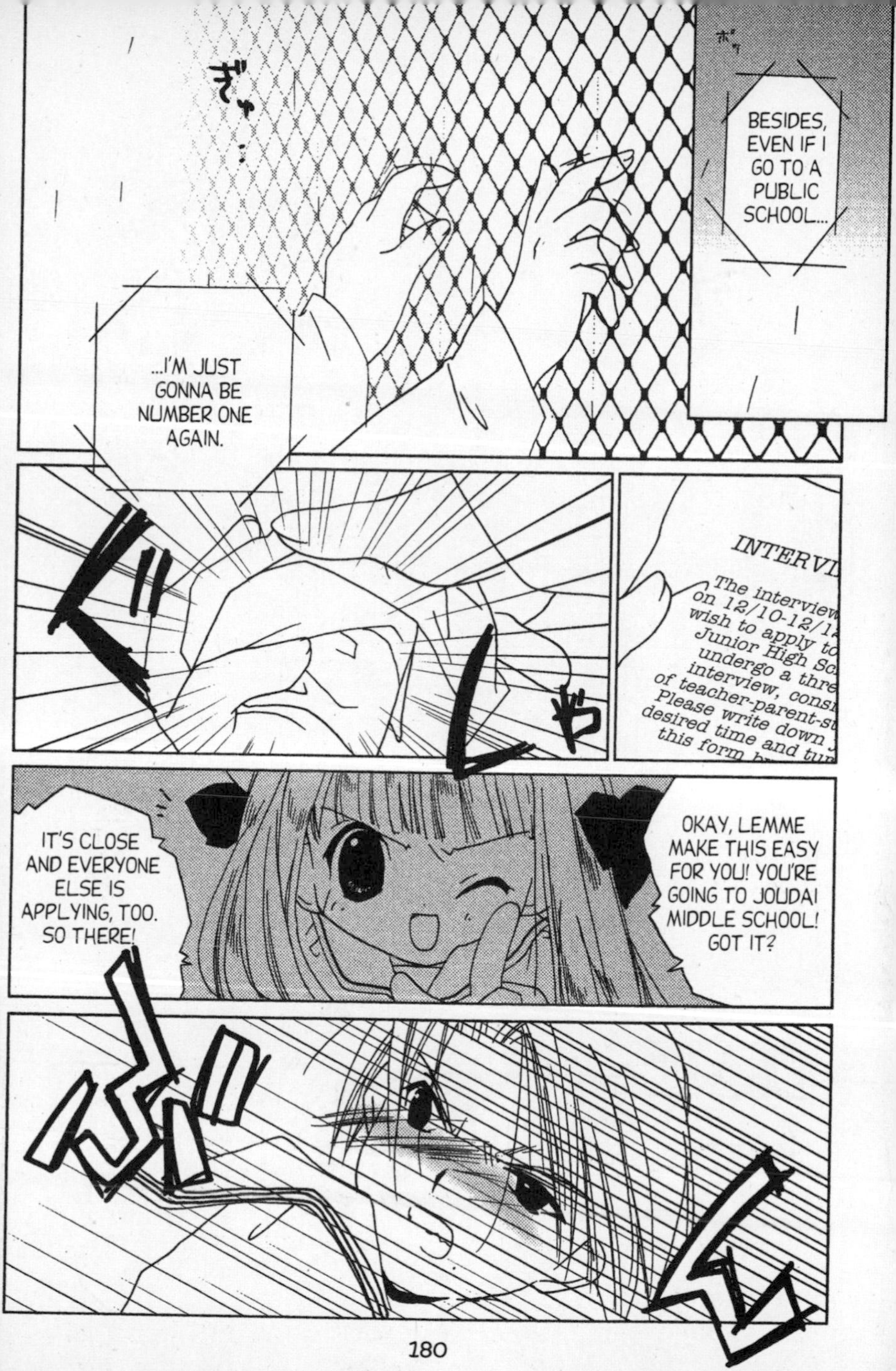
BESIDES, EVEN IF I GO TO A PUBLIC SCHOOL...
...I'M JUST GONNA BE NUMBER ONE AGAIN.
INTERVI
The interview
on 12/10-12/1
wish to apply t
Junior High Sc
undergo a thre
interview, consi
of teacher-parent-s
Please write down
desired time and tu
OKAY, LEMME MAKE THIS EASY FOR YOU! YOU'RE GOING TO JOUDAI MIDDLE SCHOOL! GOT IT?
IT'S CLOSE AND EVERYONE ELSE IS APPLYING, TOO. SO THERE!

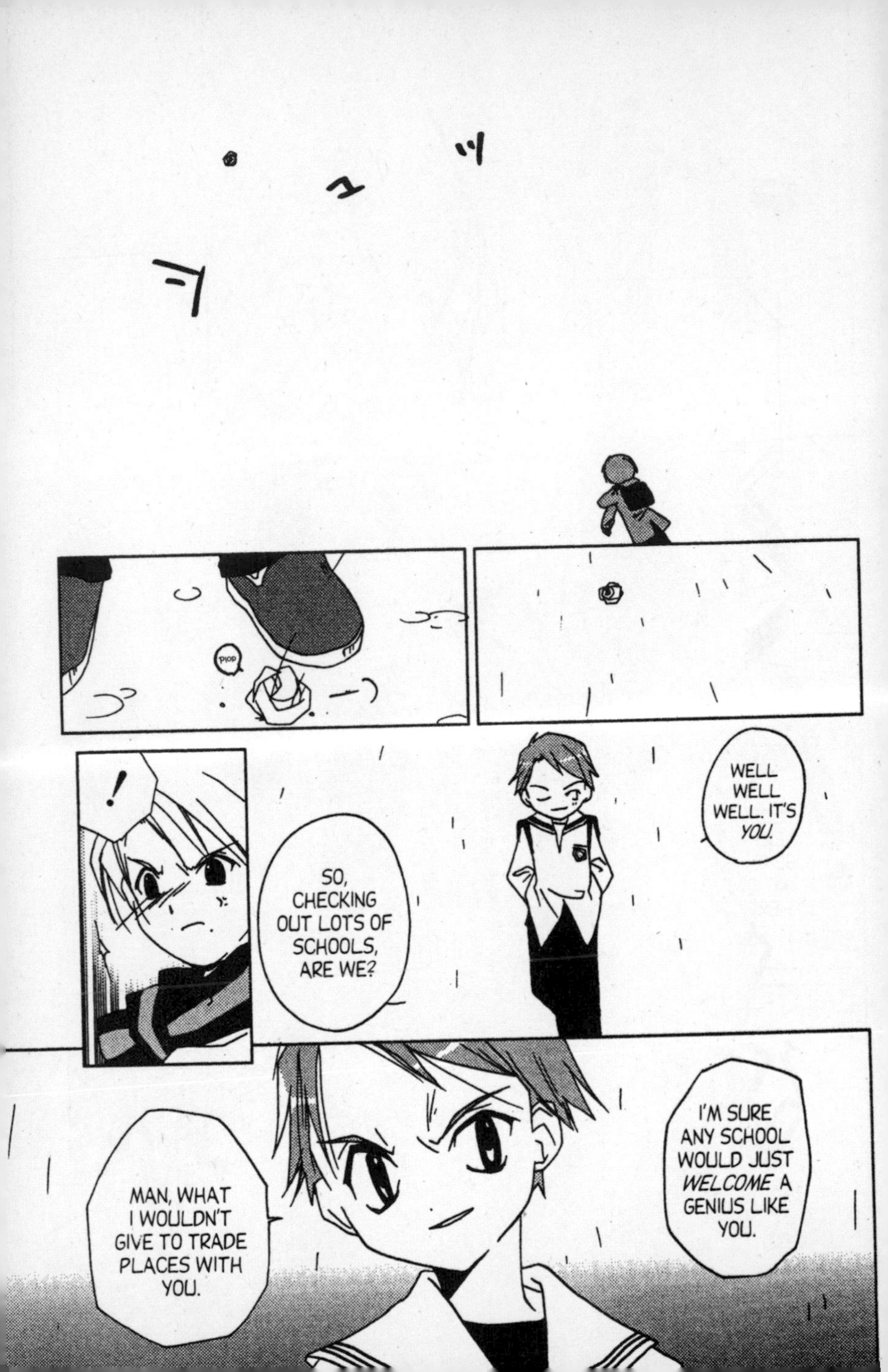
PLOP
WELL WELL WELL. IT'S *YOU.*
SO, CHECKING OUT LOTS OF SCHOOLS, ARE WE?
!
I'M SURE ANY SCHOOL WOULD JUST *WELCOME* A GENIUS LIKE YOU.
MAN, WHAT I WOULDN'T GIVE TO TRADE PLACES WITH YOU.

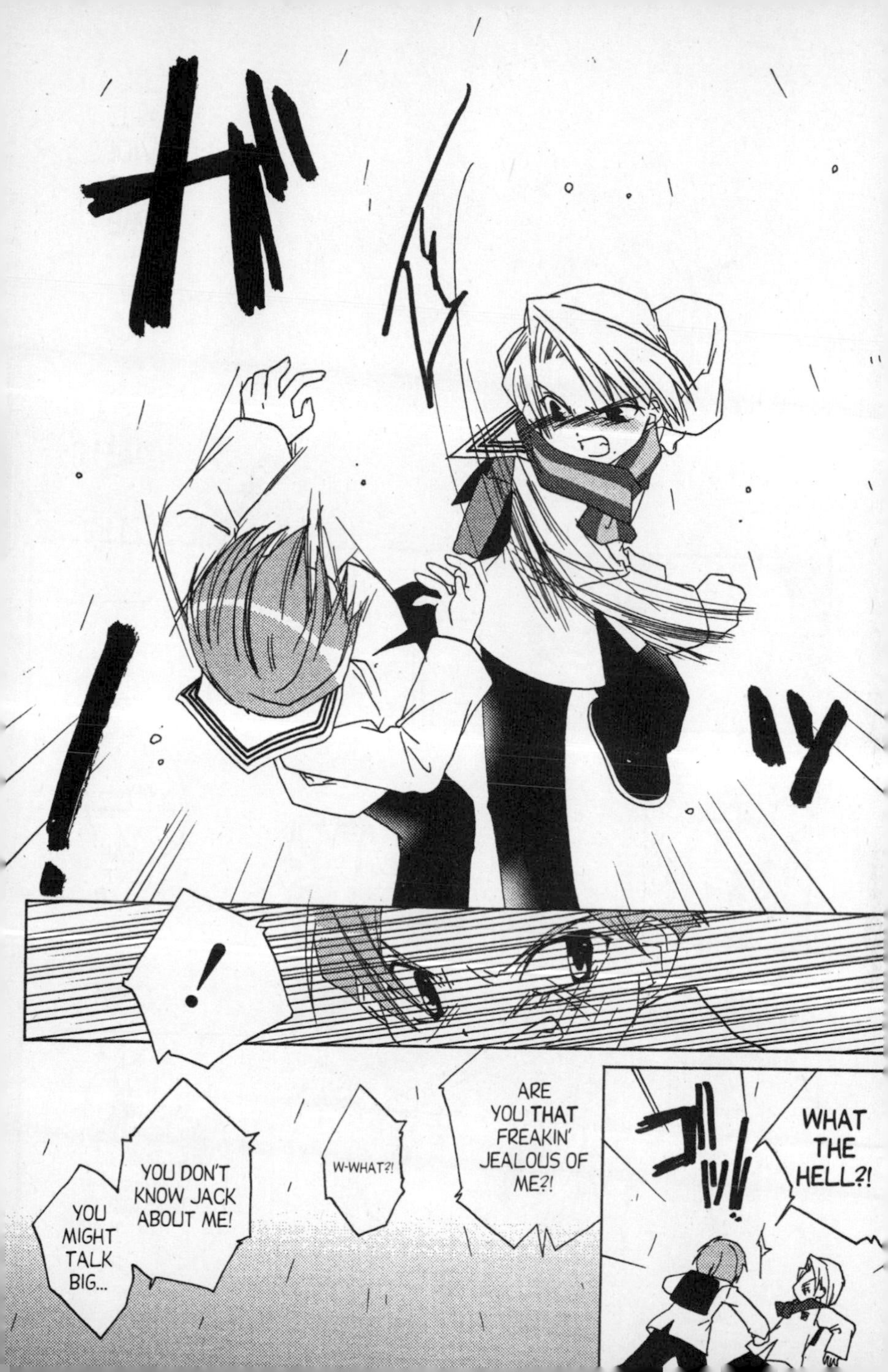
ガッ!
!
WHAT THE HELL?!
ゴッ!!
ARE YOU THAT FREAKIN' JEALOUS OF ME?!
W-WHAT?!
YOU DON'T KNOW JACK ABOUT ME!
YOU MIGHT TALK BIG...

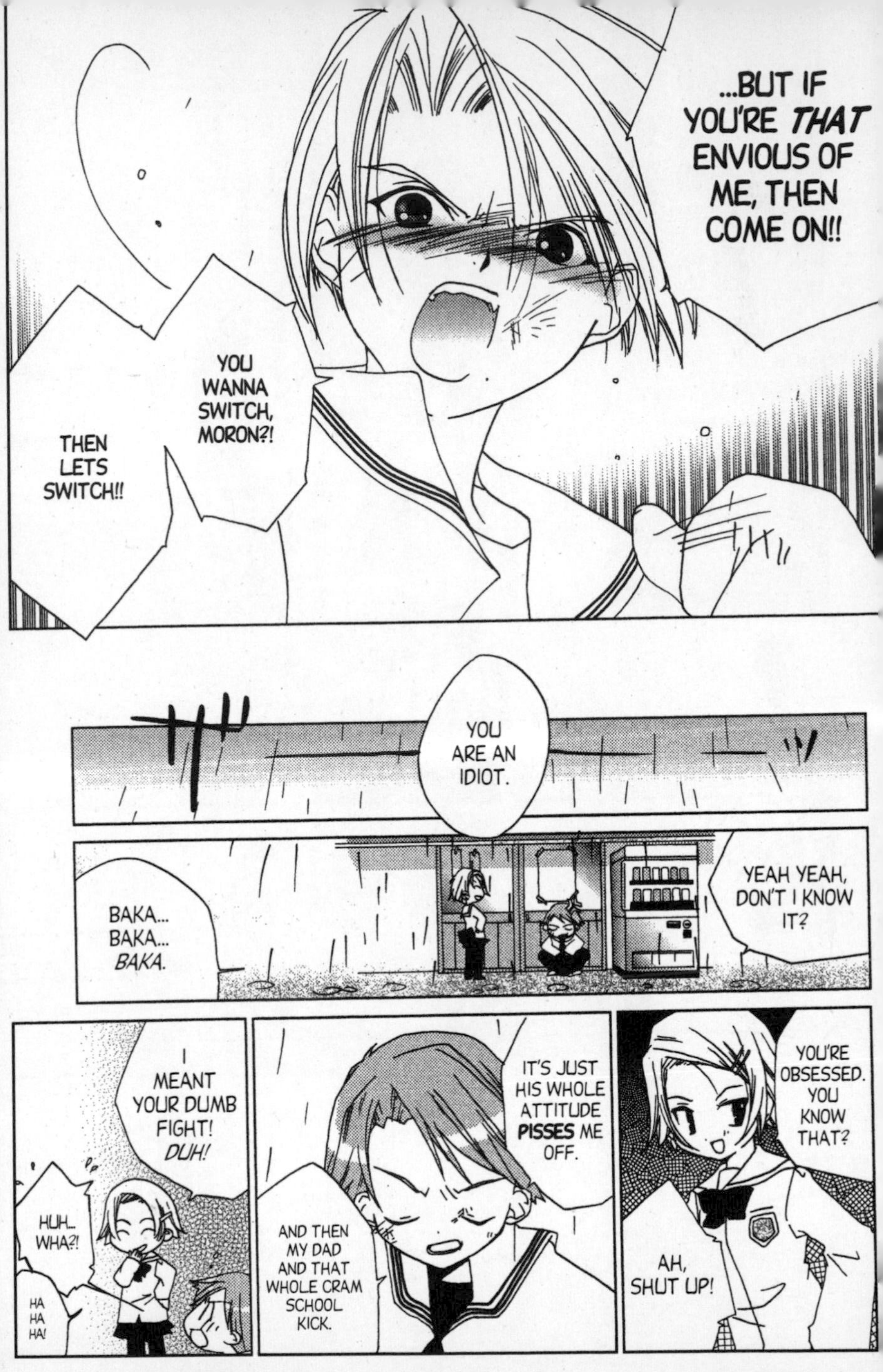

...BUT IF YOU'RE *THAT* ENVIOUS OF ME, THEN COME ON!!
YOU WANNA SWITCH, MORON?!
THEN LETS SWITCH!!
YOU ARE AN IDIOT.
YEAH YEAH, DON'T I KNOW IT?
BAKA... BAKA... *BAKA.*
YOU'RE OBSESSED. YOU KNOW THAT?
AH, SHUT UP!
IT'S JUST HIS WHOLE ATTITUDE **PISSES** ME OFF.
AND THEN MY DAD AND THAT WHOLE CRAM SCHOOL KICK.
I MEANT YOUR DUMB FIGHT! *DUH!*
HUH.. WHA?!
HA HA HA!

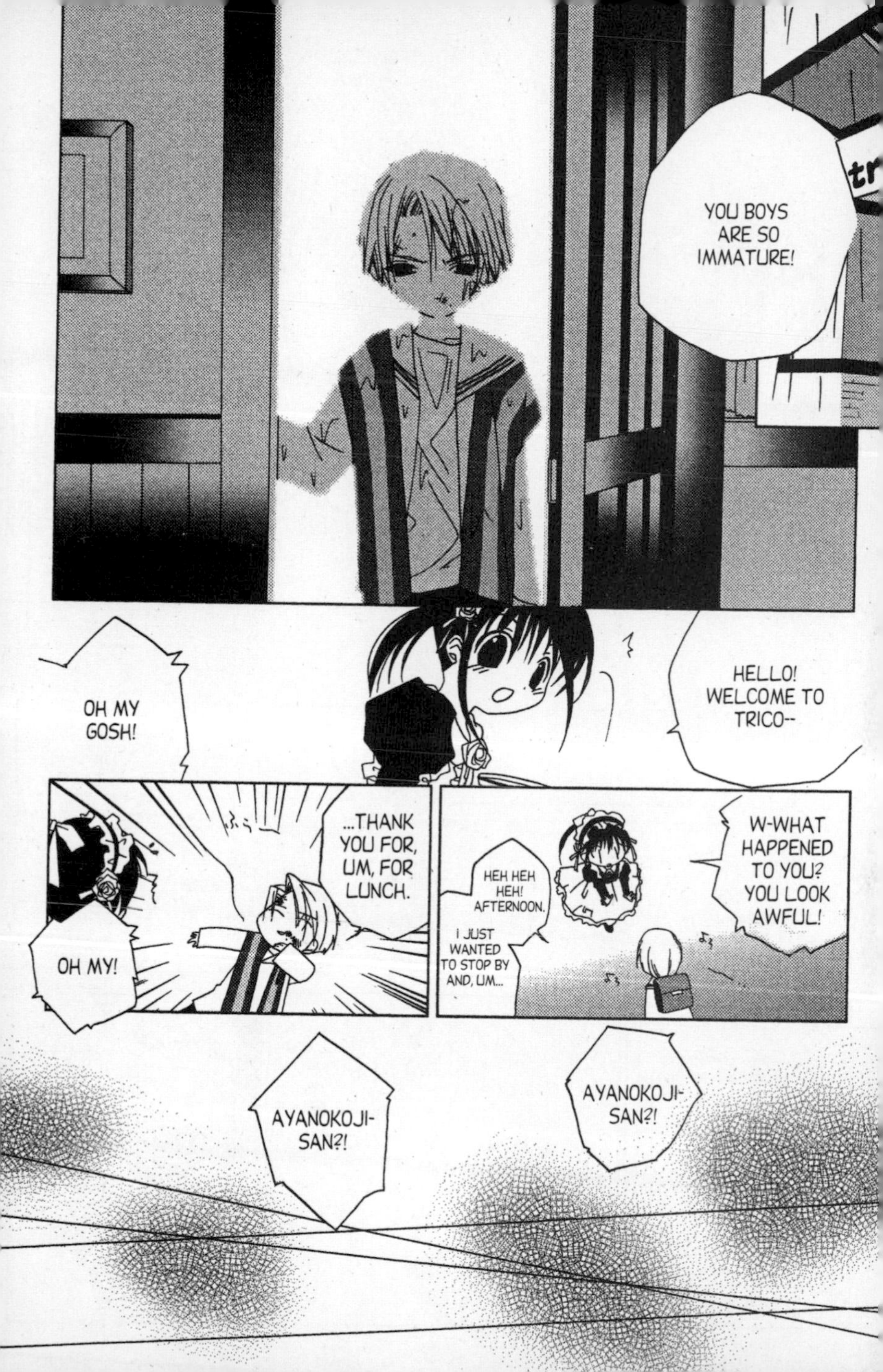
YOU BOYS ARE SO IMMATURE!
HELLO! WELCOME TO TRICO--
OH MY GOSH!
W-WHAT HAPPENED TO YOU? YOU LOOK AWFUL!
HEH HEH HEH! AFTERNOON.
I JUST WANTED TO STOP BY AND, UM...
...THANK YOU FOR, UM, FOR LUNCH.
OH MY!
AYANOKOJI-SAN?!
AYANOKOJI-SAN?!

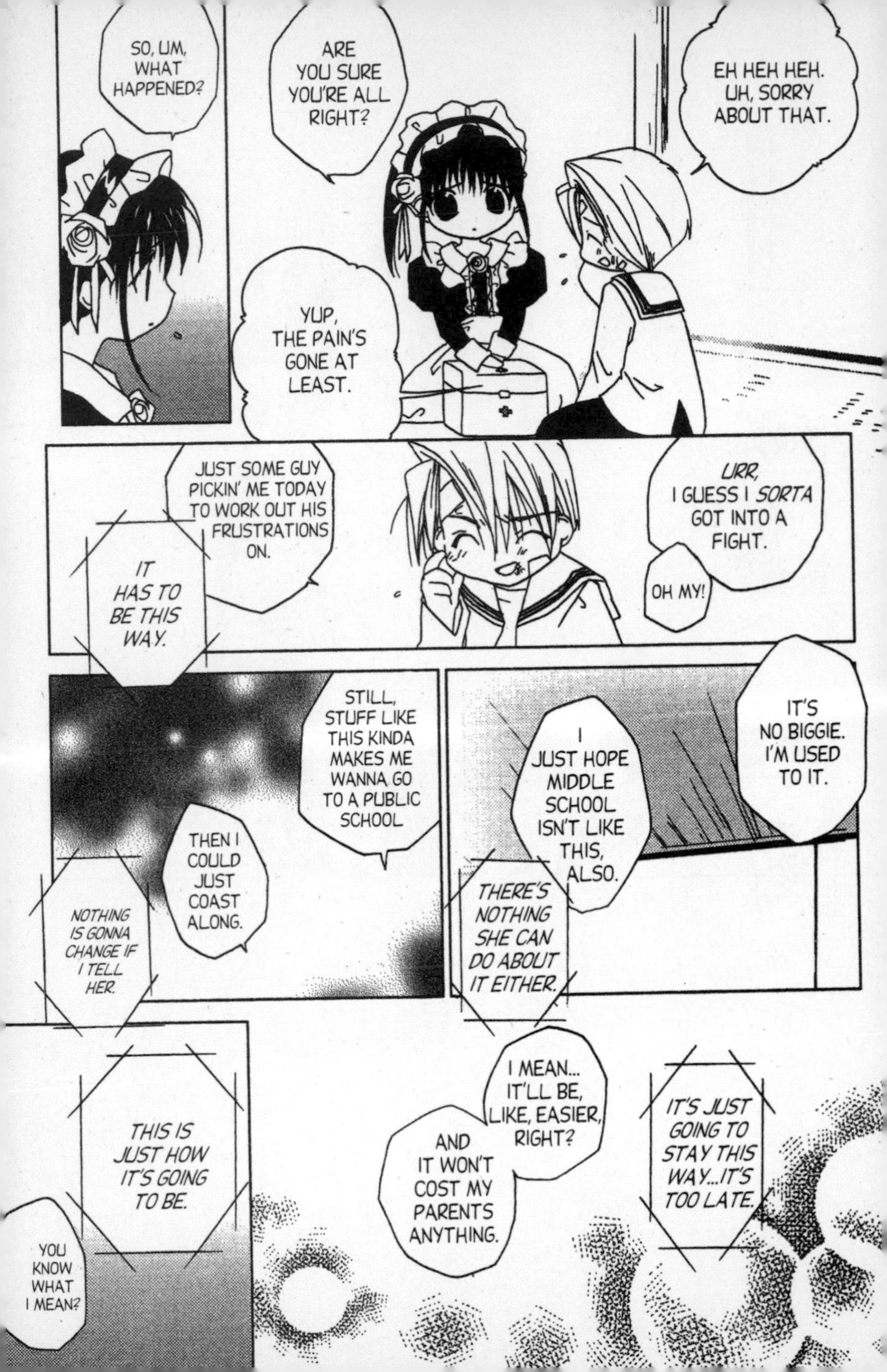
EH HEH HEH. UH, SORRY ABOUT THAT.
ARE YOU SURE YOU'RE ALL RIGHT?
YUP, THE PAIN'S GONE AT LEAST.
SO, UM, WHAT HAPPENED?
URR, I GUESS I SORTA GOT INTO A FIGHT.
OH MY!
JUST SOME GUY PICKIN' ME TODAY TO WORK OUT HIS FRUSTRATIONS ON.
IT HAS TO BE THIS WAY.
IT'S NO BIGGIE. I'M USED TO IT.
I JUST HOPE MIDDLE SCHOOL ISN'T LIKE THIS, ALSO.
THERE'S NOTHING SHE CAN DO ABOUT IT EITHER.
STILL, STUFF LIKE THIS KINDA MAKES ME WANNA GO TO A PUBLIC SCHOOL
THEN I COULD JUST COAST ALONG.
NOTHING IS GONNA CHANGE IF I TELL HER.
IT'S JUST GOING TO STAY THIS WAY...IT'S TOO LATE.
I MEAN... IT'LL BE, LIKE, EASIER, RIGHT?
AND IT WON'T COST MY PARENTS ANYTHING.
THIS IS JUST HOW IT'S GOING TO BE.
YOU KNOW WHAT I MEAN?

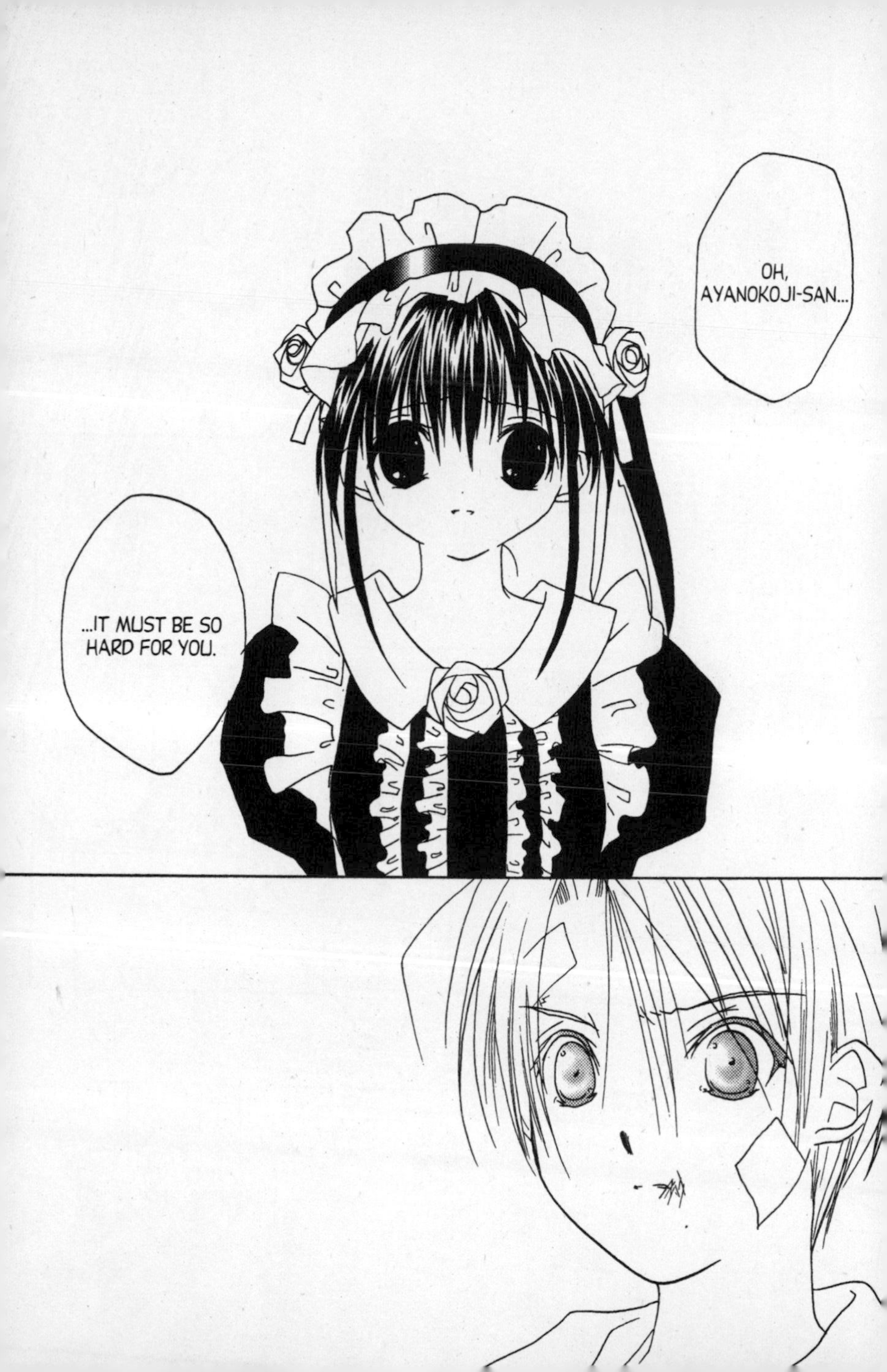
OH, AYANOKOJI-SAN...
...IT MUST BE SO HARD FOR YOU.

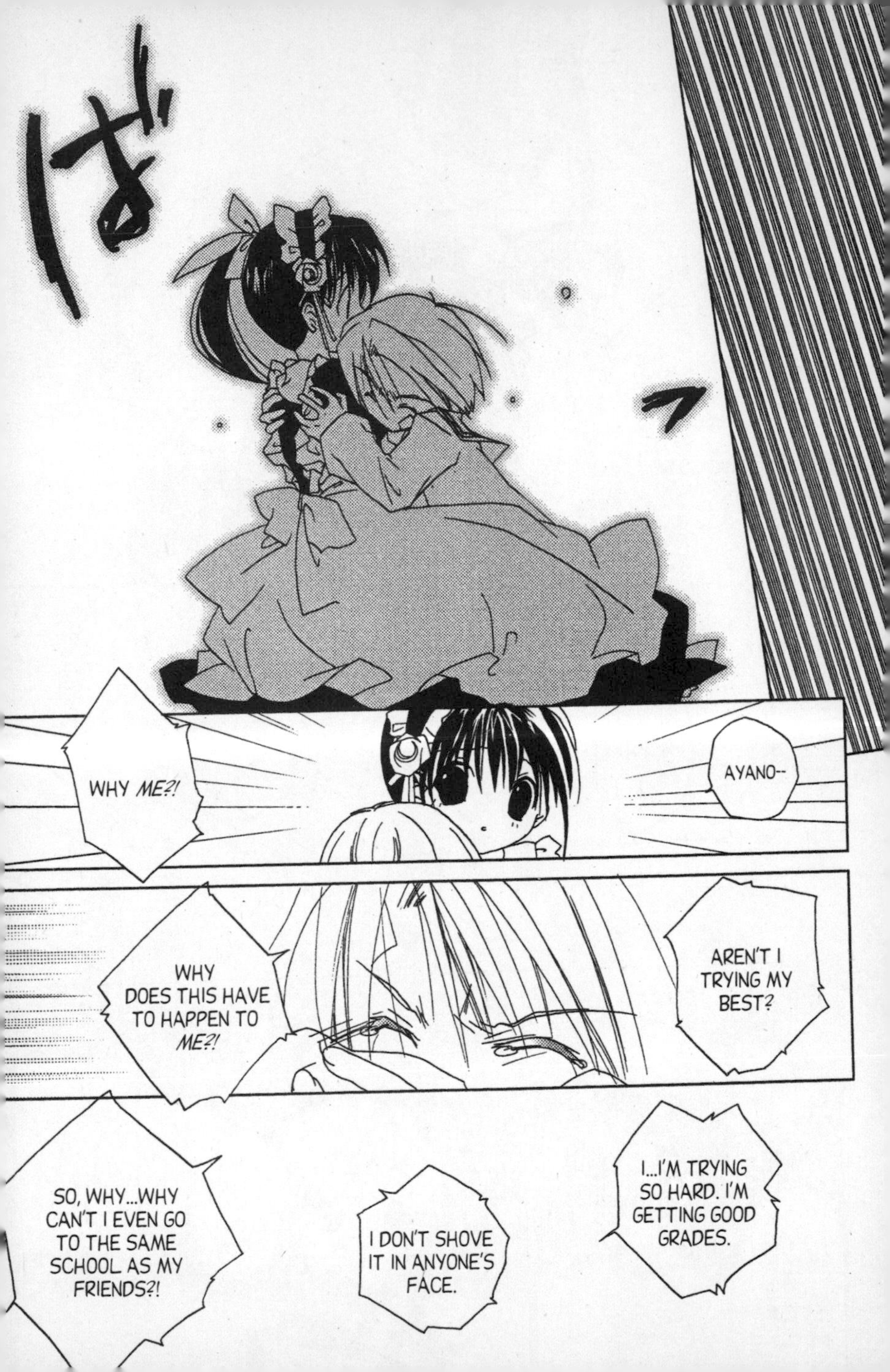
ば
AYANO--
WHY *ME?!*
AREN'T I TRYING MY BEST?
WHY DOES THIS HAVE TO HAPPEN TO *ME?!*
I...I'M TRYING SO HARD. I'M GETTING GOOD GRADES.
I DON'T SHOVE IT IN ANYONE'S FACE.
SO, WHY...WHY CAN'T I EVEN GO TO THE SAME SCHOOL AS MY FRIENDS?!

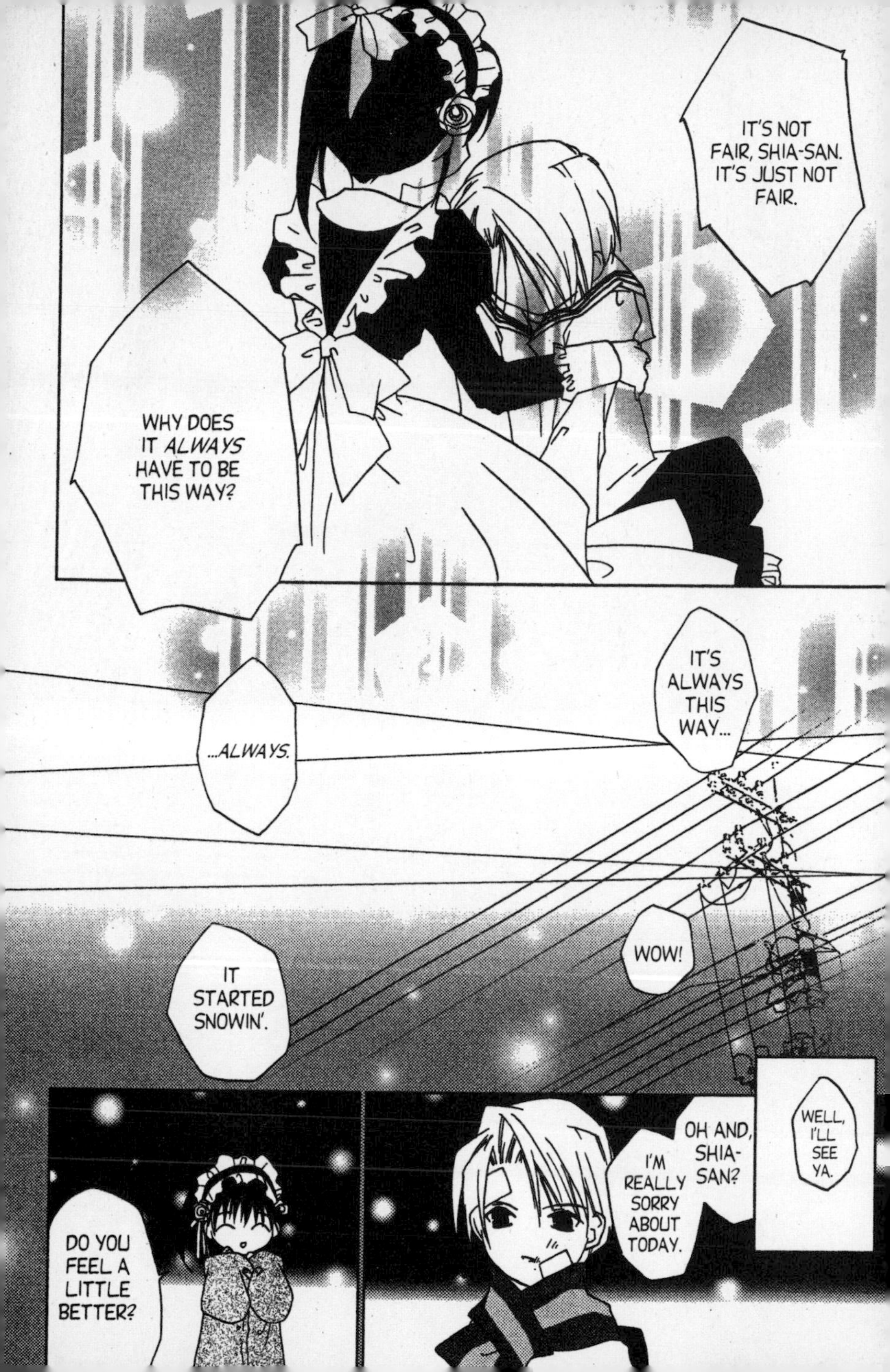
IT'S NOT FAIR, SHIA-SAN. IT'S JUST NOT FAIR.
WHY DOES IT *ALWAYS* HAVE TO BE THIS WAY?
IT'S ALWAYS THIS WAY...
...*ALWAYS.*
WOW!
IT STARTED SNOWIN'.
WELL, I'LL SEE YA.
OH AND, SHIA-SAN?
I'M REALLY SORRY ABOUT TODAY.
DO YOU FEEL A LITTLE BETTER?

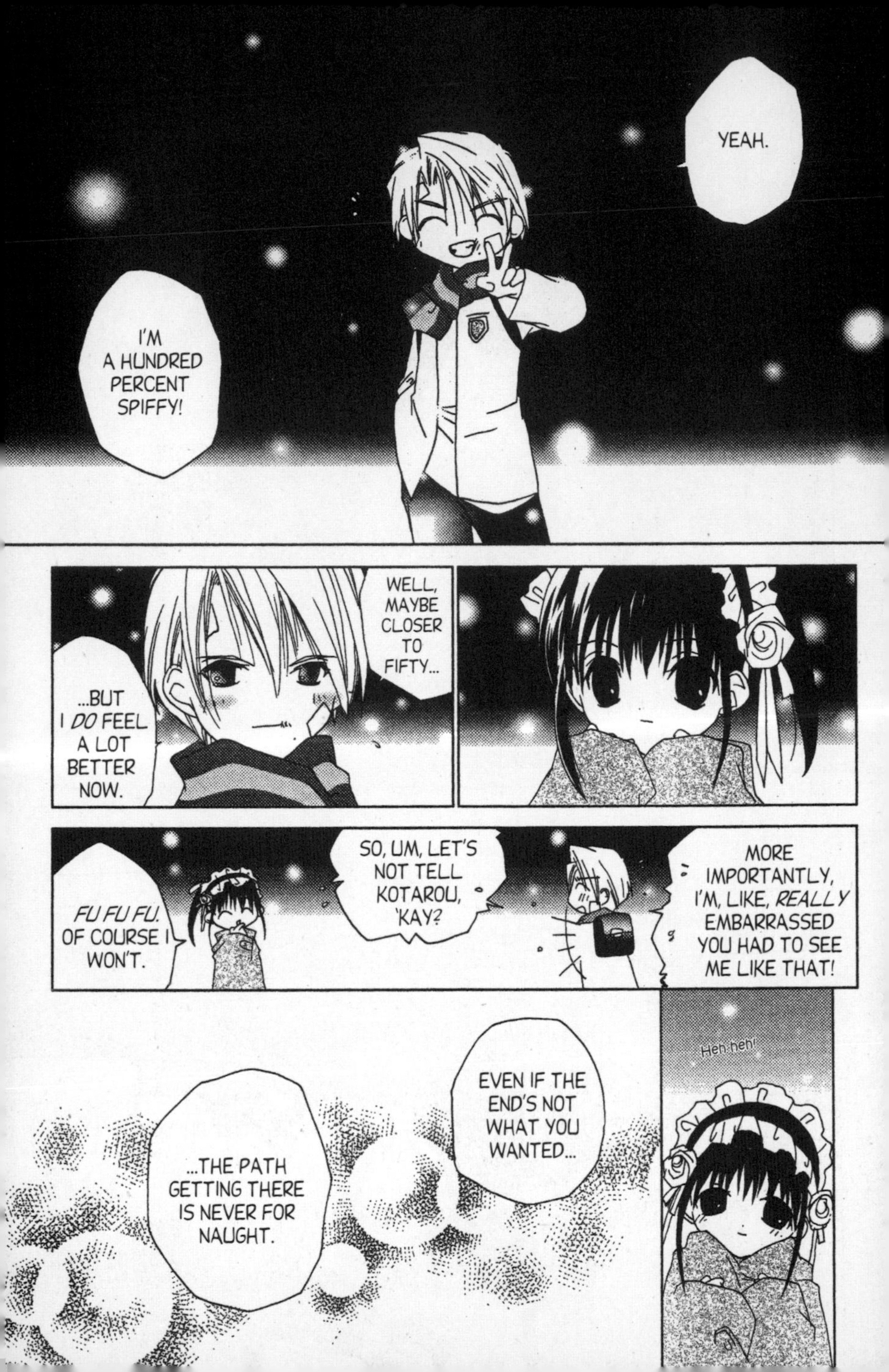
YEAH.
I'M A HUNDRED PERCENT SPIFFY!
WELL, MAYBE CLOSER TO FIFTY...
...BUT I *DO* FEEL A LOT BETTER NOW.
MORE IMPORTANTLY, I'M, LIKE, *REALLY* EMBARRASSED YOU HAD TO SEE ME LIKE THAT!
SO, UM, LET'S NOT TELL KOTAROU, 'KAY?
FU FU FU. OF COURSE I WON'T.
Heh heh!
EVEN IF THE END'S NOT WHAT YOU WANTED...
...THE PATH GETTING THERE IS NEVER FOR NAUGHT.

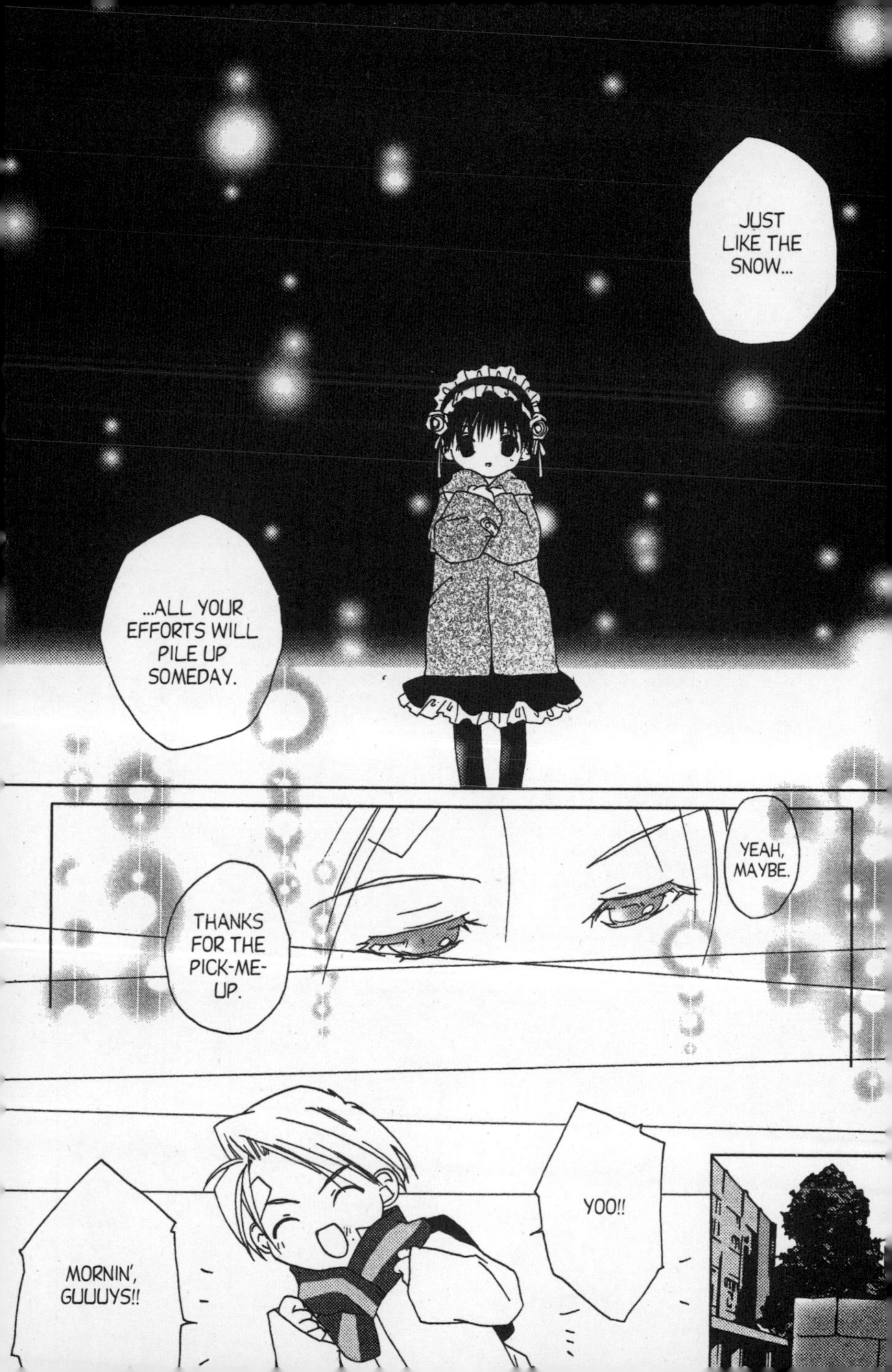
JUST LIKE THE SNOW...
...ALL YOUR EFFORTS WILL PILE UP SOMEDAY.
YEAH, MAYBE.
THANKS FOR THE PICK-ME-UP.
YOO!!
MORNIN', GUUUYS!!

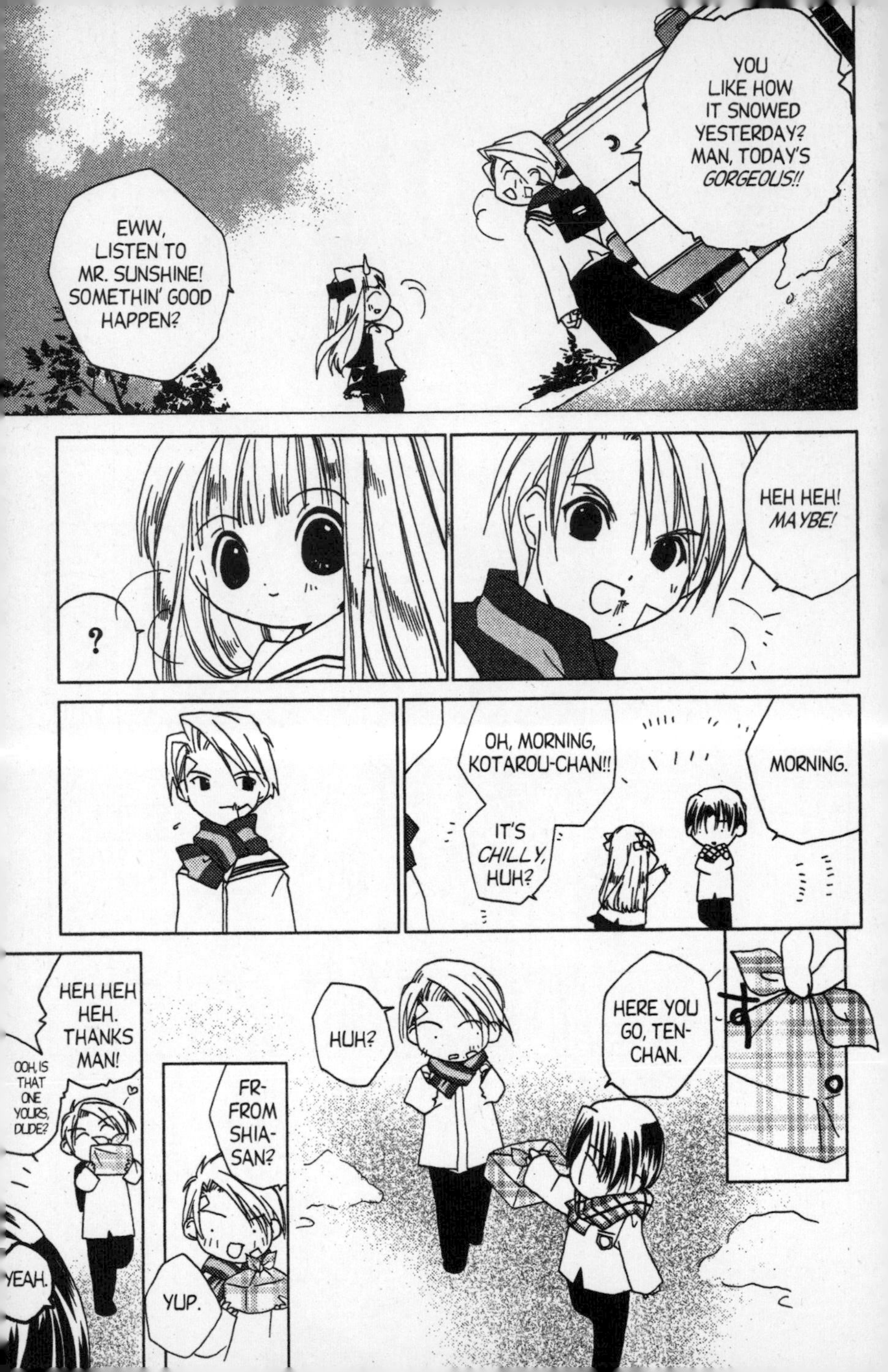
YOU LIKE HOW IT SNOWED YESTERDAY? MAN, TODAY'S *GORGEOUS!!*
EWW, LISTEN TO MR. SUNSHINE! SOMETHIN' GOOD HAPPEN?
HEH HEH! *MAYBE!*
?
MORNING.
OH, MORNING, KOTAROU-CHAN!!
IT'S *CHILLY,* HUH?
HERE YOU GO, TEN-CHAN.
HUH?
FR-FROM SHIA-SAN?
YUP.
HEH HEH HEH. THANKS MAN!
OOH, IS THAT ONE YOURS, DUDE?
YEAH.

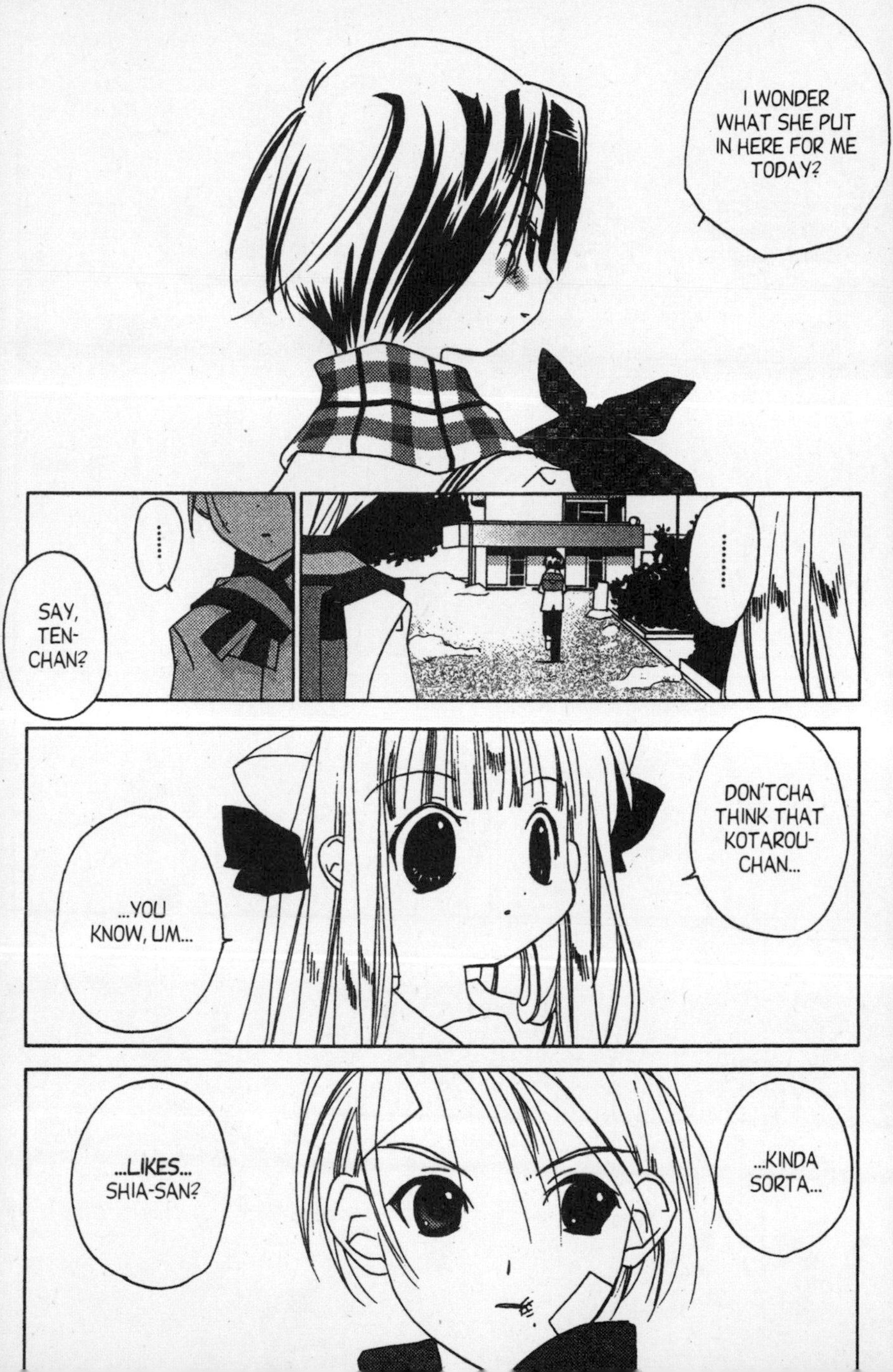
I WONDER WHAT SHE PUT IN HERE FOR ME TODAY?
....
......
SAY, TEN-CHAN?
DON'TCHA THINK THAT KOTAROU-CHAN...
...YOU KNOW, UM...
...KINDA SORTA...
...LIKES... SHIA-SAN?

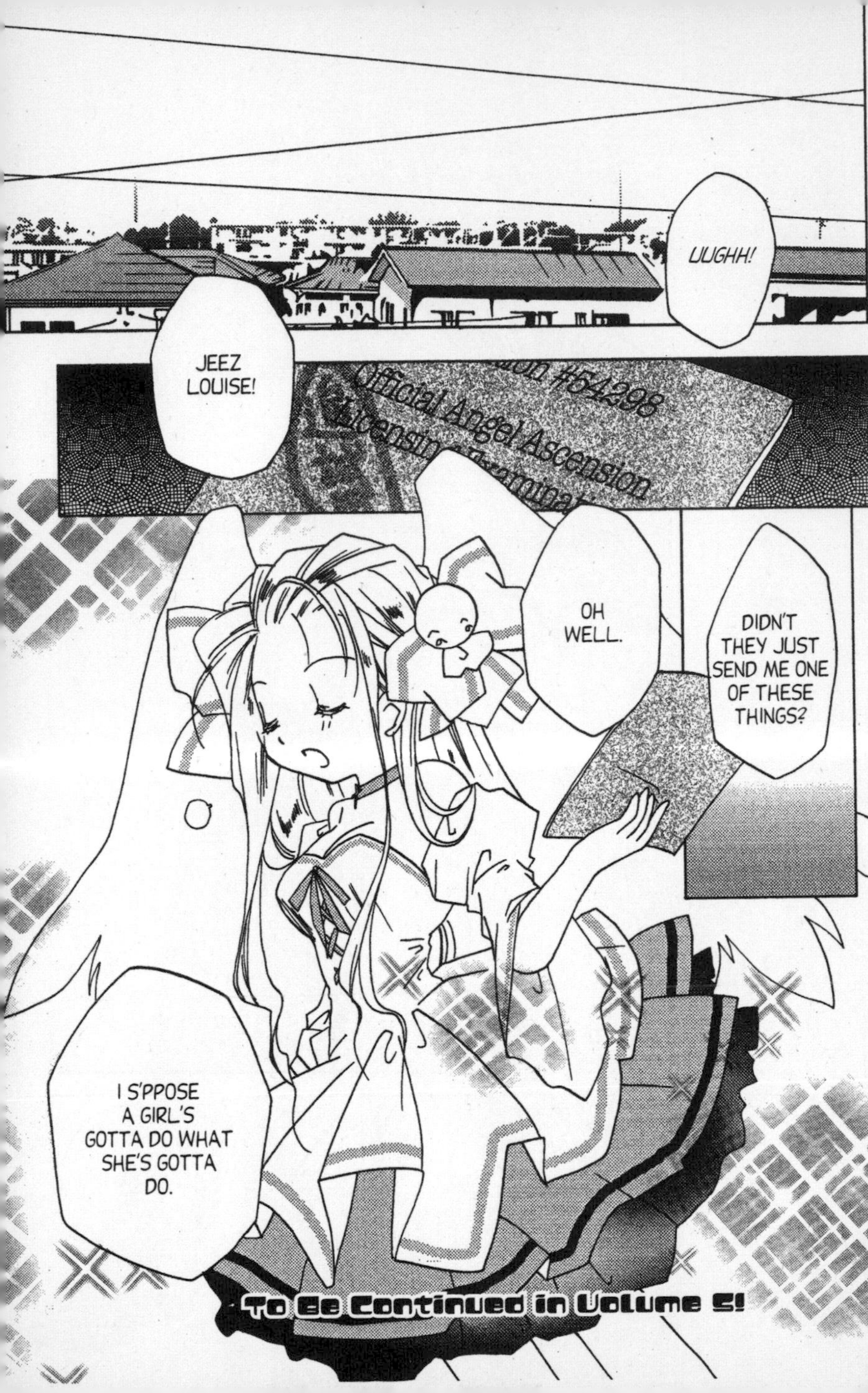
UUGHH!
JEEZ LOUISE!
Official Angel Ascension
DIDN'T THEY JUST SEND ME ONE OF THESE THINGS?
OH WELL.
I S'PPOSE A GIRL'S GOTTA DO WHAT SHE'S GOTTA DO.
To Be Continued in Volume 5!

★ HEYAS AND HELLO, GANG!

WELL, YOU JUST GOT THROUGH THE FOURTH VOLUME AND I JUST WANT TO THANK YOU SO VERY, VERY MUCH FOR CONTINUING TO SUPPORT US!

I KNOW THAT I STILL HAVE A LOT TO LEARN, BUT I AM GOING TO KEEP ON TRYING! SO, DON'T GIVE UP ON ME, PLEASE?!

★ NOW, LET'S GET THIS STRAIGHT. I MIGHT BE DRAWING A MANGA ABOUT MIDDLE SCHOOL EXAMS, BUT I'VE NEVER ACTUALLY TAKEN THEM. I'VE DEFINITELY DONE RESEARCH ON THEM, BUT I'M SURE THAT I'M BOUND TO BE MISSING SOMETHING.

★ IF THERE IS ANYONE OUT THERE WHO *HAS* TAKEN THEM AND CAN THINK OF SOMETHING THAT NEEDS TO BE INCLUDED OR VICE VERSA, PLEASE WRITE ME AND LET ME KNOW!

PLEEEEEEASE?!

★ ON THAT NOTE, I HOPE TO SEE YOU ALL AGAIN IN VOLUME 5!

2001.10.

KOGE

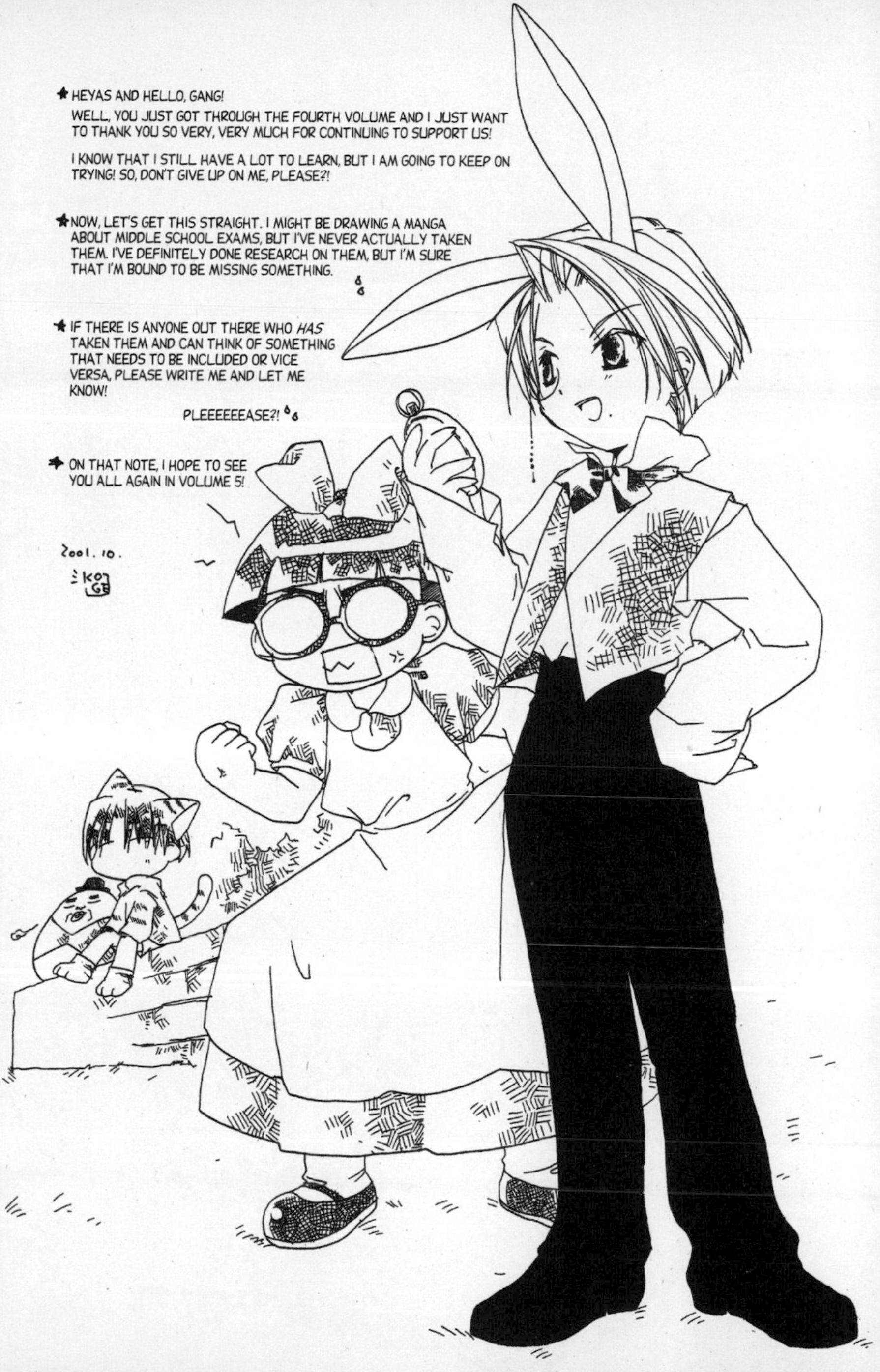

以下次巻。

THERE'S SURE TO BE
MORE NEXT TIME!

KOGE

In the Next Volume of...

PITA-TEN

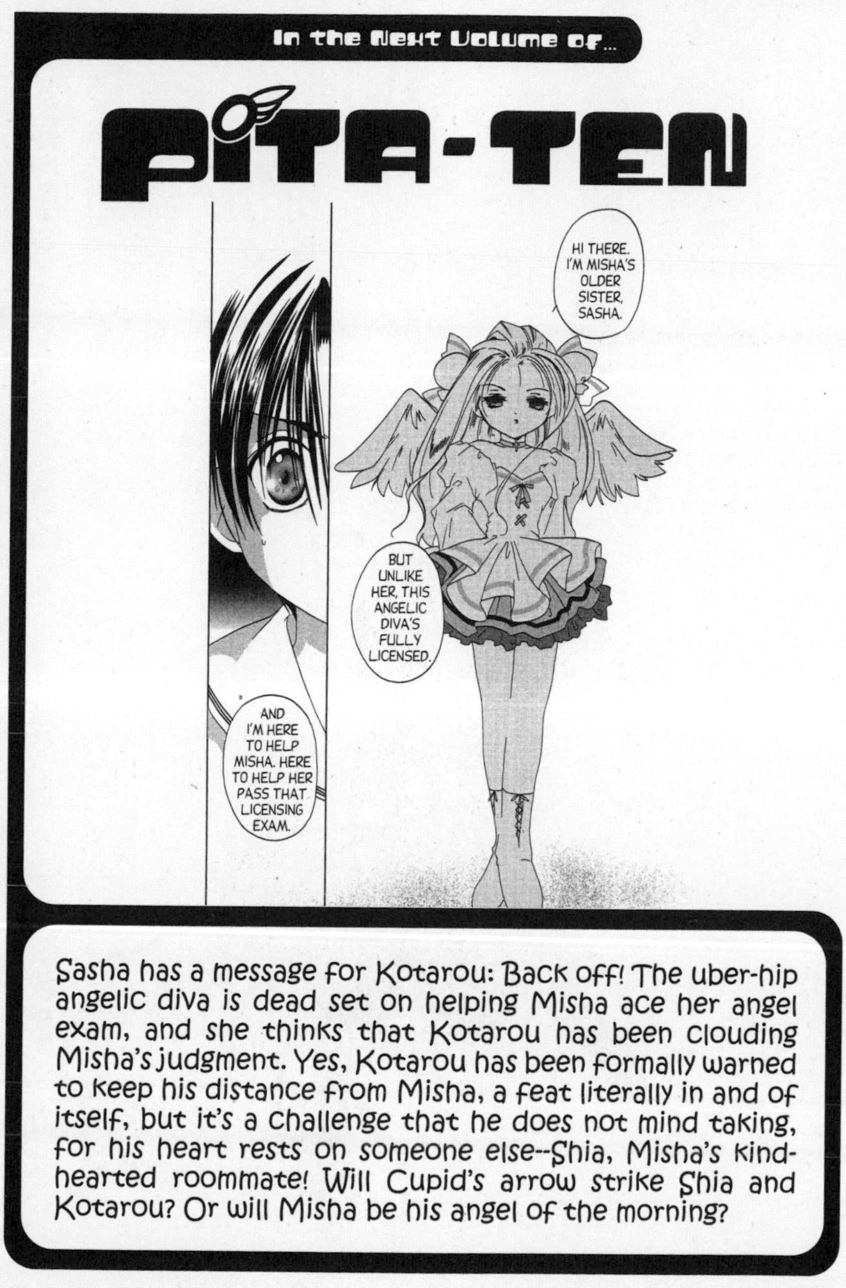
HI THERE. I'M MISHA'S OLDER SISTER, SASHA.
BUT UNLIKE HER, THIS ANGELIC DIVA'S FULLY LICENSED.
AND I'M HERE TO HELP MISHA. HERE TO HELP HER PASS THAT LICENSING EXAM.

Sasha has a message for Kotarou: Back off! The uber-hip angelic diva is dead set on helping Misha ace her angel exam, and she thinks that Kotarou has been clouding Misha's judgment. Yes, Kotarou has been formally warned to keep his distance from Misha, a feat literally in and of itself, but it's a challenge that he does not mind taking, for his heart rests on someone else--Shia, Misha's kind-hearted roommate! Will Cupid's arrow strike Shia and Kotarou? Or will Misha be his angel of the morning?

ALSO AVAILABLE FROM TOKYOPOP®

ALSO AVAILABLE FROM 🎧 TOKYOPOP®

MANGA

.HACK//LEGEND OF THE TWILIGHT
ANGELIC LAYER
BABY BIRTH
BRAIN POWERED
BRIGADOON
B'TX
CANDIDATE FOR GODDESS, THE
CARDCAPTOR SAKURA
CARDCAPTOR SAKURA - MASTER OF THE CLOW
CHRONICLES OF THE CURSED SWORD
CLAMP SCHOOL DETECTIVES
CLOVER
COMIC PARTY
CORRECTOR YUI
COWBOY BEBOP
COWBOY BEBOP: SHOOTING STAR
CRAZY LOVE STORY
CRESCENT MOON
CROSS
CULDCEPT
CYBORG 009
D•N•ANGEL
DEMON DIARY
DEMON ORORON, THE
DIGIMON
DIGIMON TAMERS
DIGIMON ZERO TWO
DRAGON HUNTER
DRAGON KNIGHTS
DRAGON VOICE
DREAM SAGA
DUKLYON: CLAMP SCHOOL DEFENDERS
ET CETERA
ETERNITY
FAERIES' LANDING
FLCL
FLOWER OF THE DEEP SLEEP
FORBIDDEN DANCE
FRUITS BASKET
G GUNDAM
GATEKEEPERS
GIRL GOT GAME
GIRLS' EDUCATIONAL CHARTER
GUNDAM BLUE DESTINY
GUNDAM SEED ASTRAY
GUNDAM WING
GUNDAM WING: BATTLEFIELD OF PACIFISTS
GUNDAM WING: ENDLESS WALTZ

GUNDAM WING: THE LAST OUTPOST (G-UNIT)
HANDS OFF!
HARLEM BEAT
IMMORTAL RAIN
I.N.V.U.
INITIAL D
INSTANT TEEN: JUST ADD NUTS
JING: KING OF BANDITS
JING: KING OF BANDITS - TWILIGHT TALES
JULINE
KARE KANO
KILL ME, KISS ME
KINDAICHI CASE FILES, THE
KING OF HELL
KODOCHA: SANA'S STAGE
LEGEND OF CHUN HYANG, THE
MAGIC KNIGHT RAYEARTH I
MAGIC KNIGHT RAYEARTH II
MAN OF MANY FACES
MARMALADE BOY
MARS
MARS: HORSE WITH NO NAME
MINK
MIRACLE GIRLS
MODEL
MY LOVE
NECK AND NECK
ONE
ONE I LOVE, THE
PEACH GIRL
PEACH GIRL: CHANGE OF HEART
PITA-TEN
PLANET LADDER
PLANETES
PRINCESS AI
PSYCHIC ACADEMY
QUEEN'S KNIGHT, THE
RAGNAROK
RAVE MASTER
REALITY CHECK
REBIRTH
REBOUND
RISING STARS OF MANGA
SAILOR MOON
SAINT TAIL
SAMURAI GIRL REAL BOUT HIGH SCHOOL
SEIKAI TRILOGY, THE
SGT. FROG
SHAOLIN SISTERS

04.23.04Y

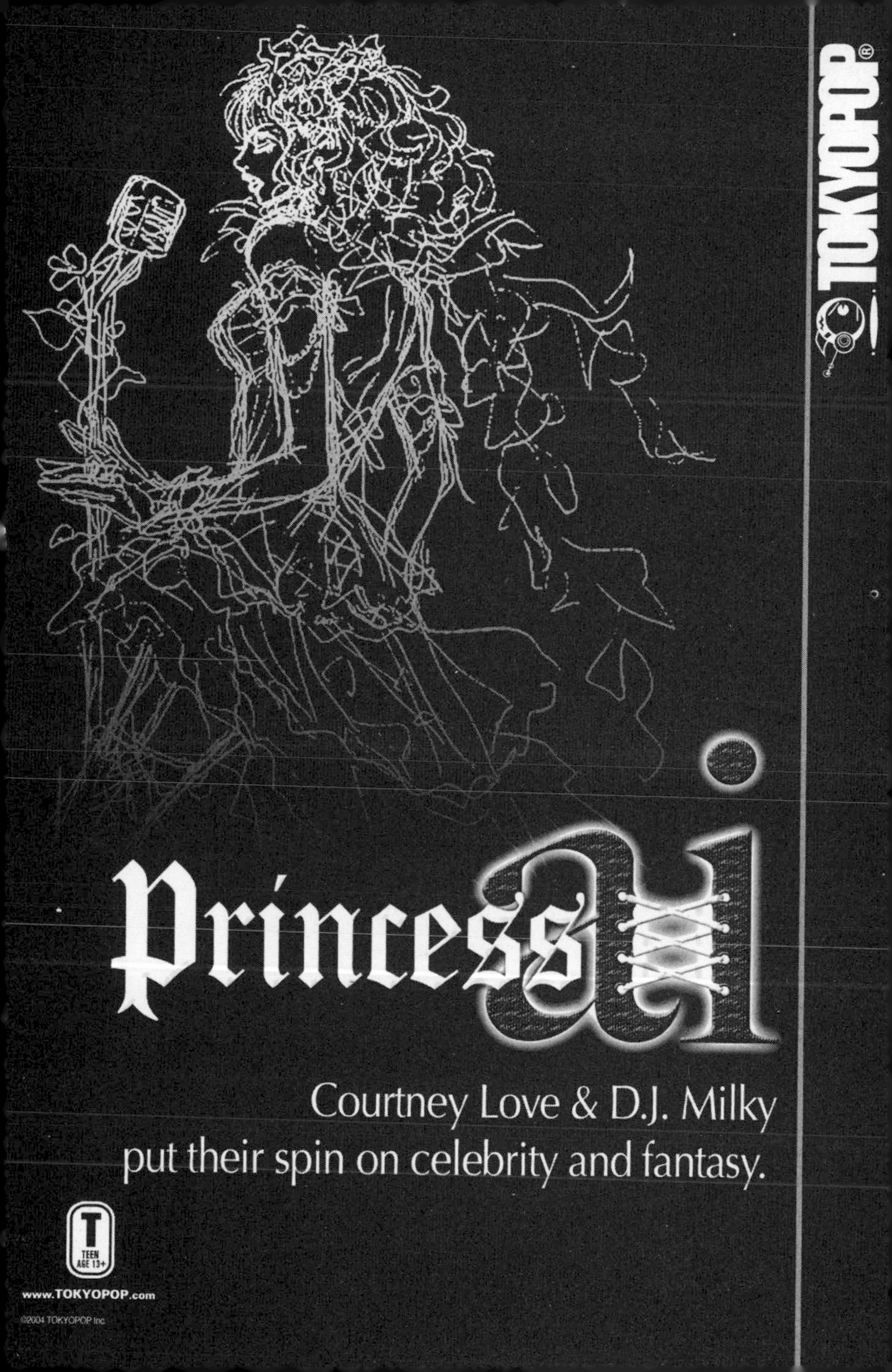
TOKYOPOP®
Princess ai
Courtney Love & D.J. Milky
put their spin on celebrity and fantasy.
T
TEEN
AGE 13+
www.TOKYOPOP.com
©2004 TOKYOPOP Inc.

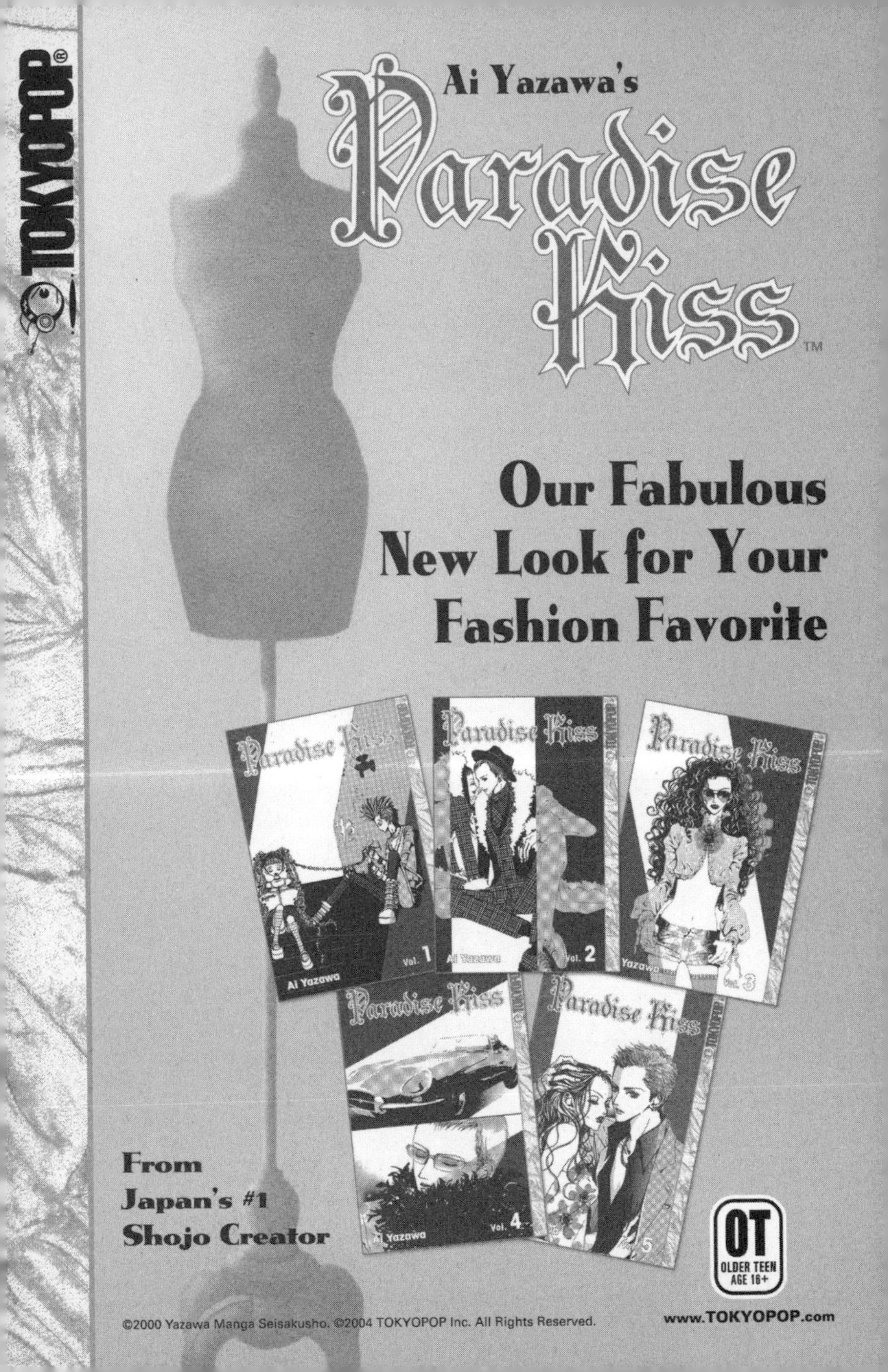
TOKYOPOP®
Ai Yazawa's
Paradise Kiss™
Our Fabulous
New Look for Your
Fashion Favorite
Paradise Kiss
Vol. 1
Ai Yazawa
Paradise Kiss
Vol. 2
Paradise Kiss
Vol. 3
Paradise Kiss
Vol. 4
Ai Yazawa
Paradise Kiss
5
From
Japan's #1
Shojo Creator
OT
OLDER TEEN
AGE 16+
©2000 Yazawa Manga Seisakusho. ©2004 TOKYOPOP Inc. All Rights Reserved.
www.TOKYOPOP.com

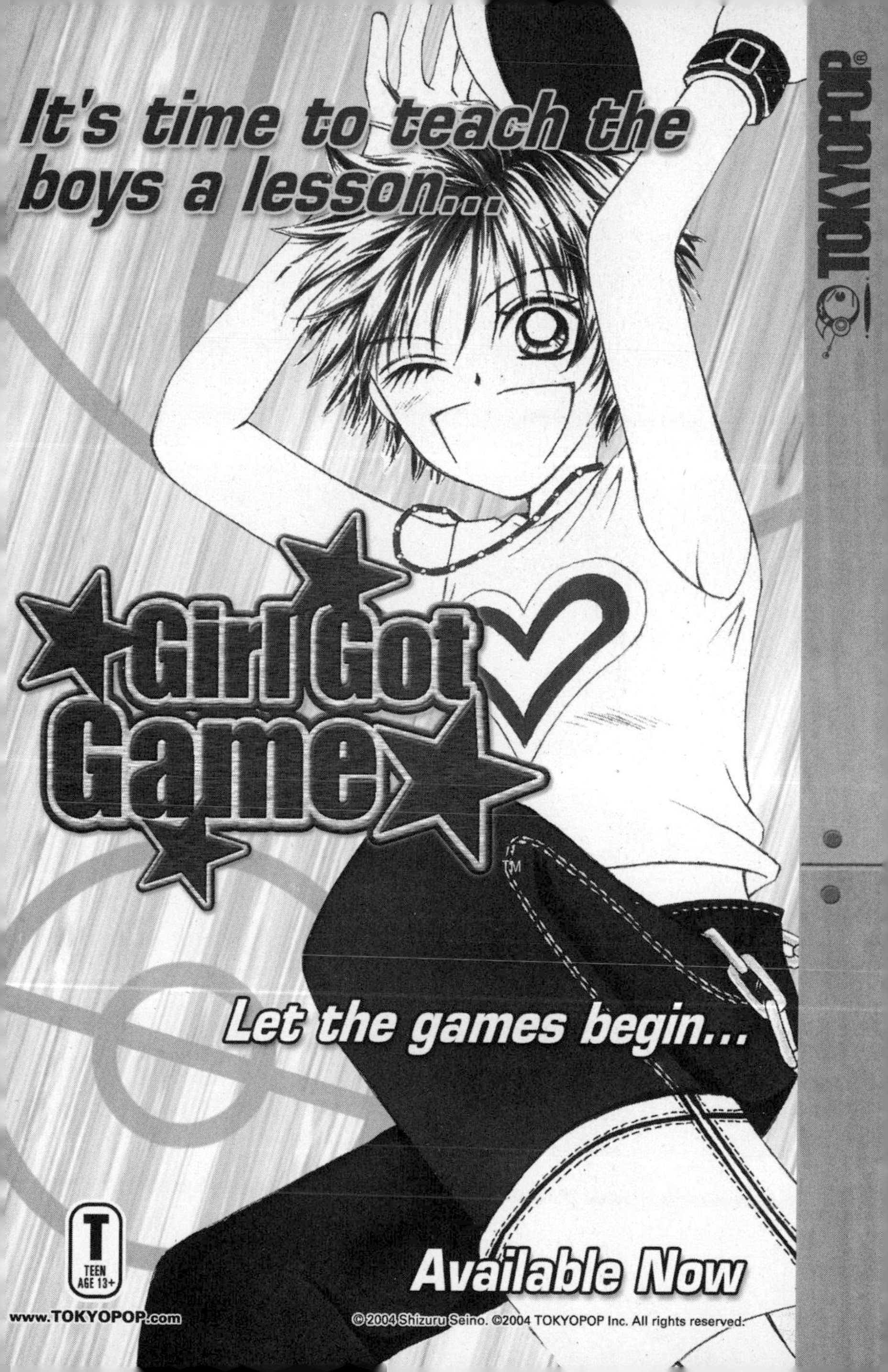
It's time to teach the boys a lesson...
TOKYOPOP®
Girl Got Game™
Let the games begin...
T TEEN AGE 13+
Available Now
www.TOKYOPOP.com
© 2004 Shizuru Seino. ©2004 TOKYOPOP Inc. All rights reserved.

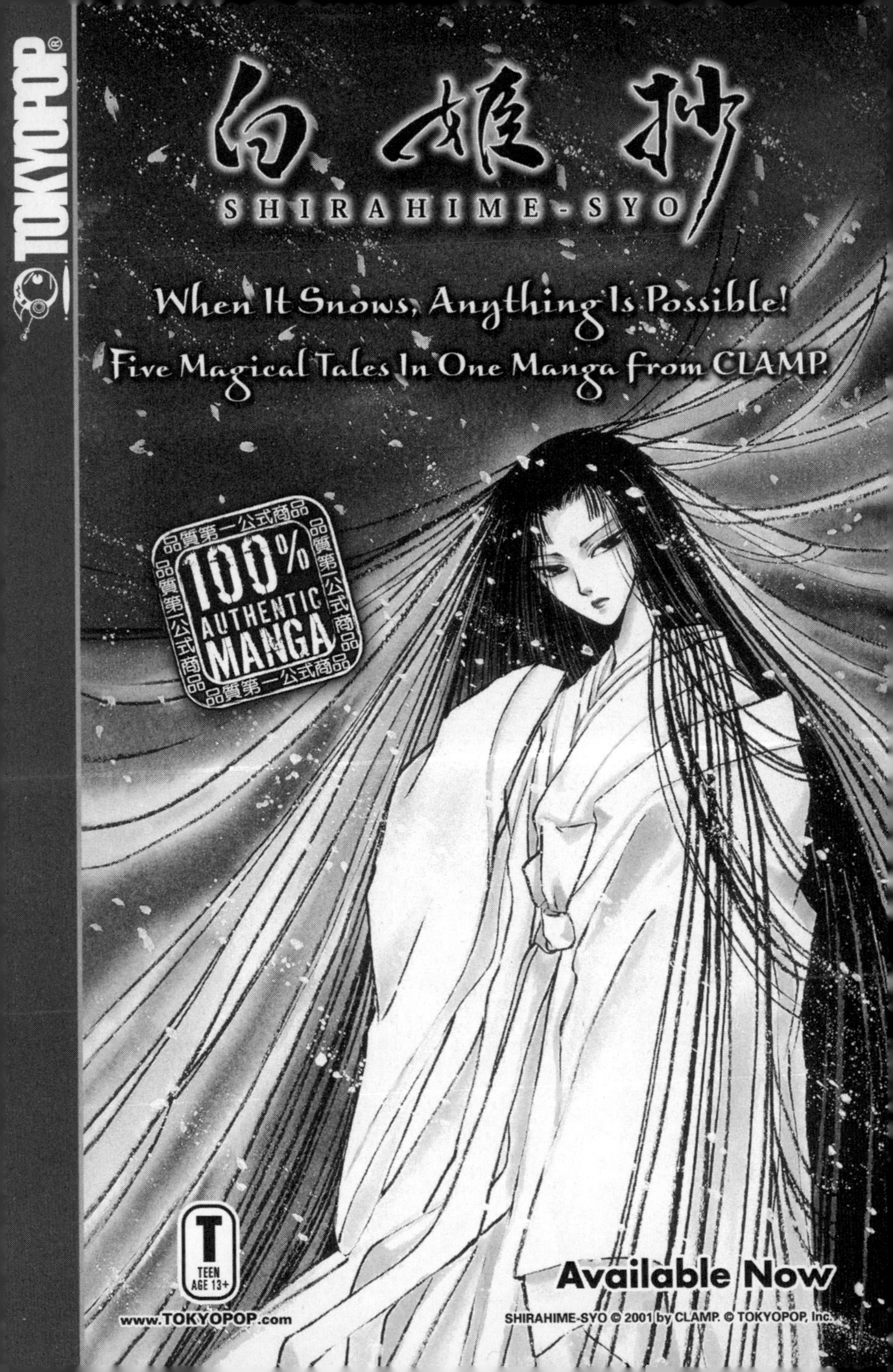
TOKYOPOP
白姫抄
SHIRAHIME-SYO
When It Snows, Anything Is Possible!
Five Magical Tales In One Manga from CLAMP.
品質第一公式商品
100% AUTHENTIC MANGA
T
TEEN
AGE 13+
Available Now
www.TOKYOPOP.com
SHIRAHIME-SYO © 2001 by CLAMP. © TOKYOPOP, Inc.

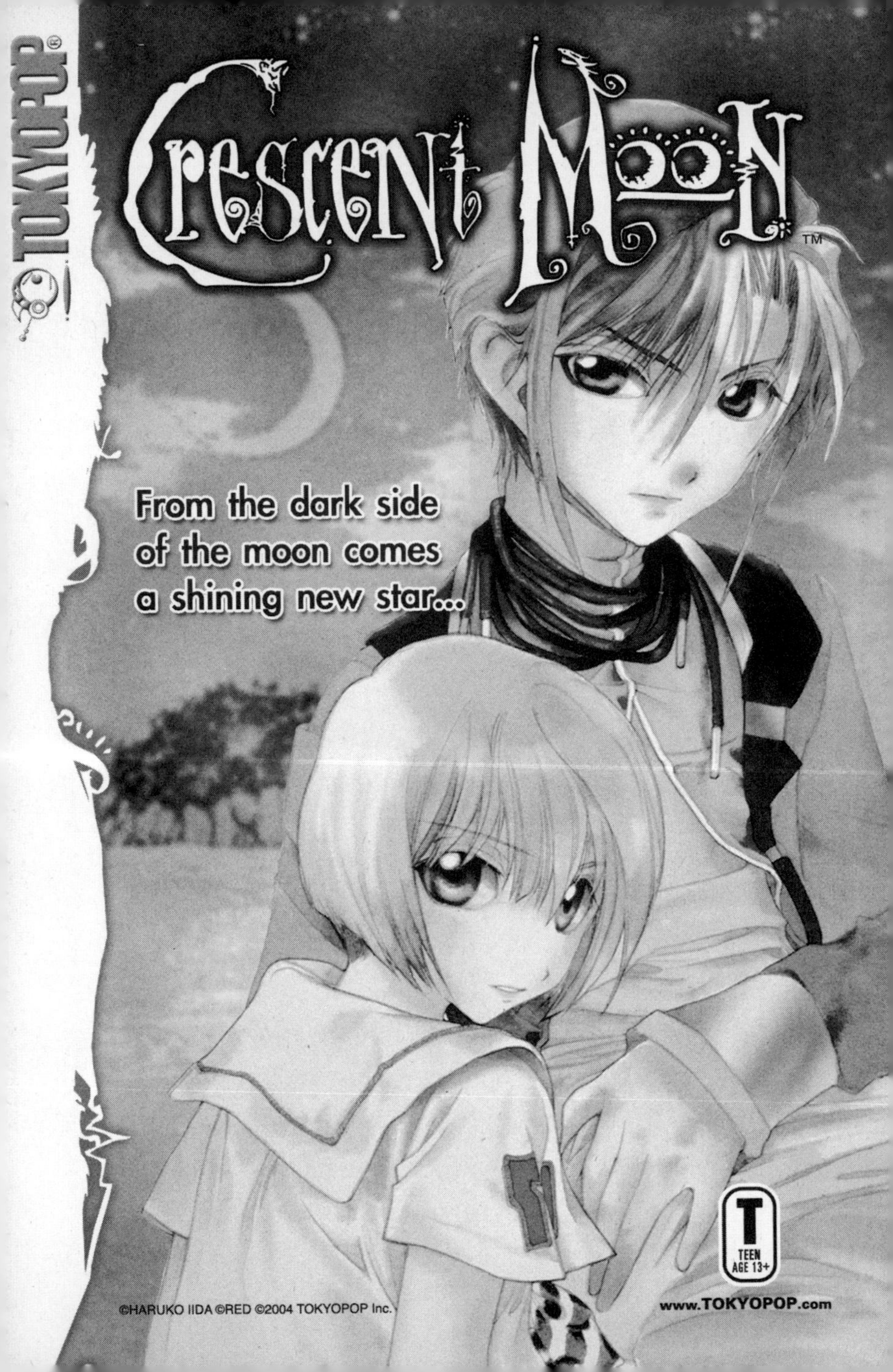
TOKYOPOP®
Crescent Moon™
From the dark side of the moon comes a shining new star...
T TEEN AGE 13+
©HARUKO IIDA ©RED ©2004 TOKYOPOP Inc.
www.TOKYOPOP.com

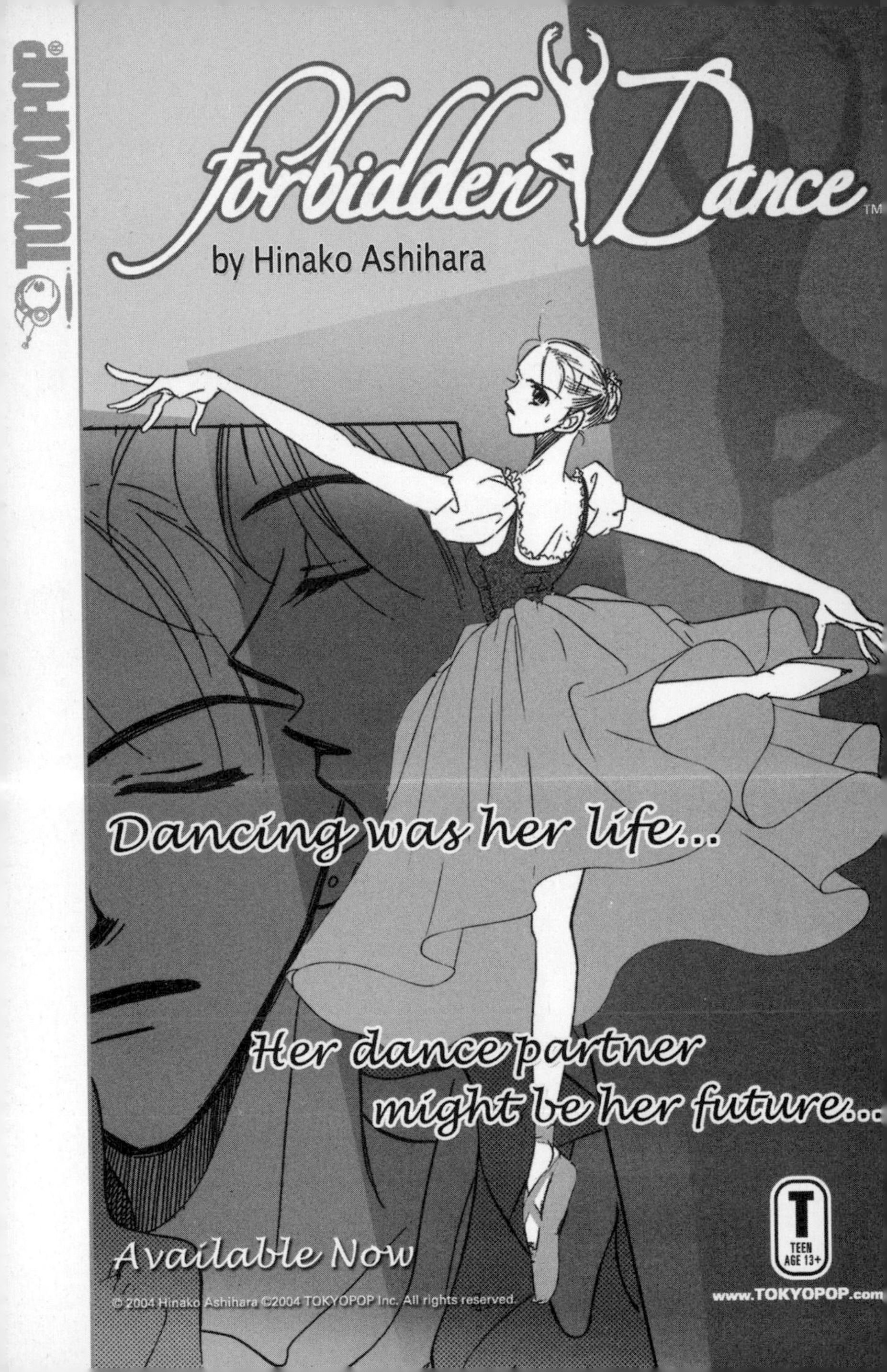
TOKYOPOP
Forbidden Dance™
by Hinako Ashihara
Dancing was her life...
Her dance partner
might be her future...
Available Now
© 2004 Hinako Ashihara ©2004 TOKYOPOP Inc. All rights reserved.
T
TEEN
AGE 13+
www.TOKYOPOP.com

STOP!

This is the back of the book.
You wouldn't want to spoil a great ending!

This book is printed "manga-style," in the authentic Japanese right-to-left format. Since none of the artwork has been flipped or altered, readers get to experience the story just as the creator intended. You've been asking for it, so TOKYOPOP® delivered: authentic, hot-off-the-press, and far more fun!

DIRECTIONS

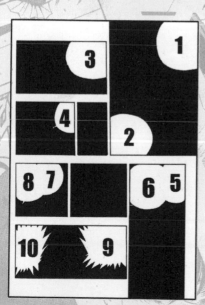

If this is your first time reading manga-style, here's a quick guide to help you understand how it works.

It's easy… just start in the top right panel and follow the numbers. Have fun, and look for more 100% authentic manga from TOKYOPOP®!